INTERNATIONAL MONETARY FUND

WORLD ECONOMIC OUTLOOK

A Long and Difficult Ascent

2020
OCT

Cover and Design: IMF CSF Creative Solutions Division
Composition: AGS, An RR Donnelley Company

Cataloging-in-Publication Data

Joint Bank-Fund Library

Names: International Monetary Fund.
Title: World economic outlook (International Monetary Fund)
Other titles: WEO | Occasional paper (International Monetary Fund) | World economic and financial surveys.
Description: Washington, DC : International Monetary Fund, 1980- | Semiannual | Some issues also have thematic titles. | Began with issue for May 1980. | 1981-1984: Occasional paper / International Monetary Fund, 0251-6365 | 1986-: World economic and financial surveys, 0256-6877.
Identifiers: ISSN 0256-6877 (print) | ISSN 1564-5215 (online)
Subjects: LCSH: Economic development—Periodicals. | International economic relations—Periodicals. | Debts, External—Periodicals. | Balance of payments—Periodicals. | International finance—Periodicals. | Economic forecasting—Periodicals.
Classification: LCC HC10.W79

HC10.80

ISBN 978-1-51355-605-5 (English Paper)
     978-1-51355-814-1 (English ePub)
     978-1-51355-815-8 (English PDF)

The *World Economic Outlook* (WEO) is a survey by the IMF staff published twice a year, in the spring and fall. The WEO is prepared by the IMF staff and has benefited from comments and suggestions by Executive Directors following their discussion of the report on September 30, 2020. The views expressed in this publication are those of the IMF staff and do not necessarily represent the views of the IMF's Executive Directors or their national authorities.

Recommended citation: International Monetary Fund. 2020. *World Economic Outlook: A Long and Difficult Ascent.* Washington, DC, October.

Publication orders may be placed online, by fax, or through the mail:
International Monetary Fund, Publication Services
P.O. Box 92780, Washington, DC 20090, USA
Tel.: (202) 623-7430 Fax: (202) 623-7201
E-mail: publications@imf.org
www.imfbookstore.org
www.elibrary.imf.org

CONTENTS

Online Tables—Statistical Appendix

Figures

ASSUMPTIONS AND CONVENTIONS

A number of assumptions have been adopted for the projections presented in the *World Economic Outlook* (WEO). It has been assumed that real effective exchange rates remained constant at their average levels during July 24 to August 21, 2020, except for those for the currencies participating in the European exchange rate mechanism II (ERM II), which are assumed to have remained constant in nominal terms relative to the euro; that established policies of national authorities will be maintained (for specific assumptions about fiscal and monetary policies for selected economies, see Box A1 in the Statistical Appendix); that the average price of oil will be $41.69 a barrel in 2020 and $46.70 a barrel in 2021 and will remain unchanged in real terms over the medium term; that the six-month London interbank offered rate (LIBOR) on US dollar deposits will average 0.7 percent in 2020 and 0.4 percent in 2021; that the three-month euro deposit rate will average –0.4 percent in 2020 and –0.5 percent in 2021; and that the six-month Japanese yen deposit rate will yield, on average, 0.0 percent in 2020 and 2021. These are, of course, working hypotheses rather than forecasts, and the uncertainties surrounding them add to the margin of error that would, in any event, be involved in the projections. The estimates and projections are based on statistical information available through September 28, 2020.

The following conventions are used throughout the WEO:

. . .   to indicate that data are not available or not applicable;

–   between years or months (for example, 2019–20 or January–June) to indicate the years or months covered, including the beginning and ending years or months; and

/   between years or months (for example, 2019/20) to indicate a fiscal or financial year.

"Billion" means a thousand million; "trillion" means a thousand billion.

"Basis points" refers to hundredths of 1 percentage point (for example, 25 basis points are equivalent to ¼ of 1 percentage point).

Data refer to calendar years, except in the case of a few countries that use fiscal years. Please refer to Table F in the Statistical Appendix, which lists the economies with exceptional reporting periods for national accounts and government finance data for each country.

For some countries, the figures for 2019 and earlier are based on estimates rather than actual outturns. Please refer to Table G in the Statistical Appendix, which lists the latest actual outturns for the indicators in the national accounts, prices, government finance, and balance of payments indicators for each country.

What is new in this publication:

- Following the recent release of the 2017 International Comparison Program (ICP) survey for new purchasing-power-parity benchmarks, the WEO's estimates of purchasing-power-parity weights and GDP valued at purchasing power parity have been updated. For more details, see Box 1.1 in the October 2020 WEO at http://www.imf.org/external/pubs/ft/weo/2020/02/index.htm.

- Starting with the October 2020 WEO, data and forecasts for Bangladesh and Tonga are presented on a fiscal year basis.

- Data for West Bank and Gaza are now included in the WEO. West Bank and Gaza is added to the Middle East and Central Asia regional group.

In the tables and figures, the following conventions apply:

- If no source is listed on tables and figures, data are drawn from the WEO database.

- When countries are not listed alphabetically, they are ordered on the basis of economic size.

- Minor discrepancies between sums of constituent figures and totals shown reflect rounding.

As used in this report, the terms "country" and "economy" do not in all cases refer to a territorial entity that is a state as understood by international law and practice. As used here, the term also covers some territorial entities that are not states but for which statistical data are maintained on a separate and independent basis.

Composite data are provided for various groups of countries organized according to economic characteristics or region. Unless noted otherwise, country group composites represent calculations based on 90 percent or more of the weighted group data.

The boundaries, colors, denominations, and any other information shown on the maps do not imply, on the part of the IMF, any judgment on the legal status of any territory or any endorsement or acceptance of such boundaries.

FURTHER INFORMATION

Corrections and Revisions

The data and analysis appearing in the *World Economic Outlook* (WEO) are compiled by the IMF staff at the time of publication. Every effort is made to ensure their timeliness, accuracy, and completeness. When errors are discovered, corrections and revisions are incorporated into the digital editions available from the IMF website and on the IMF eLibrary (see below). All substantive changes are listed in the online table of contents.

Print and Digital Editions

Print

Print copies of this WEO can be ordered from the IMF bookstore at imfbk.st/29296.

Digital

Multiple digital editions of the WEO, including ePub, enhanced PDF, and HTML, are available on the IMF eLibrary at http://www.elibrary.imf.org/OCT20WEO.

Download a free PDF of the report and data sets for each of the charts therein from the IMF website at www.imf.org/publications/weo or scan the QR code below to access the WEO web page directly:

Copyright and Reuse

Information on the terms and conditions for reusing the contents of this publication are at www.imf.org/external/terms.htm.

DATA

This version of the *World Economic Outlook* (WEO) is available in full through the IMF eLibrary (www.elibrary.imf.org) and the IMF website (www.imf.org). Accompanying the publication on the IMF website is a larger compilation of data from the WEO database than is included in the report itself, including files containing the series most frequently requested by readers. These files may be downloaded for use in a variety of software packages.

The data appearing in the WEO are compiled by the IMF staff at the time of the WEO exercises. The historical data and projections are based on the information gathered by the IMF country desk officers in the context of their missions to IMF member countries and through their ongoing analysis of the evolving situation in each country. Historical data are updated on a continual basis as more information becomes available, and structural breaks in data are often adjusted to produce smooth series with the use of splicing and other techniques. IMF staff estimates continue to serve as proxies for historical series when complete information is unavailable. As a result, WEO data can differ from those in other sources with official data, including the IMF's International Financial Statistics.

The WEO data and metadata provided are "as is" and "as available," and every effort is made to ensure their timeliness, accuracy, and completeness, but these cannot be guaranteed. When errors are discovered, there is a concerted effort to correct them as appropriate and feasible. Corrections and revisions made after publication are incorporated into the electronic editions available from the IMF eLibrary (www.elibrary.imf.org) and on the IMF website (www.imf.org). All substantive changes are listed in detail in the online tables of contents.

For details on the terms and conditions for usage of the WEO database, please refer to the IMF Copyright and Usage website (www.imf.org/external/terms.htm).

Inquiries about the content of the WEO and the WEO database should be sent by mail, fax, or online forum (telephone inquiries cannot be accepted):

World Economic Studies Division
Research Department
International Monetary Fund
700 19th Street, NW
Washington, DC 20431, USA
Fax: (202) 623-6343
Online Forum: www.imf.org/weoforum

PREFACE

The analysis and projections contained in the *World Economic Outlook* are integral elements of the IMF's surveillance of economic developments and policies in its member countries, of developments in international financial markets, and of the global economic system. The survey of prospects and policies is the product of a comprehensive interdepartmental review of world economic developments, which draws primarily on information the IMF staff gathers through its consultations with member countries. These consultations are carried out in particular by the IMF's area departments—namely, the African Department, Asia and Pacific Department, European Department, Middle East and Central Asia Department, and Western Hemisphere Department—together with the Strategy, Policy, and Review Department; the Monetary and Capital Markets Department; and the Fiscal Affairs Department.

The analysis in this report was coordinated in the Research Department under the general direction of Gita Gopinath, Economic Counsellor and Director of Research. The project was directed by Gian Maria Milesi-Ferretti, Deputy Director, Research Department, and Malhar Nabar, Division Chief, Research Department; Oya Celasun, Division Chief, Research Department directed Chapter 3.

The primary contributors to this report are Philip Barrett, John Bluedorn, Christian Bogmans, Benjamin Carton, Francesca Caselli, Johannes Eugster, Francesco Grigoli, Florence Jaumotte, Toh Kuan, Weicheng Lian, Weifeng Liu, Adil Mohommad, Andrea Pescatori, Evgenia Pugacheva, Damiano Sandri, Marina Tavares, Nico Valckx, and Simon Voigts.

Other contributors include Gavin Asdorian, Srijoni Banerjee, Eric Bang, Thomas Brand, Luisa Calixto, Sophia Chen, Wenjie Chen, Gabriela Cugat, Sonali Das, Federico Diez, Angela Espiritu, Niels-Jakob Hansen, Jinjin He, Mandy Hemmati, Youyou Huang, Benjamin Hunt, Christopher Johns, Jaden Jonghyuk Kim, Lama Kiyasseh, Eduard Laurito, Jungjin Lee, Claire Mengyi Li, Chiara Maggi, Susanna Mursula, Futoshi Narita, Savannah Newman, Cynthia Nyanchama Nyakeri, Emory Oakes, Nicola Pierri, Yiyuan Qi, Daniela Rojas Fernandez, Max Rozycki, Susie Xiaohui Sun, Nicholas Tong, Shan Wang, Julia Xueliang Wang, Yarou Xu, Hannah Leheng Yang, and Huiyuan Zhao.

Joseph Procopio from the Communications Department led the editorial team for the report, with production and editorial support from Christine Ebrahimzadeh, and editorial assistance from Lucy Scott Morales, James Unwin, Harold Medina (and team), and Vector Talent Resources.

The analysis has benefited from comments and suggestions by staff members from other IMF departments, as well as by Executive Directors following their discussion of the report on September 30, 2020. However, both projections and policy considerations are those of the IMF staff and should not be attributed to Executive Directors or to their national authorities.

FOREWORD

More than one million lives have been lost to COVID-19 since the start of the year and the toll continues to rise. Many more have suffered serious illness. Close to 90 million people are expected to fall into extreme deprivation this year.

These are difficult times, yet there are some reasons to be hopeful. Testing has been ramped up, treatments are improving, and vaccine trials have proceeded at an unprecedented pace, with some now in the final stage of testing. International solidarity has strengthened along some dimensions, from rolling back trade restrictions on medical equipment to enhancing financial assistance for vulnerable countries. And recent data suggest that many economies have started to recover at a faster pace than anticipated after reopening from the Great Lockdown.

We are projecting a somewhat less severe though still deep recession in 2020, relative to our June forecast. The revision is driven by second quarter GDP outturns in large advanced economies, which were not as negative as we had projected; China's return to growth, which was stronger than expected; and signs of a more rapid recovery in the third quarter. Outturns would have been much weaker if it weren't for sizable, swift, and unprecedented fiscal, monetary, and regulatory responses that maintained disposable income for households, protected cash flow for firms, and supported credit provision. Collectively these actions have so far prevented a recurrence of the financial catastrophe of 2008-09.

While the global economy is coming back, the ascent will likely be long, uneven, and uncertain. Indeed, compared to our forecast in June, prospects have worsened significantly in some emerging market and developing economies where infections are rising rapidly. Consequently, emerging market and developing economies, excluding China, are projected to incur a greater loss of output over 2020-21 relative to the pre-pandemic projected path when compared to advanced economies. These uneven recoveries significantly worsen the prospects for global convergence in income levels.

Moreover, recovery is not assured while the pandemic continues to spread. With renewed upticks in COVID-19 infections in places that had reduced local transmission to low levels, re-openings have paused, and targeted shutdowns are being reinstated. Economies everywhere face difficult paths back to pre-pandemic activity levels.

Preventing further setbacks will require that policy support is not prematurely withdrawn. The path ahead will require skillful domestic policies that manage trade-offs between lifting near-term activity and addressing medium-term challenges. The October 2020 *Global Financial Stability Report* highlights such trade-offs for monetary policy. Sustaining the recovery will also require strong international cooperation on health and financial support for countries facing liquidity shortfalls. Finding the right policy mix is daunting, but the experience of the past few months provides grounds for cautious optimism that the priorities laid out in this report can be achieved.

A key aspect of combating the health crisis is to ensure that all innovations, be they in testing, treatments, or vaccines, are produced at scale for the benefit of all countries. Advance purchase commitments for vaccines under trial can help spur this process for manufacturers who may otherwise hesitate to bear the upfront cost. This effort should include a strong multilateral component to help distribute doses to all countries at affordable prices. More generally, the global community will need to continue helping countries with limited health care capacity through sharing equipment, know-how, and through financial support from international health agencies.

At the national level, governments have already responded with a variety of fiscal countermeasures that include efforts to cushion income losses, incentivize hiring, expand social assistance, guarantee credit, and inject equity into firms. These measures have prevented widespread firm bankruptcies and have helped employment rebound partially. Employment and labor force participation, however, remain well below pre-pandemic levels, and many more millions of jobs are at risk the longer this crisis continues. To preserve jobs, it is important for governments, where possible, to continue to support viable but still vulnerable firms with moratoria on debt service and equity-like support. Over time, once the recovery has taken a strong hold, policies should shift gradually to facilitating reallocation of workers from sectors likely to shrink on a long-term basis (travel) to growing sectors (e-commerce). Along the transition, workers will need to be supported, including through income transfers, retraining, and reskilling programs.

Advanced economies have generally been able to deliver larger direct spending and liquidity support relative to GDP than others constrained by elevated debt and higher borrowing costs. Those constrained countries will need to create room for immediate spending needs by prioritizing crisis countermeasures and reducing poorly targeted subsidies. Some will require additional help from creditors and donors through debt restructuring, grants, and concessional financing, building on important initiatives under way. The IMF has been central to these initiatives through its joint call with the World Bank on debt service suspension for low-income countries, its call for reform of the international debt architecture, and its extension of funding at unprecedented speed to several member countries.

Further complicating the task that countries face is the need to address challenges coming out of the pandemic. In this report we are releasing medium-term growth projections for the first time since the crisis started. While uncertainty remains substantial, growth is expected to moderate significantly, following the projected rebound in global activity in 2021. Both advanced and emerging market economies are likely to register significant losses of output relative to their pre-pandemic forecasts. Small states as well as tourism-dependent and commodities-based economies are in a particularly difficult spot.

Most economies will experience lasting damage to supply potential, reflecting scars from the deep recession this year and the need for structural change. The persistent output losses imply a major setback to living standards relative to what was expected before the pandemic. Not only will the incidence of extreme poverty rise for the first time in over two decades, but inequality is set to increase because the crisis has disproportionately affected women, the informally employed, and those with relatively lower educational attainment, as discussed in Chapter 2 of this report. The loss of human capital accumulation after widespread school closures poses an additional challenge.

Moreover, sovereign debt levels are set to increase significantly even as downgrades to potential output imply a smaller tax base that makes it harder to service the debt. On the plus side, the prospects of low interest rates over a longer period, alongside the projected rebound in growth in 2021, can help alleviate debt service burdens in many countries. To ensure that debt remains on a sustainable path over the medium-term governments may need to increase the progressivity of their taxes and ensure that corporations pay their fair share of taxes while eliminating wasteful spending.

Near-term support policies should be designed with a view toward placing economies on paths of stronger, equitable, and sustainable growth. As discussed in Chapter 3 of this report, policymakers can simultaneously aim to mitigate climate change and bolster the recovery from the COVID-19 crisis. This can be achieved through a comprehensive package that includes a sizable green public infrastructure push, a gradual rise in carbon prices, and compensation for lower income households to make the transition fair. More generally, expanding the safety net where gaps exist can ensure the most vulnerable are protected while supporting near-term activity, as already seen, for example, in many advanced economies where disposable income remained relatively stable even as GDP registered record collapses. And investments in health and education (including to remedy losses incurred during the pandemic) can help achieve participatory and inclusive growth. The October 2020 *Fiscal Monitor* makes a strong case for public investment in these times of heightened uncertainty.

We have already had significant policy innovations in the past few months: the establishment of the European Union pandemic recovery package fund, the launch of asset purchases by emerging market central banks, and the novel use of digital technologies to deliver social assistance in places like sub-Saharan Africa. Such actions have prevented even more extreme collapses and are a powerful reminder that effective, well-designed policies protect people and collective economic well-being. Building on these actions, policies for the next stage of the crisis must seek lasting improvements in the global economy that create secure, prosperous futures for all.

Gita Gopinath
Economic Counsellor and Director of Research

EXECUTIVE SUMMARY

The global economy is climbing out from the depths to which it had plummeted during the Great Lockdown in April. But with the COVID-19 pandemic continuing to spread, many countries have slowed reopening and some are reinstating partial lockdowns to protect susceptible populations. While recovery in China has been faster than expected, the global economy's long ascent back to pre-pandemic levels of activity remains prone to setbacks.

Global Growth Outlook and Risks

Near-term outlook. Global growth is projected at –4.4 percent in 2020, a less severe contraction than forecast in the June 2020 *World Economic Outlook* (WEO) *Update*. The revision reflects better-than-anticipated second quarter GDP outturns, mostly in advanced economies, where activity began to improve sooner than expected after lockdowns were scaled back in May and June, as well as indicators of a stronger recovery in the third quarter. Global growth is projected at 5.2 percent in 2021, a little lower than in the June 2020 WEO *Update*, reflecting the more moderate downturn projected for 2020 and consistent with expectations of persistent social distancing. Following the contraction in 2020 and recovery in 2021, the level of global GDP in 2021 is expected to be a modest 0.6 percent above that of 2019. The growth projections imply wide negative output gaps and elevated unemployment rates this year and in 2021 across both advanced and emerging market economies.

Medium-term outlook. After the rebound in 2021, global growth is expected to gradually slow to about 3.5 percent into the medium term. This implies only limited progress toward catching up to the path of economic activity for 2020–25 projected before the pandemic for both advanced and emerging market and developing economies. It is also a severe setback to the projected improvement in average living standards across all country groups. The pandemic will reverse the progress made since the 1990s in reducing global poverty and will increase inequality. People who rely on daily wage labor and are outside the formal safety net faced sudden income losses when mobility restrictions were imposed. Among them, migrant workers who live far from home had even less recourse to traditional support networks. Close to 90 million people could fall below the $1.90 a day income threshold of extreme deprivation this year. In addition, school closures during the pandemic pose a significant new challenge that could set back human capital accumulation severely.

The subdued outlook for medium-term growth comes with a significant projected increase in the stock of sovereign debt. Downward revisions to potential output also imply a smaller tax base over the medium term than previously envisaged, compounding difficulties in servicing debt obligations.

The baseline projection assumes that social distancing will continue into 2021 but will subsequently fade over time as vaccine coverage expands and therapies improve. Local transmission is assumed to be brought to low levels everywhere by the end of 2022. The medium-term projections also assume that economies will experience scarring from the depth of the recession and the need for structural change, entailing persistent effects on potential output. These effects include adjustment costs and productivity impacts for surviving firms as they upgrade workplace safety, the amplification of the shock via firm bankruptcies, costly resource reallocation across sectors, and discouraged workers' exit from the workforce. The scarring is expected to compound forces that dragged productivity growth lower across many economies in the years leading up to the pandemic—relatively slow investment growth weighing on physical capital accumulation, more modest improvements in human capital, and slower efficiency gains in combining technology with factors of production.

Risks. The uncertainty surrounding the baseline projection is unusually large. The forecast rests on public health and economic factors that are inherently difficult to predict. A first layer relates to the path of the pandemic, the needed public health response, and the associated domestic activity disruptions, most notably for contact-intensive sectors. Another source of uncertainty is the extent of global spillovers from soft demand, weaker tourism, and lower remittances.

A third set of factors comprises financial market sentiment and its implications for global capital flows. Moreover, there is uncertainty surrounding the damage to supply potential—which will depend on the persistence of the pandemic shock, the size and effectiveness of the policy response, and the extent of sectoral resource mismatches.

Progress with vaccines and treatments, as well as changes in the workplace and by consumers to reduce transmission, may allow activity to return more rapidly to pre-pandemic levels than currently projected, without triggering repeated waves of infection. And an extension of fiscal countermeasures into 2021 could also lift growth above the forecast, which factors in only the measures implemented and announced so far.

However, the risk of worse growth outcomes than projected remains sizable. If the virus resurges, progress on treatments and vaccines is slower than anticipated, or countries' access to them remains unequal, economic activity could be lower than expected, with renewed social distancing and tighter lockdowns. Considering the severity of the recession and the possible withdrawal of emergency support in some countries, rising bankruptcies could compound job and income losses. Deteriorating financial sentiment could trigger a sudden stop in new lending (or failure to roll over existing debt) to vulnerable economies. And cross-border spillovers from weaker external demand could amplify the impact of country-specific shocks.

Policy Priorities: Near-Term Imperatives, Medium-Term Challenges

Besides combating the deep near-term recession, policymakers have to address complex challenges to place economies on a path of higher productivity growth while ensuring that gains are shared evenly and debt remains sustainable. Many countries already face difficult trade-offs between implementing measures to support near-term growth and avoiding a further buildup of debt that will be hard to service down the road, considering the crisis's hit to potential output. Policies to support the economy in the near term should therefore be designed with an eye to guiding economies to paths of stronger, equitable, and resilient growth.

Tax and spending measures should privilege initiatives that can help lift potential output, ensure participatory growth that benefits all, and protect the vulnerable. The additional debt incurred to finance such endeavors is more likely to pay for itself down the road by increasing the size of the economy and future tax base than if the borrowing were done to finance ill-targeted subsidies or wasteful current spending. Investments in health, education, and high-return infrastructure projects that also help move the economy to lower carbon dependence can further those objectives. Research spending can facilitate innovation and technology adoption—the principal drivers of long-term productivity growth. Moreover, safeguarding critical social spending can ensure that the most vulnerable are protected while also supporting near-term activity, given that the outlays will go to groups with a higher propensity to spend their disposable income than more affluent individuals. In all instances, adhering to the highest standards of debt transparency will be essential to avoid future rollover difficulties and higher sovereign risk premiums that raise borrowing costs across the economy.

Given the global nature of the shock and common challenges across countries, strong multilateral efforts are needed to fight the health and economic crisis. A key priority is funding advance purchase commitments at the global level for vaccines currently under trial to incentivize rapid scaling up of production and worldwide distribution of affordable doses (for example, by bolstering multilateral initiatives for vaccine development and manufacture, including the Coalition for Epidemic Preparedness Innovations and Gavi, the Vaccine Alliance). This is particularly important given the uncertainty and risk of failure in the search for effective and safe vaccines. A related priority is to help countries with limited health care capacity.

Beyond assistance with medical equipment and know-how, several emerging market and developing economies—in particular low-income countries—require support from the international community through debt relief, grants, and concessional financing. Where debt restructuring is needed, creditors and low-income-country and emerging market borrowers should quickly agree on mutually acceptable terms. The global financial safety net can further help countries deal with external funding shortfalls. Since the onset of the crisis, the IMF has expeditiously provided funding from its various lending facilities to about 80 countries at unprecedented speed.

For many countries, sustaining economic activity and helping individuals and firms most in need—while ensuring that debt remains sustainable—is a daunting task, given high public debt, the spending needs triggered by the crisis, and the hit to public revenues. Governments should do all that they can to combat the health crisis and mitigate the deep downturn while being ready to adjust policy strategy as the pandemic and its impact on activity evolve. Where fiscal rules may constrain action, their temporary suspension would be warranted, combined with a commitment to a gradual consolidation path after the crisis abates to restore compliance with the rules over the medium term. Room for immediate spending needs could be created by prioritizing crisis countermeasures and reducing wasteful and poorly targeted subsidies. Extending maturities on public debt and locking in low interest rates to the extent possible would help reduce debt service and free up resources to be redirected toward crisis mitigation efforts. Although adopting new revenue measures during the crisis will be difficult, governments may need to consider raising progressive taxes on more affluent individuals and those relatively less affected by the crisis (including increasing tax rates on higher income brackets, high-end property, capital gains, and wealth) as well as changes to corporate taxation that ensure firms pay taxes commensurate with profitability. Countries should also cooperate on the design of international corporate taxation to respond to the challenges of the digital economy.

With the pandemic continuing to spread, all countries—including those where infections appear to have peaked—need to ensure that their health care systems can cope with elevated demand. This means securing adequate resources and prioritizing health care spending as needed, including on testing; contact tracing; personal protective equipment; life-saving equipment, such as ventilators; and facilities, such as emergency rooms, intensive care units, and isolation wards.

Countries where infections continue to rise need to contain the pandemic with mitigation measures that slow transmission. As Chapter 2 shows, lockdowns are effective in bringing down infections. Mitigation measures—a much-needed investment in public health—set the stage for an eventual economic recovery from the downturn brought on by mobility constraints. Economic policy in such cases should limit the damage by cushioning income losses for affected people and firms while also supporting resource reallocation away from contact-intensive sectors that are likely to be constrained for an extended period of time. Retraining and reskilling should be pursued to the extent feasible so that workers can look for jobs in other sectors. Because the transition may take a while, displaced workers will need extended income support as they retrain and search for jobs. Complementing such measures, broad-based accommodative monetary

and fiscal responses—where fiscal space exists—can help prevent deeper and longer-lasting downturns, even if their ability to stimulate spending is initially hampered by mobility restrictions.

As countries reopen, policies must support the recovery by gradually removing targeted support, facilitating the reallocation of workers and resources to sectors less affected by social distancing, and providing stimulus where needed to the extent possible. Some fiscal resources freed from targeted support should be redeployed to public investment—including in renewable energy, improving the efficiency of power transmission, and retrofitting buildings to reduce their carbon footprint. Moreover, as lifelines are unwound, social spending should be expanded to protect the most vulnerable where gaps exist in the safety net. In those cases, authorities could enhance paid family and sick leave, expand eligibility for unemployment insurance, and strengthen health care benefit coverage as needed. Where inflation expectations are anchored, accommodative monetary policy can help during the transition by containing borrowing costs.

Beyond the pandemic, multilateral cooperation is needed to defuse trade and technology tensions between countries and address gaps—for instance in services trade—in the rules-based multilateral trading system. Countries must also act collectively to implement their climate change mitigation commitments. As discussed in Chapter 3, joint action—particularly by the largest emitters—that combines steadily rising carbon prices with a green investment push is needed to reduce emissions consistent with limiting increases in global temperature to the targets of the 2015 Paris Agreement. A broadly adopted, growth-friendly mitigation package could raise global activity through investment in green infrastructure over the near term, with modest output costs over the medium term as economies transition away from fossil fuels toward cleaner technologies. Relative to unchanged policies, such a package would significantly boost incomes in the second half of the century by avoiding damages and catastrophic risks from climate change. Moreover, health outcomes would begin to improve immediately in many countries thanks to reduced local air pollution. The global community should also take urgent steps to strengthen its defenses against calamitous health crises, for example by augmenting stockpiles of protective equipment and essential medical supplies, financing research, and ensuring adequate ongoing assistance to countries with limited health care capacity, including through support of international organizations.

CHAPTER 1

GLOBAL PROSPECTS AND POLICIES

Global Economy Climbing Out of the Depths, Prone to Setbacks

The months after the release of the June 2020 *World Economic Outlook* (WEO) *Update* have offered a glimpse of how difficult rekindling economic activity will be while the pandemic surges. During May and June, as many economies tentatively reopened from the Great Lockdown, the global economy started to climb from the depths to which it had plunged in April. But with the pandemic spreading and accelerating in places, many countries slowed reopening, and some are reinstating partial lockdowns. While the swift recovery in China has surprised on the upside, the global economy's long ascent back to pre-pandemic levels of activity remains prone to setbacks.

- *Activity picked up in May and June as economies reopened.* The strengthening from the trough in April was most evident, not surprisingly, in retail sales, where discretionary consumer spending rose with reopening (Figure 1.1). Firms, however, remained cautious in responding to this revival: industrial production in many countries is still well below December levels.
- *Second quarter GDP outturns, on balance, delivered positive surprises.* As economies reopened and released constraints on spending, overall activity normalized faster than anticipated in the June 2020 WEO *Update*. GDP outturns for the second quarter surprised on the upside in China (where, after lockdowns eased in early April, public investment helped boost activity to return to positive growth in the second quarter) and the United States and euro area (where both economies contracted at a historic pace in the second quarter, but less severely than projected, with government transfers supporting household incomes). The news, however, was not uniformly positive. Second quarter GDP was weaker than projected, for instance, where domestic demand plunged following a very sharp compression in consumption and a collapse in investment (such as in India), where the pandemic continued to spread (such as in Mexico), where soft external demand weighed particularly heavily on exporting

sectors (for example, in Korea), and where significant weakening of remittance flows weighed on domestic spending (for example, in the Philippines).

- *Global trade* began recovering in June as lockdowns were eased (Figure 1.2). China is an important contributor. Its exports recovered from deep declines earlier in the year, supported by an earlier restart of activity and a strong pickup in external demand for medical equipment and for equipment to support the shift to remote working.
- *The pandemic continues to spread.* By late September, the number of confirmed infections worldwide exceeded 33 million, with over a million deaths—up from more than 7 million infections and 400,000 deaths at the time of the June 2020 WEO *Update.* Confirmed cases rose dramatically in the United States, Latin America, India, and South Africa. Moreover, there were renewed upticks in places that had previously flattened the infection curve: Australia, Japan, Spain, and France.
- *Reopening has stalled.* Confronting renewed upticks, countries slowed their reopening during August and reinstated partial lockdowns in some cases (Figure 1.3).

The deep wounds to the global economy from the pandemic recession are further evident in labor market indicators and inflation outcomes.

- *Labor market.* According to the International Labour Organization, the global reduction in work hours in the second quarter of 2020 compared with the fourth quarter of 2019 was equivalent to the loss of 400 million full-time jobs, deepening from equivalent 155 million full-time jobs lost in the first quarter. Women in the labor force, particularly those informally employed, have been disproportionately affected by the pandemic and lockdowns needed to slow the spread of the virus: the International Labour Organization estimates that 42 percent of informally employed women work in severely affected sectors of the economy, compared with about 32 percent of men in informal employment. Consistent with the pattern for global activity

Figure 1.1. Industrial Production and Retail Sales
(Index, December 2019 = 100; seasonally adjusted)

Retail sales have generally recovered stronger than industrial production.

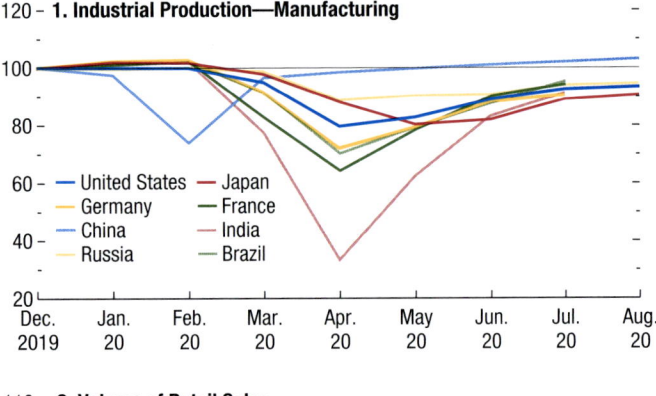

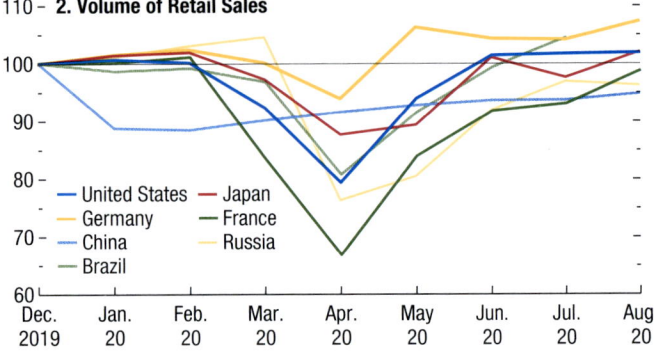

Sources: Haver Analytics; and IMF staff calculations.

Figure 1.2. Global Activity Indicators
(Three-month moving average, annualized percent change; deviations from 50 for manufacturing PMI, unless noted otherwise)

Global trade and industrial production picked up as lockdowns were eased.

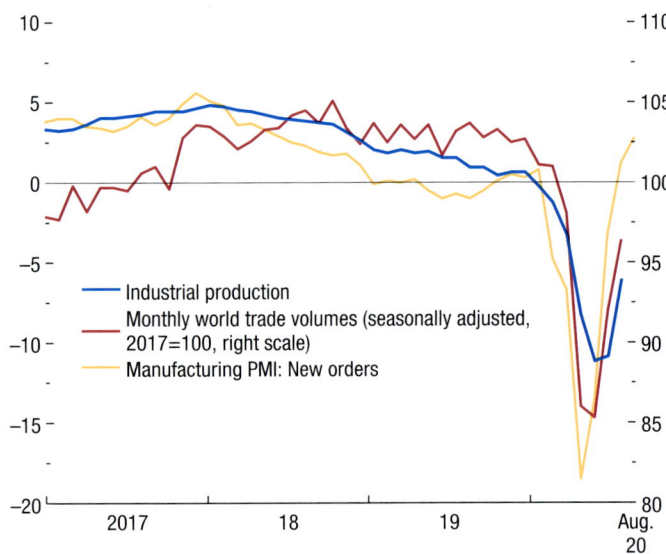

Sources: CPB Netherlands Bureau for Economic Policy Analysis; Haver Analytics; Markit Economics; and IMF staff calculations.
Note: PMI = purchasing managers' index.

and trade, employment and labor force indicators have improved since May. For example, the unemployment rate fell substantially and job creation increased in the United States, applications to Germany's *Kurzarbeit* reduced-hours work program slowed sharply in May and continued declining steadily throughout August, and female labor force participation had partially recovered in Japan as of July after close to 1 million women left the labor force from January to April.

- *Inflation.* While prices of such items as medical supplies increased and commodity prices lifted from their April trough (Commodities Special Feature; Figure 1.4), the effects of weak aggregate demand appear to have outweighed the impact of supply interruptions.[1] In sequential terms, inflation in

---

[1] The assessment is subject to an important caveat. The basket of goods and services used to measure consumer price inflation may not be representative of actual consumption patterns during the pandemic and may underestimate the true increase in the cost of living.

advanced economies remains below pre-pandemic levels (Figure 1.5). In emerging market and developing economies inflation declined sharply in the initial stages of the pandemic, although it has since picked up in some countries (India, for example, reflecting supply disruptions and a rise in food prices).

A unique recession. The downturn triggered by the COVID-19 pandemic has been very different from past recessions. In previous downturns, service-oriented sectors have tended to suffer smaller growth declines than manufacturing. In the current crisis, the public health response needed to slow transmission, together with behavioral changes, has meant that service sectors reliant on face-to-face interactions—particularly wholesale and retail trade, hospitality, and arts and entertainment—have seen larger contractions than manufacturing (Figure 1.6). The scale of disruption indicates that, without a vaccine and effective therapies to combat the virus, such sectors face a particularly difficult path back to any semblance of normalcy.

A strong rebound in the third quarter, but slowing momentum entering the fourth quarter. High-frequency indicators suggest a strong, albeit partial, rebound in

Figure 1.3. Government Lockdowns and Economic Responses to COVID-19: Global Index

Reopening has slowed as new infections have increased.

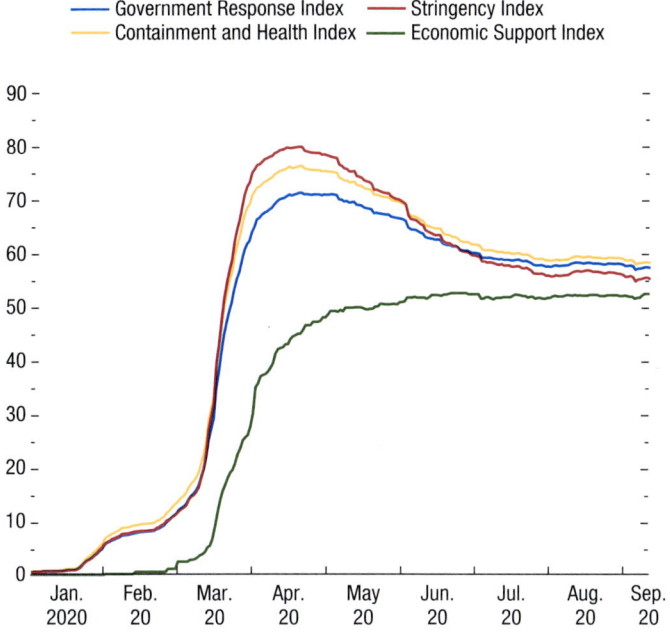

Source: Oxford COVID-19 Government Response Tracker.

Figure 1.4. Commodity Prices
(Deflated using US consumer price index; 2014 = 100)

Commodity prices have lifted since April.

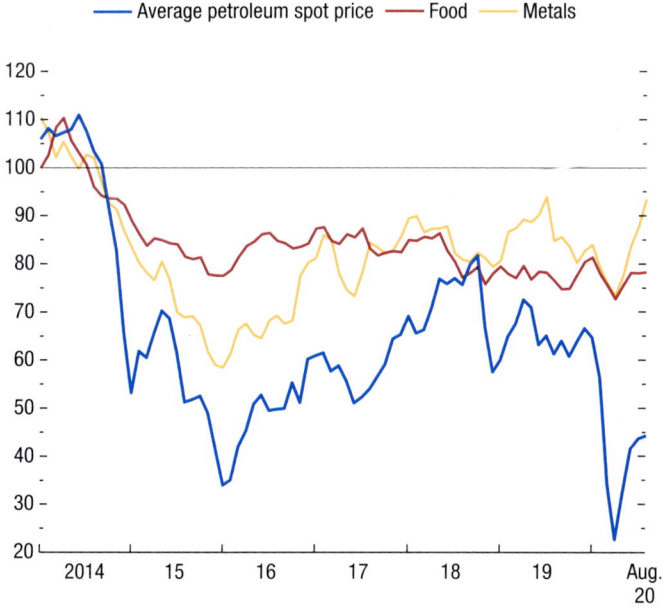

Sources: IMF, Primary Commodity Price System; and IMF staff calculations.

Figure 1.5. Global Inflation
(Three-month moving average; annualized percent change)

Inflation generally remains below pre-pandemic levels.

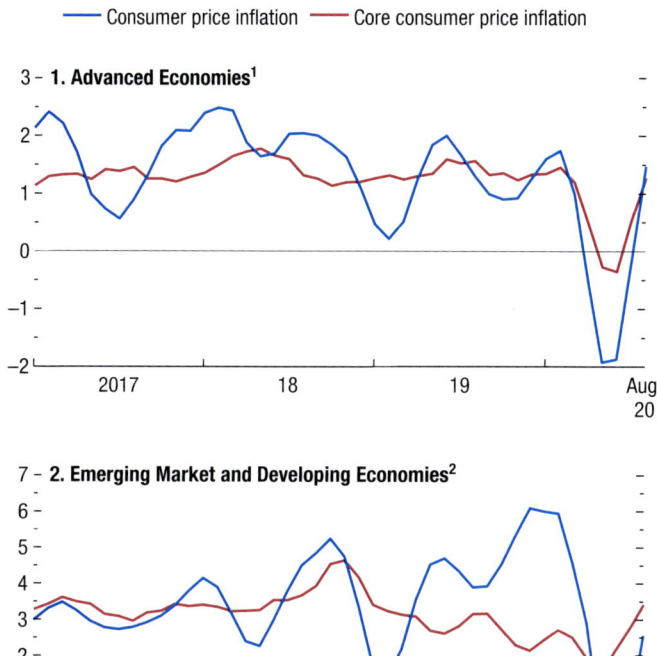

Sources: Consensus Economics; Haver Analytics; and IMF staff calculations.
Note: Country lists use International Organization for Standardization (ISO) country codes.
[1]Advanced economies are AUT, BEL, CAN, CHE, CZE, DEU, DNK, ESP, EST, FIN, FRA, GBR, GRC, HKG, IRL, ISR, ITA, JPN, KOR, LTU, LUX, LVA, NLD, NOR, PRT, SGP, SVK, SVN, SWE, TWN, USA.
[2]Emerging market and developing economies are BGR, BRA, CHL, CHN, COL, HUN, IDN, IND, MEX, MYS, PER, PHL, POL, ROU, RUS, THA, TUR, ZAF.

activity in the third quarter, after the trough in the second quarter. However, momentum going into the fourth quarter appears to be slowing. Business surveys of purchasing managers show firms in the United States, euro area, China, and Brazil, for example, expanded output successively in July and August compared with the previous month, whereas the opposite was true elsewhere (for instance, in India, Japan, and Korea)—(Figure 1.7). For September, these indicators point to stronger activity in manufacturing but some setback for services, most likely reflecting the increase in infections. Other high-frequency data suggest a leveling off in activity—as reflected, for example, in daily consumer spending in the United States (see the Opportunity Insights Economic Tracker 2020).

Figure 1.6. Sectoral Growth and the Business Cycle

In the COVID-19 recession, service sectors have seen larger contractions than has manufacturing.

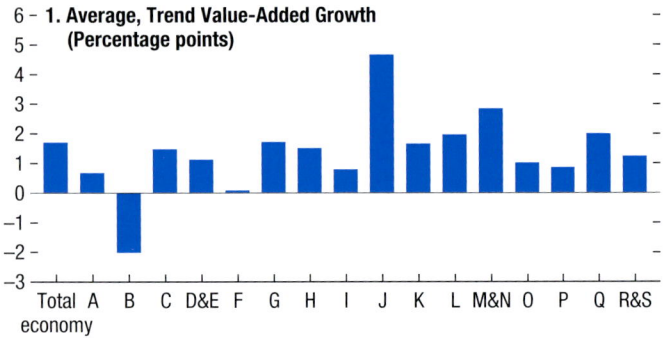

1. **Average, Trend Value-Added Growth**
   (Percentage points)

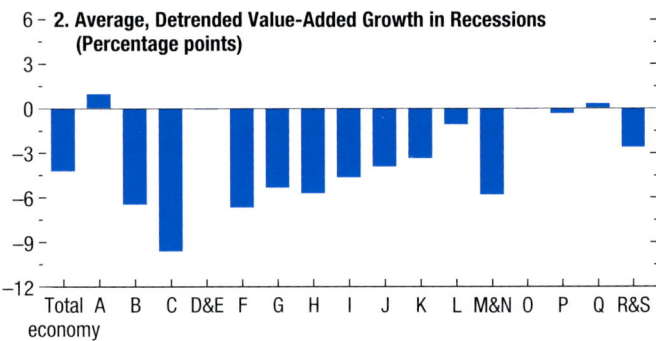

2. **Average, Detrended Value-Added Growth in Recessions**
   (Percentage points)

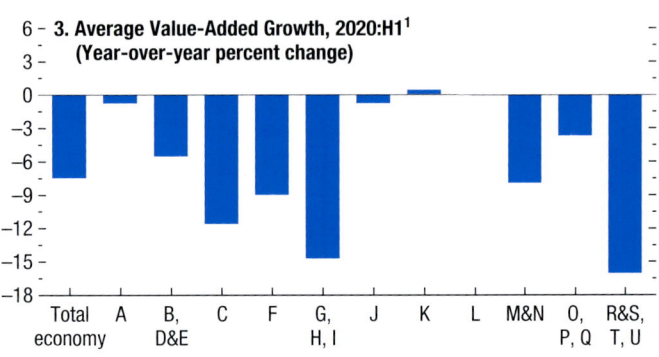

3. **Average Value-Added Growth, 2020:H1[1]**
   (Year-over-year percent change)

Sources: EU KLEMS; Organisation for Economic Co-operation and Development; US Bureau of Economic Analysis; and IMF staff calculations.
Note: Underlying data in panels 1 and 2 are annual for 1995–2017. Sector groupings in panel 3 are slightly different from those in panels 1 and 2 because of reporting differences in the quarterly sectoral national data. Recessions are years of negative total value-added growth. "Total economy" indicates value added for the economy as a whole. Country sample comprises Austria, Belgium, Finland, France, Germany, Italy, Japan, Luxembourg, the Netherlands, Spain, the United Kingdom, and the United States. Sectors are ISIC rev.4: A = agriculture, forestry, and fishing; B = mining and quarrying; C = manufacturing; D&E = utilities; F = construction; G = wholesale and retail trade; H = transportation; I = accommodation and food services; J = information and communication; K = financial and insurance activities; L = real estate; M&N = professional and administrative services; O = public administration and defense; P = education; Q = human health and social work; R&S = arts, entertainment, recreation, and other services; T = activities of households as employers and undifferentiated goods-and-services-producing activities of households for own use; U = activities of extraterritorial organizations and bodies.
[1]Excludes Japan due to lack of sectoral detail. 2020:Q1 year-over-year growth is used for the United States in panel 3 calculations due to lack of data on 2020:Q2.

Figure 1.7. Purchasing Managers' Indices, 2020
(Index; 50+ = expansion)

Business surveys of purchasing managers suggest a strong but only partial rebound in activity after the trough in the second quarter.

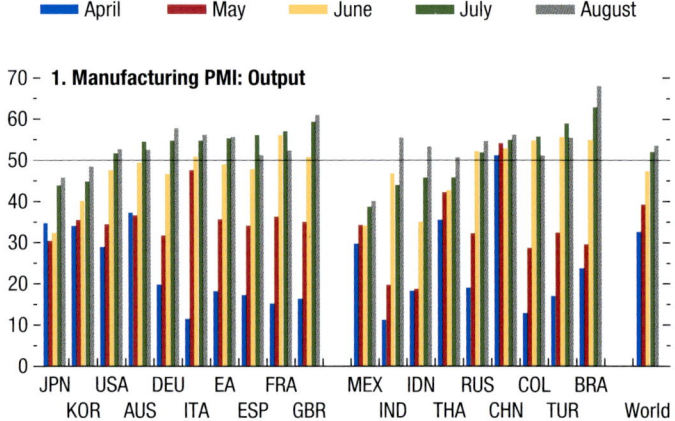

1. **Manufacturing PMI: Output**

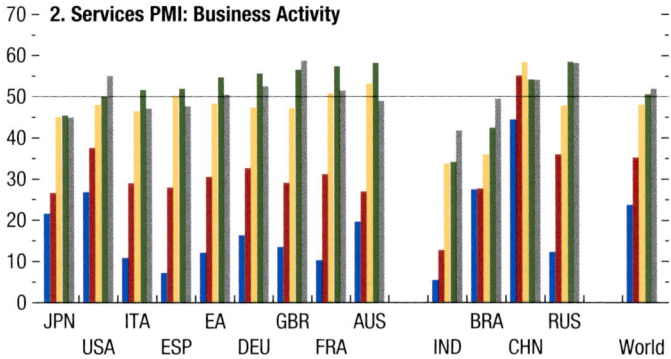

2. **Services PMI: Business Activity**

Sources: IHS Markit; and IMF staff calculations.
Note: EA = euro area; PMI = purchasing managers' indices. Data labels use International Organization for Standardization (ISO) country codes.

Moreover, weekly initial jobless claims in the United States continued close to 1 million into late September, indicating sustained widespread layoffs and adverse impacts on household income.

Massive policy support has prevented worse outcomes. The bleak numbers that mark the COVID-19 recession would have constituted far worse signposts had massive policy support not thwarted further slides in activity. As discussed in the October 2020 *Fiscal Monitor*, discretionary revenue and spending measures announced so far in advanced economies amount to more than 9 percent of GDP, with another 11 percent in various forms of liquidity support, including equity injections, asset purchases, loans, and credit guarantees. The response in emerging market and developing economies is smaller but still sizable: about 3.5 percent of GDP in discretionary budget measures and more than 2 percent in liquidity support.

New policy initiatives have also helped lift sentiment. Beyond their sheer scale, the novelty of the policy actions has also supported sentiment. Prominent examples of new initiatives include the €750 billion European Union pandemic recovery package–fund (more than half of it grant-based) and a wide range of temporary lifeline policies worldwide. The latter have included cash and in-kind transfers to affected firms and households; wage subsidies to maintain employment; expanded unemployment insurance coverage; tax deferrals; and regulatory initiatives to ease classification rules and provisioning requirements for banks' nonperforming loans, together with the release of buffers to help absorb losses. Central bank actions in advanced economies have involved more diverse, larger scales of asset purchases and relending facilities, supporting credit provision to a wide range of borrowers. The Federal Reserve also announced changes in its monetary policy strategy, moving to a flexible average inflation target of 2 percent over time. Emerging market central banks' responses combined interest rate cuts, new relending facilities, and, for the first time in many cases, asset purchases (see Chapter 2 of the October 2020 *Global Financial Stability Report* [GFSR]).

Financial conditions have generally continued to ease. These aggressive policy countermeasures have played a vital role in supporting sentiment and preventing further amplification of the COVID-19 shock through the financial system. Financial conditions have eased since June for advanced economies and for most emerging market and developing economies, implying a continuing disconnect between financial markets and the real economy that partly reflects the unprecedented policy support (as discussed in the October 2020 GFSR).

- Equity markets in advanced economies have mostly regained (and in some cases exceeded) their levels from the start of the year, sovereign bond yields are broadly unchanged or have declined further since June (as seen in Italy since the European Union's pandemic recovery package was established and the European Central Bank's pandemic emergency purchase program was expanded), and corporate spreads have dropped further, particularly for high-yield credit (benefiting, in the United States, from the Federal Reserve's targeted lending facilities), as shown in Figure 1.8. The decline in interest rates reflects a combination of a lower return on

Figure 1.8. Advanced Economies: Monetary and Financial Market Conditions
(Percent, unless noted otherwise)

Financial conditions imply a continuing disconnect between financial markets and the real economy.

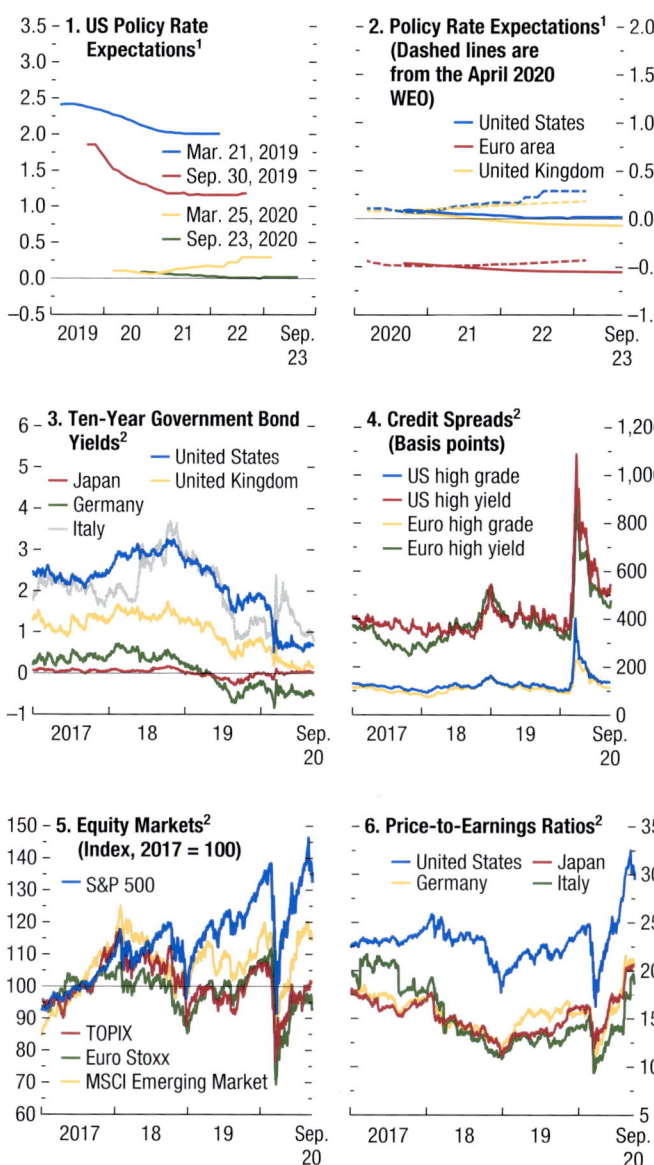

Sources: Bloomberg Finance L.P.; Haver Analytics; Refinitiv Datastream; and IMF staff calculations.
Note: MSCI = Morgan Stanley Capital International; S&P = Standard & Poor's; TOPIX = Tokyo Stock Price Index; WEO = *World Economic Outlook*.
[1]Expectations are based on the federal funds rate futures for the United States, the sterling overnight interbank average rate for the United Kingdom, and the euro interbank offered forward rate for the euro area; updated September 23, 2020.
[2]Data are through September 23, 2020.

safe assets (consistent with expectations of central bank policy rates remaining low into the foreseeable future) and compression of risk premiums—as shown in panels 1 through 4 of Figure 1.8.

- Sovereign yields in emerging markets have generally declined in recent months. Spreads over US Treasury securities, which had begun falling after the Federal Reserve's aggressive actions in March to offset tighter financial conditions and dollar liquidity shortages, have continued to compress since June in line with stronger risk appetite (Figure 1.9). Equity markets in emerging market and developing economies have also generally firmed up since June (notably in China). Steps to support dollar liquidity (such as central bank swap lines), together with the recovery under way in China, have helped rekindle portfolio flows to some emerging markets after the sharp reversal in March (Figure 1.10). Nonetheless, as noted in the October 2020 GFSR, the recovery in portfolio flows is uneven, with some countries continuing to experience large outflows.
- Among major currencies, the dollar depreciated by over 4 ½ percent in real effective terms between April and late September, reflecting improving global risk sentiment and concerns about the impact of rising COVID-19 cases on the speed of the US recovery. During the same period, the euro appreciated by close to 4 percent on improving economic prospects and slower increases in COVID-19 cases. The currencies of commodity exporters among advanced economies strengthened as commodity prices firmed. Most emerging market currencies recovered between April and June, after the severe pressures during the market turmoil in March. Since then the Chinese renminbi has strengthened and the currencies of other Asian emerging market economies have generally remained stable in real effective terms. In contrast, the Russian ruble depreciated on geopolitical factors and the currencies of countries severely affected by the pandemic or with a vulnerable external or fiscal position (such as Argentina, Brazil, and Turkey) have also weakened (Figure 1.11).

Considerations for the Forecast

Fundamental uncertainty regarding the pandemic and associated factors. The full extent of the contraction in the second quarter of 2020 has become clearer since the June 2020 WEO *Update*, providing a more informed basis for the near-term forecast. But the persistence

Figure 1.9. Emerging Market Economies: Monetary and Financial Conditions

Emerging market sovereign spreads over US Treasury securities declined after the Federal Reserve's actions in March to offset tighter financial conditions and dollar liquidity shortages.

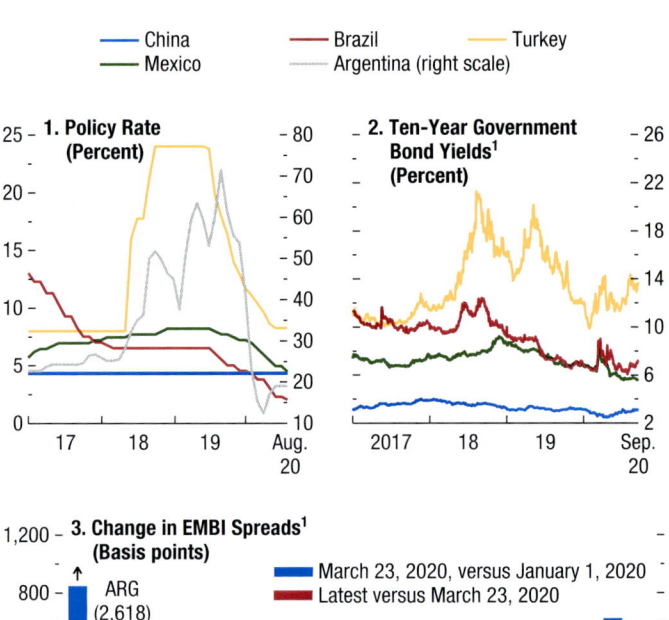

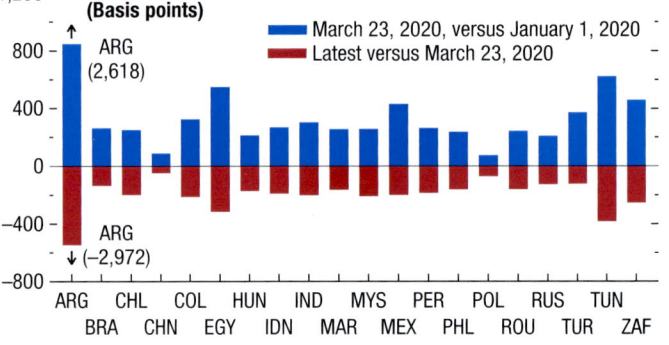

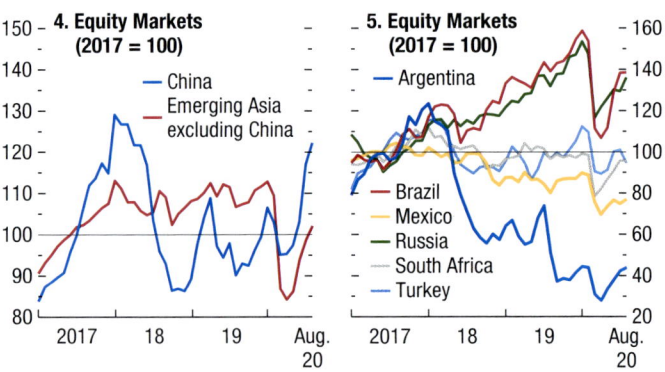

Sources: Bloomberg Finance L.P.; Haver Analytics; IMF, *International Financial Statistics;* Refinitiv Datastream; and IMF staff calculations.
Note: EMBI = J.P. Morgan Emerging Markets Bond Index. Data labels use International Organization for Standardization (ISO) country codes.
[1]Data are through September 22, 2020.

Figure 1.10. Emerging Market Economies: Capital Flows

The recovery in portfolio flows to emerging markets has been uneven, with some continuing to experience large outflows.

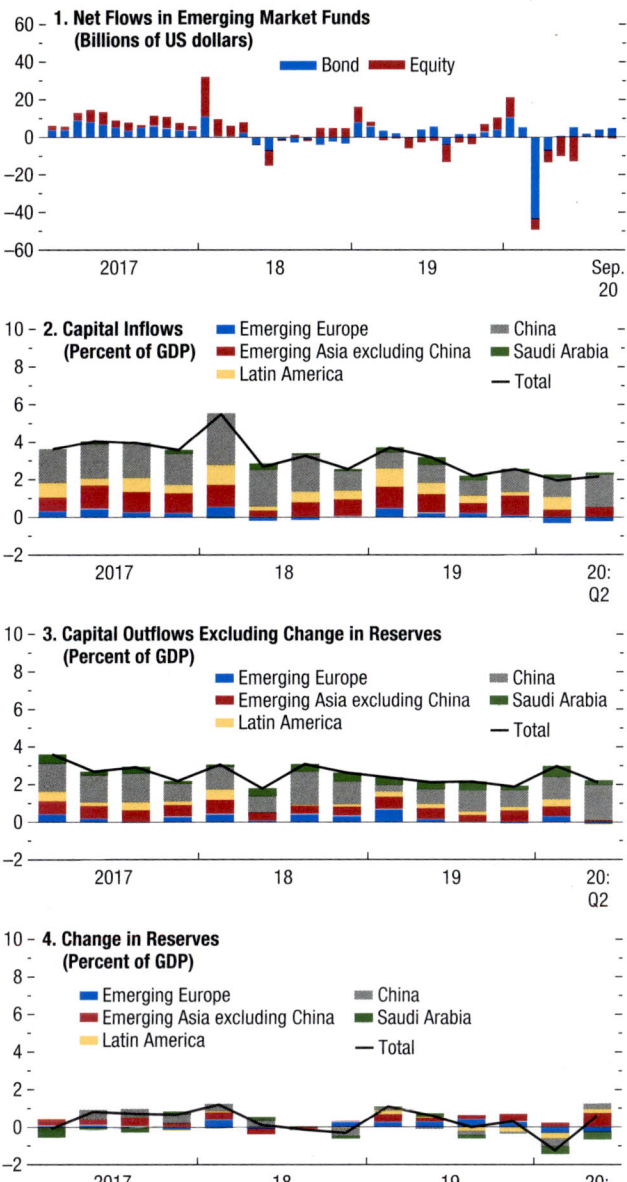

Sources: EPFR Global; Haver Analytics; IMF, *International Financial Statistics;* and IMF staff calculations.
Note: Capital inflows are net purchases of domestic assets by nonresidents. Capital outflows are net purchases of foreign assets by domestic residents. Emerging Asia excluding China comprises India, Indonesia, Malaysia, the Philippines, and Thailand; emerging Europe comprises Hungary, Poland, Romania, Russia, and Turkey; Latin America comprises Brazil, Chile, Colombia, Mexico, and Peru.

Figure 1.11. Real Effective Exchange Rate Changes, April–September 2020
(Percent)

Major currency movements have reflected shifts in risk sentiment.

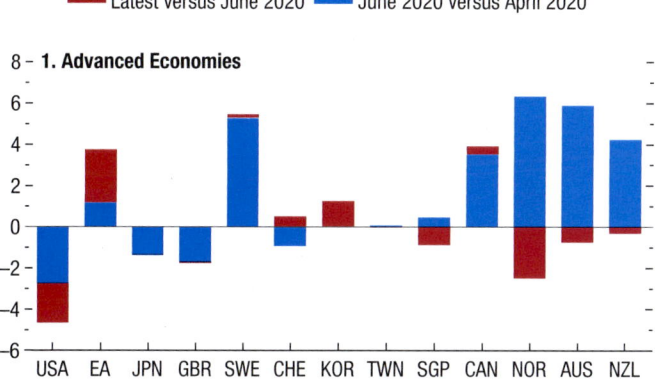

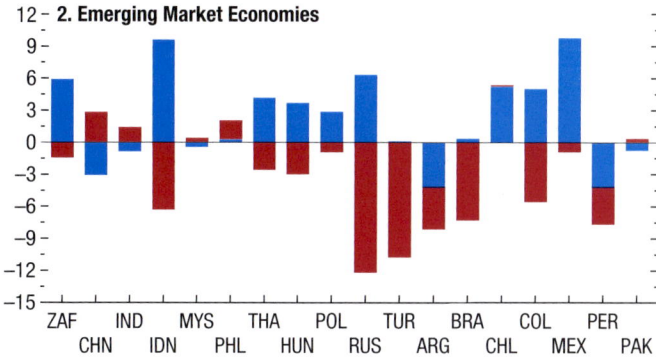

Source: IMF staff calculations.
Note: EA = euro area. Latest data available are for September 25, 2020. Data labels use International Organization for Standardization (ISO) country codes.

of the shock remains uncertain and relates to factors inherently difficult to predict, including the path of the pandemic, the adjustment costs it imposes on the economy, the effectiveness of the economic policy response, and the evolution of financial sentiment.

The baseline forecast rests on the following considerations and assumptions:

- *Stronger-than-anticipated GDP outturns in the second quarter.* The developments discussed in the previous section suggest that the worst may be over for now, but nothing is assured while the pandemic worsens and stalls reopening. A slightly less severe hit to activity than previously projected for the second quarter implies an upward revision to the 2020 forecast. But other considerations weigh on the forecast for 2021 and beyond.

- *Persistent social distancing and enhanced workplace safety standards.* The baseline projection assumes that social distancing will continue into 2021 but will then fade over time as vaccine coverage expands and therapies improve, with local transmission brought to low levels everywhere by the end of 2022. Vaccine trials have progressed at an unprecedented rate, and some have reached the final testing phase prior to approval or rejection. Nonetheless, even after approval, vaccine coverage is likely to expand only gradually as it will take time to scale up production and distribute adequate doses worldwide at affordable prices. In countries where infection rates appear to have gone past their peak, persistent behavioral changes, together with enhanced workplace hygiene and safety standards, are assumed to keep new infections at a level that allows health care systems to cope with the caseload and without requiring a return to economy-wide lockdowns. For other countries where infections are still rising, the baseline also assumes the possibility of renewed lockdowns for particular zones, even if stringent nationwide shutdowns are not repeated.
- *Scarring.* As in the WEO forecasts in April and June, the baseline also assumes that the deep downturn this year will damage supply potential to varying degrees across economies. The impact will depend on various factors discussed in the section on the medium-term growth outlook, including the extent of firm closures, exit of discouraged workers from the labor force, and resource mismatches (sectoral, occupational, and geographic).
- *Policy support and financial conditions.* Fiscal policy settings in the baseline reflect the $6 trillion direct tax and spending measures announced and implemented worldwide so far in response to the crisis (see the October 2020 *Fiscal Monitor*). Major central banks are assumed to maintain their current settings throughout the forecast horizon to the end of 2025. The baseline forecast is consistent with financial conditions remaining broadly at current levels.
- *Commodity prices.* Average petroleum spot prices per barrel are projected at $41 in 2020 and $43.8 in 2021, higher than in the April and June forecasts. Oil futures curves indicate that prices are expected to rise thereafter toward $48, some 25 percent below the 2019 average. Nonfuel commodity prices are expected to rise faster than assumed in April and June.

Partial Recovery from Deep Recession Expected in 2021

Global growth is projected at –4.4 percent in 2020, 0.8 percentage point above the June 2020 WEO *Update* forecast (Table 1.1). The stronger projection for 2020 compared with the June 2020 WEO *Update* reflects the net effect of two competing factors: the upward impetus from better-than-anticipated second quarter GDP outturns (mostly in advanced economies) versus the downdraft from persistent social distancing and stalled reopenings in the second half of the year. As explained in Box 1.1, the global growth forecast and the forecast for regional aggregates in Table 1.1 use an updated set of purchasing-power-parity weights for individual economies following the release of the 2017 survey of the International Comparison Program.[2]

As discussed, a recovery has taken root in the third quarter of 2020. It is expected to strengthen gradually over 2021. The recovery is likely to be characterized by persistent social distancing until health risks are addressed (as discussed in Chapter 2)—and countries may have to again tighten mitigation measures depending on the spread of the virus (see also Online Annex 1.2 of the October 2020 *Fiscal Monitor*). Global growth is projected at 5.2 percent in 2021, 0.2 percentage point lower than in the June 2020 WEO *Update*. The projected 2021 rebound following the deep 2020 downturn implies a small expected increase in global GDP over 2020–21 of 0.6 percentage point relative to 2019.

Growth in the *advanced economy* group is projected at –5.8 percent in 2020, 2.3 percentage points stronger than in the June 2020 WEO *Update*. The upward revision reflects, in particular, the better-than-foreseen US and euro area GDP outturns in the second quarter. In 2021 the advanced economy growth rate is projected to strengthen to 3.9 percent, leaving 2021 GDP for the group some 2 percent below what it was in 2019. The US economy is projected to contract by 4.3 percent, before growing at 3.1 percent in 2021. A deeper contraction of 8.3 percent is projected for

---

[2]The main shift in global weights compared with the previous set is an increase of 3 percentage points in the relative weight of advanced economies (from 40 percent to 43 percent for 2019), offset by a reduction in the relative weight of emerging market and developing economies, most notably China and India. Because the new set increases the weight attached to slower-growing advanced economies, the aggregation of the June 2020 WEO *Update* country forecasts with the new purchasing-power-parity weights yields a slightly lower projection for world growth in 2020 (–5.2 percent) than the one shown in June (–4.9 percent).

Table 1.1. Overview of the *World Economic Outlook* Projections
(Percent change, unless noted otherwise)

	2019	Projections		Difference from June 2020 WEO *Update*[1]		Difference from April 2020 WEO[1]	
		2020	2021	2020	2021	2020	2021
World Output	2.8	**−4.4**	**5.2**	**0.8**	**−0.2**	**−1.1**	**−0.5**
Advanced Economies	1.7	**−5.8**	**3.9**	**2.3**	**−0.9**	**0.3**	**−0.6**
United States	2.2	−4.3	3.1	3.7	−1.4	1.6	−1.6
Euro Area	1.3	−8.3	5.2	1.9	−0.8	−0.8	0.5
Germany	0.6	−6.0	4.2	1.8	−1.2	1.0	−1.0
France	1.5	−9.8	6.0	2.7	−1.3	−2.6	1.5
Italy	0.3	−10.6	5.2	2.2	−1.1	−1.5	0.4
Spain	2.0	−12.8	7.2	0.0	0.9	−4.8	2.9
Japan	0.7	−5.3	2.3	0.5	−0.1	−0.1	−0.7
United Kingdom	1.5	−9.8	5.9	0.4	−0.4	−3.3	1.9
Canada	1.7	−7.1	5.2	1.3	0.3	−0.9	1.0
Other Advanced Economies[2]	1.7	−3.8	3.6	1.1	−0.6	0.8	−1.0
Emerging Market and Developing Economies	3.7	**−3.3**	**6.0**	**−0.2**	**0.2**	**−2.1**	**−0.5**
Emerging and Developing Asia	5.5	−1.7	8.0	−0.9	0.6	−2.7	−0.5
China	6.1	1.9	8.2	0.9	0.0	0.7	−1.0
India[3]	4.2	−10.3	8.8	−5.8	2.8	−12.2	1.4
ASEAN-5[4]	4.9	−3.4	6.2	−1.4	0.0	−2.8	−1.5
Emerging and Developing Europe	2.1	−4.6	3.9	1.2	−0.3	0.6	−0.3
Russia	1.3	−4.1	2.8	2.5	−1.3	1.4	−0.7
Latin America and the Caribbean	0.0	−8.1	3.6	1.3	−0.1	−2.9	0.2
Brazil	1.1	−5.8	2.8	3.3	−0.8	−0.5	−0.1
Mexico	−0.3	−9.0	3.5	1.5	0.2	−2.4	0.5
Middle East and Central Asia	1.4	−4.1	3.0	0.4	−0.5	−1.3	−1.0
Saudi Arabia	0.3	−5.4	3.1	1.4	0.0	−3.1	0.2
Sub-Saharan Africa	3.2	−3.0	3.1	0.2	−0.3	−1.4	−1.0
Nigeria	2.2	−4.3	1.7	1.1	−0.9	−0.9	−0.7
South Africa	0.2	−8.0	3.0	0.0	−0.5	−2.2	−1.0
Memorandum							
Low-Income Developing Countries	5.3	−1.2	4.9	−0.2	−0.3	−1.6	−0.7
Middle East and North Africa	0.8	−5.0	3.2	0.7	−0.5	−1.8	−1.0
World Growth Based on Market Exchange Rates	2.4	−4.7	4.8	1.4	−0.5	−0.5	−0.6
World Trade Volume (goods and services)	1.0	**−10.4**	**8.3**	**1.5**	**0.3**	**0.6**	**−0.1**
Imports							
Advanced Economies	1.7	−11.5	7.3	1.7	0.1	0.0	−0.2
Emerging Market and Developing Economies	−0.6	−9.4	11.0	0.0	1.6	−1.2	1.9
Exports							
Advanced Economies	1.3	−11.6	7.0	2.0	−0.2	1.2	−0.4
Emerging Market and Developing Economies	0.9	−7.7	9.5	1.6	0.2	1.9	−1.5
Commodity Prices (US dollars)							
Oil[5]	−10.2	−32.1	12.0	9.0	8.2	9.9	5.7
Nonfuel (average based on world commodity import weights)	0.8	5.6	5.1	5.4	4.3	6.7	5.7
Consumer Prices							
Advanced Economies	1.4	0.8	1.6	0.5	0.5	0.3	0.1
Emerging Market and Developing Economies[6]	5.1	5.0	4.7	0.5	0.1	0.3	0.2
London Interbank Offered Rate (percent)							
On US Dollar Deposits (six month)	2.3	0.7	0.4	−0.2	−0.2	0.0	−0.2
On Euro Deposits (three month)	−0.4	−0.4	−0.5	0.0	−0.1	0.0	−0.1
On Japanese Yen Deposits (six month)	0.0	0.0	0.0	0.0	0.1	0.1	0.1

Source: IMF staff estimates.

Note: Real effective exchange rates are assumed to remain constant at the levels prevailing during July 24–August 21, 2020. Economies are listed on the basis of economic size. The aggregated quarterly data are seasonally adjusted. WEO = *World Economic Outlook.*

[1]Difference based on rounded figures for the current, June 2020 WEO *Update*, and April 2020 WEO forecasts. Global and regional growth figures are based on new purchasing-power-parity weights derived from the recently released 2017 International Comparison Program survey (see Box) and are not comparable to the figures reported in the April 2020 WEO.

[2]Excludes the Group of Seven (Canada, France, Germany, Italy, Japan, United Kingdom, United States) and euro area countries.

[3]For India, data and forecasts are presented on a fiscal year basis, and GDP from 2011 onward is based on GDP at market prices with fiscal year 2011/12 as a base year.

Table 1.1 *(continued)*
(Percent change, unless noted otherwise)

	Year over Year				Q4 over Q4[7]			
			Projections				Projections	
	2018	2019	2020	2021	2018	2019	2020	2021
World Output	**3.5**	**2.8**	**−4.4**	**5.2**	**3.1**	**2.7**	**−2.6**	**3.7**
Advanced Economies	**2.2**	**1.7**	**−5.8**	**3.9**	**1.7**	**1.5**	**−4.9**	**3.8**
United States	3.0	2.2	−4.3	3.1	2.5	2.3	−4.1	3.2
Euro Area	1.8	1.3	−8.3	5.2	1.1	1.0	−6.6	4.8
Germany	1.3	0.6	−6.0	4.2	0.3	0.4	−5.2	4.6
France	1.8	1.5	−9.8	6.0	1.4	0.8	−6.7	4.0
Italy	0.8	0.3	−10.6	5.2	0.1	0.1	−8.0	3.4
Spain	2.4	2.0	−12.8	7.2	2.1	1.8	−10.8	6.6
Japan	0.3	0.7	−5.3	2.3	−0.3	−0.7	−2.3	0.7
United Kingdom	1.3	1.5	−9.8	5.9	1.4	1.1	−6.4	3.7
Canada	2.0	1.7	−7.1	5.2	1.8	1.5	−5.9	4.9
Other Advanced Economies[2]	2.7	1.7	−3.8	3.6	2.3	2.1	−4.2	5.0
Emerging Market and Developing Economies	**4.5**	**3.7**	**−3.3**	**6.0**	**4.3**	**3.8**	**−0.5**	**3.6**
Emerging and Developing Asia	6.3	5.5	−1.7	8.0	6.1	5.1	2.2	3.6
China	6.7	6.1	1.9	8.2	6.6	6.0	5.8	3.9
India[3]	6.1	4.2	−10.3	8.8	5.5	3.1	−4.0	1.4
ASEAN-5[4]	5.3	4.9	−3.4	6.2	5.3	4.6	−2.1	5.2
Emerging and Developing Europe	3.3	2.1	−4.6	3.9	. . .	. . .	. . .	. . .
Russia	2.5	1.3	−4.1	2.8	2.9	2.2	−4.5	2.8
Latin America and the Caribbean	1.1	0.0	−8.1	3.6	−0.2	−0.3	−6.5	2.1
Brazil	1.3	1.1	−5.8	2.8	0.8	1.6	−4.7	1.7
Mexico	2.2	−0.3	−9.0	3.5	1.2	−0.8	−7.0	2.7
Middle East and Central Asia	2.1	1.4	−4.1	3.0	. . .	. . .	. . .	. . .
Saudi Arabia	2.4	0.3	−5.4	3.1	4.3	−0.3	−5.2	6.6
Sub-Saharan Africa	3.3	3.2	−3.0	3.1	. . .	. . .	. . .	. . .
Nigeria	1.9	2.2	−4.3	1.7	. . .	. . .	. . .	. . .
South Africa	0.8	0.2	−8.0	3.0	0.2	−0.6	−5.5	1.0
Memorandum								
Low-Income Developing Countries	5.1	5.3	−1.2	4.9	. . .	. . .	. . .	. . .
Middle East and North Africa	1.2	0.8	−5.0	3.2	. . .	. . .	. . .	. . .
World Growth Based on Market Exchange Rates	3.1	2.4	−4.7	4.8	2.6	2.3	−3.0	3.7
World Trade Volume (goods and services)	**3.9**	**1.0**	**−10.4**	**8.3**	. . .	. . .	. . .	. . .
Imports								
Advanced Economies	3.6	1.7	−11.5	7.3	. . .	. . .	. . .	. . .
Emerging Market and Developing Economies	5.0	−0.6	−9.4	11.0	. . .	. . .	. . .	. . .
Exports								
Advanced Economies	3.5	1.3	−11.6	7.0	. . .	. . .	. . .	. . .
Emerging Market and Developing Economies	4.1	0.9	−7.7	9.5	. . .	. . .	. . .	. . .
Commodity Prices (US dollars)								
Oil[5]	29.4	−10.2	−32.1	12.0	9.5	−6.1	−26.1	6.2
Nonfuel (average based on world commodity import weights)	1.3	0.8	5.6	5.1	−2.3	4.9	10.3	−0.5
Consumer Prices								
Advanced Economies	2.0	1.4	0.8	1.6	1.9	1.4	0.8	1.5
Emerging Market and Developing Economies[6]	4.9	5.1	5.0	4.7	4.5	5.1	3.5	4.1
London Interbank Offered Rate (percent)								
On US Dollar Deposits (six month)	2.5	2.3	0.7	0.4	. . .	. . .	. . .	. . .
On Euro Deposits (three month)	−0.3	−0.4	−0.4	−0.5	. . .	. . .	. . .	. . .
On Japanese Yen Deposits (six month)	0.0	0.0	0.0	0.0	. . .	. . .	. . .	. . .

[4]Indonesia, Malaysia, Philippines, Thailand, and Vietnam.

[5]Simple average of prices of UK Brent, Dubai Fateh, and West Texas Intermediate crude oil. The average price of oil in US dollars a barrel was $61.39 in 2019; the assumed price, based on futures markets, is $41.69 in 2020 and $46.70 in 2021.

[6]Excludes Venezuela. See country-specific note for Venezuela in the "Country Notes" section of the Statistical Appendix.

[7]For World Output, the quarterly estimates and projections account for approximately 90 percent of annual world output at purchasing-power-parity weights. For Emerging Market and Developing Economies, the quarterly estimates and projections account for approximately 80 percent of annual emerging market and developing economies' output at purchasing-power-parity weights.

Table 1.2. Overview of the *World Economic Outlook* Projections at Market Prices
(Percent change)

		Projections		Difference from June 2020 WEO *Update*[1]		Difference from April 2020 WEO[1]	
	2019	2020	2021	2020	2021	2020	2021
World Output	2.4	−4.7	4.8	1.4	−0.5	−0.5	−0.6
Advanced Economies	1.7	−5.8	3.8	2.3	−1.0	0.4	−0.7
Emerging Market and Developing Economies	3.6	−3.0	6.2	0.1	0.1	−1.7	−0.6
Emerging and Developing Asia	5.7	−0.7	8.0	−0.4	0.4	−1.7	−0.7
Emerging and Developing Europe	2.1	−4.5	3.8	1.3	−0.5	0.7	−0.3
Latin America and the Caribbean	−0.5	−8.1	3.6	1.3	−0.1	−2.8	0.2
Middle East and Central Asia	1.0	−5.7	3.2	0.3	−0.4	−2.1	−1.1
Sub-Saharan Africa	2.8	−3.5	3.1	0.2	−0.3	−1.5	−0.9
Memorandum							
Low-Income Developing Countries	5.1	−1.4	4.7	−0.1	−0.3	−1.6	−0.7

Source: IMF staff estimates.

Note: The aggregate growth rates are calculated as a weighted average, where a moving average of nominal GDP in US dollars for the preceding three years is used as the weight. WEO = *World Economic Outlook*.

[1]Difference based on rounded figures for the current, June 2020 WEO *Update*, and April 2020 WEO forecasts.

the euro area in 2020, reflecting a sharper downturn than in the United States in the first half of the year. The growth bounce-back of 5.2 percent projected for 2021 is accordingly stronger from a lower base. Asian advanced economies are projected to have somewhat more moderate downturns than those of Europe, in light of the more contained pandemic, also reflected in smaller GDP declines during the first half of 2020.

Among *emerging market and developing economies*, growth is forecast at −3.3 percent in 2020, 0.2 percentage point weaker than in the June 2020 WEO *Update*, strengthening to 6 percent in 2021. Prospects for China are much stronger than for most other countries in this group, with the economy projected to grow by about 10 percent over 2020–21 (1.9 percent this year and 8.2 percent next year). Activity normalized faster than expected after most of the country reopened in early April, and second quarter GDP registered a positive surprise on the back of strong policy support and resilient exports.

For many *emerging market and developing economies excluding China*, prospects continue to remain precarious. This reflects a combination of factors: the continuing spread of the pandemic and overwhelmed health care systems; the greater importance of severely affected sectors, such as tourism; and the greater dependence on external finance, including remittances. All emerging market and developing economy regions are expected to contract this year, including notably emerging Asia, where large economies, such as India and Indonesia, continue to try to bring the pandemic under control. Revisions to the forecast are particularly large for India, where GDP contracted much more severely than

expected in the second quarter. As a result, the economy is projected to contract by 10.3 percent in 2020, before rebounding by 8.8 percent in 2021. Regional differences remain stark, with many countries in Latin America severely affected by the pandemic facing very deep downturns, and large output declines expected for many countries in the Middle East and Central Asia region and oil-exporting countries in sub-Saharan Africa affected by low oil prices, civil strife, or economic crises. Growth for emerging market and developing economies excluding China is projected at −5.7 percent for 2020 and 5 percent for 2021. The projected rebound in 2021 is not sufficient to regain the 2019 level of activity by next year. Growth among low-income developing countries is projected at −1.2 percent in 2020, strengthening to 4.9 percent in 2021. Higher population growth and low starting levels of income imply that even this more modest contraction compared with most emerging market economies will take a very heavy toll on living standards, especially for the poor (Box 1.2).

Table 1.2 provides alternative projections for global and key group aggregate growth rates using GDP at market exchange rates as weights.[3] The market exchange rate weights allocate significantly higher global GDP shares to slower-growing advanced economies than the purchasing-power-parity weights used in Table 1.1. Because of the difference in weights the global growth projection (−4.7 percent for 2020 and 4.8 percent for 2021) is lower than in Table 1.1.

[3]Specifically, the projections use a three-year trailing moving average of nominal US dollar GDP as weights.

Unemployment. The growth projections imply wide negative output gaps this year and in 2021 as well as elevated unemployment rates across both advanced and emerging market economies (Annex Tables 1.1.1 to 1.1.5). Including those in reduced-hours work programs and those counted in involuntary part-time employment, the share of workers underemployed in some advanced economies is significantly higher than the fraction of headline unemployed. Labor market data are less comprehensive for emerging market economies. Nonetheless, based on surveys and available official estimates, unemployment rates in several emerging market economies are projected to increase significantly this year.

Medium-Term Growth Reflects Damage to Supply Potential

After the rebound in 2021, the baseline forecast for the global economy envisages growth to slow to about 3.5 percent into the medium term. This implies that both advanced and emerging market and developing economies will only modestly progress toward the 2020–25 path of economic activity projected before the COVID-19 pandemic (Figure 1.12), pointing to a severe setback to the projected pace of improvement in average living standards across all country groups (Figure 1.13).

Medium-term projections incorporate the expected impact of the COVID-19 shock on supply potential. As noted, the projections rely on economies adapting and operating in ways compatible with social distancing for the initial forecast years and being affected by scarring (including through bankruptcies, lower labor force participation, and obstacles to resource reallocation). This may entail large structural change, including redeploying resources away from sectors where activity will be constrained by distancing, workplace changes to raise safety standards, and the adoption of new technologies that support remote working. As firms make the needed adjustments to modes of production and distribution while consumers adapt to new modes of consumption (such as increasingly shifting to

Figure 1.12. GDP Losses: 2019–21 versus 2019–25
(Percent difference between January 2020 WEO Update and October 2020 WEO projections)

Over the medium term, advanced and emerging market and developing economies will only modestly progress toward the 2020–25 path of economic activity projected before the COVID-19 pandemic.

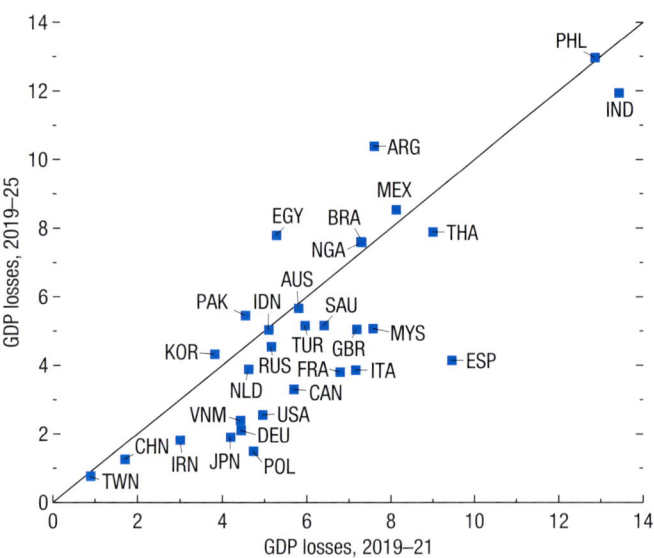

Source: IMF staff estimates.
Note: WEO = *World Economic Outlook.* Data labels use International Organization for Standardization (ISO) country codes.

Figure 1.13. Per Capita GDP: Cumulative Growth, 2019–25
(Percent)

Subdued medium-term growth prospects imply a severe setback to the projected pace of improvement in average living standards across all country groups.

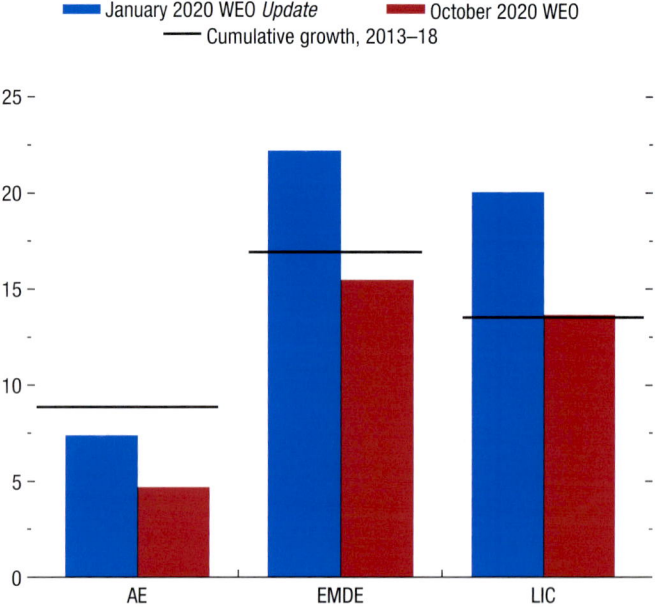

Source: IMF staff estimates.
Note: AE = advanced economy; EMDE = emerging market and developing economy; LIC = low-income country; WEO = *World Economic Outlook.*

online purchases), the changes are expected to have persistent effects on potential output across economies.

Among the 10 largest advanced economies, potential GDP in the medium term is expected, on average, to remain 3.5 percent below what had been projected in the January 2020 WEO (pre-pandemic) forecast. Among the 10 largest emerging markets, the decline is even larger, at 5.5 percent, on average.

In the *advanced economy* group, growth is expected to slow to 1.7 percent over the medium term. Beyond the impact of the pandemic on potential growth, the macroeconomic effects of demographic change (aging and slower population growth) weigh on the medium-term forecast for the group.

Among *emerging market and developing economies*, growth is projected to decline to 4.7 percent by 2025, well below the 5.6 percent average of 2000–19. Key features shaping the medium-term outlook for the group include the structural slowdown in China that preceded the pandemic and is expected to continue following the strong cyclical rebound in 2021; a subdued path for commodity prices; weak prospects for external demand related to the expected moderation in advanced economy growth; and, for tourism-dependent economies, persistently lower cross-border travel.

Challenges to Debt Sustainability

The subdued outlook for medium-term growth comes with a significant projected increase in the stock of sovereign debt—which was high to begin with. Downward revisions to potential output also imply a smaller tax base over the medium term than previously envisaged, compounding difficulties in servicing debt obligations.

As discussed in the October 2020 *Fiscal Monitor*, sovereign debt to GDP in advanced economies is projected to rise by 20 percentage points to about 125 percent of GDP by the end of 2021. Over the same period, sovereign debt to GDP in emerging market and developing economies is projected to rise by more than 10 percentage points to about 65 percent of GDP.

Although low interest rates are expected to contain debt service, this is a mitigating factor mostly for advanced economies with a large fraction of negative-yielding sovereign bonds. The ratio of sovereign debt service to tax revenue is anticipated to increase for several emerging markets and low-income countries (Figure 1.14).

Figure 1.14. Ratio of Public Debt Service Costs to Government Tax Revenue
(Share of countries in group, percent)

The ratio of sovereign debt service to tax revenue is anticipated to increase for several emerging markets and developing economies.

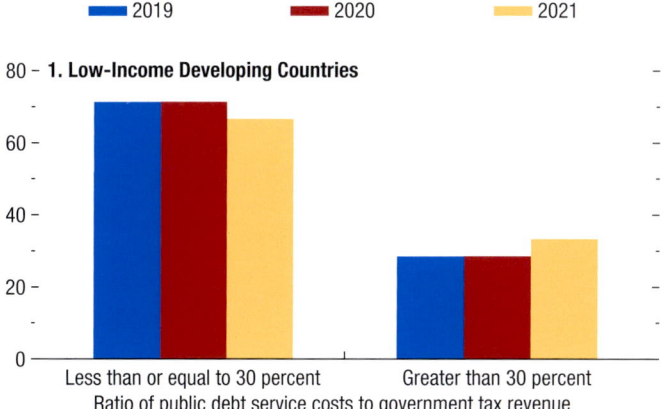

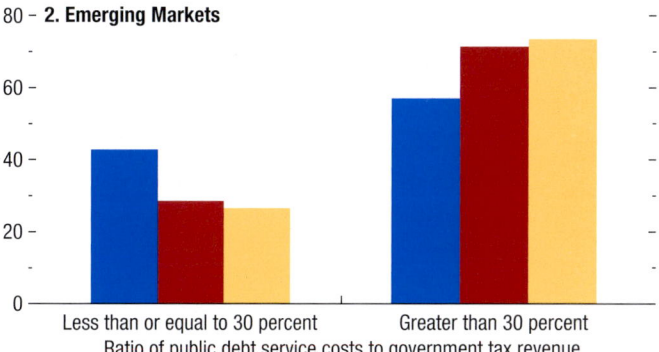

Source: IMF staff estimates.
Note: Shares by country groups are calculated based on countries for which data are available.

The high fraction of tax revenue absorbed by debt service will necessarily mean that there is less revenue left over for critical areas, including social spending needs. These needs will be elevated after the crisis period to address rising poverty, tackle growing inequality, and correct setbacks to human capital accumulation.

Poverty, Inequality, and Setbacks to Human Capital Accumulation

Poverty. The pandemic will reverse the progress made since the 1990s in reducing global poverty. People who rely on daily wage labor and are outside the formal safety net faced sudden income losses when mobility restrictions were imposed. Among them, migrant workers who live far from home had even less recourse to traditional support networks. As a consequence, close to 90 million people could fall below the $1.90 a day income threshold of extreme deprivation this year (Box 1.2, October 2020 *Fiscal Monitor*, and WB 2020a).

Inequality. As discussed in Chapter 2, the pandemic is having particularly adverse effects on economically more vulnerable people, including younger workers and women. The burden of the crisis has fallen unevenly across sectors. Differentiating jobs based on attributes that make them amenable to telework, workers most affected by the pandemic are employed in accommodation and food services, transportation, retail, and wholesale (Brussevich, Dabla-Norris, and Khalid 2020). Moreover, younger workers, those in less secure work arrangements, and those employed in small and medium enterprises appear more vulnerable to layoffs. In general, low-wage earners are at an appreciably higher risk of losing their jobs than those in upper quintiles of the wage distribution (see, for example, Shibata 2020 on the United States). Similar outcomes are seen in emerging market and developing economies, where informally employed workers are more likely to become unemployed than those with formal contracts (see, for example, Jain and others 2020 on South Africa).

Such developments will exacerbate preexisting trends. Entering the crisis, income inequality had risen significantly compared with the early 1990s in many advanced economies and among some fast-growing emerging market and developing economies (Figure 1.15; also see Annex 1.1 of the October 2020 *Fiscal Monitor*). These developments reflect a combination of factors, including skill-biased technological change that favored those with high educational attainment, the decline of unions, the increase in firms' monopsony power in the labor market because of rising market concentration and the associated decrease in the bargaining power of employees, and regressive tax policy changes that have resulted in lower marginal taxes on the highest earners as well as lower corporate taxes over the past several years.

Human Capital Accumulation. An additional aspect, with bearing on the current labor market outcomes of parents and prospects for their children, follows from the extensive school closures during the pandemic. UNESCO (2020) estimates that more than 1.6 billion learners worldwide have been affected by school and

Figure 1.15. Change in Income Inequality since 1990
(Change in Gini coefficient for disposable income[1])

Entering the COVID-19 pandemic, income inequality had risen significantly compared with the early 1990s in many advanced economies and among some fast-growing emerging market and developing economies.

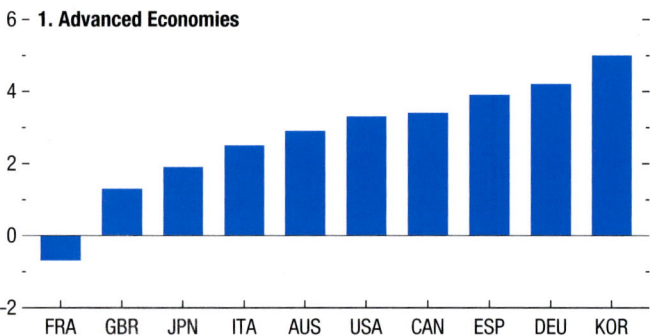

1. Advanced Economies

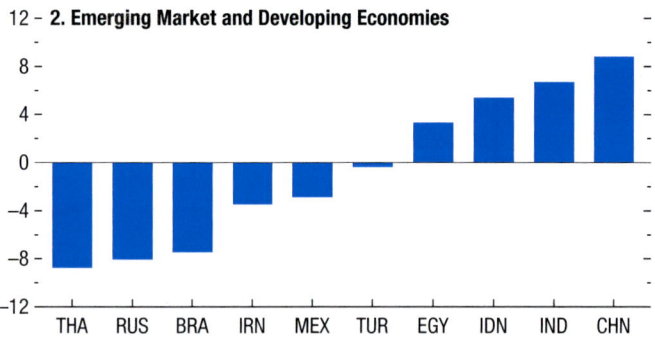

2. Emerging Market and Developing Economies

Sources: IMF Fiscal Affairs Department Gini database; Standardized World Income Inequality database; and IMF staff calculations.
Note: Data labels use International Organization for Standardization (ISO) country codes.
[1]Change is calculated as latest available minus Gini coefficient in 1990.

university closures. Gaps in childcare limit parents' ability to work, particularly that of mothers (see Chapter 2). For children, schooling interruptions reduce learning opportunities. This is particularly true for underprivileged students, whose parents may not be as well placed as affluent parents to provide supplementary instruction for their children. Evidence suggests that the loss of learning increases with the duration of interruption (Quinn and Polikoff 2017). Online and distance learning can act as a temporary bridge, but are not an effective substitute (Baytiyeh 2018).

School closures exacerbate fundamental divisions in the access to nutrition and safe environments for children. Because many schools provide free or subsidized meals to children from low-income households, closures may result in greater food insecurity and poorer nutrition for children from those homes (Anderson, Gallagher, and Ramirez Ritchie 2017; Ralston and others 2017). Children home from school are also more likely to be exposed to violence and exploitation. In some countries, past evidence suggests school closures are associated with earlier marriages, children forced into militias, sexual exploitation, teen pregnancies, and child labor (Korkoyah and Wreh 2015; UNDP 2015; UNESCO 2020).

The closures are likely to have long-lasting consequences for future social and economic outcomes absent actions to try to regain the human capital accumulation lost. Lower lifetime schooling is associated with lower lifetime income (Card 1999). Interrupted schooling is also associated with lower earnings trajectories (Light 1995; Holmlund, Liu, and Skans 2008).

In short, the subdued medium-term growth outlook for the global economy comes with the prospect of elevated debt, more poverty, higher inequality, and severe setbacks to human capital accumulation. Policymakers will also have to confront additional complexities related to the outlook for inflation and trade, the subject of the next two sections.

Inflation Is Expected to Remain Low

As with the growth outlook, considerable uncertainty surrounds the inflation projections for the projection horizon. Competing forces will shape price developments in the years ahead (see Ebrahimy, Igan, and Martinez Peria 2020).

- Price pressures could increase, for example, due to the release of pent-up demand as consumers increase spending on items that they had been forced to delay consuming because of lockdowns and restrictions on movement. They could also increase due to higher production costs from persistent supply disruptions. The credibility of monetary policy frameworks can also affect price developments. Credibility can suffer where central banks are regarded as conducting monetary policy to keep government borrowing costs low rather than to ensure price stability ("fiscal dominance"). In those contexts, inflation expectations can increase very quickly once governments begin running large fiscal deficits.
- Counterbalancing such forces are those that will weigh on demand. These include a persistent increase in consumers' precautionary saving prompted by higher perceived risk of joblessness

and falling sick; transfers of purchasing power to lenders with lower propensities to spend as borrowers service the high debt incurred during the pandemic; and concerns about the limits of monetary policy's ability to stimulate demand (particularly in advanced economies), which cause inflation expectations to slide and lead to disinflation.

A sectoral decomposition of inflation in the period leading up to the pandemic and in the first six months of the pandemic offers clues about what to expect. Across a sample of advanced economies and large emerging market economies, the decline in inflation appears broad-based (Freitag and Lian, forthcoming). It reflects weak price pressures in sectors where price developments have historically responded to aggregate demand (furnishing, housing excluding energy, recreation, restaurants, and hotels) as well as in "noncyclical" sectors, where price movements typically are less sensitive to demand fluctuations (clothing and footwear, communications, education, health, transportation services, and miscellaneous goods and services), as shown in Figure 1.16. With aggregate demand expected to be relatively weak and economies projected to operate with considerable slack into 2022, price pressures in the cyclically sensitive sectors are expected to stay muted. Moreover, inflation in the noncyclical group has been on a long-standing downward trend. The trend is expected to continue, given that these sectors are unlikely to experience supply constraints or rising unit labor costs on account of slowing innovation.

Market participants generally expect subdued inflation in advanced economies (Figure 1.17). Among emerging market economies, inflation expectations remain relatively low compared with historical averages. Even as some emerging market central banks have embarked on asset purchases, these actions have so far not unanchored inflation expectations. Possible reasons include more credible monetary policy frameworks and communications explaining that the actions are also intended to support market functioning, consistent with price stability mandates.

In line with the subdued outlook for activity, inflation is expected to remain relatively low over the forecast horizon. Inflation in the advanced economy group is projected at 0.8 percent in 2020, rising to 1.6 percent in 2021 as the recovery gains hold, and broadly stabilizing thereafter at 1.9 percent. In the emerging market and developing economy group,

Figure 1.16. Contribution to Headline Inflation
(Percentage points)

The decline in inflation appears broad based, encompassing sectors where price developments have historically responded to aggregate demand as well as in those in which price movements typically are less sensitive to demand fluctuations.

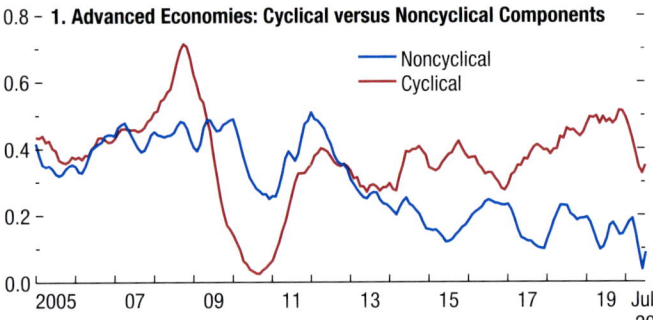

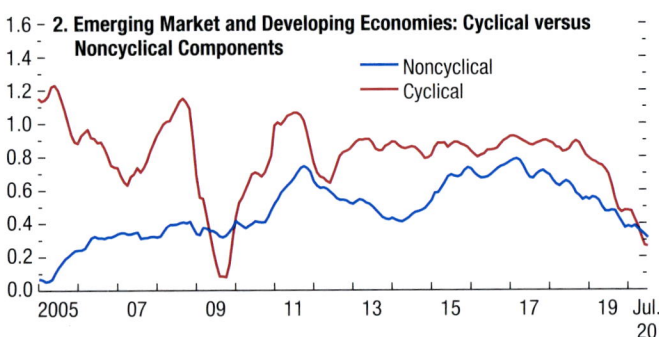

Sources: Eurostat; Haver Analytics; Organisation for Economic Co-operation and Development; and IMF staff calculations.
Note: The figure plots the time fixed effects of regressions in which three-month trailing averages of contributions to headline inflation are regressed on country and time fixed effects, with the weights being the GDP in purchasing-power-parity terms. The contribution of a component is defined as its year-on-year price change multiplied by its weight in the headline consumer price index basket. Country fixed effects account for different timing of countries entering the sample, and the time fixed effects are normalized to equal the contribution in January 2005. Cyclical components include furnishing, household equipment and routine household maintenance, housing (excluding utilities whenever the data permit), recreation and culture, and restaurants and hotels. Noncyclical components include clothing and footwear, communication, education, health, and miscellaneous goods and services. The definition of cyclical components follows the results of Stock and Watson (2019), except that furnishing, household equipment, and routine household maintenance are not included in their construction of cyclically sensitive inflation. Food and energy components are excluded to better reveal underlying trends. Transportation services are a noncyclical component in Stock and Watson (2019) and excluded here, as it was volatile in 2020 for advanced economies, and cannot be constructed without being combined with the fuel component for many emerging market and developing economies. The post–global financial crisis downward trend of noncyclical components remains if transportation services are included. Advanced economies comprise Austria, Belgium, Cyprus, the Czech Republic, Denmark, Estonia, Finland, France, Germany, Greece, Iceland, Ireland, Italy, Japan, Latvia, Lithuania, Luxembourg, Malta, the Netherlands, Norway, Portugal, Slovenia, South Korea, Spain, Sweden, Switzerland, the United Kingdom, and the United States. Emerging market and developing economies comprise Algeria, Chile, China, Colombia, Egypt, Hungary, India, Kazakhstan, Malaysia, Morocco, Myanmar, Nigeria, Pakistan, Peru, the Philippines, Poland, Qatar, Romania, Russia, Serbia, Slovak Republic, South Africa, Thailand, Ukraine, the United Arab Emirates, and Vietnam.

Figure 1.17. Five-Year, Five-Year Inflation Swaps
(Percent; market-implied average inflation rate expected over the five-year period starting five years from date shown)

Inflation in advanced economies is generally expected to remain subdued.

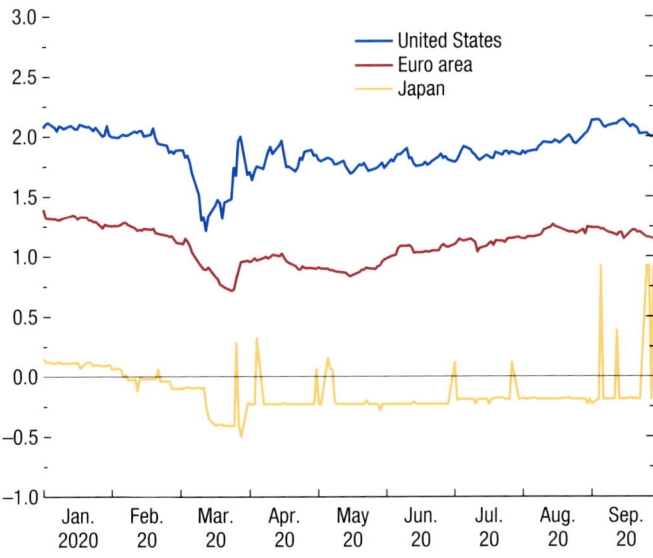

Sources: Bloomberg Finance L.P.; and IMF staff calculations.

inflation is projected at 5 percent this year, declining to 4.7 percent next year, and moderating thereafter to 4 percent over the medium term, below the historical average for the group.

Subdued Trade Flows, Smaller Deficits and Surpluses

Global trade growth is projected to weaken significantly. Global trade is expected to contract by over 10 percent this year—a pace similar to during the global financial crisis in 2009, despite the contraction in activity being much more pronounced this year. The current recession reflects a particularly sharp contraction in contact-intensive sectors with much smaller trade intensity than manufacturing, which generally contracts sharply in recessions as demand for capital goods and consumer durables plummets. As noted in the 2020 *External Sector Report*, the expected decline in trade volumes largely reflects weak final demand from consumers and firms in the synchronized global downturn. Trade restrictions (for example on medical supplies) and supply chain disruptions are expected to play limited roles in accounting for the collapse.

Consistent with the projected recovery in global activity, trade volumes are expected to grow by about 8 percent in 2021 and by slightly more than 4 percent, on average, in subsequent years. Subdued trade volumes also reflect, in part, possible shifts in supply chains as firms reshore production to reduce perceived vulnerabilities from reliance on foreign producers. A reflection of this anticipated development is that foreign direct investment flows as a share of global GDP are expected to remain well below their levels of the pre-pandemic decade (Figure 1.18, panel 1).

While all countries are expected to suffer large drops in exports and imports, the incidence is uneven. The trade outlook is particularly bleak for tourism-dependent economies, where restrictions on international travel, together with consumers' fear of contagion, are likely to weigh heavily on tourism activity even in situations where the pandemic appears contained for now (economies in the Caribbean, for example). Balance of payments data for the first half of the year show a collapse in net revenues from tourism and travel for countries in which these sectors play an important role (for instance, Greece, Iceland, Portugal, and Turkey; Figure 1.18, panel 2). And as Figure 1.18, panel 3 shows, countries where tourism and travel account for a larger share of GDP are projected to suffer larger declines in activity during 2020–21 compared with pre-COVID-19 forecasts. In addition, oil exporters have suffered a severe terms-of-trade shock with the decline in oil prices and face a more difficult external outlook.

Remittances. Remittance flows contracted sharply during the early lockdown period but have shown signs of recovery. Nonetheless, the risk of a decline in payments and transfers from migrant workers back to their home countries is very significant, particularly for such countries as Bangladesh, Egypt, Guatemala, Pakistan, the Philippines, and those in sub-Saharan Africa more broadly.

Global current account deficits and surpluses are projected to shrink in 2020 to the lowest level in the past two decades and to remain broadly stable thereafter (Figure 1.19). Among creditor countries, surpluses are projected to decline in east Asia and to a lesser extent in Germany and the Netherlands, reflecting the weaker external environment, while the surplus in oil exporters is projected to turn into a modest deficit. These offset a modest increase in the projected surplus for China. Among debtor countries, smaller deficits

are projected for Latin America, despite negative terms-of-trade shocks, mainly reflecting pronounced weakness in domestic demand, as well as for India and the United Kingdom on the back of lower oil prices and weak domestic demand. Creditor and debtor positions as a share of GDP are instead projected

Figure 1.18. Global Trade Volume Growth, Global Outward Foreign Direct Investment, and Travel-Related Trade Services

The contraction in global trade in 2020 reflects a sharp collapse in tourism and travel. Countries where these sectors account for a larger share of GDP are projected to suffer bigger declines in activity during 2020–21 compared with pre-pandemic forecasts.

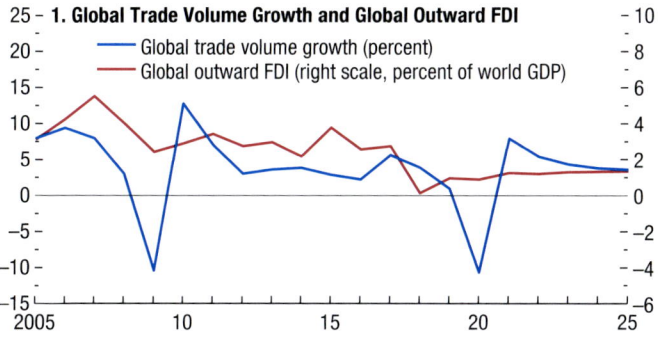

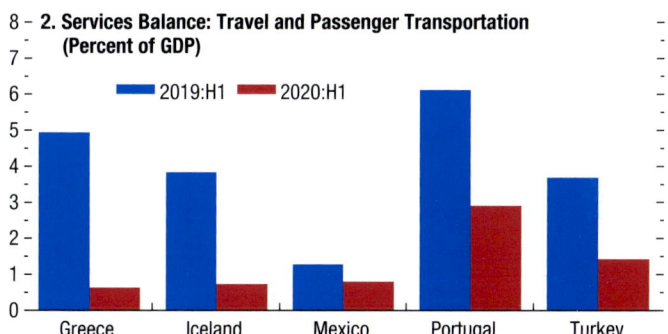

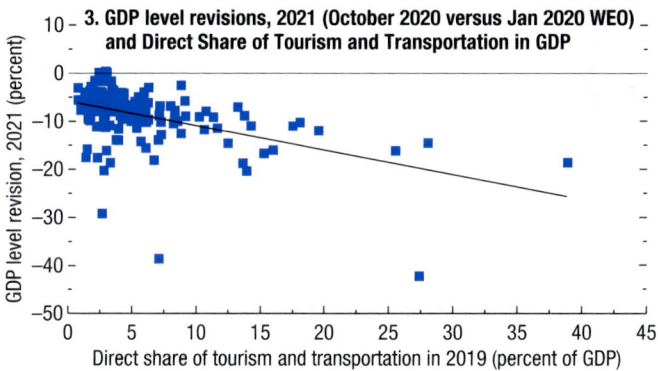

Sources: World Travel and Tourism Council; and IMF staff estimates.
Note: FDI = foreign direct investment; WEO = *World Economic Outlook.*

Figure 1.19. Current Account and International Investment Positions
(Percent of world GDP)

Global current account deficits and surpluses are projected to shrink in 2020 to the lowest level in the past two decades.

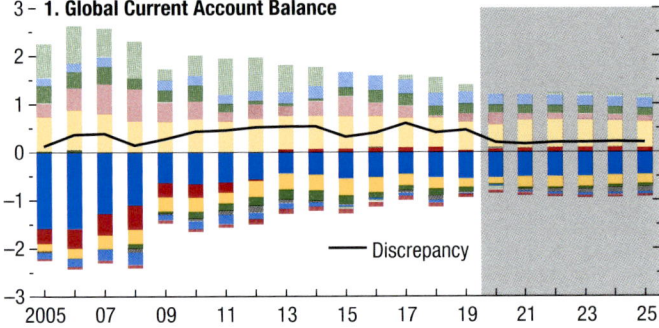

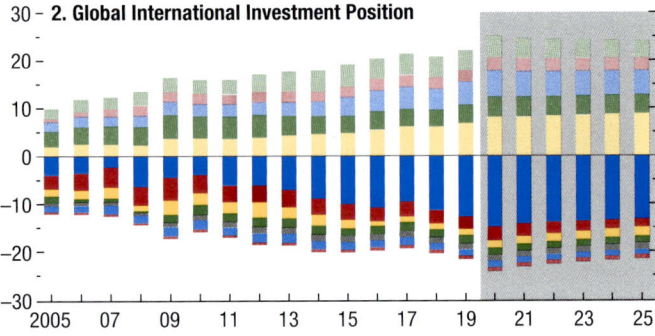

Source: IMF staff estimates.
Note: Adv. Asia = advanced Asia (Hong Kong SAR, Korea, Singapore, Taiwan Province of China); Afr. and ME = Africa and the Middle East (Democratic Republic of the Congo, Egypt, Ethiopia, Ghana, Jordan, Kenya, Lebanon, Morocco, South Africa, Sudan, Tanzania, Tunisia); CEE = central and eastern Europe (Belarus, Bulgaria, Croatia, Czech Republic, Hungary, Poland, Romania, Slovak Republic, Turkey, Ukraine); Em. Asia = emerging Asia (India, Indonesia, Pakistan, Philippines, Thailand, Vietnam); Eur. creditors = European creditors (Austria, Belgium, Denmark, Finland, Germany, Luxembourg, Netherlands, Norway, Sweden, Switzerland); Euro debtors = euro area debtors (Cyprus, Greece, Ireland, Italy, Portugal, Spain, Slovenia); Lat. Am. = Latin America (Argentina, Brazil, Chile, Colombia, Mexico, Peru, Uruguay); Oil exporters = Algeria, Azerbaijan, Iran, Kazakhstan, Kuwait, Nigeria, Oman, Qatar, Russia, Saudi Arabia, United Arab Emirates, Venezuela; Other adv. = other advanced economies (Australia, Canada, France, Iceland, New Zealand, United Kingdom).

to widen in 2020: the increase in the ratios follows from the drop in the denominator, reflecting the sharp decline in activity. The ratios are then projected to gradually shrink over the projection horizon as GDP recovers and current account imbalances remain subdued.

Significant Risks of More Severe Growth Outcomes

Fundamental uncertainty regarding the evolution of the pandemic makes it difficult to provide a quantitative assessment of the balance of risks around the baseline forecast described above.

On the *upside:*

- *The recession could turn out to be less severe* than projected if economic normalization proceeds faster than currently expected in areas that have reopened, without rekindling infections.

- *Extensions of fiscal countermeasures.* The current forecast factors in only the measures implemented and announced so far. As such, the overall fiscal policy stance in advanced and emerging market economies is expected to turn significantly less accommodative in 2021, in line with the projected handoff to private-activity-led growth (Figure 1.20). Extensions of fiscal countermeasures would lift global growth above the projected baseline in 2021.

- *Faster productivity growth* could be engendered by changes in production, distribution, and payment

Figure 1.20. Fiscal Stance, 2019–21
(Change in structural primary fiscal balance, percent of potential GDP)

Extensions of fiscal countermeasures represent an upside risk to global growth.

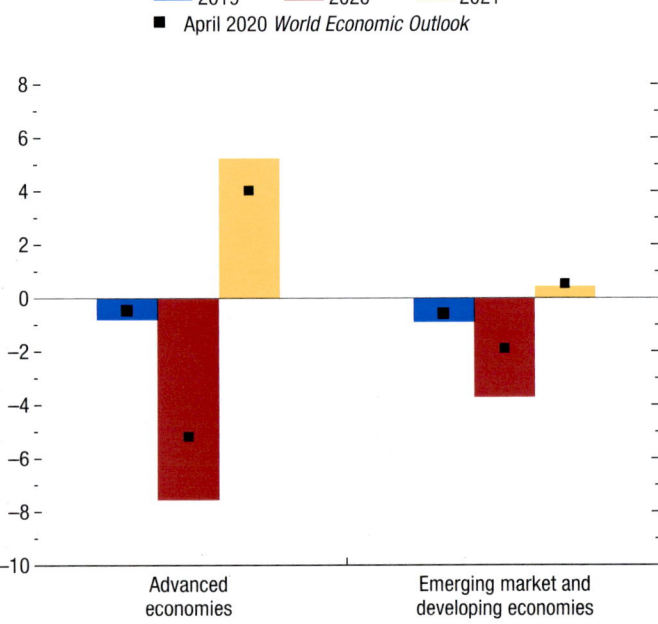

Source: IMF staff estimates.

systems—from new techniques in medicine to new data-enabled services and remote working across broader sectors of the economy.

- *Advances in therapies* may allow health care systems to better manage infection loads, while changes in the workplace and by consumers to reduce transmission may allow activity to return more quickly to pre-pandemic levels without triggering repeated waves of infection.

- *Production of a safe, effective vaccine* would prevail over all other upside risk factors. If produced at the needed scale and distributed worldwide at affordable prices, such a vaccine would lift sentiment and yield better growth outcomes than in the baseline, including by allowing for a fuller recovery in contact-intensive sectors and travel. Some of these aspects are featured in Scenario Box 1, which presents growth projections under alternative scenarios.

Downside risks, however, remain significant. They include the following:

- *Outbreaks* could recur in places. If the virus resurges, and progress on treatments and vaccines is slower than anticipated or countries' access to them remains unequal, economic activity could be lower than expected, with renewed social distancing and tighter lockdowns. Cross-border spillovers from weaker external demand could further magnify the impact of country- or region-specific shocks on global growth.

- *Premature withdrawal of policy support*, or poor targeting of measures because of design and implementation challenges, could lead to the dissolution of otherwise viable and productive economic relationships, exacerbating misallocation.

- *Financial conditions may again tighten*, as in March, exposing vulnerabilities. A sudden stop in new lending (or failure to roll over existing debt) would tip some economies into debt crises and slow activity further.

- *Liquidity shortfalls and insolvencies.* Deep recessions invariably entail widespread liquidity shortfalls as firms suffer immediate revenue losses but still have to meet payroll expenses, cover fixed costs, and fulfill debt service obligations. Prolonged liquidity shortfalls can readily translate into bankruptcies and firm closures. This time around, there have been a few prominent bankruptcies, for example in retail and rental car sectors, and the rate of corporate bond defaults more broadly is at its highest since

the global financial crisis (June 2020 GFSR *Update*). However, the aggressive and swift policy countermeasures have so far likely prevented even more widespread bankruptcies. But considering the severity of the recession and the possible withdrawal of some of the emergency support in some countries, the risk of a wider cross-section of firms experiencing deep liquidity shortfalls and bankruptcies is tangible (Box 1.3). Such events would lead to large job and income losses, further weakening demand. At the same time, they would deplete bank capital buffers and constrain credit supply, compounding the downturn.

- *Intensifying social unrest.* Instances of social unrest increased globally in 2019 before declining during the early part of the pandemic (Box 1.4). While ultimate causes vary across countries, in many cases, these include declining trust in established institutions and lack of representation in governance structures, as well as a perceived disconnect between leaders' priorities and the problems faced by the public. In June, social unrest increased in the United States and quickly spread worldwide in protests against institutional racism and racial inequality. More widespread or longer-lived protests could hurt sentiment and further weigh on activity. Intensifying social unrest may also complicate the political economy of reform efforts, to the detriment of medium-term growth or the sustainability of public finances.

- *Geopolitical tensions.* While seeming to de-escalate during the pandemic (Figure 1.21), geopolitical tensions could again flare up. Moreover, frayed ties among the OPEC+ coalition of oil producers (Organization of the Petroleum Exporting Countries, including Russia and other non-OPEC oil exporters) pose risks for global oil supply. A renewed plunge in prices as seen in March would severely hurt activity in oil exporters and lead to weaker growth than projected.

- *Trade policy uncertainty and technology frictions.* Despite the recent reaffirmation of the Phase One trade deal between the United States and China signed at the start of the year, tensions between the world's two largest economies remain elevated on numerous fronts. Moreover, the United Kingdom's transitional arrangement with the European Union expires on December 31, 2020. If the two sides fail to agree and ratify a trade deal before then, trade barriers between them are set to rise significantly,

Figure 1.21. Geopolitical Risk Index
(Index)

Geopolitical tensions seemed to de-escalate during the pandemic but could again flare up.

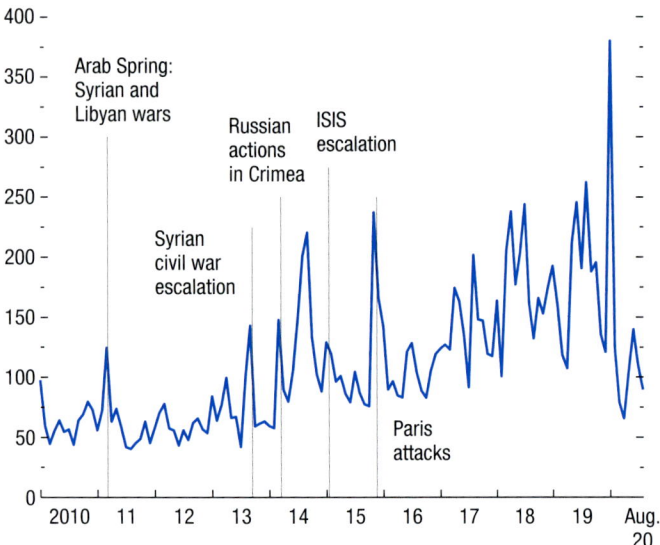

Source: Caldara and Iacoviello 2018.
Note: The Caldara and Iacoviello Geopolitical Risk index reflects automated text-search results of the electronic archives of 11 national and international newspapers. The index is calculated by counting the number of articles related to geopolitical risk in each newspaper for each month (as a share of the total number of news articles) and normalized to average a value of 100 over the 2000–09 decade. ISIS = Islamic State.

Figure 1.22. Share of World Imports Affected by Countries' Own Import Restrictions
(Percent)

The bulk of the distortionary tariff and nontariff barriers instituted over the past two years remain in place.

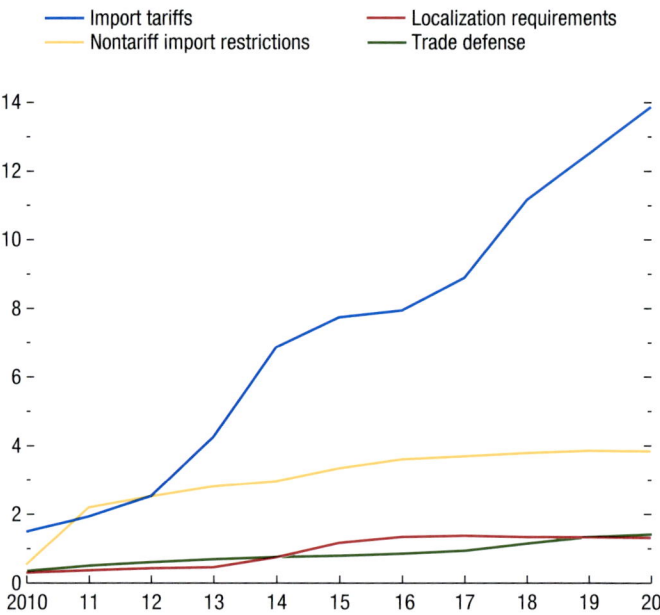

Source: Global Trade Alert.

which would increase business costs and could disrupt long-standing cross-border production arrangements. In addition, the bulk of the distortionary tariff and nontariff barriers instituted over the past two years remain in place (Figure 1.22). The World Trade Organization Appellate Body has ceased functioning because of the impasse over appointments, casting doubt over the enforceability of World Trade Organization legal commitments. Moreover, with the spread of trade disputes to the technology domain, global supply chains face additional threats from a bifurcation of technology standards and platforms. On the positive side, the trade agreement between Canada, Mexico, and the United States came into force on July 1, helping to lower near-term trade policy uncertainty (Figure 1.23). But lingering frictions (for example, on aluminum, rules of origin in the auto sector, and dairy trade) could hamper implementation. Trade policy uncertainty could increase again in these

contexts or in discussions involving other trading partners, weighing on global growth.

- *Weather-related natural disasters.* The increased frequency and intensity of weather-related natural disasters, such as tropical storms, floods, heat waves, droughts, and wildfires has inflicted a devastating humanitarian toll and widespread livelihood loss on many regions in recent years (for example, Australia, the Caribbean, eastern and southern Africa, south Asia). Climate change, a principal driver of more frequent and intense weather-related disasters, already has had visible impacts—and not just in regions where the disasters strike. The disasters could also contribute to cross-border migration and financial stress (for example, in the insurance sector) or add to disease burdens. Moreover, they can have persistent effects long after the event itself (as seen, for example, in parts of eastern Africa, where heavy rainfall in late 2019 and earlier this year have contributed to an extreme locust infestation—the worst in decades—that has imperiled food supplies in the region).

Figure 1.23. Policy Uncertainty and Trade Tensions
(Index)

Trade policy uncertainty has declined recently, but trade tensions remain elevated.

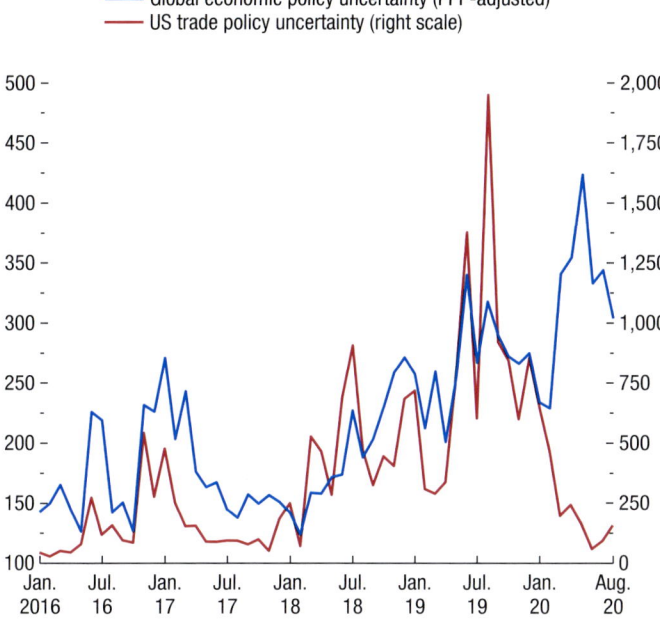

Source: Baker, Bloom, and Davis 2016.
Note: The Baker Bloom Davis Index of Global Economic Policy Uncertainty (GEPU) is a GDP-weighted average of national EPU indices for 20 countries: Australia, Brazil, Canada, Chile, China, France, Germany, Greece, India, Ireland, Italy, Japan, Korea, Mexico, the Netherlands, Russia, Spain, Sweden, the United Kingdom, and the United States. Mean GEPU from 1997 to 2015 = 100; mean US trade policy uncertainty index from 1985 to 2010 = 100. PPP = purchasing power parity.

Figure 1.24. Output Gap Projections, 2020–23
(Percent)

Economies are expected to operate well below capacity over 2020 and 2021.

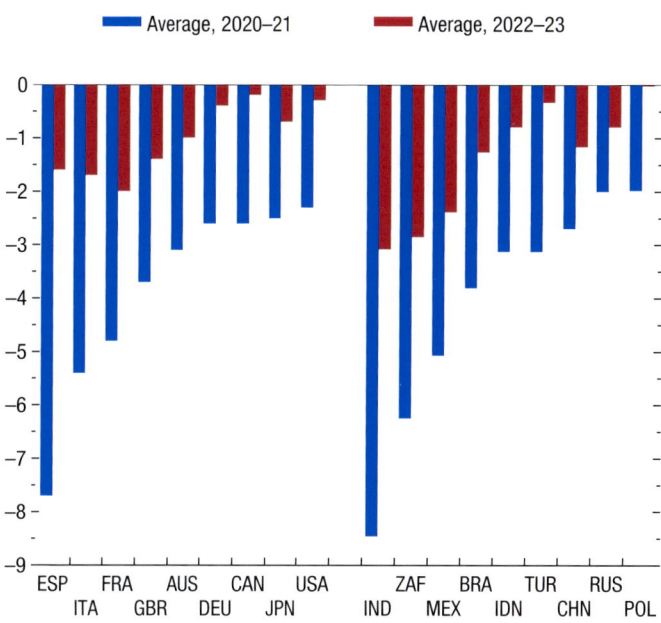

Source: IMF staff estimates.
Note: Data labels use International Organization for Standardization (ISO) country codes.

Near-Term Policy Priorities: Ensure Adequate Resources for Health Care, Limit Economic Damage

The global economy is in the grip of the most devastating public health crisis and its worst recession in decades. All major economies are expected to operate well below capacity over 2020 and 2021 (Figure 1.24). Moreover, downside risks are significant. The immediate dual priority for policy is to ensure adequate resources for health care systems and to limit the economic damage.

Difficult Trade-Offs: Near-Term Imperatives, Medium-Term Challenges

Besides combating the deep near-term recession, policymakers will have to address complex challenges to place economies on a path of higher productivity

growth while ensuring that gains are shared evenly and debt remains sustainable. Many countries already face very difficult trade-offs between implementing measures to support near-term growth and avoiding a further buildup of debt that will be difficult to service down the road, considering the crisis's hit to potential output. Policies to support the economy in the near term should therefore be designed with an eye to furthering these broader objectives of guiding economies to paths of stronger, equitable, and resilient growth.

Tax and spending measures should privilege initiatives that can help lift potential output, ensure participatory growth that benefits all, and protect the vulnerable. The additional debt incurred to finance such endeavors is more likely to pay for itself down the road by increasing the overall size of the economy and future tax base than if the borrowing were done to finance ill-targeted subsidies or wasteful current spending. Investments in health, education, and high-return infrastructure projects that also help move the economy to lower carbon dependence can further those objectives. Research spending can facilitate innovation and technology adoption, the principal drivers of long-term productivity growth. Moreover, safeguarding critical social spending can ensure the most vulnerable are protected while also supporting near-term activity, since the outlays will go to groups with a higher propensity to spend their disposable income than more affluent individuals. In all instances, adhering to the highest standards of debt transparency will be essential to avoid future rollover difficulties and higher sovereign risk premiums that raise borrowing costs across the economy.

Enhancing Multilateral Cooperation

The global nature of the shock, its cross-border spillovers, and the resulting shared challenges point to a need for significant multilateral efforts toward fighting the health and economic crisis.

Multilateral cooperation to support health care systems. National efforts on health will have to be supplemented with extensive multilateral cooperation. A key priority is to fund advance purchase commitments of vaccines undergoing trials to encourage rapid scaling up of the manufacture and distribution of affordable doses worldwide (examples of such coordinated, multilateral initiatives include the Coalition for Epidemic Preparedness Innovations and Gavi, the Vaccine Alliance). The uncertainty and risk of failure associated with the search for effective and safe vaccines make global funding particularly important. A related priority is to support countries with limited health care capacity. Their ability to avoid a catastrophic human toll depends critically on the international community stepping up medical assistance to them. Countries should also continue to remove trade restrictions on essential medical supplies and share information on the pandemic as well as on the search for vaccines and therapies.

Financial support for constrained countries. Beyond assistance with medical equipment and know-how, several emerging market and developing economies—low-income countries in particular—require support from the international community through debt relief, grants, and concessional financing. Building on the Group of Twenty initiative for a temporary standstill on official debt service payments by low-income countries, private creditors should extend similar treatment as well so that those countries can conserve international liquidity and direct resources to priority health care spending and relief measures. Where debt restructuring

is needed, all creditors and low-income country and emerging market borrowers should quickly agree on mutually acceptable terms. The global financial safety net can further help countries facing external funding shortfalls. As part of its response to the COVID-19 crisis, the IMF has expanded its lending toolkit to include a renewable and replenishable credit line for members with strong policy frameworks and fundamentals, provided new financing through other lending facilities, temporarily increased access limits to its emergency financing facilities, and improved its ability to provide grant-based debt service relief.

National-Level Policies

Creating room to accommodate elevated spending on crisis countermeasures. A sizable and aggressive economic policy response is already under way in several countries, notably in advanced economies where their status as issuers of reserve currencies provides more latitude for countering the crisis compared with emerging market and developing economies. The longer this crisis persists, the greater will be the fiscal demands on governments—including by way of health care spending, unemployment benefits, cash transfers, and countercyclical initiatives to revive activity. While the crisis lasts, governments should do all that they can to mitigate the deep downturn and be ready to adapt strategy to respond to the evolution of the pandemic and its impact on activity. Where fiscal rules may constrain action, temporary suspension of the rules would be warranted, combined with a commitment to a gradual consolidation path after the crisis abates to restore compliance with the rules over the medium term. Room for immediate spending needs could be created by prioritizing crisis countermeasures and reducing wasteful and poorly targeted subsidies. Prudent debt management—extending maturities on government borrowing and locking in low interest rates to the extent possible—can save debt service expenses and free up resources within the fiscal envelope to redirect toward crisis mitigation efforts (see also the recommendations in IMF 2020). Although instituting new revenue measures during the crisis will be difficult, governments may need to consider raising progressive taxes on more affluent individuals and those relatively less affected by the crisis (including increasing tax rates on higher income brackets, high-end property, capital gains, and wealth) as well as changes to corporate taxation that ensure firms pay taxes commensurate with profitability (see also Chapter 1 of the October 2020 *Fiscal Monitor*). Countries should also cooperate on the design of international corporate taxation to respond to the challenges of the digital economy. While implementing such initiatives, fiscal authorities should also clearly communicate their commitment to ensuring that public finances remain on a sustainable footing, drawing up credible consolidation plans that can be implemented after the crisis recedes.

These policy objectives are shared across all countries confronting the health and economic crisis, with particularly severe impacts on those heavily dependent on tourism, oil exports, and external remittances. The magnitude of the challenge is in general far greater in countries that entered this crisis with large preexisting vulnerabilities, limited policy space, and a high degree of informality that limits the extent to which relief measures can reach vulnerable people through existing tax registries and banking channels. Such features typically correlate with tighter borrowing constraints. Without strong external support, those economies—particularly low-income countries with fragile health care systems, food and medical supply shortages, and volatile security situations—could be overwhelmed by the health and economic crisis.

Resources for health care. With the pandemic continuing to spread, all countries—including those where infections appear to have peaked—need to ensure that their health care systems can cope with the elevated demand for their services. This means securing adequate resources and prioritizing health care spending as needed, including on testing; contact tracing; personal protective equipment; life-saving equipment, such as ventilators; and facilities such as emergency rooms, intensive care units, and isolation wards.

Policies to limit economic damage where the pandemic is accelerating. The foremost priority in countries where infections continue to rise unabated is to slow transmission. As Chapter 2 shows, lockdowns are effective in bringing down infections. A necessary investment in public health, they pave the way for eventual economic recovery from the severe downturn brought on by mobility constraints.

- Economic policy countermeasures in such cases should limit the damage by cushioning income losses for people and firms. Among particularly effective measures in this regard are targeted temporary tax breaks for affected people and firms, wage subsidies for furloughed workers, cash transfers, allowances for postponements of financial payments,

and paid sick and family leave. Expanded eligibility criteria for unemployment insurance and better coverage of self-employed workers should also be considered among efforts to strengthen the broader safety net. Such measures have already supported disposable income in many advanced economies and, to an extent, across emerging market and developing economies, preventing even further deep declines in spending. Where needed, temporary credit guarantees and loan restructuring can help solvent-but-illiquid firms remain afloat and preserve employment relationships likely to remain viable after the pandemic fades.

- At the same time, retraining and reskilling should be pursued to the extent feasible so that workers can look for jobs in other sectors, as needed. Because the transition may take a while, displaced workers will need extended income support as they retrain and search for jobs.

- Complementing the targeted measures, broad-based monetary, financial regulatory, and fiscal responses can help prevent deeper and longer-lasting downturns, even if mobility restrictions hamper their ability to stimulate spending to the extent typical in other recessions. These broader responses can boost credit provision (for example, through central bank liquidity support and targeted relending facilities for affected firms or regulatory actions to temporarily ease loan classification standards and provisioning requirements). Increases in borrowing costs can be contained through central bank policy rate cuts where interest rates are not already at their effective lower bound, or through asset purchases and forward guidance where interest rates are already at that limit. Among emerging market central banks that launch asset purchases, it is important to communicate clearly the objectives of the program and its consistency with price stability objectives. Doing so would mitigate the risks of perceived fiscal dominance, inflation, and capital flight. Fiscal stimulus through public infrastructure investment or across-the-board tax cuts (where financing constraints permit) can support confidence, protect corporate cash flow, and limit bankruptcies.

As the pandemic evolves, its effects on different sectors become more obvious, and policymakers learn more about what is most effective, the economic policy response for limiting the damage will have to adjust as well. It will need to avoid locking people and inputs into sectors unlikely to return to pre-pandemic vitality, while at the same time supporting the vulnerable.

Supporting the recovery where reopening is under way. As noted earlier, many economies that began reopening in May and June have since slowed or paused that process. Workplace closures remain, but are not as widespread as a few months ago. As countries reopen, policies must support the recovery by gradually removing targeted support, continuing to facilitate reallocation to sectors less affected by social distancing, and providing stimulus to the extent possible.

- The unwinding of measures such as wage subsidies, cash transfers, enhanced unemployment benefits, and credit guarantees for small and medium enterprises should be calibrated to the pace of the recovery and start only after activity picks up durably. Premature scaling back of such lifelines, especially while infections are surging and may require renewed containment measures, risks pushing the economy back into recession. Moreover, the pace at which particular measures are unwound depends on the structure of the economy. For instance, in economies with a large share of self-employed people and significant informality, cash and in-kind transfers to households may need to continue for longer while other measures are scaled back. In economies where medium and large enterprises account for a large share of employment, credit guarantees and liquidity support for firms and wage subsidies for employed workers may need to be maintained to avoid sudden increases in joblessness, even as other lifelines are gradually withdrawn.
- As fiscal resources are freed from targeted support, some should be redeployed to public investment. Examples include investments in renewable energy, improvements in the efficiency of power transmission, and retrofitting buildings to reduce their carbon footprint (see also Chapter 2 of the October 2020 *Fiscal Monitor*). Moreover, as lifelines are unwound, social spending should be expanded to protect the most vulnerable. For example, where gaps exist and as needed, authorities could enhance safety net measures, such as paid and family sick leave, expanded eligibility for unemployment insurance, and strengthened health care benefit coverage.
- Complementing these efforts, hiring subsidies and additional spending on retraining, coupled with income support for displaced workers, can help smooth the transition. Measures to reduce labor market rigidities that deter firms from hiring can also help reallocate employment toward growing sectors. Moreover, an important part of the reallocation will involve balance sheet repair (see details in the section on policies to address medium- and long-term challenges).
- During the transition, where inflation expectations are anchored, accommodative monetary policy can help by ensuring that borrowing costs remain low and credit conditions supportive. The prospects of relatively low inflation over the medium term suggest that central banks have room to allow the recovery to take root firmly before they exit their current settings.

Limiting the damage in countries with large informal sectors. Many of the measures discussed so far rely on well-established tax registries and widespread access to bank accounts to ensure that relief reaches those who need it. But such infrastructure is often missing in economies with a large share of informal employment. In those countries, government relief can be delivered through digital payment systems, for instance as was done in Benin and Côte d'Ivoire (see also Díez and others 2020). In some countries, centralized databases with assigned identification numbers have been used to provide targeted assistance to market traders, taxi drivers, and others most affected during shutdowns (for example, in Togo). Additional challenges arise where individuals do not have mobile phones or identification numbers and may therefore not be covered by digital payments. In such cases, workarounds to deliver relief can include in-kind support of food, medicine, and other essentials delivered through local governments, community organizations, and specialized stores that stock subsidized goods (Prady 2020).

To counter further shocks, policymakers should also strengthen mechanisms for automatic, timely, and temporary support in downturns. As discussed in the April 2020 WEO, rules-based fiscal stimulus triggered by deteriorating macroeconomic conditions—such as temporary targeted cash transfers to liquidity-constrained low-income households that activate when unemployment or jobless claims rise above a certain threshold—can help dampen downturns.

Policies to Address Medium- and Long-Term Challenges

The COVID-19 pandemic is a transformational event unlike any seen since World War II. The damages to supply potential, the buildup of debt, and implications for inequality discussed above are likely to exacerbate issues that predate the pandemic, and the setback to human capital accumulation is a new challenge. This section discusses policy priorities to address these challenges.

Catalyzing Stronger, Environmentally Sustainable Growth

Productivity growth had already slowed across both advanced and emerging market and developing economies in the 15 years before the pandemic, going back to before the global financial crisis (Adler and others 2017; October 2018 WEO, Chapter 2). The damage to supply potential in the medium-term projections reflects in part a continuation of forces that had dragged productivity growth lower in the years leading up to the pandemic: relatively slow investment growth weighing on physical capital accumulation, more modest improvements in human capital, and slower efficiency gains in combining technology with available factors of production, partly reflecting sectoral mismatches.

Policy initiatives that can counteract these forces include repairing balance sheets and disposing of distressed debt so that investment can recover quickly. Policymakers should also address labor market rigidities and reduce barriers to entry that may hamper redeployment of resources to growing sectors. In this regard, the corporate sector shake-up induced by the pandemic—particularly the exit of smaller firms—risks reinforcing the trend of broad-based increases in concentration and market power across the economy (Chapter 3 of the April 2019 WEO), posing a threat to dynamism and innovation. Competition policy frameworks and scrutiny of corporate mergers need to ensure that such developments do not lead to abuses of market power and that small start-ups can continue competing on a level playing field with incumbents.

Facilitating new growth opportunities, including to speed the transition to a low-carbon economy. In addition, as discussed in Chapter 3, a green investment push to increase reliance on renewables, improve efficiency of the grid, and retrofit buildings to increase energy conservation could also spur capital spending in such sectors as construction materials and energy-efficient heating systems, while speeding the transition to a lower-carbon growth path. The European Union's agreement to target 30 percent of the Next Generation recovery fund to climate-change-related spending is a

step in this direction. More broadly, efforts to promote investment in new growth areas would also help with the post-pandemic reorganization of the economy as firms take advantage of new opportunities. An emerging cluster of growth opportunities during the pandemic relates to the accelerated shift to e-commerce, increasing digitalization of the economy, and possible innovation of new data-enabled services. Another cluster relates to medicine and biotechnology.

Boosting Human Capital Accumulation

The global loss of learning as schools and universities stay closed for a large part of 2020 is likely to be one of the most enduring legacies of the COVID-19 crisis. Virtual learning may not be an adequate substitute, even in locations with widespread high-speed internet connectivity where consumers have adequate access to online learning and supplementary instruction is available at home. Loss of learning can have long-lasting consequences on individuals' lifetime earning potential and economy-wide productivity growth. Policymakers will have to devise makeup strategies for use when the pandemic is under control and it is safe to resume full-time schooling. Options could include setting aside funding to accommodate adjustments to the length of the school year, training teachers on remedial approaches to correct learning losses, and instituting or expanding supplementary after-school tutoring programs (see WB 2020b). At the same time, educational and vocational programs will need to accommodate training needs in jobs that are likely to be in high demand (emergency first responders, nurses, and lab technicians and digital literacy more broadly, so that more and more people can take advantage of teleworking opportunities). Even with these adaptations in vocational programs, take-up may still fall short if the training involves acquiring a substantively different and challenging set of skills, raising the possibility of a persistent increase in dropouts and large numbers of people in neither education, employment, nor training.

Making Gains More Equitable

The setback to human capital accumulation is one dimension along which inequality is likely to increase as a result of the pandemic, as already discussed. Among the social spending measures beyond education to counter the increase in inequality are strengthening social assistance (for example, conditional cash transfers, food stamps and in-kind nutrition, medical payments for low-income households), expanding social insurance (relaxing eligibility criteria for unemployment insurance, extending the coverage of paid family and sick leave), and investments in retraining and reskilling programs to boost reemployment prospects for displaced workers.

Resolving Debt Overhangs

The scope for actions to boost productivity growth, accelerate the transition to a low-carbon economy, and reduce inequality is limited in many instances because elevated debt levels entering the crisis are set to rise further.

Sovereign debt overhang. Governments with large debt stocks will need to consider options to raise revenues and gradually decrease expenditures over the medium term. These include measures to increase progressivity in the tax code discussed earlier. Efforts to expand the tax base can include reducing corporate tax breaks, applying tighter caps on personal income tax deductions, instituting value-added taxes where not part of the code, and improving the coverage of tax registries and electronic filing of returns. On the spending side, scaling back such outlays as poorly targeted and wasteful subsidies would help with consolidation. In some cases, restructuring of sovereign debt may be needed to alleviate financing pressures and restore debt sustainability, although this brings its own challenges, including potentially long-lasting impacts on a sovereign's credibility. Where available, collective action clauses may need to be activated to speed up the process. Restructuring options could include maturity extensions, interest rate reductions, principal reductions (haircuts), and other debt swaps (with renegotiated terms).

Corporate debt overhang. Resolving the likely large corporate debt overhang coming out the crisis will first require triaging business cases into those that are considered ultimately viable and can be restructured versus those that are unviable. In the case of systemically important firms, equity injections may be considered. If a firm's business model appears viable over the medium term, restructuring its balance sheet and providing liquidity support are appropriate. Special out-of-court restructuring frameworks may need to be strengthened (or established) to help deal

with the expected high number of cases. Standardized restructuring solutions and incentives (deadlines for agreements, fines for creditors, threat of liquidation to debtors) will be needed to expedite restructuring (Liu, Garrido, and DeLong 2020). To help deal with a potential rise in nonperforming loans, supervisors should enhance regulatory oversight (for example, through more robust provisioning, write-offs, and income recognition), whereas banks should strengthen their internal nonperforming loan management capabilities. The development of distressed debt markets can be supported by increasing access to debtor information, removing regulatory barriers (for example, enabling nonbanks to own and manage nonperforming loans) and improving the quality of collateral valuations. Tax rules that inhibit debt restructurings or write-offs should also be amended (Aiyar and others 2015; Awad and others 2020).

The scale of the COVID-19 shock and potential for larger spillovers from bankruptcies than in normal recessions argue for providing more ample solvency support than usual, except for firms that were already insolvent before the crisis began. Tax measures, such as loss carrybacks, could help support previously viable firms. For large firms, support can take the form of direct equity injections or junior debt claims with warrants that allow the public purse to benefit from eventual return to profitability. For unlisted small and medium enterprises, where direct equity injections are not an option, support could involve grants today that are partially recovered by a temporarily higher corporate tax rate in future.

Where long-lived or structural shifts in consumption and production chains are taking place and a firm's medium-term prospects are poor, liquidation to enable reallocation of capital and labor to better uses may be needed. For firms rendered unviable by persistent structural changes, it is essential to have an efficient and equitable corporate bankruptcy framework that can apportion losses across investors, banks, and owners.

Multilateral Policies to Ensure a Sustained Global Recovery

Beyond the current pandemic, as noted in the section on risks, intensifying trade and technology tensions between countries could drag global growth starkly lower than the baseline projection.

Effective multilateral cooperation to defuse these tensions and address gaps in the rules-based multilateral trading system would go a long way toward preventing such outcomes.

Countries must also act collectively to implement their climate change mitigation commitments. As discussed in Chapter 3, joint action—particularly by the largest emitters—that combines a green investment push, together with steadily rising carbon prices, is needed to achieve emission reductions consistent with limiting global temperature increases to the targets of the 2015 Paris Agreement. A broadly adopted, growth-friendly mitigation package could raise global activity through investment in green infrastructure over the near term, with modest output costs over the medium term as economies transition away from fossil fuels toward cleaner technologies. Relative to unchanged policies, such a package would significantly boost incomes in the second half of the century by avoiding damages and catastrophic risks from climate change. The global community should also take urgent steps to strengthen its defenses against calamitous health crises, for instance by augmenting stockpiles of protective equipment and essential medical supplies, financing research, and ensuring adequate ongoing assistance to countries with limited health care capacity, including through support of international organizations.

Scenario Box 1. Alternative Scenarios

Here, the G20 Model[1] is used to estimate the potential impact on activity of two alternative paths for the evolution of the fight against COVID-19. In the first alternative—the downside—containing the virus proves to be a more difficult and protracted struggle until a vaccine is widely available. In the second alternative—the upside—it is assumed that all dimensions of the fight against the virus go well.

Downside Scenario: Containment Proves Much More Difficult

For the downside scenario (red line in Scenario Figure 1), it is assumed that measures to contain the spread—either mandated or voluntary—slightly increase the direct drag on activity in the second half of 2020 as the virus proves more difficult to contain. Further, it is assumed that in 2021 progress on all fronts in the fight against the virus proves to be slower than assumed in the baseline, including progress on vaccines, treatments, and adherence to social distancing guidelines to contain the virus's spread. This leads to a deterioration in activity in contact-intensive sectors, with the associated income effects spilling over to other sectors. These domestic demand effects are then amplified via trade. Financial conditions are also assumed to tighten, with corporate spreads rising in advanced economies and both corporate and sovereign spreads widening in emerging market economies. The increase in 2020 is quite mild but grows to be more substantive in 2021 as the weakness in activity persists. Financial conditions gradually return to baseline beyond 2022. Fiscal authorities in advanced economies are assumed to respond with an increase in transfers beyond standard automatic stabilizers, while those in emerging market economies are assumed to be more constrained, with only automatic stabilizers operating. Monetary authorities in advanced economies with constraints on conventional policy space are assumed to use unconventional measures to contain increases in long-term interest rates. The more protracted weakness in activity is assumed to create additional, persistent damage to economies'

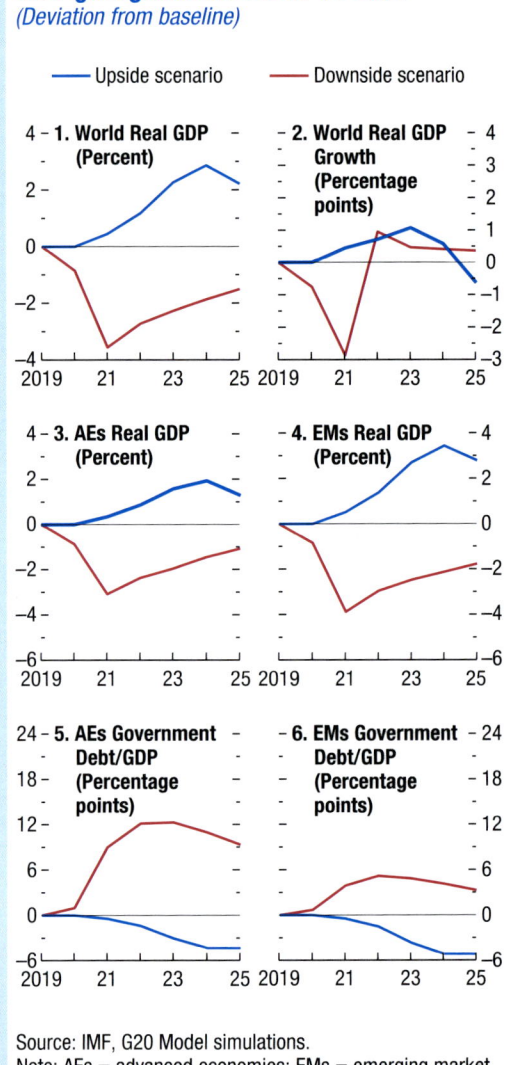

Scenario Figure 1. Alternative Evolutions in the Fight against the COVID-19 Virus
(Deviation from baseline)

Source: IMF, G20 Model simulations.
Note: AEs = advanced economies; EMs = emerging market economies.

The authors of this box are Ben Hunt and Susanna Mursula.
[1]The G20 Model is a global, structural model of the world economy, capturing international spillovers and key economic relationships among the household, corporate, and government sectors, including monetary policy.

supply capacity, with a loss in productive capital, a persistent rise in the natural rate of unemployment, and temporarily weaker productivity growth. These scarring effects are assumed to be largely felt in 2022 and beyond. Panel 1 in Scenario Figure 2 contains a decomposition of the impact on global GDP of the four key layers of the downside scenario.

Relative to the baseline, global growth in 2020 is roughly ¾ percentage point weaker and almost 3 percentage points weaker in 2021 under the downside scenario. Emerging market economies are more

Scenario Box 1 *(continued)*

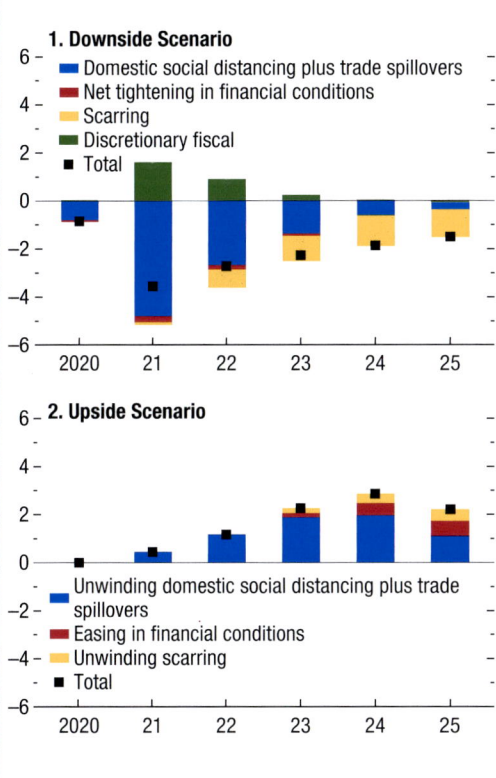

Scenario Figure 2. Downside and Upside Scenarios: Global Real GDP
(Percent deviation from baseline)

1. Downside Scenario

- Domestic social distancing plus trade spillovers
- Net tightening in financial conditions
- Scarring
- Discretionary fiscal
- Total

2. Upside Scenario

- Unwinding domestic social distancing plus trade spillovers
- Easing in financial conditions
- Unwinding scarring
- Total

Source: IMF G20 simulations.

Upside Scenario: All Dimensions of the Fight against the Virus Go Well

Under the upside scenario, (blue line in Scenario Figure 1) it is assumed that all things in the fight against COVID-19 go much better than assumed in the baseline. On the treatment front, advances quickly start to reduce the fatality rate, reducing fear and helping to restore confidence. An early and substantial ramp-up in investment in vaccine production capabilities and cooperation agreements in the associated global supply chain lead to earlier, widespread vaccine availability. Complete openness and transparency in the underlying science increase confidence in vaccine efficacy and safety, leading to widespread vaccinations. All these advances will allow activity in the contact-intensive sectors, which have been most adversely affected, to bounce back more quickly than assumed in the baseline. In addition, the overall improvement in confidence will lead to higher spending across other sectors as uncertainty about future income prospects subsides. More buoyant activity will in turn lead to improved prospects for firms and less deterioration in fiscal positions, driving an easing in risk premiums. Further, the faster bounce-back will lead to fewer bankruptcies, less labor market dislocation, and a milder slowing in productivity growth than assumed in the baseline. The improvements in these supply side factors start in 2023 and grow. On the policy front, with the improvement in activity, fiscal withdrawal is assumed to be only in terms of automatic stabilizers, and monetary authorities everywhere are assumed to be able to accommodate the faster growth without imperiling their price stability objectives. Panel 2 in Scenario Figure 2 contains a decomposition of the impact on global GDP of the three key layers under the upside scenario.

Global growth under the upside scenario gradually accelerates relative to the baseline, with growth roughly ½ percentage point higher in 2021, rising to roughly 1 percentage point higher by 2023. In 2024 the pickup moderates, with growth slightly below baseline by 2025. Although both advanced and emerging market economies see marked improvements in activity, emerging market economies benefit more, as the baseline assumes that the impact of limited progress in measures to fight the virus falls more heavily on these economies. Further, the difference is magnified by the larger relative easing in risk premiums and a larger unwinding of the scarring embedded in the baseline.

negatively impacted than are advanced economies, given that limited fiscal space constrains their ability to support incomes. Consequently, even tighter financial conditions for emerging market economies exacerbate the difference, which is further reinforced by more substantive scarring. After 2021 growth rises above baseline for several years, but the level of global GDP is still roughly 1.5 percent below baseline by the end of the *World Economic Outlook* horizon in 2025. The negative impact on the level of GDP is roughly twice as large for emerging market economies as for advanced economies. The more protracted negative impact on activity, combined with the additional fiscal expenditures to support incomes, leads to a marked increase in public indebtedness. Debt-to-GDP ratios rise by well above 10 percentage points, on average, for advanced economies, but by a more modest 5 percentage points for emerging market economies by 2022.

Scenario Box 1 *(continued)*

By 2025 the level of global GDP is roughly 2 percent above the baseline, with the improvement in emerging market economies almost double that in advanced economies. The faster growth leads to an improvement in fiscal positions, with both advanced and emerging market economies seeing debt-to-GDP ratios falling by roughly 5 percentage points by the end of the *World Economic Outlook* horizon. Should fiscal authorities also take advantage of the stronger upside growth to unwind discretionary measures faster than assumed in the baseline, debt-to-GDP positions could improve even more.

Box 1.1. Revised *World Economic Outlook* Purchasing-Power-Parity Weights

The International Comparison Program (ICP), maintained and published by the World Bank in coordination with the Organisation for Economic Co-operation and Development and other international organizations, released new purchasing power parities (PPPs) for the reference year 2017 in May 2020 for the 176 economies that participated. Revised results for the preceding reference year, 2011, and estimates of annual PPPs for 2012–16 were also released.[1] PPPs are used to convert different currencies to a common currency and equalize their purchasing power by eliminating differences in price levels between economies. They show, with

reference to a base economy (the United States), the relative price of a given basket of goods and services across economies.

Estimates of regional and world output and growth, along with forecasts, are key macroeconomic indicators reported in many of the IMF's flagship publications, including the *World Economic Outlook* (WEO). The revised PPPs used in the October 2020 WEO are based on 2011–17 data from the ICP 2017 survey, which are then extended forward and backward by using the growth rates in relative GDP deflators (the GDP deflator of a country divided by the GDP deflator of the United States). These generate PPP-based GDP, which is used as weights to compute regional and global real GDP growth and other real sector aggregates, including inflation.[2]

The authors of this box are Jungjin Lee and Evgenia Pugacheva, with contributions from Angela Espiritu and Mahnaz Hemmati.
[1]See ICP 2017 Report for more information on the results and methodology of the 2017 ICP exercise.

[2]See WEO FAQ for more information on the aggregation method and use of PPPs in the WEO.

Table 1.1.1. Changes in World GDP Shares from Purchasing-Power-Parity Revisions
(Percent, unless noted otherwise)

	(1)	(2)	(3)	(4)	(5)	(6)	(7)	(8)
	World GDP Share						Difference[2]	USD GDP Share
	New (ICP 2017)			Old (ICP 2011)				
	2011	2017	2019[1]	2011	2017[1]	2019[1]	2019	2019
Advanced Economies	**45.3**	**44.0**	**43.1**	**45.2**	**41.3**	**40.3**	**2.8**	**59.1**
United States	16.3	16.1	15.9	16.3	15.2	15.1	0.9	24.4
Euro Area[3]	13.2	12.9	12.5	13.2	11.5	11.2	1.3	15.2
Japan	4.8	4.3	4.1	4.8	4.2	4.0	0.0	5.8
Other Advanced Economies[4]	7.0	6.9	6.8	6.9	6.6	6.5	0.3	8.4
Emerging Market and Developing Economies	**54.7**	**56.0**	**56.9**	**54.8**	**58.7**	**59.7**	**−2.8**	**40.9**
Emerging and Developing Asia	26.5	29.9	31.5	26.7	32.4	34.1	−2.6	24.1
China	14.4	16.3	17.4	14.5	18.1	19.2	−1.8	16.8
India	5.9	6.8	7.1	6.1	7.5	7.8	−0.7	3.5
Emerging and Developing Europe	7.5	7.6	7.6	7.7	7.2	7.1	0.5	4.5
Russia	3.4	3.1	3.1	3.6	3.2	3.1	0.0	1.9
Latin America and the Caribbean	8.7	8.0	7.6	8.7	7.7	7.2	0.3	5.9
Brazil	3.1	2.5	2.4	3.1	2.5	2.4	−0.1	2.1
Mexico	2.0	2.0	2.0	2.0	1.9	1.8	0.1	1.4
Middle East and Central Asia	9.0	7.4	7.1	8.7	8.4	8.1	−0.9	4.5
Saudi Arabia	1.7	1.3	1.2	1.4	1.4	1.3	−0.1	0.9
Sub-Saharan Africa	3.0	3.1	3.1	3.1	3.1	3.1	0.0	2.0
Nigeria	0.9	0.8	0.8	0.9	0.9	0.9	−0.1	0.5
South Africa	0.7	0.6	0.6	0.7	0.6	0.6	0.0	0.4

Sources: June 2020 WEO *Update*; and IMF staff calculations.
Note: New shares are based on the June 2020 WEO *Update* revised with ICP 2017; old shares are from the June 2020 WEO *Update*; ICP = International Comparison Program; USD = US dollar; WEO = *World Economic Outlook*.
[1]Extrapolations.
[2]Difference between column 3 and column 6; percentage points.
[3]Aggregate of member countries.
[4]Excludes the Group of Seven and euro area countries.

Box 1.1 *(continued)*

PPP Weight Changes for Regions and Economies

Table 1.1.1 shows that the share of emerging market and developing economies in world GDP rises, while that of advanced economies falls during 2011–19 based on ICP 2017 (columns 1–3), as was the case based on ICP 2011 (columns 4–6). However, the focus here is on the weight revisions for a given year, with the main change being a shift in the relative weight of advanced economies, whose share of the global economy for 2019 is now estimated at 43 percent—higher than the previous calculation of 40 percent. Looking at changes for different regions and economies, euro area countries and the United States are estimated to have higher shares in 2019 than before. Meanwhile, revisions for China and India together mostly account for the smaller shares of emerging Asia and emerging market and developing economies as a whole in new weights. Latin America and the Caribbean and emerging Europe have a slightly larger global weight, while the Middle East and Central Asia region has a smaller global weight. The weight of sub-Saharan Africa is virtually unchanged.

The country shares in world GDP used as weights to derive world output growth could differ, depending on whether the GDP shares are valued at PPP or market exchange rates.[3] Revisions in PPPs notwithstanding, emerging market and developing economies represent a much smaller fraction of global GDP at market exchange rates of 41 percent than at PPP of 57 percent for 2019, reflecting their more limited purchasing power in international markets.

Factors behind PPP Weight Revision

Sizable discrepancies can arise between PPPs from a new cycle and extrapolated PPPs from a previous cycle as the new cycle brings forth additional and updated information on the world. The six-year gap between ICP cycles resulted in notable differences for some economies.[4] One of the assumptions underlying PPP extrapolations for GDP is that the structure of each country's economy is similar to that of the

numeraire country and changes in the same way over time. In practice, however, structures and changes can be very different. This is significant, particularly when developing economies are compared with an advanced economy. For example, the Chinese economy has been developing rapidly in recent years, and its structure has changed in a significantly different way from that of the United States.

Although the ICP provides revised 2011 PPP values with ICP 2017 results, 2011 revisions are small, and the new 2017 estimates drive the changes in PPP paths over 2011–17 compared with those extrapolated from the 2011 ICP vintage. Figure 1.1.1 shows that China's 2019 GDP share has been revised down, with the PPP conversion rate depreciating relative to previous estimates. This implies that the increase in overall prices in China was underestimated with extrapolation derived from ICP 2011. In ICP 2017, the relative price level in China in 2019 is now higher, and GDP converted at the PPP rate is therefore smaller. This in turn leads to a lower 2019 PPP share for China in the global economy using

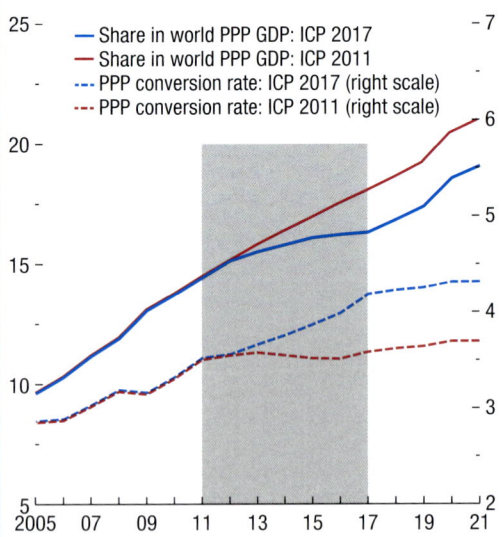

Figure 1.1.1. Purchasing-Power-Parity Revision for China
(Percent; local currency per US dollar on right scale)

Sources: June 2020 *World Economic Outlook Update*; IMF staff calculations.
Note: Shaded area denotes the years of the new estimates from the ICP 2017 survey. ICP = International Comparison Program; PPP = purchasing power parity.

---

[3]Table 1.1 of the WEO report presents both measures of world output.

[4]While the extrapolation methodology used is robust, the estimates based on extrapolation—for example, the 2017 value derived from ICP 2011—should not be expected to match the corresponding year in the new ICP 2017 survey. See McCarthy (2013) and Deaton and Aten (2017).

Box 1.1 *(continued)*

ICP 2017 (17.4 percent) compared with the share estimated using ICP 2011 (19.2 percent). This implies that increases in overall prices exceed differences in GDP deflators.

Impact of PPP Revision on Aggregate Growth

As an illustration of how the change in weights can affect the calculation of aggregate growth rates, Table 1.1.2 compares the aggregation of the June 2020 WEO *Update* country forecasts based on ICP 2011 with those based on ICP 2017. The lower weight of fast-growing emerging Asia and the larger weight of advanced economies under ICP 2017 imply that global growth calculated with the new weights is slightly lower. Average global growth is estimated at 3.2 percent for 2018–19 and 3.6 percent for 2011–17,

some 0.1 percentage point lower than with the old weights. For 2020 the aggregation of the June 2020 WEO *Update* country forecasts with the new weights yields an aggregate global growth rate projection of –5.2 percent for 2020 (compared with the projection of –4.9 percent in the June 2020 WEO *Update,* which used the old weights).[5] The reduction in the relative weight of its fastest-growing region also implies slightly lower average growth for emerging market and developing economies using the ICP 2017 weights compared with the estimate using the ICP 2011 weights.

[5]GDP share and aggregate growth calculations based on ICP 2017 presented here are based on the most recent data of the June 2020 WEO *Update* and may differ from the final estimates in the October 2020 WEO.

Table 1.1.2. Revisions to Real GDP Growth of *World Economic Outlook* Aggregates
(Percent, unless noted otherwise)

	2011–17	2018	2019	2020	2021
June 2020 WEO Revised with ICP 2017					
World	3.6	3.5	2.8	–5.2	5.4
Advanced Economies	1.9	2.2	1.7	–8.1	4.8
Emerging Market and Developing Economies	5.0	4.5	3.6	–3.1	5.8
June 2020 WEO Based on ICP 2011					
World	3.7	3.6	2.9	–4.9	5.4
Advanced Economies	1.9	2.2	1.7	–8.0	4.8
Emerging Market and Developing Economies	5.1	4.5	3.7	–3.0	5.9
Difference (percentage points)					
World	–0.05	–0.08	–0.08	–0.24	–0.04
Advanced Economies	0.00	0.00	0.00	–0.07	0.04
Emerging Market and Developing Economies	–0.04	–0.03	–0.05	–0.13	–0.05

Sources: June 2020 WEO *Update*; and IMF staff calculations.
Note: ICP = International Comparison Program; WEO = *World Economic Outlook.*

Box 1.2. Inclusiveness in Emerging Market and Developing Economies and the Impact of COVID-19

This box documents the possible implications of the pandemic for poverty reduction, improvements in life expectancy, and progress toward greater equality in emerging market and developing economies. The number of people in extreme poverty is likely to rise substantially this year, for the first time in more than 20 years, and income inequality, on average, across these economies could rise back to levels seen in 2008, reversing gains since the global financial crisis. Life expectancy is less likely to be affected, although there are downside risks related to the fragile state of health care systems and interruptions in treatments of other life-threatening illnesses.

In the two decades prior to the COVID-19 crisis, emerging market and developing economies grew by 4.1 percent on average—one percentage point higher than during the preceding two decades (1980–99). With slowing population growth, per capita growth shows a sharper contrast: 2.4 percent in 2000–19 versus 1.0 percent in 1980–99. A key question is how much progress has been made in the past 20 years toward enhancing inclusiveness (in poverty reduction, improvements in life expectancy, and greater equality) within countries.[1]

With the pandemic, real GDP in emerging market and developing economies is expected to decline by 3.3 percent in 2020. This crisis is disproportionately affecting vulnerable workers, putting at risk much of the progress achieved before the crisis and likely exacerbating remaining gaps. Against this backdrop, a second key question is how the pandemic will affect inclusiveness in these economies.

Stocktaking: Progress on Inclusiveness prior to the Pandemic

Remarkable progress was made on poverty reduction since 2000 until the pandemic started.[2]

The share of people living on less than $1.90 a day (in 2011 purchasing-power-parity terms) in the total population declined from 25 percent in 2002 to 12 percent in 2018, on average, with stronger progress in low-income developing countries (Figure 1.2.1, panel 1).[3] On top of improvements in the extensive margin of poverty (headcount measure), the poverty gap index (how far below the poverty line the poor in a given country fall) points to improvements in the intensive margin (average distance from $1.90 a day among people living in poverty), indicating that the average annual money transfer per person living in poverty necessary to end extreme poverty declined from $240 to $184 (for perfectly targeted transfers).

Health-related indicators also showed significant progress before the crisis. Life expectancy exhibited strong "convergence"—levels substantially increased for almost all emerging market and developing economies, and the increase was stronger for countries with lower life expectancy, most of which are low-income developing countries (Figure 1.2.1, panel 2).[4] The convergence can also be seen within countries: inequality in life expectancy across people in a country was reduced, though to a lesser extent. Other health indicators also showed significant progress, including mortality under age five, maternal mortality, and access to clean water. Nevertheless, challenges remain in health care systems in many of these economies and make them particularly vulnerable to the pandemic (see WB 2019).

Despite advances in poverty reduction and improvement in life expectancy, progress in reducing income inequality has been slow over the past two decades. The Gini coefficient (a measure of statistical dispersion intended to represent income inequality) declined only gradually, by 3 percentage points—from 44 to 41, on average—during this period (Figure 1.2.2, panel 1). Wide gaps with respect to the average level of advanced economies remain for many emerging market and developing economies, while some others in this country group have already reached that level. Progress has been weaker for low-income developing countries, with one-third of them seeing an increase in income inequality. Similarly, the Palma ratio shows that the total income of the top 10 percent is twice as large as the total income of the bottom 40 percent in

---

The authors of this box are Gabriela Cugat and Futoshi Narita, with contributions from the authors of Brussevich, Dabla-Norris, and Khalid (2020) and Bannister and Mourmouras (2017) as well as Albe Gjonbalaj. This box is part of a research project on macroeconomic policy in low-income countries supported by the United Kingdom's Foreign, Commonwealth and Development Office (FCDO). The views expressed here do not necessarily represent the views of the FCDO.

[1]For further discussion focused on low-income developing countries, see Fabrizio and others (2017); Chapter 1 of the April 2020 *Sub-Saharan Africa Regional Economic Outlook* discusses progress made in sub-Saharan African countries.

[2]For further discussion, see WB (2018).

[3]As the data examined in this box are mostly sparse, data points for a given year are averaged over the year and the previous four years.

[4]For further discussion, see UNDP (2019).

Box 1.2 *(continued)*

Figure 1.2.1. Positive Developments

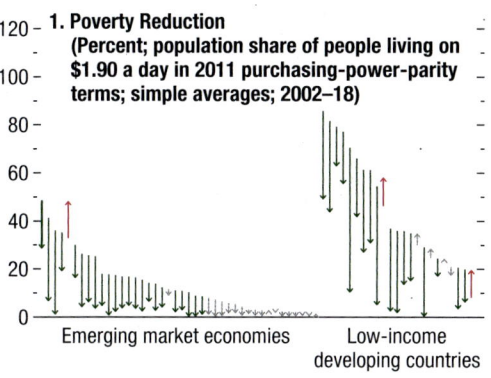

1. Poverty Reduction
   (Percent; population share of people living on
   $1.90 a day in 2011 purchasing-power-parity
   terms; simple averages; 2002–18)

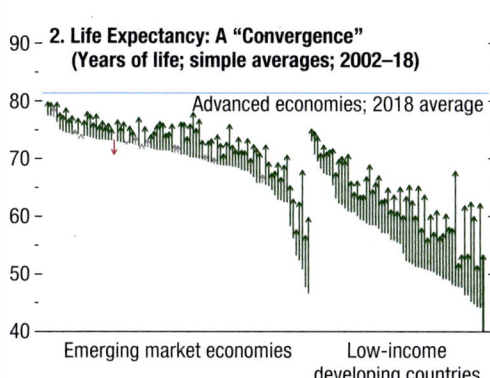

2. Life Expectancy: A "Convergence"
   (Years of life; simple averages; 2002–18)

Source: World Bank, World Development Indicators
database.
Note: Each arrow represents a country, beginning at the
level of the corresponding variable in 2002 and ending at the
level in 2018. Green (red) color indicates improvements
(deteriorations) larger than half a standard deviation. Data
points for a given year are averaged over the year and the
previous four years.

Figure 1.2.2. Remaining Gaps

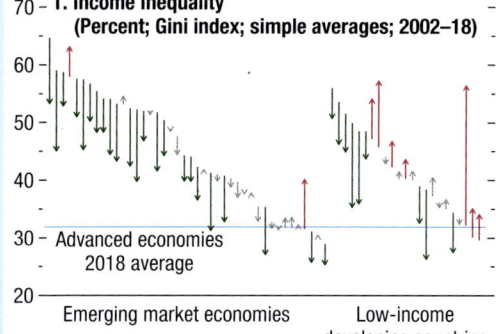

1. Income Inequality
   (Percent; Gini index; simple averages; 2002–18)

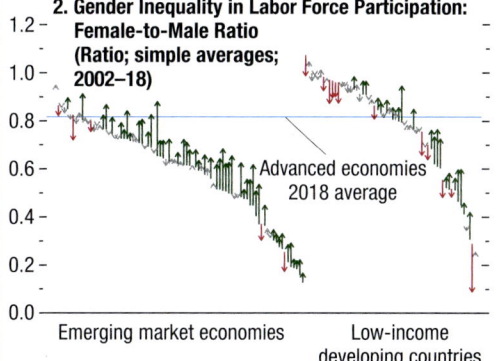

2. Gender Inequality in Labor Force Participation:
   Female-to-Male Ratio
   (Ratio; simple averages;
   2002–18)

Sources: International Labour Organization; World Bank,
World Development Indicators database; and IMF staff
calculations.
Note: Each arrow represents a country, beginning at the
level of the corresponding variable in 2002 and ending at the
level in 2018. Green (red) color indicates improvements
(deteriorations) larger than half a standard deviation. Data
points for a given year are averaged over the year and the
previous four years. The definition of the Gini index varies
depending on household surveys across countries (for
example, income or consumption).

emerging market and developing economies, whereas
the difference is only 25 percent for advanced economies, on average.

Several other dimensions of inclusiveness, related to
inequality of opportunity, have also seen slow progress.
The share of inactive youth (that is, youth not in
education nor in employment) has hovered around
20 percent.[5] Inequality in education (that is, inequality in the distribution of years of schooling within a
country) has only marginally declined, leaving wide
gaps in most of these economies compared with the

average in advanced economies.[6] Gender equality has
been promoted in recent years, but the gender gap
remains high in labor force participation (Figure 1.2.2,
panel 2).[7] In some economies, lack of progress in
female labor force participation is related to higher

---

[5]For a discussion of youth labor markets in these economies,
see Ahn and others (2019). For a discussion of labor market
policies in these economies, see Duval and Loungani (2019).

[6]The education inequality index is compiled by the United
Nations Human Development Report Office. For further discussion, see UNDP (2019).

[7]For a discussion of gender inequality in economic issues,
see Brussevich and others (2018), Ostry and others (2018), and
Sahay and Cihak (2018).

Box 1.2 *(continued)*

female enrollment in education. However, educational attainment of women also remains lower than that of men in most of these economies, especially in low-income countries.

The Impact of the Pandemic on Inclusiveness

The COVID-19 pandemic is expected to both halt the improving trends and widen existing gaps in inclusiveness. The World Bank estimates that, compared with pre-pandemic projections, the COVID-19 pandemic will increase the global share of people living on less than $1.90 a day by 1.14 percentage points, which represents almost 90 million people newly living in extreme poverty—the first increase since 1998.[8] In terms of life expectancy, the COVID-19 impact is currently projected to be moderate.[9] However, downside risk factors are related to more fragile health care systems than in advanced economies and interruptions in other health services to treat and prevent HIV, malaria, and tuberculosis (see Hogan and others 2020). Income inequality widened during past pandemics, especially over the medium term (see Furceri and others 2020). Furthermore, the impact on inequality is expected to be much larger than in the past because the COVID-19 crisis and associated containment measures are disproportionately affecting the most vulnerable (see Adams and others 2020 and Shibata 2020). Gender equality is also being undermined and could experience a sharp setback under the current circumstances (see Alon and others 2020 and Georgieva and others 2020).

Although it is difficult to quantify distributional impacts of the pandemic on many economies in a comparable way, a parsimonious estimate based on lower telework ability for lower-paying jobs indicates a strong setback in progress made on income inequality since the global financial crisis. Brussevich, Dabla-Norris, and Khalid 2020 estimate the degree of telework ability across 35 economies and finds that it is generally lower for low-income earners than high-income earners (Figure 1.2.3, panel 1). Other real-time survey data also show that more tele-workable sectors saw a smaller loss of employment

[8]See WB (2020a). The estimate corresponds to the baseline projection without change in inequality.

[9]With younger populations (of a median age of 27 years) being less vulnerable to the disease so far, the mortality burden is several times smaller than in advanced economies (Decerf and others 2020).

Figure 1.2.3. Telework Ability and Income Inequality

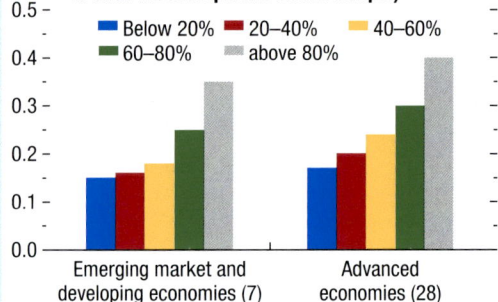

1. **Telework Ability, by Income Quintile**
(Index ranging from zero to 1; simple averages divided by the number of economies in parentheses in *x*-axis labels; each bar corresponds to the average divided by workers in each income quintile in the sample)

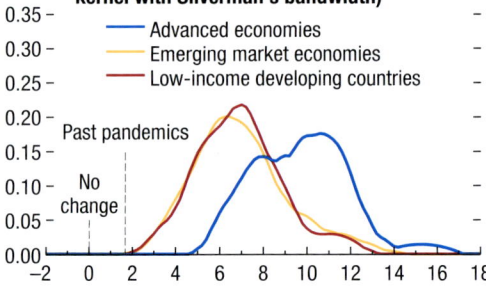

2. **Estimated Impact on Income Inequality**
(Percent change in the Gini index; estimated density using the Epanechnikov kernel with Silverman's bandwidth)

Sources: Bick, Blandin, and Mertens 2020; Brussevich and others 2020; World Bank, World Development Indicators database; and IMF staff calculations.
Note: In panel 2, the impact on the Gini index is estimated by distributing the aggregate income shock (based on the IMF's real GDP projections) to the income quintile shares, in proportion to telework ability, whose magnitude is calibrated using the estimated coefficient of telework ability in the regression of employment loss across sectors using the data by Bick, Blandin, and Mertens (2020, Appendix Table C1). Percent changes in the Gini index are obtained as the changes in an approximated Gini index based only on the income quintile shares. The (closest) economy group average is used when the telework ability index is missing. Data points for a given year are averaged over the year and the previous four years. The vertical line for "past pandemics" corresponds to 1¼ percent, based on the findings of Furceri and others (2020) on the net Gini index.

Box 1.2 *(continued)*

from February to May 2020 in the United States (see Bick, Blandin, and Mertens 2020). Extrapolating these findings to emerging market and developing economies, the aggregate decrease in income (taken from the IMF's latest real GDP projections) can be distributed among the groups of people divided by income quintiles for each economy, in proportion to telework ability.[10] The resultant impact (without reflecting any redistribution policies or other factors) on the income shares by income quintile are used to estimate a percent change in the Gini coefficient in 2020. These show that the average Gini coefficient for emerging market and developing economies would increase by 2.6 percentage points to 42.7, broadly comparable to the level in 2008, implying that gains since the global financial crisis could be reversed (Figure 1.2.3, panel 2).

A simple welfare measure that goes beyond GDP indicates that there was good progress before the pandemic and that a strong reversal due to this crisis can be expected. The measure, proposed by Jones and Klenow (2016), takes into account four factors: (1) real consumption per capita, (2) life expectancy, (3) leisure time, and (4) consumption inequality.[11] Combining these factors, the average welfare improvement in 56 emerging market and developing economies with available data from 2002 to 2019 was equivalent to a 6 percent increase in annual consumption levels in every year (Figure 1.2.4). This exceeded per capita real GDP growth in the same period by 1.3 percentage points. The excess welfare growth stems almost entirely from longer life expectancy. A setback in welfare in 2020 could exceed 8 percent, driven in

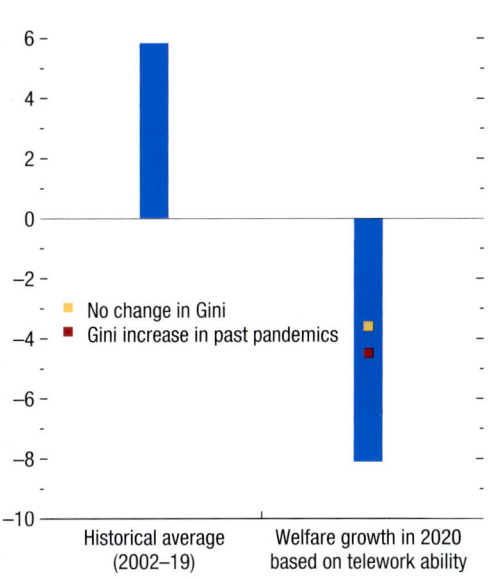

Figure 1.2.4. Beyond GDP Welfare Growth
(Percent; annualized per capita growth relative to 2002; simple averages across 45 economies)

No change in Gini
Gini increase in past pandemics

Historical average (2002–19)

Welfare growth in 2020 based on telework ability

Sources: Penn World Table (9.1); World Bank, World Development Indicators database; and IMF staff calculations.
Note: The welfare measure is based on Jones and Klenow (2016, equation 7). For different scenarios on inequality in 2020, the "no change in Gini" scenario uses the latest observations; the "Gini increase in past pandemic" scenario applies a 1¼ percent increase to all economies, based on the findings of Furceri and others (2020) on the net Gini index; and the "telework ability" scenario is based on parsimonious estimates using various levels of telework ability across income groups within countries (see Figure 1.2.3, panel 2). Macroeconomic data are extrapolated from the IMF's latest projections. The impacts on life expectancy and employment are estimated using a multigroup susceptible-infected-removed model. Data points for a given year are averaged over the year and the previous four years.

---

[10]How the shock affects the income quintile shares depending on telework ability is calibrated using the estimated coefficient of telework ability in the regression of employment loss across sectors using the data from Bick and others (2020, Appendix Table C1). The (closest) economy group average is used when the telework ability index is missing.

[11]See Jones and Klenow (2016), which proposes a welfare measure in percent of annual consumption, based on the lifetime expected utility of an imaginary person just before she or he is born in a country in a given year, under many strong assumptions that are needed to compute this measure for a large set of countries with only aggregate-level data. See the online appendix of Jones and Klenow (2016) for a detailed discussion on caveats regarding this measure. In addition, for an extension to reflect net welfare losses from environmental issues, see Bannister and Mourmouras (2017).

large part by the excess change in inequality, as indicated by parsimonious estimates.

Since 2000 emerging market and developing economies have made appreciable progress in poverty reduction and increasing life expectancy. COVID-19 threatens to set back such progress, particularly in terms of poverty reduction, and to widen existing gaps in terms of income inequality, access to education, and gender equality. Redistribution policies and measures to support affected people and firms are essential to mitigate sizable adverse impacts on inequality and on welfare more generally.

Box 1.3. Rising Small and Medium Enterprise Bankruptcy and Insolvency Risks: Assessment and Policy Options

The COVID-19 recession will affect small and medium enterprises (SMEs) particularly hard. These firms typically are more vulnerable than their larger counterparts, reflecting, among other factors, their limited buffers and access to credit. However, the effects of the current crisis on SMEs are likely to be even more severe than in previous crises because SMEs are most prevalent among the hardest-hit sectors, such as restaurants, hotels, and arts and entertainment. Consequently, liquidity and solvency risks are bound to increase, putting both SME jobs and debt at risk. This box assesses jobs at risk and discusses policy options to address rising bankruptcy risks among SMEs. Using the same data and framework, Chapter 1 of the October 2020 *Global Financial Stability Report* assesses implications for financial stability, with particular focus on SME debt at risk.

The analysis builds on the methodology proposed by Gourinchas and others (2020) and uses Orbis data for SMEs across 21 (mostly advanced) economies.[1] To assess the liquidity risks, the analysis considers whether a firm has enough cash available at the end of 2020 to cover its operational and financial expenses, under the assumption that it can roll over maturing debt but cannot take on additional debt. Likewise, for insolvency risks, the analysis focuses on whether a firm's net equity is projected to become negative at the end of 2020. The analysis shows that firms in distress account for 9 to 13 percent of total SME (in sample) employment, depending on the stress measure chosen—insolvency or illiquidity. This represents almost a doubling of SME jobs at risk due to liquidity risks (and a 50 percent increase due to insolvency risks) vis-à-vis a scenario without COVID-19 (see Figure 1.3.1, panel 1). Using illiquidity as a distress measure, the share of jobs at risk climbs to 30 and 40 percent for the "arts and entertainment" and "food and accommodation" sectors, respectively, reflecting their comparatively larger drop in output and greater job intensity (Figure 1.3.1, panel 2).[2]

The authors of this box are Federico Díez and Chiara Maggi.
[1]The countries included are Australia, Austria, Belgium, the Czech Republic, Finland, France, Germany, Greece, Hungary, Ireland, Italy, Japan, Korea, Poland, Portugal, Romania, the Slovak Republic, Slovenia, Spain, Sweden, and the United Kingdom.
[2]Accounting for the massive government support provided by most countries dampens these projections. This support is difficult to quantify because it has come in multiple forms

Figure 1.3.1. Small and Medium Enterprises' Liquidity and Solvency Concerns under COVID-19 in 2020

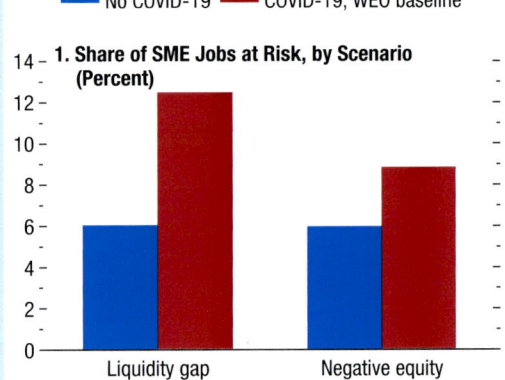

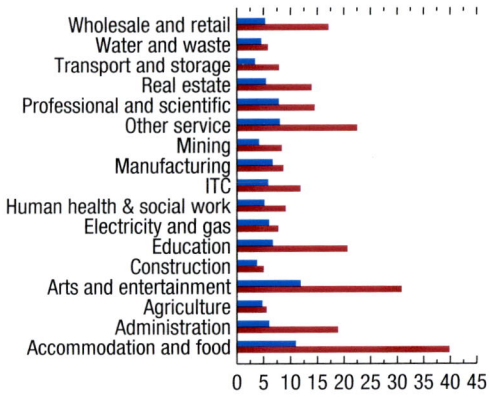

Sources: Orbis; and IMF staff calculations.
Note: The bars measure the share of SME jobs at risk due to firms facing a liquidity gap or negative equity under a scenario without COVID-19 in 2020 (blue bars) and with COVID-19 using the WEO baseline projections at the country level (red bars). Data are aggregated from the firm to the country level using sectoral weights, and across countries using GDP weights. ITC = information technology and communication; SME = small and medium enterprise; WEO = *World Economic Outlook*.

with widely different take-up rates across firms and countries. Bearing these limitations in mind, preliminary simulations suggest that the announced government support could have significantly dampened the rise in liquidity shortages and insolvency rates in some European countries (Chapter 3 of the October 2020 *Regional Economic Outlook: Europe*).

Box 1.3 *(continued)*

The large projected increased risks call for further government support. While standard advice involves providing liquidity to illiquid but solvent firms, and restructuring insolvent firms to facilitate swift resource reallocation, this time is different. The magnitude of the shock, the uncertainty about its duration, and the macro-financial amplifiers associated with mass bankruptcies justify ampler-than-usual recourse to solvency support. This comes over and above the need to cut the legal and financial costs of bankruptcy procedures to alleviate risks of overwhelming bankruptcy courts.

The multiple ways governments provide solvency support to firms can involve important trade-offs—such as balancing the reach and cost-effectiveness of support, minimizing unwarranted bankruptcies, and containing fiscal costs, as well as promoting firms (and jobs) preservation and resource reallocation. Figure 1.3.2 shows the impact on projected insolvency rates of two illustrative options—giving all SMEs 5 percent of their pre-pandemic annual revenues (accounting for more than 4 percent of GDP) in the form of either government loans or equity(-like) injections. Only the equity(-like) injections would reduce insolvency risks—and, further, they would reduce the share of jobs at risk by almost 3 percentage points relative to panel 1 of Figure 1.3.1.[3] This benefit comes at the cost of greater fiscal risks, particularly if firms still end up defaulting, given that equity(-like) claims would then be junior to debt claims.

Overall, rising risks and the associated drag on the recovery make a case for extending support to firms for longer and for equity(-like) interventions—at least in countries with available fiscal space. For larger firms, options include direct equity injections or junior debt claims together with warrants, for example. For SMEs, combining grants with a temporarily higher future

[3]Both types of policy imply a cash transfer of a similar amount and thereby are equally effective at easing liquidity risks.

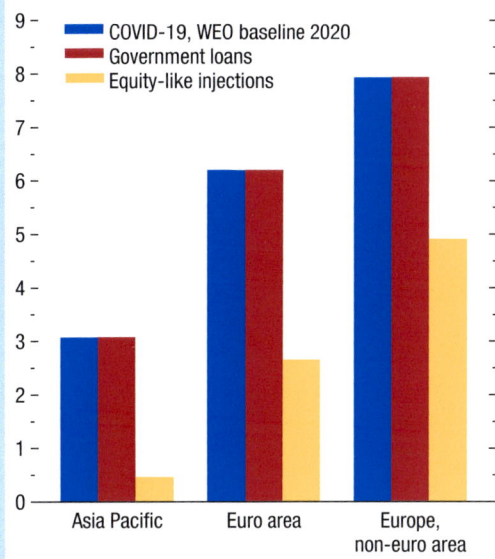

Figure 1.3.2. Change in Share of Small and Medium Enterprises with Negative Equity, by Policy Scenario and Region
(Percentage points)

Sources: Orbis; and IMF staff calculations.
Note: The bars measure the change in the share of SME firms with negative equity under a scenario with no policy intervention (blue bars), government loans (red bars), and equity-like injections (yellow bars). The changes are computed comparing the WEO baseline scenario with COVID-19 to a counterfactual scenario for 2020 without COVID-19. Data are aggregated from the firm to the country level using sectoral weights, and across countries using GDP weights. SME = small and medium enterprise; WEO = *World Economic Outlook*.

corporate tax rate would act like an equity injection; such an approach could raise tax administration challenges and would need to be carefully calibrated. All these options would entail larger fiscal risks, however, given that equity-like injections into SMEs may attract not only viable firms but also those that are unviable and gambling for resurrection.

Box 1.4. Social Unrest during COVID-19

Social unrest has decreased in recent months as mobility has declined. This is consistent with past experience immediately following epidemics. However, unrest was high and rising before the COVID-19 crisis started. As the crisis passes, unrest may yet reemerge in countries where progress on underlying social and political issues has stalled and where the crisis exposes or exacerbates preexisting problems.

Social unrest has fallen markedly as lockdowns and social distancing have been introduced. The Reported Social Unrest Index (RSUI), which counts media reports of social unrest, has fallen dramatically since March 2020.[1] The frequency of major unrest events—defined by country-specific spikes in the RSUI—fell to its lowest in almost five years. The decline in social unrest corresponds closely with a generalized decline in mobility driven by regulations, such as shelter-in-place orders and voluntary social distancing, as shown in Figure 1.4.1 (in line with the findings of Chapter 2). Notable exceptions include the United States, where protests against police violence grew rapidly at the start of June (Figure 1.4.2), and Lebanon.[2]

Before the COVID-19 outbreak, unrest had been rising for several years. Late 2019 and early 2020 saw major protests, most notably in the Middle East and South America but also elsewhere, including in Belarus, Bolivia, Chile, France, Hong Kong Special Administrative Region, India, Iran, and Iraq. This was the continuation of a longer trend since 2016 (Figure 1.4.1), which itself reversed a gradual decline in unrest following a peak after the Arab Spring of 2011.

Historically, countries with more epidemics experience more frequent unrest. Table 1.4.1. presents cross-sectional evidence on the number of social unrest events and epidemics since 1990. Data on epidemics are from EM-DAT, a database reporting information on the timing and location of more than 1,200 country-year epidemic events since 1990. The results show a positive and statistically significant cross-country relationship between the two variables. This result holds within regions and is robust for both the frequency and severity of epidemics.

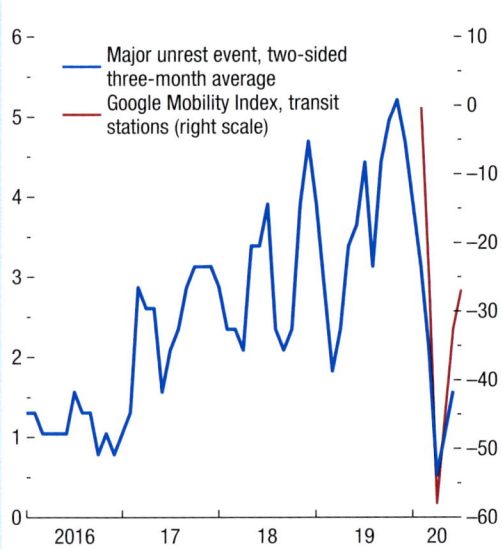

Figure 1.4.1. Monthly Share of Countries Experiencing Unrest Implied by the Reported Social Unrest Index
(Percent; percent deviation from baseline on right scale)

Sources: Factiva; Google Community Mobility Reports; and IMF staff calculations.
Note: The Google mobility index is a simple average of all countries' transit mobility deviation from baseline, expressed monthly.

However, this cross-sectional relationship is likely not causal. For example, common factors, such as geography or income level, may lead to more unrest and more or more serious epidemics. To explore this possibility, Table 1.4.2. presents results from a dynamic panel regression.[3] This accounts for some of the common drivers, including country- and time-specific effects and recent protests. The results show very weak

---

The authors of this box are Philip Barrett and Sophia Chen. Luisa Calixto provided research assistance.

[1] The RSUI is a measure of social unrest constructed from media reports. Details about the index and how it can be used to identify major events are discussed in Barrett and others (2020).

[2] That media reports reacted strongly in the US case is also evidence that this approach still captures protests despite other newsworthy events.

[3] Specifically, the linear probability model: $y_{i,t} = \alpha_i + \eta_t + \sum_{j=1}^{n} \beta_j x_{i,t}^j + \gamma' z_{i,t} + e_{i,t}$, in which $y_{i,t}$ is an indicator for a social unrest event in country i in year t, α_i and η_t are country and time fixed effects, $x_{i,t}^j$ is an indicator variable that takes a value of 1 if the latest disaster occurred j periods prior (in practice we group past lags together to improve power), and $z_{i,t}$ is a vector of controls. Nonlinear models are avoided to admit a wide battery of country and time fixed effects. Barrett and others (2020) shows that recent social unrest both domestically and in neighboring countries is correlated with higher future social unrest, so these are included as controls. This short-term analysis does not preclude longer-term effects of epidemics on unrest, such as those identified in the October 2020 *Asia and Pacific Regional Economic Outlook*.

Box 1.4 *(continued)*

Figure 1.4.2. Daily Protest Articles for the United States, April–June 2020
(Index, April 2020 = 100)

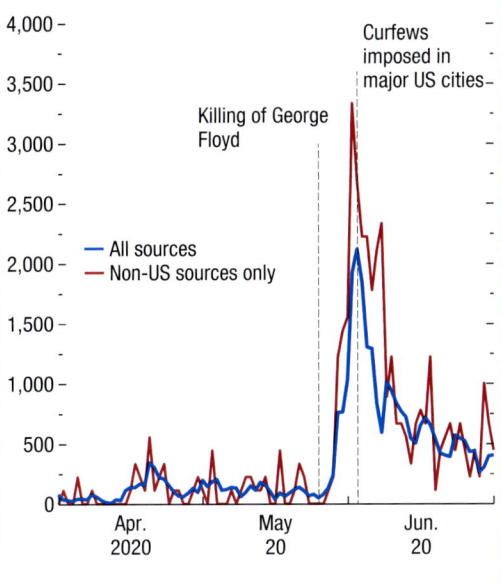

Sources: Factiva; and IMF staff calculations.

statistical evidence of a higher likelihood of unrest following epidemics. On the contrary, in any given country, the likelihood of social unrest drops slightly following epidemics (see especially specifications 2 and 3). The COVID-19 experience so far is consistent with this historical pattern.

Recent history also includes few examples of unrest obviously caused by epidemics. Concerns over public health have rarely been a primary driver of major episodes of social unrest in the past two decades,

despite numerous (often viral) epidemics during this period. While specific demands vary, the purported motives of protesters in events as diverse as the Arab Spring of 2011, unrest in Latin America in late 2019, anti-austerity protests in Europe following the Great Recession, and a variety of episodes in Asia are all at least superficially related to dissatisfaction about social or political issues, not public health. At the same time, several major public health crises have occurred, albeit of smaller scale than the COVID-19 episode, including SARS (2002–04), the H5N1 avian flu (2003–present), the H1N1 swine flu (2009–10), MERS (2012–present), and the West African Ebola epidemic (2013–16).

Several factors may explain the lack of a short-term link from epidemics to unrest. Humanitarian crises likely impede the communication and transportation needed to organize major protests. Public opinion may favor cohesion and solidary in times of duress. Or incumbent regimes may take advantage of an emergency to consolidate power and suppress dissent.

Unrest is likely to reemerge as the pandemic eases. This analysis shows that unrest was elevated before the COVID-19 crisis began but has declined as the crisis has continued. It is reasonable to expect that, as the crisis fades, unrest may reemerge in locations where it previously existed, not because of the COVID-19 crisis per se, but simply because underlying social and political issues have not been tackled. The threats may also be bigger where the crisis exposes or exacerbates problems, such as a lack of trust in institutions, poor governance, poverty, or inequality.[4]

[4]A large body of literature discusses how such factors can lead to political instability (Alesina and Perotti 1996) and civil conflicts (surveyed by Blattman and Miguel 2010).

Table 1.4.1. Cross-Sectional Regressions
(Cross-sectional relationship between social unrest and epidemics)

	Dependent Variable: Number of Social Unrest Events, 1990–2019			
	(1)	(2)	(3)	(4)
Number of Epidemics	0.056***	0.044**		
	(0.013)	(0.019)		
Deaths from Epidemics			0.0002***	0.0001*
			(0.00005)	(0.0001)
Region Fixed Effects	No	Yes	No	Yes
Observations	128	128	128	128
R^2	0.080	0.109	0.058	0.097
Adjusted R^2	0.072	0.072	0.050	0.060

Sources: EM-DAT; Reported Social Unrest Index; and IMF staff calculations.
Note: Robust standard errors shown in parenthesis.
*$p < .05$; **$p < .01$; ***$p < .001$.

Box 1.4 *(continued)*

Table 1.4.2. Dynamic Regressions: Epidemics
(Conditional probabilities of social unrest following epidemics)

	Dependent Variable: Social Unrest Event					
	(1)	(2)	(3)	(4)	(5)	(6)
Epidemic, Current Month		−0.003	−0.006**	0.0003	0.002	0.003
		(0.003)	(0.003)	(0.003)	(0.004)	(0.005)
Epidemic, Last 2–3 Months		−0.003	−0.006*	−0.001	−0.001	−0.003
		(0.003)	(0.003)	(0.003)	(0.005)	(0.005)
Epidemic, Last 4–6 Months		−0.005*	−0.009***	−0.003	−0.003	−0.003
		(0.003)	(0.003)	(0.003)	(0.004)	(0.005)
Months since Last Social Unrest Event					0.00000	−0.00000
					(0.00002)	(0.00003)
Months since Last Social Unrest Event, Neighboring Country						0.00002
						(0.00003)
Constant	0.014***	0.015***				
	(0.001)	(0.001)				
Country Fixed Effects		No	Yes	Yes	Yes	Yes
Time Fixed Effects		No	No	Yes	Yes	Yes
R^2	0.014	0.015	0.019	0.036	0.044	0.049
Observations	27,223	27,223	27,223	27,223	17,893	14,952

Sources: EM-DAT; Reported Social Unrest Index; and IMF staff calculations.
Note: All specifications also include further lags of epidemics with no robust statistical patterns. Double-clustered standard errors are shown in parenthesis.
$*p < .05$; $**p < .01$; $***p < .001$.

Special Feature: Commodity Market Developments and Forecasts

Despite heightened volatility, the IMF's primary commodity price index remained broadly stable between February and August 2020, the respective reference periods for the April 2020 and October 2020 WEOs (Figure 1.SF.1, panel 1). This reflects two distinct phases: between February and April the index fell by 24 percent as the COVID-19 pandemic intensified; between April and August the index recovered by about 31 percent, as many countries eased lockdown measures and economic activity resumed. The rebound, however, has varied across commodities, depending on conditions in end-use sectors and regions affected by the outbreak and on the storability and supply elasticity of a commodity. Prices of energy and some agricultural raw materials rebounded later than metals' prices. Food prices were less affected, even though changes were widely dispersed across agricultural commodities. This special feature also includes an in-depth analysis of coal.

Energy Prices Recovered after April

Oil prices declined by 60 percent between February and April 2020 as the pandemic led to a collapse in global oil demand and concerns about storage capacity (see Figure 1.SF.2). In March OPEC+ (Organization of the Petroleum Exporting Countries, including Russia and other non-OPEC oil exporters) could not agree on supply cuts to restore order to the market, but as the oil price fall intensified, in mid-April the cartel decided to curb production by 9.7 million barrels a day in May and June (later extended until July) by 7.7 million barrels a day until December 2020 and by 5.8 million barrels a day until April 2022. US crude oil producers were also hurt as the front-month futures price for the West Texas Intermediate blend briefly went to –$37 in April. Protracted low oil prices led to shut-ins, sharply reduced drilling activity, and a surge in US shale producer bankruptcy filings. This resulted in an unprecedented 2 million barrel a day decrease in US crude oil production in May 2020.

Thanks to supply reductions, from late April onward, oil prices recovered from the mid-$10s to more than $40 a barrel by early June, but into August they remained about $25 below early January prices. As a result, many oil firms have suffered large losses,

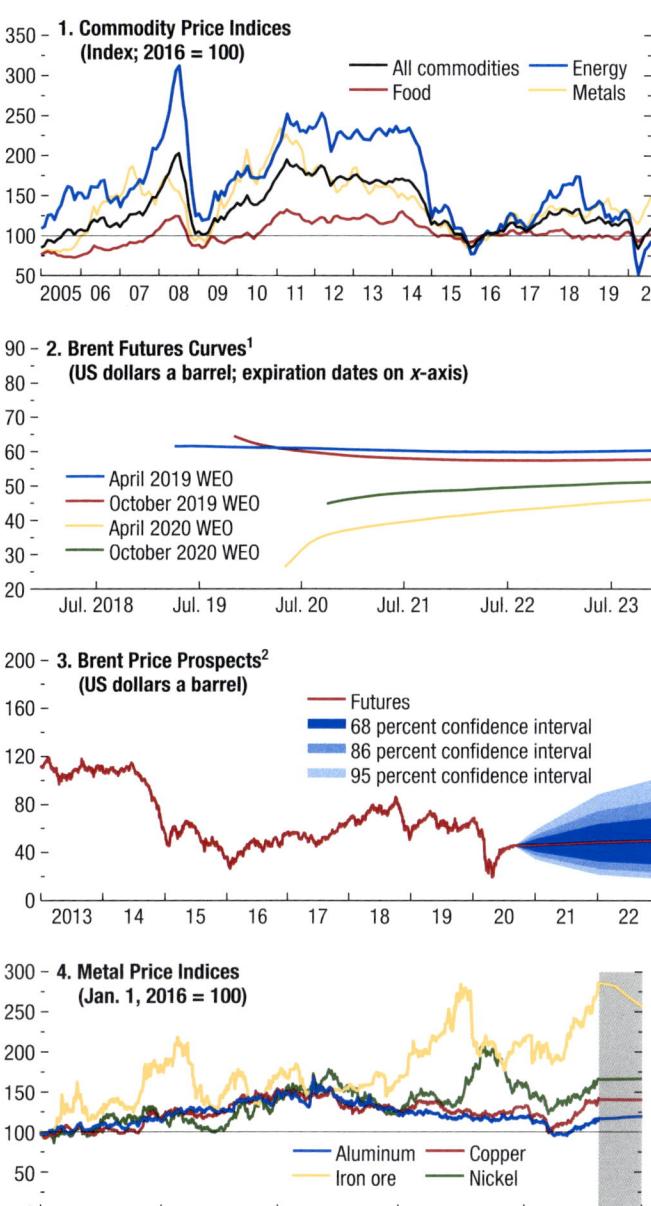

Figure 1.SF.1. Commodity Market Developments

1. Commodity Price Indices
(Index; 2016 = 100)
All commodities · Energy · Food · Metals

2. Brent Futures Curves[1]
(US dollars a barrel; expiration dates on *x*-axis)
April 2019 WEO · October 2019 WEO · April 2020 WEO · October 2020 WEO

3. Brent Price Prospects[2]
(US dollars a barrel)
Futures · 68 percent confidence interval · 86 percent confidence interval · 95 percent confidence interval

4. Metal Price Indices
(Jan. 1, 2016 = 100)
Aluminum · Copper · Iron ore · Nickel

Sources: Bloomberg Finance L.P.; IMF, Primary Commodity Price System; Refinitiv Datastream; and IMF staff estimates.
Note: WEO = *World Economic Outlook.*
[1]WEO futures prices are baseline assumptions for each WEO and are derived from futures prices. October 2020 WEO prices are based on August 21, 2020, closing.
[2]Derived from prices of futures options on August 27, 2020.

Figure 1.SF.2. Oil Storage Capacity Utilization Rates
(Percent)

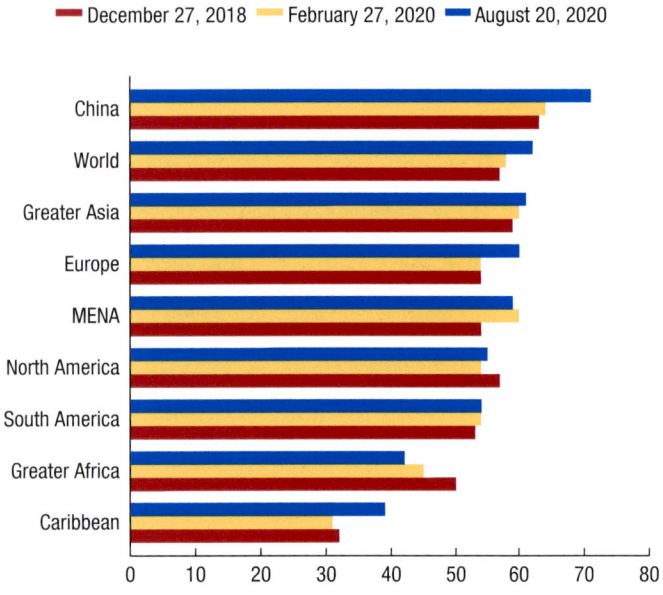

Figure 1.SF.3. Global Driving and Walking Mobility Indices
(Index; Jan. 13, 2020 = 100)

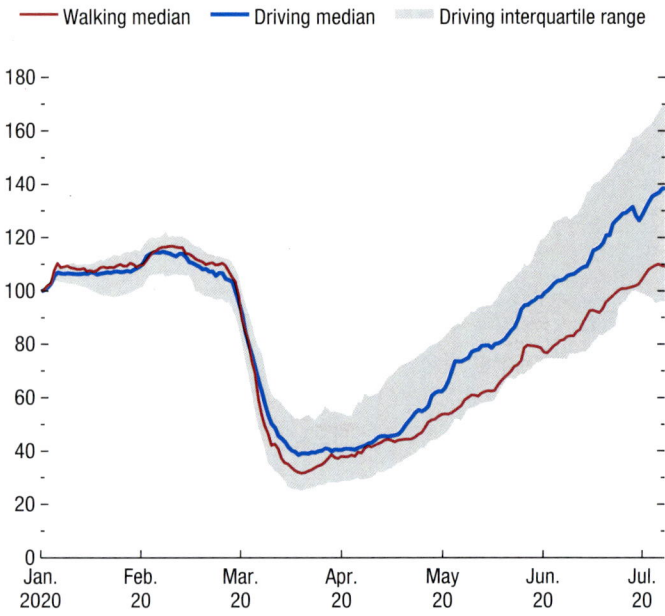

Sources: URSA Space Systems; and IMF staff calculations.
Note: MENA = Middle East and North Africa. Countries and regions as defined by URSA.

Sources: Apple; and IMF staff calculations.
Note: Data are the seven-day moving average of Apple Mobility Indices.

massive layoffs, and asset write-downs as they reassess price outlooks and investments.

On the demand side, the COVID-19 outbreak drove oil prices sharply down as travel restrictions strongly reduced global demand for liquid fuels in the first half of 2020. On one hand, road traffic has recovered in many countries (see Figure 1.SF.3); on the other hand, air traffic volume—especially international flights—remains subdued. As a result, the International Energy Agency expects oil demand for this year to be down by 8.1 million barrels a day, to 91.9 million barrels a day, and to rebound by 5.2 million barrels a day in 2021—a significant revision up from –9.3 million barrels a day for 2020 in its April forecast.

In the natural gas market, spot prices have hovered around record lows in recent months amid large inventories left in place after a mild winter, weak demand, and subdued oil prices. This led oil producers to burn off large amounts of unwanted natural gas as a byproduct of oil extraction—equivalent to 400 metric tons of carbon dioxide (CO_2) in 2019, the most since 2009, according to the World Bank. In late August natural gas prices increased due to an expected rise in winter demand, supply uncertainty in Asia, and technical trading patterns. Competing with natural

gas for electricity generation, coal has also experienced significant downward price pressure, although supply disruptions in South Africa and strong demand from Indian industrial buyers supported South African coal prices, while Australian prices have been depressed by China's apparent tightening of import restrictions and by Japan's intention to phase out inefficient coal-fired power plants by 2030 (see the section on coal).

As of early September, oil futures contracts indicate that Brent prices will increase to $50 by the end of 2023, highlighting near-term demand concerns (Figure 1.SF.1, panel 2). Baseline assumptions, also based on futures prices, suggest average annual prices of $41.7 a barrel in 2020—a decrease of 32 percent from the 2019 average—and $46.7 a barrel in 2021 for the IMF's average petroleum spot prices. Currently, the oil market is characterized by elevated uncertainty as the COVID-19 pandemic is not yet under control (Figure 1.SF.1, panels 2 and 3). Risks, however, are broadly balanced. Upside risks to prices include escalating geopolitical events in the Middle East and faster containment of the pandemic as well as excessive cuts in oil and gas upstream investments and further bankruptcies in the energy sector. The biggest downside risk is a renewed slowdown in global economic

Figure 1.SF.4. Commodity Prices during the COVID-19 Pandemic
(Percent)

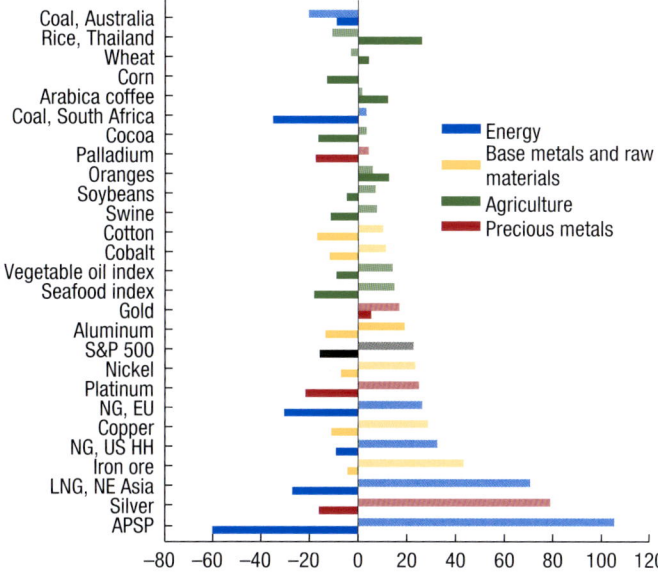

Sources: Argus; Bloomberg L.P.; IMF, Primary Commodity Price System; Thomson Reuters Datastream; and IMF staff calculations.
Note: Dark fill sections represent the percent change in commodity prices for February–April 2020, while light fill sections represent the percent change for April–August 2020. APSP = Average petroleum spot price; AU = Australia; EU = Europe; HH = Henry Hub; LNG = liquefied natural gas; NE = northeast; SA = South Africa; US = United States.

activity as large inventories remain a concern. Other downside risks for oil prices include stronger oil production growth in several non-OPEC+ countries, a faster normalization of Libya's oil production, and a breakdown of the OPEC+ agreement. In the medium and long term, global policy actions to lower CO_2 emissions present a further downside risk to oil demand (see Box 1.SF.1).

Metal Prices Recovered amid an Uncertain Economic Outlook

Base metal prices increased by 18.2 percent between February and August 2020. Slow global industrial activity weighed heavily on prices in the first quarter of 2020 (see Figure 1.SF.4). Since then, supply disruptions in mining related to COVID-19 and a resurgence in industrial activity in China—which accounts for half of base metal demand—have helped metal prices return to pre-pandemic levels. Unprecedented stimulus measures and a stock market surge also boosted sentiment toward metals. Precious metal prices

continued to rise due to increasing demand for safe-haven assets amid concerns that a second wave of COVID-19 infections would cause protracted monetary policy stimulus.

Among base metals, iron ore prices increased the most between February and August, by 37.0 percent, reaching a year high, while copper prices increased by 14.4 percent amid growing optimism over China's economic recovery, falling inventories, and supply disruptions in key producing countries (Chile and Peru). Aluminum (+3.0 percent), whose supply has been more insulated from the pandemic as it is mostly sourced domestically, did not rally as global automotive sales slumped. The price of nickel and cobalt, key inputs for stainless steel and batteries in electric vehicles, increased by 14.6 percent and fell by 1.9 percent, respectively.

The IMF annual base metal price index is projected to increase by 0.8 percent on an annual average basis in 2020 and by a further 3.0 percent in 2021 on concerns surrounding the long-term impact of the pandemic. The possibility of a second wave of COVID-19, the sustainability of strong China demand, and tensions between China and the United States are the major risks to metal prices falling. These more than offset the risk of supply disruptions in major metal-producing countries. The precious metals index is expected to increase by 28.4 percent in 2020 and by 10.4 percent in 2021 due to the effects of heightened global uncertainty and continued accommodative monetary policies.

Food Prices Declined amid Ample Global Supplies

The IMF's food and beverage price index increased by 0.7 percent, reflecting pandemic-induced changes in demand and supply conditions, with different effects on food prices depending on the region and the agricultural commodity. As COVID-19 slowed economic activity, demand for agricultural raw materials and animal feed initially declined. Prices of most staple crops, including wheat, maize, soybeans, and palm oil, have been stable or have declined since the beginning of the pandemic due to large global supplies and the initial collapse of crude oil prices (see Figure 1.SF.4).

Led by pork, the meat price index fell by 7.1 percent from the April baseline. Amplified by large seasonal farm supply, wholesale pork prices declined by 4.5 percent as several meat processing facilities in the United States closed after employees were infected by the coronavirus. The resulting drop in processing capacity reduced supply to retail channels and drove a wedge between wholesale and retail prices, which generally increased.[1] The wholesale price decline spilled over to other meats and seafood, which saw similar downward trends.

Staple food prices, such as for wheat and rice rallied, initially driven by consumer stockpiling, but, given ample supply, as the initial surge in demand passed, prices retrenched. Overall, though, the price of rice is still up by 12.6 percent. Corn prices plummeted by 13.0 percent on ethanol demand destruction, with prices reaching a 10-year low in May. Soybean prices declined by 13.0 percent beginning in February on account of ample global supplies, notwithstanding the fact that China ramped up buying in June as part of the 2020 US-China trade deal.

Food prices are projected to increase slightly, by 0.4 percent year over year in 2020 and then increase 4.3 percent in the year thereafter on tighter supply conditions (meats, for example), in part related to expected delays in the supply chain. Further supply chain disruptions and export restrictions in large food exporters are a significant source of upside risk. Renewed tensions between the United States and China could disrupt food trade and lower US food prices while increasing them in competing exporters.

Coal: Past, Present, and Future

Many countries are taking steps to reduce their dependence on fossil fuels, especially coal, as they seek to pursue a more sustainable future. Because of its high carbon intensity, coal accounts for just under half of global CO_2 emissions and nearly three-quarters of all power sector CO_2 emissions. In the absence of pollution mitigation systems, it contributes to local air pollution, with potentially severe damaging effects on human health (Smith, Mehta, and Maeusezahl-Feuz 2004). The unprecedented drop in electricity demand in 2020 favored renewables over traditional fossil fuel sources, such as coal and natural gas. In Europe, where electricity consumption fell by more than 10 percent in April, the share of coal (fossil fuels) in power generation declined to

below 8 (30) percent—a historical low. As electricity demand recovered, use of coal resumed globally.

So why is coal still popular if it has large negative externalities? Which economies and economic sectors are most dependent on coal? Some countries moved away from coal in the past. How did they do it, and is this replicable? Will the pandemic speed or slow the demise of coal? These questions are explored by looking at the use of coal throughout history, until the recent pandemic, and its trends in production and consumption across countries.

Coal Usage, Industrialization, and Energy Transition to Fossil Fuels

The Heydays

The use of coal took off during the industrial revolution in 18th century England and then spread to continental Europe and the United States during the 19th and 20th centuries. A series of technological innovations (including the steam engine and coal-fueled furnaces for steel production) radically transformed manufacturing, coal mining, and transportation (for example, steam locomotives and steamships). This spurred rapid economic growth, industrialization, and urbanization, which drastically increased demand. The transition to coal in Europe also helped reverse a pattern of excessive deforestation from centuries of intensive wood harvesting—a major energy transition that saw industrial economies moving away from biomass (that is, wood fuel).[2,3] Hence, until the early interwar period, coal consumption and its share in the energy mix grew unabated in almost every country.

Decline and Renaissance

During the 1930s and especially after World War II cleaner fossil fuel alternatives—such as oil and, later, natural gas—increasingly displaced coal in the transportation, residential, and commercial sectors and even in power generation (Figure 1.SF.5). Coal, especially the low-grade sulfurous variety, was cheap but a major

---

[1]The harmonized consumer price subindex for food and nonalcoholic beverages, for instance, increased by 4.5 percent between February and June in the United States and by 1.3 percent in the euro area. In China, on the other hand, the food consumer price subindex fell by 9.7 percent.

[2]Indeed, forest cover in Europe today is higher than it has been in a century (Fuchs and others 2015). Afforestation notwithstanding, primeval forests in western Europe are extremely rare. For a vivid depiction of a preindustrial Italian forest, see "Hunting in the Pontine Marshes" by Horace Vernet (1833).

[3]Similarly, the rise of the American oil industry in the 19th century helped save several whale species from extinction as kerosene lamps quickly displaced whale oil lamps and candles in the 19th century.

Figure 1.SF.5. Coal, 1850–2017

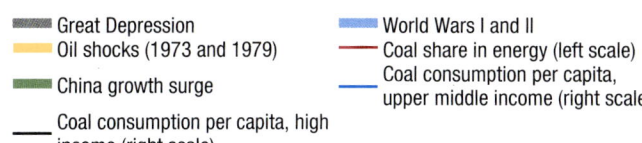

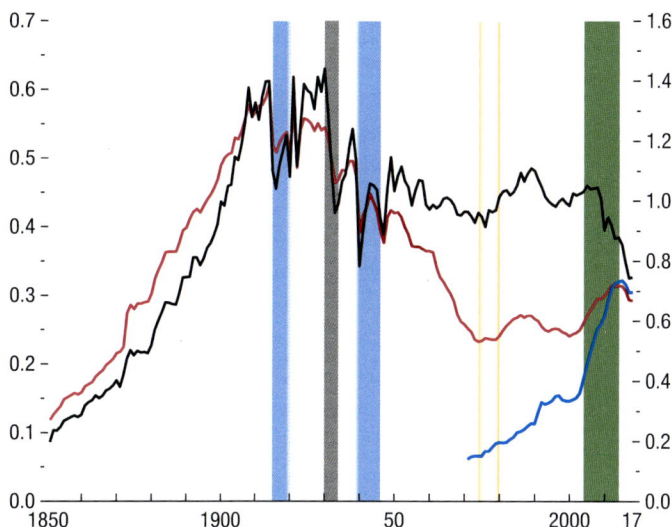

Sources: B.R. Mitchell; Maddison Project Database (2018); United Nations; and IMF staff calculations.
Note: China growth surge is defined as the years between 2003 and 2011, when annual GDP growth exceeded 12 percent, except in 2009. Income categories are as defined by the World Bank.

Figure 1.SF.6. Decomposition of Change in World Coal Intensity
(Percent)

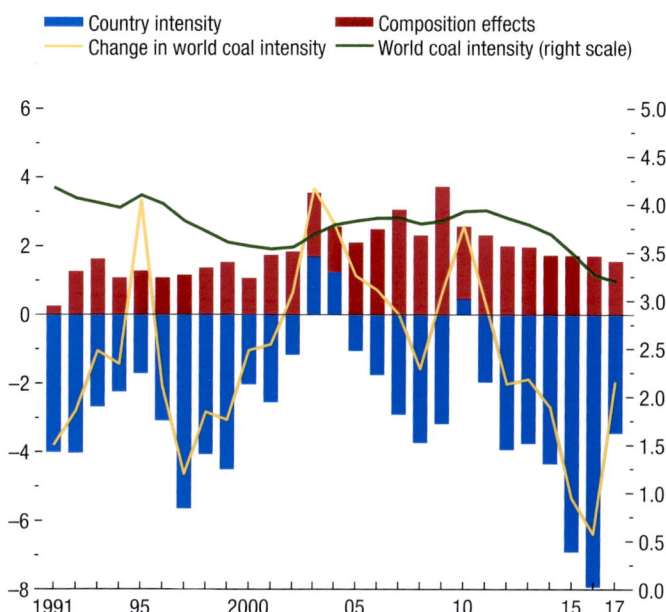

Sources: International Energy Agency; World Bank, *World Development Indicators*; and IMF staff calculations.

cause of air pollution and environmental damage.[4] Hence, per capita coal consumption, and especially the coal share in the energy mix, declined rapidly—and was further pushed down by the expanding motor vehicle industry's thirst for gasoline.

That coal decline was surprisingly interrupted in the 1970s and then partially reversed by three significant factors (Figure 1.SF.5): (1) energy security concerns (because of the twin oil shocks of the 1970s), (2) the growing electrification of energy end-uses, and (3) fast economic growth in emerging markets. The combination of (1) and (2) contributed to increased demand for coal for power generation in many advanced economies that wanted to reduce dependence on oil because of energy security concerns.[5] Later, at the turn of the

century, as economic growth shifted to markets with higher coal intensity (that is, coal consumption per unit of GDP) and income elasticity of coal demand (such as China and India), coal demand in emerging markets surged, more than offsetting declining coal usage in advanced economies.[6] As a result, global per capita coal consumption, its energy share, and even coal intensity increased again: the coal renaissance (Figure 1.SF.6).

Today, the top five coal-consuming countries (China, India, United States, Russia, Japan) account for 76.7 percent of global coal consumption (Figure 1.SF.7). China accounts for about half of global coal consumption after industrial and power generation coal demand grew particularly fast in the mid-2000s following an infrastructure boom. In fact, today, driven by China, emerging markets, where industry coal demand is still important, account for the lion's share—76.8 percent—of coal consumption. Globally, industry takes about 20 percent of total coal consumption (Table 1.SF.1).

In advanced economies, coal demand is predominantly associated with power generation because of the decline of

[4]During the Great Smog of London (December 5–9, 1952), due to weather conditions, air pollutants from the combustion of coal and diesel-powered buses for public transportation covered the city in a blanket of smog. UK government medical reports estimate that 4,000 people died as a direct result of the smog and 100,000 more were made ill.

[5]The share of coal in energy troughed in 1973, globally.

[6]China and India increasingly relied on coal to satisfy their rising energy needs as economic activity accelerated (Steckel, Edenhofer, and Jakob 2015).

Figure 1.SF.7. Coal Consumption, by Country
(Percent)

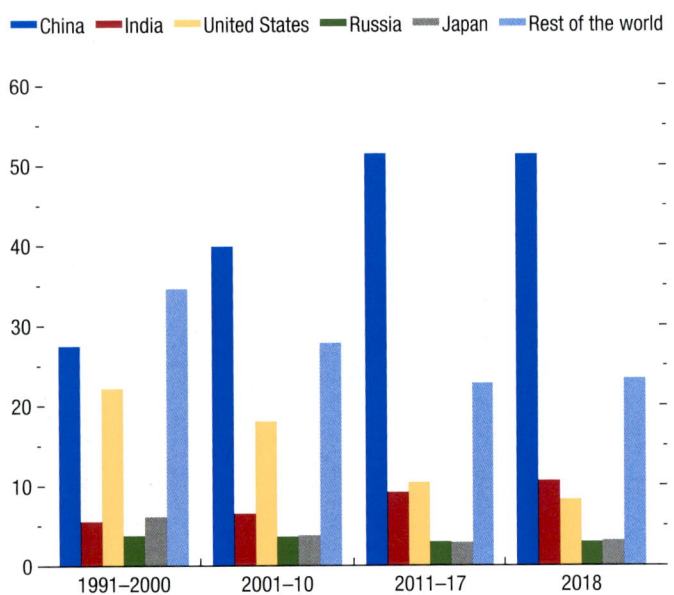

Sources: International Energy Agency, *World Energy Balances*; and IMF staff calculations.

Table 1.SF.1. Coal Consumption, by Sector
(Percent)

	OECD	Non-OECD	Total
Power Generation	20.1	50.7	70.8
Industry	2.2	19.4	21.6
Others	0.9	6.7	7.6
Total	23.2	76.8	100.0

Sources: International Energy Agency; and IMF staff calculations.
Note: "Others" consist of residential and commercial and nonenergy use. OECD = Organisation for Economic Co-operation and Development.

coal-intensive industries, such as steel and cement. Given that the electrification of economic systems is ongoing, energy demand from power generation is expected to increase in advanced economies, where total energy demand is flattening.[7] Whereas no significant economical alternatives to coking coal exist in the industrial sector (for example, in making steel and cement), low-carbon alternatives compete with coal for investment in new power plants. This is more relevant in emerging markets, where power generation capacity is expected to grow the most.

Coal's Negative Externalities: Health, Environment, and Carbon Emissions

Coal-fired thermal power plants release several substances—including sulfur dioxide, nitrogen oxide, particulate matter, and mercury—into the air and rivers, streams, and lakes. These emissions are hazardous to human health (toxins) and degrade the environment (pollutants).[8] Air pollution from the combustion of coal and other fossil fuels was long considered the most serious environmental problem in advanced economies.[9] In Europe and the United States, for example, regulations were rolled out beginning in the 1980s and 1990s to incentivize the adoption of environmental pollution mitigation technologies, such as scrubbers, thereby curtailing emissions from coal plants.[10] Other countries decided to (slowly) steer away from the use of coal altogether, with nuclear, hydropower, natural gas, and—more recently—renewable energy slowly displacing coal.

Though steps have been taken to mitigate coal's direct environmental impact, the combustion of coal also emits CO_2. Coal is more carbon intense than any other primary energy fuel. This means that replacing coal with other energy sources decarbonizes the energy system, and the degree to which that happens depends on the substitute. To rank energy sources by carbon intensity, their emission factors can be compared, expressed in tons of CO_2 per unit of electricity generated, which considers both the intrinsic carbon intensity of the fuel per unit of energy and the average efficiency of the generation technology. When burned to generate both heat and electricity, coal is 2.2 times as carbon intense as natural gas— the only realistic fossil fuel alternative in the power sector (Figure 1.SF.8). With its high emission factor and large share in world energy consumption, coal contributes about 44 percent of all CO_2 emissions and 72 percent of all power sector emissions (Figure 1.SF.9).[11]

---

[7]There has been a steady increase in the role of electricity as energy service provider. In 2017 power generation accounted for about 41 percent of total energy demand, up from 26 percent in 1971.

[8]Emissions from coal combustion can damage the respiratory, cardiovascular, and nervous systems of the human body (Smith, Mehta, and Maeusezahl-Feuz 2004).

[9]According to Fouquet (2011), by 1880 the mining, transportation, and combustion of coal in the British economy had imposed external damages close to 20 percent of GDP.

[10]An important milestone in this context has been the United Nations Convention on Long-Range Transboundary Air Pollution, the first treaty to deal with air pollution on a regional basis, which entered into force in 1983.

[11]According to the International Energy Agency, the share of energy in total greenhouse gas emissions was 74.2 percent in 2015. The remainder constitutes greenhouse gas emissions from agriculture, deforestation, and land conversion more broadly.

Figure 1.SF.8. Emission Factors
(Metric tons of carbon dioxide a megawatt-hour)

Sources: International Energy Agency; and IMF staff calculations.

Figure 1.SF.9. Average Annual Carbon Dioxide Emissions
(Metric tons of carbon dioxide)

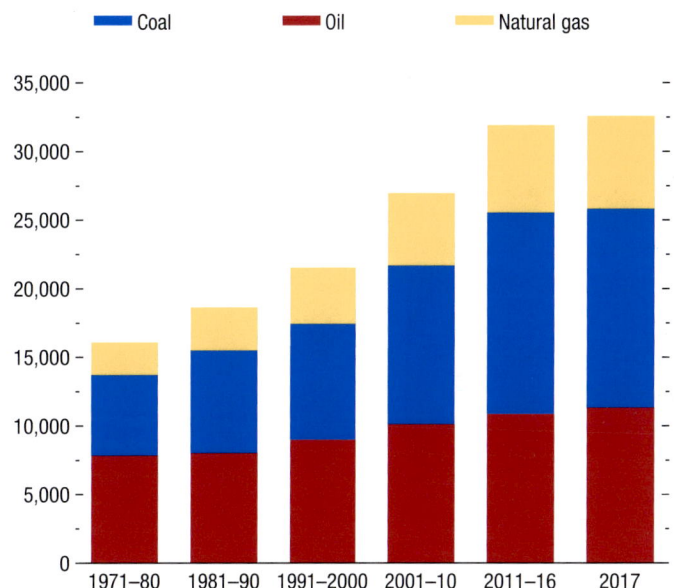

Sources: International Energy Agency; and IMF staff calculations.

How Fast and When Do Countries Lessen Their Dependence on Coal?

With the introduction and rise of new energy sources, especially after World War II, the energy mix in many countries broadened and they became less dependent on coal. Currently, per capita coal consumption has already peaked in 73 out of the 84 countries whose share of coal in total energy consumption at some point crossed 5 percent. Irrespective of their absolute dependence reached at peak consumption, the average annual decline across these countries was 2.3 percent between 1971 and 2017 (Figure 1.SF.10). This implies that it takes, on average, 43 years to phase out coal after the peak in coal consumption per capita has been reached.

Contrasting the energy mix of countries across income groups reveals stark differences (Table 1.SF.2). Poor countries rely primarily on biomass for their energy needs, while middle-income countries have a strong dependence on coal.[12] At high incomes, the coal share in energy decreases as nuclear and natural gas options grow.

The quality ladder hypothesis may help explain the observed relationship between income and the

[12]See the relationship between income level and biomass consumption in Chapter 1 of the October 2018 WEO.

energy mix. The hypothesis states that as income rises, energy sources are chosen not just for affordability and availability but increasingly for their efficiency, convenience, low environmental impact, and safety.[13] Biofuels occupy the low rungs of that ladder; coal, oil, and hydro the middle rungs; and capital-intensive sources, such as nuclear, natural gas, and renewables, the upper rungs. The low price of coal-fired power generation (Figure 1.SF.11) is consistent with the notion that coal plays an important role in the energy mix of lower-middle- and upper-middle-income countries as an affordable and often abundant energy source (Table 1.SF.2).[14,15] Country-specific endowments of competing energy sources, such as hydropower potential, could also influence the attractiveness of coal during different stages of development.

[13]See Stokey (1998) for a theory model on demand for environmental quality.

[14]Even today, the marginal cost of operating a coal-fired power plant is one of the lowest. The cost of wind and solar has substantially declined at the plant level, but a full ramp-up of renewables in the electricity grid faces decreasing returns due to their intermittency.

[15]A common way to compare alternative options for electrical energy production is the levelized cost of electricity, which is defined as the present value of the price of the produced electrical energy (usually expressed in units of cents per kilowatt-hour), considering the economic life of the plant and the costs incurred in the construction, operation and maintenance, and fuel costs.

Figure 1.SF.10. Coal Phaseouts

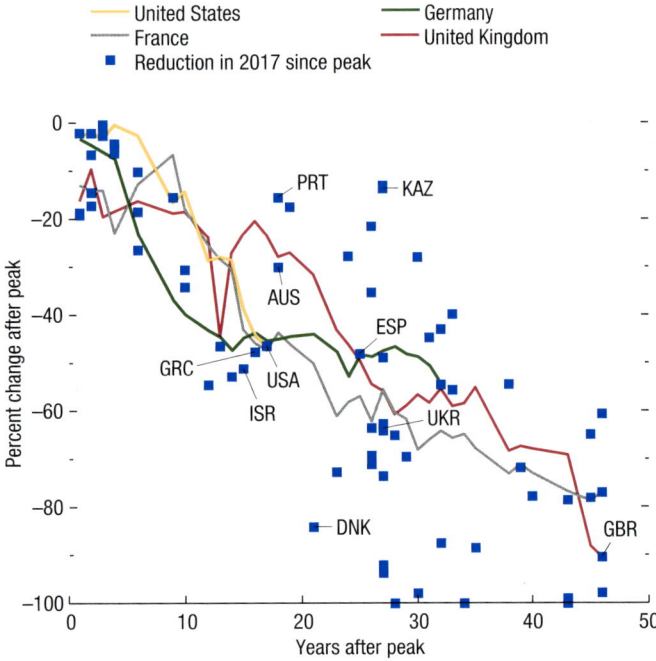

Sources: International Energy Agency; and IMF staff calculations.
Note: For each country, coal peak is defined as the year with the highest coal consumption per capita. Blue square = coal consumption per capita reduction in 2017 since peak. Coal phaseout paths for selected countries are shown in the figure. Data labels use International Organization for Standardization (ISO) country codes.

Empirical Analysis

A panel regression is used to test for the relationship between income per capita and coal dependence, which is defined as the share of coal in total primary energy supply (*relative* coal dependence) or as coal consumption per capita (*absolute* coal dependence). The analysis controls for country-specific factors, including the share of manufacturing in nominal value added, coal reserves per capita, and hydropower potential (see Online Annex I, available at www.imf.org/en/Publications/WEO, for a more detailed discussion).

Results strongly support the presence of an inverse U-shaped relationship between income and the share of coal in the energy mix, with coal attaining its maximum share at an income level of $9,600 per capita—that is, when a country reaches upper-middle-income status. For example, our main specification predicts that, between 1971 and 2017, income per capita contributed to reductions in the coal share of 6.4 percentage points in the United States and 5.2 percentage points in Japan and to increases of 12.2 percentage points in India and 11.3 percentage points in China.

Results also show that energy endowments, such as hydropower and coal reserves, play a quantitatively important role—more so than manufacturing and environmental regulation, for which modest effects are found. Harsher winters are also associated with higher use of coal.

Like the relationship between the coal share and income, the relationship between coal consumption per capita and income is highly nonlinear. The preferred specification shows an S-shape relationship with income per capita: at low income levels, coal consumption growth accelerates, reaches its maximum at the middle income level, and then levels off. The turning point of absolute coal dependence, after which coal consumption declines, ranges from $35,000 to $39,000.

Contrasting the turning points of the two different measures of coal dependence leads to the finding that the "share (or relative) turning point" occurs before the "per capita (or absolute) turning point." At middle and high income levels coal is indeed increasingly succeeded by faster-growing and higher-quality fuels, such as oil, nuclear, and natural gas, *causing* its share in the energy mix to decline. However, coal consumption per capita continues to grow after that (albeit at a slower pace than some other energy sources) to satisfy fast-growing energy demand. Assuming income per capita growth of 4 percent a year, it takes another 33 years to get from the share turning point to the

Table 1.SF.2. Energy Mix, by Income Groups, 2017
(Percent)

Primary Energy Share from:	Biomass	Coal	Crude Oil	Natural Gas	Hydropower	Renewables	Nuclear
Low-Income Countries	80.8	2.3	13.3	0.9	2.8	1.6	0.0
Lower-Middle-Income Countries	26.2	26.9	26.6	14.4	1.8	2.3	1.8
Upper-Middle-Income Countries	5.2	40.9	25.0	21.5	3.4	1.4	2.5
High-Income Countries	5.7	15.8	36.6	29.0	2.1	1.6	9.2
World	12.9	28.0	29.9	23.3	2.6	1.6	1.6

Sources: International Energy Agency; World Bank; and IMF staff calculations.
Note: Income groups as defined by the World Bank.

Figure 1.SF.11. Levelized Cost of Electricity for New Investment, 2019

(US dollars a megawatt-hour)

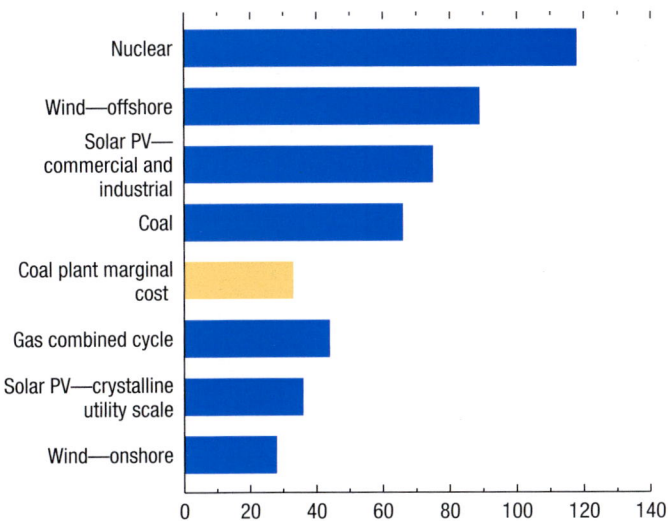

Source: Lazard 2019.
Note: Based on lower range of Lazard *Levelized Cost of Energy Comparison— Unsubsidized Analysis* estimates. Yellow bar represents the midpoint of the marginal cost of operating an existing coal power plant. PV = photovoltaic.

Table 1.SF.3. Selected Recent Fast Coal Phaseouts

Country	Year	Five-Year Reduction (Percent)	Starting Share (Percent)	Mostly Replaced by
United Kingdom	2018	−12.4	17.0	Natural Gas
Israel	2018	−9.4	29.8	Natural Gas
Greece	2018	−8.9	29.9	Natural Gas
Kazakhstan	2016	−8.1	51.3	Natural Gas
Spain	2010	−6.8	12.8	Mixed
Australia	2014	−6.5	39.7	Natural Gas
Portugal	2010	−6.3	13.5	Natural Gas
China	2017	−6.2	69.7	Mixed
Denmark	2018	−5.9	15.7	Biofuel
Ukraine	2017	−5.8	35.8	Nuclear
United States	2018	−5.3	19.6	Natural Gas

Sources: International Energy Agency; and IMF staff calculations.
Note: "Mixed" is natural gas, nuclear, and renewables.

per capita turning point. These findings are consistent with the idea that new energy fuels only slowly displace old energy fuels.

Combining estimates of the average speed of decline and the estimated time interval between the peaks in relative and absolute coal dependence, it takes, on average, 76 years to phase out coal once it reaches its largest share in the energy mix. For the United Kingdom, which is on the verge of eliminating coal, it took almost 100 years to accomplish that feat (Figure 1.SF.10). For China, whose coal share peaked in 2013, it implies at least another 38 years of coal consumption under business-as-usual conditions. Still, the United Kingdom shows the relevance of policy actions, stimulated by the introduction of carbon pricing at the utility level; the United Kingdom experienced one of the fastest declines in coal usage between 2013 and 2018 as coal was replaced by natural gas (Table 1.SF.3).[16] In the United States, instead,

a similar, but more modest, decline was driven by market forces as the shale gas revolution pushed down natural gas prices. The fastest recent transitions away from coal have been driven by natural gas, at times helped by renewables (Table 1.SF.3).

Unsurprisingly, the COVID-19 pandemic has led to a sharp reduction in coal consumption in many coal consumer countries (see Chapter 3). Given that renewables' marginal costs are extremely low, natural gas and coal accounted for most of the decline in electricity generation leading, in some regions, to record-high renewables shares in electricity production (Figure 1.SF.12). However, it is too early to declare "mission accomplished." First, the downward pressure on natural gas prices was even stronger than on coal, in part because of lack of storage for natural gas (Figure 1.SF.13). Second, where electricity demand recovered, coal usage resumed.

These considerations and the previous examples and econometric analysis suggest that a full coal phaseout will occur long after low-carbon energy sources start to gain importance in the energy mix. There are two main reasons for this persistence. First, industrial use of coal is hard to replace with other energy sources and still represents 33 percent of coal consumption in emerging markets, where most industrial sector coal usage is concentrated. Second, and most important, coal-fired power plants are long-lived assets with a minimum design lifespan of 30–40 years. This makes the obsolescence rate of a recently built coal-fired power plant very low without either large changes in the levelized cost of electricity for renewables or policy intervention.

The pandemic and its effects on economic activity are changing the medium-term outlook for coal and coal-fired power plants in various ways but, overall,

[16]In 2013 the United Kingdom became the first country in the European Union to introduce a carbon price support—a tax paid by companies that generate electricity from fossil fuels that tops Europe's emissions trading system, through which energy companies buy permits to emit carbon dioxide. The tax was initially set at £9 a metric ton of CO_2 and gradually doubled to £18.

Figure 1.SF.12. Contribution to European Electricity Generation Growth
(Year over year, percent)

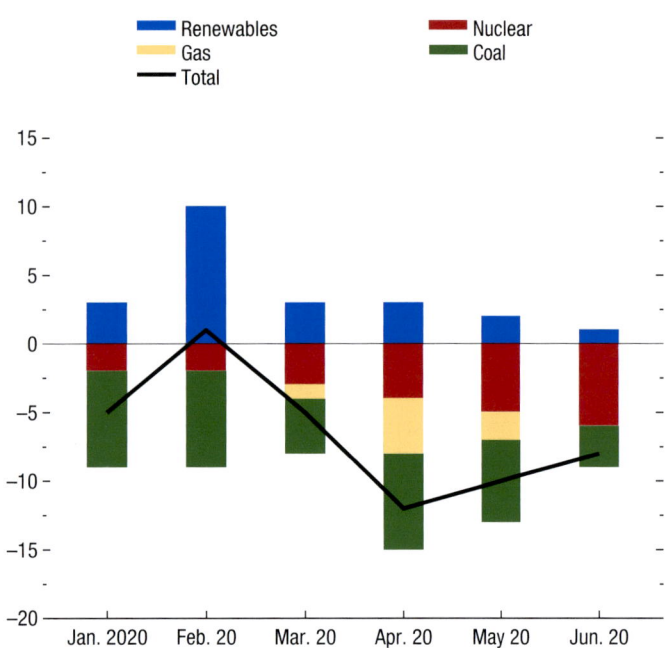

Source: EMBER.
Note: Data represent the 27 member countries of the European Union.

Figure 1.SF.13. Coal and Natural Gas Prices in 2020
(January 2–15 = 100)

Sources: IMF, Primary Commodity Price System; and IMF staff calculations.
Note: Coal index is the simple average of Australian and South African coal prices. Natural gas index is the simple average of Netherlands Title Transfer Facility and Asian liquefied natural gas prices.

the impact is unclear. On one hand, if the reduction in electricity demand turns out to be more permanent, this would likely reduce the utilization of existing coal-fired power plants, encouraging their closure, especially in advanced economies. On the other hand, in emerging markets, even if electricity demand does not fully recover to trends before the pandemic, it is still expected to grow strongly. A possible reduction in coal prices, coupled with lower wholesale electricity prices, may slow investment in renewables, to the benefit of coal, in the absence of policy intervention.

Finally, it is worth noting that, in contrast to studies examining total energy consumption, a large part of the variation in coal dependence is unexplained.[17] In part, this may reflect political economy factors leading to cross-country differences in energy policies. In some countries the value of coal reserves is multiples of GDP, raising the risk of stranded coal assets. Strong domestic mining interests in large coal consumer and producer countries, especially in Asia, including China and India, may further complicate and delay

[17]See the Commodity Special Feature of the October 2018 WEO for an analysis of energy demand.

the phaseout of coal in major coal consumer-producer countries (see Online Annex II for more detailed discussion).

Conclusions

Reducing carbon emissions from coal would go a long way toward fighting climate change. Furthermore, decarbonization of the power generation sector would amplify the benefits of a global transition to electric vehicles and electric mobility more broadly—given that electric vehicles would be charged with low-carbon electricity.

Moving away from coal usually starts in high-income nations and takes decades to complete. The pandemic may have dented coal consumption but, probably, only temporarily. Moreover, countries that have recently, or not yet, seen per capita coal consumption peak (including China, India, and Indonesia) account for the lion's share of global coal consumption, which will therefore take years to decline in the absence of significant policy actions. Further significant reductions in prices of low-carbon alternatives such as solar and wind may help, but to avoid the inter-mittency problem associated with renewables, natural gas (the closest substitute for coal) is probably needed even if electricity demand does not fully recover to its pre-pandemic trend.

Although carbon-capture and storage technology may be a viable solution, in the absence of substantial carbon pricing, it is currently expensive to retrofit existing plants or build new coal plants with such technology (see IMF 2019 for a detailed analysis of the benefits of carbon pricing). Furthermore, some claim that the CO_2 emission opportunity costs of further investment in carbon capture and storage may be large, as proven technologies, such as wind and solar, can already be used to lower carbon emissions (see, for example, Jacobson 2020). It may be wise, however, to diversify and invest in multiple mitigation strategies, as the intermittency problem of renewables, especially for a high degree of grid penetration, remains unsolved and may still require coal for power generation in some locations.

The decline in coal could be accelerated if governments were willing to compensate the losers from a coal phaseout and see the COVID-19 pandemic as an opportunity to accelerate it. In emerging markets, the degree to which coal is locked in can be minimized if capital constraints are reduced to favor investment in renewables. The international community can provide financial and technical assistance (on how to build grids with the intermittent electricity generated by renewables) and limit funding of new coal plants, at least where alternatives are available.

Box 1.SF.1. What Happened with Global Carbon Emissions in 2019?

This box updates the assessment of global carbon emissions from the October 2019 *World Economic Outlook*. Latest data for the end of 2019 show that the growth in global carbon emissions fell to below 0.5 percent, after an alarming rebound in 2017 and 2018 of more than 2 percent (Figure 1.SF.1.1).

China remains a key driver of emission growth, and its impact picked up again in 2019, after a period of gradual regression. India and other emerging markets' contribution in 2019 fell substantially, and emissions decreased in all Group of Seven economies.

The decline in global emissions in 2019 can be attributed mainly to a fall in energy intensity and

Figure 1.SF.1.1. Contribution to World Emissions, by Country/Region
(Percent change)

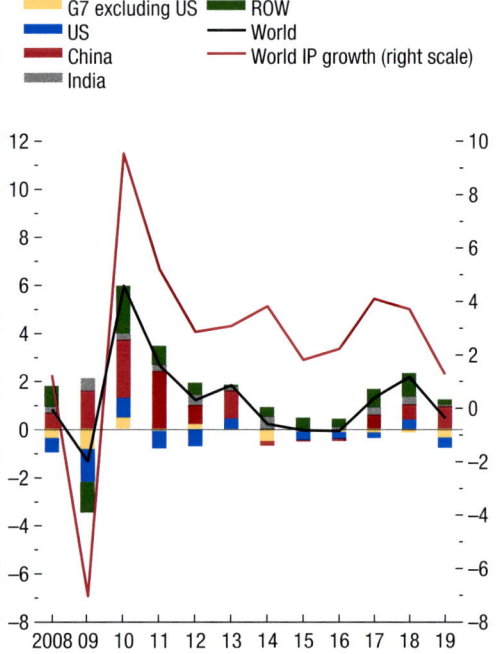

Sources: British Petroleum; International Energy Agency; and IMF staff calculations.
Note: G7 = Group of Seven (Canada, France, Germany, Italy, Japan, United Kingdom, United States); IP = industrial production; ROW = rest of the world; US = United States.

Figure 1.SF.1.2. Contribution to World Emissions, by Source
(Percent change)

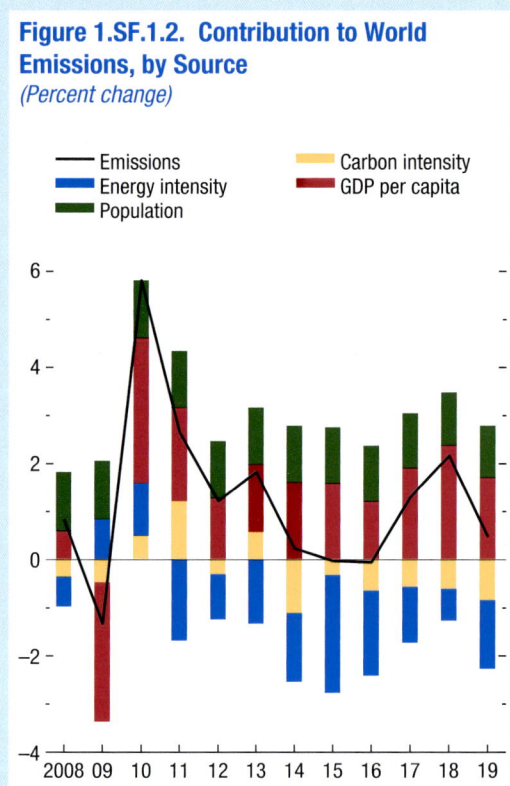

Sources: British Petroleum; International Energy Agency; World Bank, *World Development Indicators*; and IMF staff calculations.

lower income growth (Figure 1.SF.1.2).[1] This is consistent with previous years and likely reflects the cyclical slowdown in global industrial production in 2019. Decarbonization remained an important mitigation force in 2019 as wind, solar, and natural gas continued to replace coal as the energy source of choice in the power sectors of all major emitters.

In 2020 the COVID-19 pandemic and associated lockdowns will likely lead emissions to fall, although most of the reduction will likely be short-lived when normal economic growth returns. Policymakers should thus seize the crisis as an opportunity to invest in greener growth that permanently lowers emissions (Georgieva 2020).

[1]The October 2019 *World Economic Outlook* shows that total emissions can be expressed as a product of carbon intensity (carbon emissions per unit of energy), energy intensity (energy per unit of GDP), GDP per capita, and human population.

The authors of this box are Claire Li and Nico Valckx.

Annex Table 1.1.1. European Economies: Real GDP, Consumer Prices, Current Account Balance, and Unemployment
(Annual percent change, unless noted otherwise)

	Real GDP			Consumer Prices[1]			Current Account Balance[2]			Unemployment[3]		
		Projections			Projections			Projections			Projections	
	2019	2020	2021	2019	2020	2021	2019	2020	2021	2019	2020	2021
Europe	**1.6**	**−7.0**	**4.7**	**3.0**	**2.0**	**2.4**	**2.1**	**1.7**	**1.9**	...	...	...
Advanced Europe	**1.4**	**−8.1**	**5.2**	**1.3**	**0.5**	**1.0**	**2.3**	**2.1**	**2.3**	**6.6**	**8.0**	**8.5**
Euro Area[4],[5]	1.3	−8.3	5.2	1.2	0.4	0.9	2.7	1.9	2.4	7.6	8.9	9.1
Germany	0.6	−6.0	4.2	1.3	0.5	1.1	7.1	5.8	6.8	3.1	4.3	4.2
France	1.5	−9.8	6.0	1.3	0.5	0.6	−0.7	−1.9	−1.8	8.5	8.9	10.2
Italy	0.3	−10.6	5.2	0.6	0.1	0.6	3.0	3.2	3.0	9.9	11.0	11.8
Spain	2.0	−12.8	7.2	0.7	−0.2	0.8	2.0	0.5	0.9	14.1	16.8	16.8
Netherlands	1.7	−5.4	4.0	2.7	1.2	1.5	9.9	7.6	9.0	3.4	5.5	4.5
Belgium	1.4	−8.3	5.4	1.2	0.6	1.2	−1.2	0.0	−0.8	5.4	6.1	7.6
Austria	1.6	−6.7	4.6	1.5	1.2	1.8	2.6	2.4	2.5	4.5	5.8	5.5
Ireland	5.9	−3.0	4.9	0.9	−0.2	0.6	−11.4	5.0	5.5	5.0	5.6	6.2
Portugal	2.2	−10.0	6.5	0.3	0.0	1.1	−0.1	−3.1	−3.5	6.5	8.1	7.7
Greece	1.9	−9.5	4.1	0.5	−0.6	0.7	−2.1	−7.7	−4.5	17.3	19.9	18.3
Finland	1.1	−4.0	3.6	1.1	0.7	1.3	−0.5	−1.8	−0.7	6.8	8.4	8.6
Slovak Republic	2.4	−7.1	6.9	2.8	1.5	1.5	−2.9	−3.1	−4.1	5.8	7.8	7.1
Lithuania	3.9	−1.8	4.1	2.2	1.3	1.7	4.3	7.2	4.5	6.3	8.2	7.5
Slovenia	2.4	−6.7	5.2	1.6	0.5	1.8	5.7	4.5	3.9	4.6	8.0	6.0
Luxembourg	2.3	−5.8	5.9	1.7	0.4	1.4	4.5	3.8	4.3	5.4	6.5	7.0
Latvia	2.2	−6.0	5.2	2.7	0.6	1.8	−0.5	2.0	−0.8	6.3	9.0	8.0
Estonia	5.0	−5.2	4.5	2.3	0.2	1.4	2.6	4.0	2.0	4.4	7.8	6.1
Cyprus	3.2	−6.4	4.7	0.6	−0.6	1.0	−6.7	−10.6	−9.1	7.1	8.0	7.0
Malta	4.9	−7.9	4.8	1.5	0.8	1.1	9.6	7.6	8.3	3.6	4.2	4.2
United Kingdom	1.5	−9.8	5.9	1.8	0.8	1.2	−4.0	−2.0	−3.8	3.8	5.4	7.4
Switzerland	1.2	−5.3	3.6	0.4	−0.8	0.0	11.5	8.5	9.0	2.3	3.2	3.6
Sweden	1.3	−4.7	3.5	1.6	0.8	1.4	4.2	3.2	4.2	6.8	8.7	9.3
Czech Republic	2.3	−6.5	5.1	2.9	3.3	2.4	−0.4	−0.7	−0.5	2.0	3.1	3.4
Norway	1.2	−2.8	3.6	2.2	1.4	3.3	4.1	2.8	4.4	3.7	4.5	4.3
Denmark	2.3	−4.5	3.5	0.7	0.4	0.9	7.8	6.4	6.6	5.0	6.2	6.0
Iceland	1.9	−7.2	4.1	3.0	2.7	2.8	6.2	0.0	0.2	3.6	7.2	7.0
San Marino	1.1	−11.0	5.7	1.0	0.5	0.8	0.7	−4.5	−1.2	7.7	10.1	8.4
Emerging and Developing Europe[6]	**2.1**	**−4.6**	**3.9**	**6.6**	**5.2**	**5.2**	**1.4**	**−0.3**	**0.1**	...	...	...
Russia	1.3	−4.1	2.8	4.5	3.2	3.2	3.8	1.2	1.8	4.6	5.6	5.2
Turkey	0.9	−5.0	5.0	15.2	11.9	11.9	1.2	−3.7	−0.9	13.7	14.6	12.4
Poland	4.1	−3.6	4.6	2.3	3.3	2.3	0.4	3.0	1.8	3.3	3.8	5.1
Romania	4.1	−4.8	4.6	3.8	2.9	2.5	−4.6	−5.3	−4.5	3.9	7.9	6.0
Ukraine[7]	3.2	−7.2	3.0	7.9	3.2	6.0	−2.7	4.3	−3.0	8.5	11.0	9.6
Hungary	4.9	−6.1	3.9	3.4	3.6	3.4	−0.8	−1.6	−0.9	3.4	6.1	4.7
Belarus[7]	1.2	−3.0	2.2	5.6	5.1	5.1	−1.8	−3.3	−2.2	0.3	1.4	1.1
Bulgaria[5]	3.4	−4.0	4.1	2.5	1.2	1.7	4.0	1.9	2.3	4.2	5.6	4.5
Serbia	4.2	−2.5	5.5	1.9	1.5	1.9	−6.9	−6.4	−6.5	10.9	13.4	13.0
Croatia	2.9	−9.0	6.0	0.8	0.3	0.8	2.8	−3.2	−3.1	7.8	9.3	10.3

Source: IMF staff estimates.

Note: Data for some countries are based on fiscal years. Please refer to Table F in the Statistical Appendix for a list of economies with exceptional reporting periods.

[1]Movements in consumer prices are shown as annual averages. Year-end to year-end changes can be found in Tables A5 and A6 in the Statistical Appendix.
[2]Percent of GDP.
[3]Percent. National definitions of unemployment may differ.
[4]Current account position corrected for reporting discrepancies in intra-area transactions.
[5]Based on Eurostat's harmonized index of consumer prices except for Slovenia.
[6]Includes Albania, Bosnia and Herzegovina, Kosovo, Moldova, Montenegro, and North Macedonia.
[7]See country-specific notes for Belarus and Ukraine in the "Country Notes" section of the Statistical Appendix.

Annex Table 1.1.2. Asian and Pacific Economies: Real GDP, Consumer Prices, Current Account Balance, and Unemployment
(Annual percent change, unless noted otherwise)

	Real GDP			Consumer Prices[1]			Current Account Balance[2]			Unemployment[3]		
		Projections			Projections			Projections			Projections	
	2019	2020	2021	2019	2020	2021	2019	2020	2021	2019	2020	2021
Asia	**4.6**	**−2.2**	**6.9**	**2.7**	**2.5**	**2.5**	**1.8**	**1.8**	**1.3**	...	...	...
Advanced Asia	**1.2**	**−4.2**	**2.9**	**0.7**	**0.2**	**0.7**	**4.3**	**3.6**	**3.5**	**3.1**	**4.0**	**3.8**
Japan	0.7	−5.3	2.3	0.5	−0.1	0.3	3.6	2.9	3.2	2.4	3.3	2.8
Korea	2.0	−1.9	2.9	0.4	0.5	0.9	3.6	3.3	3.4	3.8	4.1	4.1
Australia	1.8	−4.2	3.0	1.6	0.7	1.3	0.6	1.8	−0.1	5.2	6.9	7.7
Taiwan Province of China	2.7	0.0	3.2	0.5	−0.1	1.0	10.7	9.6	9.8	3.8	3.9	3.8
Singapore	0.7	−6.0	5.0	0.6	−0.4	0.3	17.0	15.0	14.5	2.3	3.0	2.6
Hong Kong SAR	−1.2	−7.5	3.7	2.9	0.3	2.4	6.2	4.4	4.7	3.0	5.2	4.4
New Zealand	2.2	−6.1	4.4	1.6	1.7	0.6	−3.4	−2.0	−2.4	4.1	6.0	7.0
Macao SAR	−4.7	−52.3	23.9	2.8	1.7	1.8	34.8	−23.5	−6.7	1.7	2.3	2.0
Emerging and Developing Asia	**5.5**	**−1.7**	**8.0**	**3.3**	**3.2**	**2.9**	**0.6**	**1.0**	**0.3**	...	...	...
China	6.1	1.9	8.2	2.9	2.9	2.7	1.0	1.3	0.7	3.6	3.8	3.6
India[4]	4.2	−10.3	8.8	4.8	4.9	3.7	−0.9	0.3	−0.9	...	...	...
ASEAN-5	**4.9**	**−3.4**	**6.2**	**2.1**	**1.5**	**2.3**	**1.1**	**0.8**	**0.1**	...	...	...
Indonesia	5.0	−1.5	6.1	2.8	2.1	1.6	−2.7	−1.3	−2.4	5.3	8.0	6.8
Thailand	2.4	−7.1	4.0	0.7	−0.4	1.8	7.1	4.2	4.6	1.0	1.0	1.0
Malaysia	4.3	−6.0	7.8	0.7	−1.1	2.4	3.4	0.9	1.8	3.3	4.9	3.4
Philippines	6.0	−8.3	7.4	2.5	2.4	3.0	−0.1	1.6	−1.5	5.1	10.4	7.4
Vietnam	7.0	1.6	6.7	2.8	3.8	4.0	3.4	1.2	1.7	2.2	3.3	2.7
Other Emerging and Developing Asia[5]	**6.6**	**−1.7**	**7.8**	**5.3**	**5.3**	**5.4**	**−2.5**	**−3.4**	**−3.7**	...	...	...
Memorandum												
Emerging Asia[6]	**5.4**	**−1.7**	**8.0**	**3.2**	**3.1**	**2.8**	**0.7**	**1.1**	**0.4**	...	...	...

Source: IMF staff estimates.

Note: Data for some countries are based on fiscal years. Please refer to Table F in the Statistical Appendix for a list of economies with exceptional reporting periods.
[1]Movements in consumer prices are shown as annual averages. Year-end to year-end changes can be found in Tables A5 and A6 in the Statistical Appendix.
[2]Percent of GDP.
[3]Percent. National definitions of unemployment may differ.
[4]See country-specific note for India in the "Country Notes" section of the Statistical Appendix.
[5]Other Emerging and Developing Asia comprises Bangladesh, Bhutan, Brunei Darussalam, Cambodia, Fiji, Kiribati, Lao P.D.R., Maldives, Marshall Islands, Micronesia, Mongolia, Myanmar, Nauru, Nepal, Palau, Papua New Guinea, Samoa, Solomon Islands, Sri Lanka, Timor-Leste, Tonga, Tuvalu, and Vanuatu.
[6]Emerging Asia comprises the ASEAN-5 (Indonesia, Malaysia, Philippines, Thailand, Vietnam) economies, China, and India.

Annex Table 1.1.3. Western Hemisphere Economies: Real GDP, Consumer Prices, Current Account Balance, and Unemployment
(Annual percent change, unless noted otherwise)

	Real GDP			Consumer Prices[1]			Current Account Balance[2]			Unemployment[3]		
		Projections			Projections			Projections			Projections	
	2019	2020	2021	2019	2020	2021	2019	2020	2021	2019	2020	2021
North America	1.9	−4.9	3.3	2.0	1.6	2.7	−2.1	−2.0	−2.0	...	...	...
United States	2.2	−4.3	3.1	1.8	1.5	2.8	−2.2	−2.1	−2.1	3.7	8.9	7.3
Canada	1.7	−7.1	5.2	1.9	0.6	1.3	−2.0	−2.0	−2.4	5.7	9.7	7.9
Mexico	−0.3	−9.0	3.5	3.6	3.4	3.3	−0.3	1.2	−0.1	3.5	5.2	5.8
Puerto Rico[4]	2.0	−7.5	1.5	0.1	−1.6	0.6	...	...	...	8.3	12.0	11.5
South America[5]	−0.2	−8.1	3.6	10.1	7.9	8.6	−2.3	−0.6	−0.7	...	...	...
Brazil	1.1	−5.8	2.8	3.7	2.7	2.9	−2.8	0.3	0.0	11.9	13.4	14.1
Argentina	−2.1	−11.8	4.9	53.5	...	...	−0.9	0.7	1.2	9.8	11.0	10.1
Colombia	3.3	−8.2	4.0	3.5	2.4	2.1	−4.2	−4.0	−3.9	10.5	17.3	15.8
Chile	1.1	−6.0	4.5	2.3	2.9	2.7	−3.8	−1.6	−2.9	7.2	11.4	10.2
Peru	2.2	−13.9	7.3	2.1	1.8	1.9	−1.4	−1.1	−0.3	6.6	12.5	8.8
Venezuela	−35.0	−25.0	−10.0	19,906	6,500	6,500	8.4	−4.1	−4.1	47.6	54.4	57.3
Ecuador	0.1	−11.0	4.8	0.3	0.0	1.0	−0.1	−2.0	−0.1	3.8	8.1	5.6
Paraguay	0.0	−4.0	5.5	2.8	2.9	3.2	−1.0	−0.7	0.0	6.1	7.0	6.1
Bolivia	2.2	−7.9	5.6	1.8	1.7	4.1	−3.3	−2.6	−3.5	4.0	8.0	4.0
Uruguay	0.2	−4.5	4.3	7.9	10.0	8.2	0.6	−1.7	−3.3	8.9	9.7	9.0
Central America[6]	3.2	−5.9	3.6	2.0	1.8	2.2	−1.2	−3.1	−2.9	...	...	...
Caribbean[7]	0.7	−5.4	3.9	4.2	7.1	7.8	−2.4	−9.9	−7.5	...	...	...
Memorandum												
Latin America and the Caribbean[8]	0.0	−8.1	3.6	7.7	6.2	6.7	−1.7	−0.5	−0.8	...	...	...
Eastern Caribbean Currency Union[9]	2.8	−15.1	5.8	0.8	0.6	1.5	−7.7	−21.0	−20.5	...	...	...

Source: IMF staff estimates.

Note: Data for some countries are based on fiscal years. Please refer to Table F in the Statistical Appendix for a list of economies with exceptional reporting periods.

[1]Movements in consumer prices are shown as annual averages. Aggregates exclude Venezuela. Year-end to year-end changes can be found in Tables A5 and A6 in the Statistical Appendix.

[2]Percent of GDP.

[3]Percent. National definitions of unemployment may differ.

[4]Puerto Rico is a territory of the United States, but its statistical data are maintained on a separate and independent basis.

[5]See country-specific notes for Argentina and Venezuela in the "Country Notes" section of the Statistical Appendix.

[6]Central America refers to CAPDR (Central America, Panama, Dominican Republic) and comprises Costa Rica, Dominican Republic, El Salvador, Guatemala, Honduras, Nicaragua, and Panama.

[7]The Caribbean comprises Antigua and Barbuda, Aruba, The Bahamas, Barbados, Belize, Dominica, Grenada, Guyana, Haiti, Jamaica, St. Kitts and Nevis, St. Lucia, St. Vincent and the Grenadines, Suriname, and Trinidad and Tobago.

[8]Latin America and the Caribbean comprises Mexico and economies from the Caribbean, Central America, and South America. See country-specific notes for Argentina and Venezuela in the "Country Notes" section of the Statistical Appendix.

[9]Eastern Caribbean Currency Union comprises Antigua and Barbuda, Dominica, Grenada, St. Kitts and Nevis, St. Lucia, and St. Vincent and the Grenadines as well as Anguilla and Montserrat, which are not IMF members.

Annex Table 1.1.4. Middle Eastern and Central Asian Economies: Real GDP, Consumer Prices, Current Account Balance, and Unemployment
(Annual percent change, unless noted otherwise)

	Real GDP			Consumer Prices[1]			Current Account Balance[2]			Unemployment[3]		
		Projections			Projections			Projections			Projections	
	2019	2020	2021	2019	2020	2021	2019	2020	2021	2019	2020	2021
Middle East and Central Asia	**1.4**	**−4.1**	**3.0**	**7.8**	**9.3**	**9.3**	**0.7**	**−3.7**	**−2.7**	...	...	...
Oil Exporters[4]	**0.3**	**−6.0**	**3.3**	**6.3**	**7.3**	**8.0**	**2.9**	**−3.3**	**−2.0**	...	...	...
Saudi Arabia	0.3	−5.4	3.1	−2.1	3.6	3.7	5.9	−2.5	−1.6	5.6	...	...
Iran	−6.5	−5.0	3.2	41.0	30.5	30.0	1.1	−0.5	0.3	10.7	12.2	12.4
United Arab Emirates	1.7	−6.6	1.3	−1.9	−1.5	1.5	8.4	3.6	7.5	...	...	...
Iraq	4.4	−12.1	2.5	−0.2	0.8	1.0	1.1	−12.6	−12.1	...	...	...
Algeria	0.8	−5.5	3.2	2.0	3.5	3.8	−10.1	−10.8	−16.6	11.4	14.1	14.3
Kazakhstan	4.5	−2.7	3.0	5.2	6.9	6.2	−3.6	−3.3	−2.8	4.8	7.8	5.8
Qatar	0.8	−4.5	2.5	−0.6	−2.2	1.8	2.4	−0.6	2.6	...	...	...
Kuwait	0.4	−8.1	0.6	1.1	1.0	2.3	9.4	−6.8	−2.8	...	...	...
Oman	−0.8	−10.0	−0.5	0.1	1.0	3.4	−4.6	−14.6	−12.9	...	...	...
Azerbaijan	2.2	−4.0	2.0	2.7	3.0	3.1	9.1	−3.6	−4.4	4.8	6.5	5.8
Turkmenistan	6.3	1.8	4.6	5.1	8.0	6.0	5.1	1.0	1.8	...	...	...
Oil Importers[5]	**3.2**	**−1.1**	**2.5**	**10.3**	**12.4**	**11.3**	**−5.8**	**−4.5**	**−4.7**	...	...	...
Egypt	5.6	3.5	2.8	13.9	5.7	6.2	−3.6	−3.2	−4.2	8.6	8.3	9.7
Pakistan	1.9	−0.4	1.0	6.7	10.7	8.8	−4.9	−1.1	−2.5	4.1	4.5	5.1
Morocco	2.2	−7.0	4.9	0.2	0.2	0.8	−4.1	−7.3	−5.2	9.2	12.5	10.5
Uzbekistan	5.6	0.7	5.0	14.5	13.0	10.7	−5.6	−6.4	−7.4	...	...	...
Sudan	−2.5	−8.4	0.8	51.0	141.6	129.7	−15.1	−12.7	−10.7	22.1	25.0	22.0
Tunisia	1.0	−7.0	4.0	6.7	5.8	5.3	−8.5	−8.3	−8.7	14.9	...	...
Jordan	2.0	−5.0	3.4	0.7	−0.3	1.4	−2.3	−6.8	−5.7	19.1	...	...
Lebanon	−6.9	−25.0	...	2.9	85.5	...	−27.4	−16.3	...	...	...	...
Afghanistan	3.9	−5.0	4.0	2.3	5.4	4.8	11.7	9.5	7.8	...	...	...
Georgia	5.1	−5.0	5.0	4.9	5.3	2.5	−5.1	−10.8	−8.5	11.6	...	...
Tajikistan	7.5	1.0	6.0	7.8	8.1	7.0	−2.3	−7.1	−4.5	...	...	...
Armenia	7.6	−4.5	3.5	1.4	0.9	2.0	−8.2	−8.8	−7.3	18.9	22.3	21.1
Kyrgyz Republic	4.5	−12.0	9.8	1.1	8.0	5.5	−5.6	−13.4	−12.8	6.6	6.6	6.6
Memorandum												
Caucasus and Central Asia	4.8	−2.1	3.9	6.6	7.6	6.4	−1.5	−4.1	−3.8	...	...	...
Middle East, North Africa, Afghanistan, and Pakistan	0.9	−4.4	2.9	8.0	9.5	9.7	0.9	−3.6	−2.6	...	...	...
Middle East and North Africa	0.8	−5.0	3.2	8.2	9.4	9.9	1.3	−3.9	−2.7	...	...	...
Israel[6]	3.4	−5.9	4.9	0.8	−0.5	0.2	3.4	3.5	3.5	3.8	6.0	5.6
Maghreb[7]	2.1	−8.1	7.8	2.3	3.4	3.7	−7.0	−12.7	−12.3	...	...	...
Mashreq[8]	4.3	1.2	2.4	11.8	8.3	8.3	−6.8	−4.4	−4.7	...	...	...

Source: IMF staff estimates.

Note: Data for some countries are based on fiscal years. Please refer to Table F in the Statistical Appendix for a list of economies with exceptional reporting periods.

[1]Movements in consumer prices are shown as annual averages. Year-end to year-end changes can be found in Tables A5 and A6 in the Statistical Appendix.

[2]Percent of GDP.

[3]Percent. National definitions of unemployment may differ.

[4]Includes Bahrain, Libya, and Yemen.

[5]Includes Djibouti, Mauritania, Somalia, and West Bank and Gaza. Excludes Syria because of the uncertain political situation. See country-specific note for Lebanon in the "Country Notes" section of the Statistical Appendix.

[6]Israel, which is not a member of the economic region, is included for reasons of geography but is not included in the regional aggregates.

[7]The Maghreb comprises Algeria, Libya, Mauritania, Morocco, and Tunisia.

[8]The Mashreq comprises Egypt, Jordan, Lebanon, and West Bank and Gaza. Syria is excluded because of the uncertain political situation.

Annex Table 1.1.5. Sub-Saharan African Economies: Real GDP, Consumer Prices, Current Account Balance, and Unemployment
(Annual percent change, unless noted otherwise)

	Real GDP			Consumer Prices[1]			Current Account Balance[2]			Unemployment[3]		
		Projections			Projections			Projections			Projections	
	2019	2020	2021	2019	2020	2021	2019	2020	2021	2019	2020	2021
Sub-Saharan Africa	**3.2**	**–3.0**	**3.1**	**8.5**	**10.6**	**7.9**	**–3.6**	**–4.8**	**–4.1**	...	...	...
Oil Exporters[4]	**1.6**	**–4.1**	**2.0**	**11.7**	**13.4**	**13.3**	**–2.1**	**–3.7**	**–2.2**	...	...	...
Nigeria	2.2	–4.3	1.7	11.4	12.9	12.7	–3.8	–3.6	–2.0	...	...	...
Angola	–0.9	–4.0	3.2	17.1	21.0	20.6	5.7	–1.3	0.1	...	...	...
Gabon	3.8	–2.7	2.1	2.0	3.0	3.0	–0.3	–9.1	–6.0	...	...	...
Republic of Congo	–0.6	–7.0	–0.8	2.2	2.5	2.6	3.5	–5.7	–1.9	...	...	...
Chad	3.0	–0.7	6.1	–1.0	2.8	3.0	–4.9	–13.3	–9.7	...	...	...
Middle-Income Countries[5]	**2.2**	**–5.1**	**3.8**	**4.0**	**4.3**	**4.4**	**–3.2**	**–3.1**	**–2.9**	...	...	...
South Africa	0.2	–8.0	3.0	4.1	3.3	3.9	–3.0	–1.6	–1.8	28.7	37.0	36.5
Ghana	6.5	0.9	4.2	7.2	10.6	8.7	–2.7	–3.4	–2.9	...	...	...
Côte d'Ivoire	6.5	1.8	6.2	0.8	1.2	1.4	–2.7	–3.7	–2.9	...	...	...
Cameroon	3.9	–2.8	3.4	2.5	2.8	2.2	–4.4	–5.4	–4.5	...	...	...
Zambia	1.4	–4.8	0.6	9.8	14.5	13.3	0.6	–1.0	0.0	...	...	...
Senegal	5.3	–0.7	5.2	1.0	2.0	2.0	–7.7	–9.2	–9.9	...	...	...
Low-Income Countries[6]	**5.9**	**0.1**	**3.4**	**10.1**	**14.4**	**6.3**	**–5.9**	**–7.7**	**–7.6**	...	...	...
Ethiopia	9.0	1.9	0.0	15.8	20.2	11.5	–5.3	–4.5	–4.6	...	...	...
Kenya	5.4	1.0	4.7	5.2	5.3	5.0	–5.8	–4.9	–5.4	...	...	...
Tanzania	7.0	1.9	3.6	3.4	3.6	3.7	–2.3	–3.2	–4.4	...	...	...
Uganda	6.7	–0.3	4.9	2.9	4.2	4.8	–6.5	–8.0	–5.9	...	...	...
Democratic Republic of the Congo	4.4	–2.2	3.6	4.7	11.5	12.1	–3.8	–4.8	–4.0	...	...	...
Mali	5.1	–2.0	4.0	–2.9	0.5	1.5	–4.2	–2.0	–1.2	...	...	...
Madagascar	4.8	–3.2	3.2	5.6	4.3	5.5	–2.3	–4.2	–2.9	...	...	...

Source: IMF staff estimates.

Note: Data for some countries are based on fiscal years. Please refer to Table F in the Statistical Appendix for a list of economies with exceptional reporting periods.

[1]Movements in consumer prices are shown as annual averages. Year-end to year-end changes can be found in Table A6 in the Statistical Appendix.

[2]Percent of GDP.

[3]Percent. National definitions of unemployment may differ.

[4]Includes Equatorial Guinea and South Sudan.

[5]Includes Botswana, Cabo Verde, Eswatini, Lesotho, Mauritius, Namibia, and Seychelles.

[6]Includes Benin, Burkina Faso, Burundi, the Central African Republic, Comoros, Eritrea, The Gambia, Guinea, Guinea-Bissau, Liberia, Malawi, Mali, Mozambique, Niger, Rwanda, São Tomé and Príncipe, Sierra Leone, Togo, and Zimbabwe.

Annex Table 1.1.6. Summary of World Real per Capita Output
(Annual percent change; in constant 2017 international dollars at purchasing power parity)

	Average 2002–11	2012	2013	2014	2015	2016	2017	2018	2019	Projections 2020	2021
World	**2.4**	**1.9**	**2.0**	**2.1**	**2.1**	**2.0**	**2.6**	**2.4**	**1.6**	**−5.6**	**4.0**
Advanced Economies	**1.1**	**0.6**	**0.9**	**1.6**	**1.8**	**1.2**	**2.1**	**1.8**	**1.3**	**−6.2**	**3.6**
United States	0.9	1.5	1.2	1.8	2.3	1.0	1.7	2.4	1.7	−4.7	2.6
Euro Area[1]	0.7	−1.2	−0.5	1.1	1.7	1.6	2.4	1.7	1.2	−8.5	5.1
Germany	1.2	0.2	0.2	1.8	0.6	1.4	2.2	1.0	0.3	−6.0	4.2
France	0.6	−0.2	0.1	0.4	0.7	0.8	2.0	1.6	1.4	−10.0	5.7
Italy	−0.3	−3.3	−2.4	−0.5	0.8	1.5	1.8	1.0	0.5	−10.5	5.3
Spain	0.3	−3.0	−1.1	1.7	3.9	3.1	2.9	2.3	1.9	−12.8	7.1
Japan	0.5	1.7	2.2	0.5	1.3	0.5	2.3	0.5	0.9	−4.9	2.7
United Kingdom	0.8	0.8	1.5	1.8	1.5	1.1	1.3	0.7	0.9	−10.4	5.4
Canada	1.0	0.7	1.3	1.8	−0.1	0.0	1.9	0.6	0.2	−8.4	4.1
Other Advanced Economies[2]	2.8	1.3	1.8	2.2	1.5	1.7	2.4	2.0	1.1	−4.6	3.1
Emerging Market and Developing Economies	**4.7**	**3.7**	**3.5**	**3.1**	**2.8**	**3.0**	**3.4**	**3.2**	**2.3**	**−4.7**	**4.8**
Emerging and Developing Asia	7.3	6.0	5.9	5.8	5.8	5.8	5.7	5.5	4.6	−2.7	7.2
China	10.1	7.4	7.3	6.7	6.4	6.2	6.4	6.3	5.8	1.5	7.9
India[3]	6.1	4.2	5.1	6.2	6.8	7.1	5.9	5.0	3.0	−11.2	7.7
ASEAN-5[4]	3.9	4.9	3.7	3.4	3.7	3.9	4.3	4.2	3.8	−4.5	5.2
Emerging and Developing Europe	4.7	2.8	2.8	1.5	0.5	1.6	3.9	3.2	1.9	−4.7	3.7
Russia	5.0	3.8	1.5	−1.1	−2.2	0.0	1.8	2.6	1.4	−4.2	2.8
Latin America and the Caribbean	2.2	1.7	1.7	0.1	−0.8	−1.9	0.2	0.1	−1.3	−9.1	2.7
Brazil	2.8	1.0	2.1	−0.3	−4.4	−4.1	0.5	0.5	0.3	−6.4	2.2
Mexico	0.4	2.2	0.0	1.5	2.0	1.4	0.9	1.1	−1.4	−9.9	2.5
Middle East and Central Asia	2.3	1.3	0.4	0.3	0.5	2.3	0.0	0.0	−0.6	−6.4	1.0
Saudi Arabia	1.4	2.5	0.0	2.5	1.7	−0.6	−3.3	0.0	−1.6	−7.3	1.1
Sub-Saharan Africa	2.8	1.9	2.3	2.5	0.5	−1.2	0.4	0.6	0.4	−5.6	0.5
Nigeria	5.9	1.5	2.6	3.5	0.0	−4.2	−1.8	−0.7	−0.4	−6.7	−0.8
South Africa	2.2	0.7	0.9	0.3	−0.3	−1.1	−0.1	−0.7	−1.3	−9.4	1.5
Memorandum											
European Union	1.2	−0.9	−0.2	1.5	2.1	1.9	2.8	2.1	1.6	−7.8	5.0
Low-Income Developing Countries	3.6	2.0	3.5	3.9	2.2	1.6	2.6	2.8	2.9	−3.3	2.7
Middle East and North Africa	2.0	0.7	−0.5	−0.4	0.2	2.5	−0.9	−0.9	−1.3	−7.5	1.0

Source: IMF staff estimates.

Note: Data for some countries are based on fiscal years. Please refer to Table F in the Statistical Appendix for a list of economies with exceptional reporting periods.

[1]Data calculated as the sum of individual euro area countries.
[2]Excludes the Group of Seven (Canada, France, Germany, Italy, Japan, United Kingdom, United States) and euro area countries.
[3]See country-specific note for India in the "Country Notes" section of the Statistical Appendix.
[4]Indonesia, Malaysia, Philippines, Thailand, and Vietnam.

References

Adams, Abi, Teodora Boneva, Marta Golin, and Christopher Rauh. 2020. "Inequality in the Impact of the Coronavirus Shock: Evidence from Real Time Surveys." CEPR Discussion Paper 14665, Centre for Economic Policy Research, London.

Adler, Gustavo, Romain A. Duval, Davide Furceri, Sinem Kiliç Çelik, Ksenia Koloskova, and Marcos Poplawski-Ribeiro. 2017. "Gone with the Headwinds: Global Productivity." IMF Staff Discussion Note 17/04, International Monetary Fund, Washington, DC.

Ahn, JaeBin, Zidong An, John C. Bluedorn, Gabriele Ciminelli, Zsoka Kóczán, Davide Malacrino, Daniela Muhaj, and Patricia Neidlinger. 2019. "Work in Progress: Improving Youth Labor Market Outcomes in Emerging Market and Developing Economies." IMF Staff Discussion Note 19/02, International Monetary Fund, Washington, DC.

Aiyar, Shekhar, Wolfgang Bergthaler, Jose M. Garrido, Anna Ilyina, Andreas Jobst, Kenneth Kang, Dmitriy Kovtun, Yan Liu, Dermot Monaghan, and Marina Moretti. 2015. "A Strategy for Resolving Europe's Problem Loans." IMF Staff Discussion Note 15/19, International Monetary Fund, Washington, DC.

Alesina, Alberto, and Roberto Perotti. 1996. "Income Distribution, Political Instability, and Investment." *European Economic Review* 40 (6): 1203–28.

Alon, Titan, Matthias Doepke, Jane Olmstead-Rumsey, and Michèle Tertilt. 2020. "This Time It's Different: The Role of Women's Employment in a Pandemic Recession." Unpublished.

Anderson, Michael L., Justin Gallagher, and Elizabeth Ramirez Ritchie. 2017. "School Lunch Quality and Academic Performance." NBER Working Paper 23218, National Bureau of Economic Research, Cambridge, MA.

Awad, Rachid, Caio Ferreira, Ellen Gaston, and Luc Riedweg. 2020. "Banking Sector Regulatory and Supervisory Response to Deal with Coronavirus Impact (with Q and A)." Special Series on COVID-19, International Monetary Fund, Washington, DC.

Bannister, Geoffrey J., and Alexandros Mourmouras. 2017. "Welfare vs. Income Convergence and Environmental Externalities." IMF Working Paper 17/271, International Monetary Fund, Washington, DC.

Baker, Scott R., Nicholas Bloom, and Steven J. Davis. 2016. "Measuring Economic Policy Uncertainty." *Quarterly Journal of Economics*, 131 (4): 1593–636.

Barrett, Philip, Maximilian Appendino, Kate Nguyen, and Jorge de Leon Miranda. 2020. "Measuring Social Unrest Using Media Reports." IMF Working Paper 20/129, International Monetary Fund, Washington, DC.

Baytiyeh, Hoda. 2018. "Online Learning during Post-Earthquake School Closures." *Disaster Prevention and Management* 27 (2): 215–27.

Bick, Alexander, Adam Blandin, and Karel Mertens. 2020. "Work from Home after the COVID-19 Outbreak." Working Paper 2017, Federal Reserve Bank of Dallas, TX.

Blattman, Christopher, and Edward Miguel. 2010. "Civil War." *Journal of Economic Literature* 48 (1): 3–57.

Brussevich, Mariya, Era Dabla-Norris, Christine Kamunge, Pooja Karnane, Salma Khalid, and Kalpana Kochhar. 2018. "Gender, Technology, and the Future of Work." IMF Staff Discussion Note 18/07, International Monetary Fund, Washington, DC.

Brussevich, Mariya, Era Dabla-Norris, and Salma Khalid. 2020. "Who Will Bear the Brunt of Lockdown Policies? Evidence from Tele-Workability Measures across Countries." IMF Working Paper 20/88, International Monetary Fund, Washington, DC.

Caldara, Dario, and Matteo Iacoviello. 2018. "Measuring Geopolitical Risk." International Finance Discussion Papers 1222.

Card, David. 1999. "The Causal Effect of Education on Earnings." Chapter 30 in *Handbook of Labor Economics*, vol. 3a, edited by Orley Ashenfelter and David Card. Amsterdam: Elsevier Science.

Deaton, Angus, and Bettina Aten. 2017. "Trying to Understand the PPPs in ICP2011: Why Are the Results So Different?" *American Economic Journal: Macroeconomics* 9 (1): 243–64.

Decerf, Benoit, Francisco H. G. Ferreira, Daniel Gerszon Mahler, and Olivier Sterck. 2020. "Lives and Livelihoods: Estimates of the Global Mortality and Poverty Effects of the COVID-19 Pandemic." Policy Research Working Paper 9277, World Bank, Washington, DC.

Díez, Federico, Romain Duval, Chiara Maggi, Yi Ji, Ippei Shibata, and Marina Medes Tavares. 2020. "Options to Support the Incomes of Informal Workers during COVID-19." Special Series on COVID-19, International Monetary Fund, Washington, DC.

Duval, Romain A., and Prakash Loungani. 2019. "Designing Labor Market Institutions in Emerging and Developing Economies: Evidence and Policy Options." IMF Staff Discussion Note 19/04, International Monetary Fund, Washington, DC.

Ebrahimy, Ehsan, Deniz Igan, and Sole Martinez Peria. 2020. "The Impact of COVID-19 on Inflation: Potential Drivers and Dynamics." Special Series on COVID-19, International Monetary Fund, Washington, DC.

Fabrizio, Stefania, Davide Furceri, Rodrigo Garcia-Verdu, Bin Grace Li, Sandra V. Lizarazo, Marina Mendes Tavares, Futoshi Narita, and Adrian Peralta-Alva. 2017. "Macroeconomic Structural Policies and Income Inequality in Low-Income Developing Countries." IMF Staff Discussion Note 17/01, International Monetary Fund, Washington, DC.

Fouquet, Roger. 2011. "Long Run Trends in Energy-Related External Costs." *Ecological Economics* 70 (12): 2380–89.

Freitag, Andreas, and Weicheng Lian. Forthcoming. "Global Disinflation: Cyclical or Downward Trend?" IMF Working Paper, International Monetary Fund, Washington, DC.

Fuchs, Richard, Martin Herold, Peter H. Verburg, Jan G. P. W. Clevers, and Jonas Eberle. 2015. "Gross Changes in Reconstructions of Historic Land Cover/Use for Europe between 1900 and 2010." *Global Change Biology* 21 (1): 299–313.

Furceri, Davide, Prakash Loungani, Jonathan D. Ostry, and Pietro Pizzuto. 2020. "Will COVID-19 Affect Inequality? Evidence from Past Pandemics." COVID Economics 12, May 1, Centre for Economic Policy Research.

Georgieva, Kristalina. 2020. "Beyond the Crisis." *Finance & Development 57* (2).

Georgieva, Kristalina, Stefania Fabrizio, Cheng Hoon Lim, and Marina M. Tavares. "The COVID-19 Gender Gap." *IMFBlog*, July 21, International Monetary Fund, Washington, DC.

Google LLC. 2020. "Google COVID-19 Community Mobility Reports." https://www.google.com/covid19/mobility.

Global Economic Uncertainty. 2020. https://www.policyuncertainty.com/global_monthly.html.

Gourinchas, Pierre-Olivier, Şebnem Kalemli-Özcan, Veronika Penciakova, and Nick Sander. 2020. "COVID-19 and Business Failures." IMF Working Paper 20/207, International Monetary Fund, Washington, DC.

Hogan, Alexandra B., Britta L. Jewell, Ellie Sherrard-Smith, Juan F. Vesga, Oliver J. Watson, Charles Whittaker, and others. 2020. "Potential Impact of the COVID-19 Pandemic on HIV, Tuberculosis, and Malaria in Low-Income and Middle-Income Countries: A Modelling Study." *The Lancet Global Health,* July. https://doi.org/10.1016/S2214-109X(20)30288-6.

Holmlund, Bertil, Qian Liu, and Oskar Nordström Skans. 2008. "Mind the Gap? Estimating the Effects of Postponing Higher Education." *Oxford Economic Papers* 60 (4): 683–710.

Inklaar, Robert, Harmen de Jong, Jutta Bolt, and Jan van Zanden. 2018. "Rebasing 'Maddison': New Income Comparisons and the Shape of Long-Run Economic Development." GGDC Research Memorandum GD-174, Groningen Growth and Development Centre, University of Groningen, Netherlands.

International Energy Agency (IEA). 2018. *World Energy Outlook 2018*, Paris. https://www.iea.org/reports/world-energy-outlook-2018.

International Labour Organization (ILO). 2020. *ILO Monitor: COVID-19 and the World of Work,* 5th ed. Geneva.

International Monetary Fund (IMF). 2020. "Debt Management Responses to the Pandemic." Special Series on COVID-19, Washington, DC.

Jacobson, Mark Z. 2020. "Evaluation of Coal and Natural Gas with Carbon Capture as Proposed Solutions to Global Warming, Air Pollution, and Energy Security." Stanford University, Stanford, CA.

Jain, Ronak, Joshua Budlender, Rocco Zizzamia, and Ihsaan Bassier. 2020. "The Labor Market and Poverty Impacts of COVID-19 in South Africa." CSAE Working Paper WPS/202014, Center for the Study of African Economies, Harvard University, Cambridge, MA.

Jones, Charles I., and Peter J. Klenow. 2016. "Beyond GDP? Welfare across Countries and Time." *American Economic Review* 106 (9): 2426–57.

Korkoyah, Dala T., and Francis F. Wreh. 2015. *Ebola Impact Revealed: An Assessment of the Differing Impact of the Outbreak on the Women and Men in Liberia.* Nairobi: Oxfam.

Lakner, Christoph, Daniel Gerszon Mahler, Mario Negre, and Espen Beer Prydz. 2020. "How Much Does Reducing Inequality Matter for Global Poverty?" Global Poverty Monitoring Technical Note 13, World Bank, Washington, DC.

Lazard. 2019. *Lazard's Levelized Cost of Energy Analysis—Version 13.0,* 20. New York

Light, Audrey. 1995. "The Effects of Interrupted Schooling on Wages." *Journal of Human Resources* 30 (3): 472–502.

Liu, Yan, José Garrido, and Chanda DeLong. 2020. "Private Debt Resolution Measures in the Wake of the Pandemic." Special Series on COVID-19, International Monetary Fund, Washington, DC.

McCarthy, Paul. 2013. "Extrapolating PPPs and Comparing ICP Benchmark Results." Chapter 18 in *Measuring the Real Size of the World Economy: The Framework, Methodology and Results of the International Comparison Program.* World Bank: Washington, DC.

Opportunity Insights Economic Tracker. 2020. https://tracktherecovery.org.

Ostry, Jonathan D., Jorge Alvarez, Raphael A. Espinoza, and Chris Papageorgiou. 2018. "Economic Gains from Gender Inclusion: New Mechanisms, New Evidence." IMF Staff Discussion Note 18/06, International Monetary Fund, Washington, DC.

Prady, Delphine. 2020. "Reaching Households in Emerging and Developing Economies: Citizen ID, Socioeconomic Data, and Digital Delivery." Special Series on Fiscal Policies to Respond to COVID-19, International Monetary Fund, Washington, DC.

Quinn, David M., and Morgan Polikoff. 2017. "Summer Learning Loss: What Is It, and What Can We Do about It?" Brookings Institution, Washington, DC.

Ralston, Katherine, Katie Treen, Alisha Coleman-Jensen, and Joanne Guthrie. 2017. "Children's Food Security and USDA Child Nutrition Programs." *Economic Information Bulletin* 174, United States Department of Agriculture, Economic Research Service, Washington, DC.

Sahay, Ratna, and Martin Cihak. 2018. "Women in Finance: A Case for Closing Gaps." IMF Staff Discussion Note 18/05, International Monetary Fund, Washington, DC.

Shibata, Ippei. 2020. "The Distributional Impact of Recessions: The Global Financial Crisis and the Pandemic Recession." IMF Working Paper 20/96, International Monetary Fund, Washington, DC.

Smith, Kirk R., Sumi Mehta, and Mirjam Maeusezahl-Feuz. 2004. "Indoor Air Pollution from Household Use of Solid Fuels." In *Comparative Quantification of Health Risks: Global and Regional Burden of Disease Attributable to Selected Major Risk Factors,* edited by Majid Ezzati and others, 1435–493. Geneva: World Health Organization.

Steckel, Jan Christoph, Ottmar Edenhofer, and Michael Jakob. 2015. "Drivers for the Renaissance of Coal." *Proceedings of the National Academy of Sciences* 112 (29): E3775–81.

Stock, James H., and Mark W. Watson. 2019. "Slack and Cyclically Sensitive Inflation." NBER Working Paper 25987, National Bureau of Economic Research, Cambridge, MA.

Stokey, Nancy L. 1998. "Are There Limits to Growth? *International Economic Review* 39 (1): 1–31.

Tongia, Rahul, and Samantha Gross. 2018. "Working to Turn Ambition into Reality: The Politics and Economics of India's Turn to Renewable Power." Cross-Brookings Initiative on Energy and Climate Paper Series, Brookings Institution, Washington, DC.

Tongia, Rahul, and Samantha Gross. 2019. "Coal in India." Cross-Brookings Initiative on Energy and Climate Paper Series, Brookings Institution, Washington, DC.

United Nations Development Programme (UNDP). 2015. "Assessing Sexual and Gender Based Violence during the Ebola Crisis in Sierra Leone." New York. https://www.sl.undp.org/content/sierraleone/en/home/library/crisis_prevention_and_recovery/assessing-sexual-and-gender-based-violence-during-the-ebola-cris.html.

United Nations Development Programme (UNDP). 2019. "Human Development Report 2019: Beyond Income, Beyond Averages, Beyond Today: Inequalities in Human Development in the 21st Century." New York.

United Nations Educational, Scientific and Cultural Organization (UNESCO). 2020. "Education: From Disruption to Recovery." New York. https://en.unesco.org/covid19/educationresponse.

US Trade Policy Uncertainties. 2020. https://www.policyuncertainty.com/categorical_epu.html.

World Bank (WB). 2018. *Poverty and Shared Prosperity 2018: Piecing Together the Poverty Puzzle.* Washington, DC.

World Bank (WB). 2019. *World Bank Annual Report 2019: Ending Poverty, Investing in Opportunity.* Washington, DC.

World Bank (WB). 2020a. "Projected Poverty Impacts of COVID-19 (Coronavirus)." World Bank Brief, June 8, Washington, DC.

World Bank (WB). 2020b. "The COVID-19 Pandemic: Shocks to Education and Policy Responses." World Bank Report 148198, Washington, DC.

THE GREAT LOCKDOWN: DISSECTING THE ECONOMIC EFFECTS

To contain the coronavirus (COVID-19) pandemic and protect susceptible populations, most countries imposed stringent lockdown measures in the first half of 2020. Meanwhile, economic activity contracted dramatically on a global scale. This chapter aims to dissect the nature of the economic crisis in the first seven months of the pandemic. It finds that the adoption of lockdowns was an important factor in the recession, but voluntary social distancing in response to rising infections also contributed very substantially to the economic contraction. Therefore, although easing lockdowns can lead to a partial recovery, economic activity is likely to remain subdued until health risks abate. Meanwhile, countries should protect the most vulnerable and find ways to support economic activity compatible with social distancing, for example, by reducing contact intensity in the workplace and enhancing work from home where possible. This chapter also provides new evidence of the uneven effects of lockdowns, which are found to have a larger impact on the mobility of women and younger cohorts. This calls for targeted policy action to prevent a widening of inequality. Finally, the analysis shows that lockdowns can substantially reduce COVID-19 infections, especially if they are introduced early in a country's epidemic and are sufficiently tight. Thus, despite involving short-term economic costs, lockdowns may pave the way to a faster recovery by containing the spread of the virus and reducing the need for voluntary social distancing over time, possibly having positive overall effects on the economy. This remains an important area for future research as new data become available.

Introduction

The COVID-19 pandemic has raised unprecedented health challenges on a global scale. To contain the spread of the virus, most countries have resorted to stringent lockdown measures, closing schools and business activities and sometimes even preventing

The authors of this chapter are Francesca Caselli, Francesco Grigoli (co-lead), Weicheng Lian, and Damiano Sandri (co-lead), with support from Jungjin Lee and Xiaohui Sun. The chapter benefited from insightful comments by Yuriy Gorodnichenko and internal seminar participants.

people from leaving their homes, except for essential reasons. Meanwhile, economic activity has contracted dramatically, as discussed in Chapter 1. No country was spared, with GDP declining sharply in advanced, emerging market, and developing economies.

This chapter's first goal is to shed light on the extent to which the economic contraction was driven by the adoption of government lockdowns instead of by people voluntarily reducing social interactions for fear of contracting or spreading the virus. This issue is important to understand retrospectively the nature of the recession and to provide insights into the strength of the upcoming recovery. If lockdowns were largely responsible for the economic contraction, it would be reasonable to expect a quick economic rebound when they are lifted. But if voluntary social distancing played a predominant role, then economic activity would likely remain subdued until health risks recede.

The analysis starts by examining the cross-country association between lockdowns and economic activity across a broad sample of countries. It finds that countries that endured more stringent lockdowns experienced larger growth declines relative to pre–COVID-19 forecasts, even after controlling for the severity of the local epidemic. The chapter then assesses the impact of lockdowns using high-frequency proxies for economic activity, namely mobility indicators provided by Google and job postings provided by the website Indeed.[1] Regression results show that lockdowns have a considerable negative effect on economic activity. Nonetheless, voluntary social distancing in response to rising COVID-19 infections can also have strong detrimental effects on the economy. In fact, the analysis suggests that lockdowns and voluntary social distancing played a near comparable role in

[1]Google Community Mobility Reports provide information on daily attendance rates at various locations relative to precrisis levels. Data are available at a national level for a large set of advanced, emerging market, and developing economies. For various countries, mobility information is also available at a subnational level. Data can be downloaded at https://www.google.com/covid19/mobility/. The job site Indeed provided the IMF with anonymized information about daily job postings in 22 countries, disaggregated by job categories.

driving the economic recession. The contribution of voluntary distancing in reducing mobility was stronger in advanced economies, where people can work from home more easily and sustain periods of temporary unemployment because of personal savings and government benefits.

When looking at the recovery path ahead, the importance of voluntary social distancing as a contributing factor to the downturn suggests that lifting lockdowns is unlikely to rapidly bring economic activity back to potential if health risks remain. This is true especially if lockdowns are lifted when infections are still relatively high because, in those cases, the impact on mobility appears more modest. Further tempering the expectations of a quick economic rebound, the analysis documents that easing lockdowns tends to have a positive effect on mobility, but the impact is weaker than that of tightening lockdowns. These findings suggest that economies will continue to operate below potential while health risks persist, even if lockdowns are lifted. Therefore, policymakers should be wary of removing policy support too quickly and consider ways to protect the most vulnerable and support economic activity consistent with social distancing. These may include measures to reduce contact intensity and make the workplace safer, for example by promoting contactless payments; facilitating a gradual reallocation of resources toward less-contact-intensive sectors; and enhancing work from home, for example, by improving internet connectivity and supporting investment in information technology.

The chapter also contributes to the growing empirical evidence on the uneven effects of the crisis, with particularly acute impacts on more economically vulnerable people. Using novel anonymized and aggregated mobility indicators provided by Vodafone for some European countries, the analysis shows that lockdowns tend to have a larger effect on women's mobility than on men's, especially at the time of school closures.[2] This suggests that women carry a disproportionate burden in caring for children, which

may jeopardize their employment opportunities. Vodafone data also show that lockdowns tend to have a stronger impact on the mobility of younger cohorts, who are economically more vulnerable because they generally rely on labor income and have less stable jobs. Thus, targeted policy intervention is needed to protect the employment prospects of women and younger cohorts and prevent a widening of income inequality.

Finally, the chapter finds that lockdowns can reduce infections substantially. The effects of lockdowns on confirmed COVID-19 cases tend to materialize after a few weeks of delay, given the incubation period of the virus and testing times. This underscores the importance of early intervention, also because lockdowns are more effective in curbing infections if they are introduced early in the stage of a country's epidemic. The analysis also suggests that lockdowns must be sufficiently stringent to reduce infections significantly.

The effectiveness of lockdowns in reducing infections suggests that lockdowns may pave the way to a faster economic recovery if they succeed in containing the epidemic and thus limit the extent of voluntary social distancing. Therefore, the short-term economic costs of lockdowns could be compensated by stronger medium-term growth, possibly leading to positive overall effects on the economy. This is an important area for future research. Meanwhile, policymakers should also pursue alternative ways to contain infections that may involve lower short-term economic costs than lockdowns, such as expanding testing and contact tracing, promoting the use of face masks, and encouraging work from home. As the understanding of the virus transmission improves, countries may also be able to deploy targeted measures rather than blunt lockdowns, for example by focusing on protecting vulnerable people and restricting large indoor gatherings.

The analysis contributes to a rapidly growing literature on the pandemic and the effects of lockdowns, which is reviewed in Box 2.1. The understanding of the crisis is still evolving—some papers detect considerable effects of lockdowns while others emphasize the role of voluntary social distancing. The literature also documents the pandemic's uneven effect on vulnerable segments of the population and provides evidence of the effectiveness of lockdowns and face masks in containing infections.

---

[2]These indicators were prepared by Vodafone's Big Data and Artificial Intelligence team and were provided for the analysis in an anomymized format through a confidential agreement. To protect the privacy of individuals and minority groups, mobility indices were aggregated at the provincial level, including at least 50 customers. The data sharing protocol was subject to technical and organizational controls, including an ethical assessment of the analysis prior to its implementation.

Cross-Country Evidence on Lockdowns and Economic Activity

The analysis starts by presenting cross-country evidence on the association between lockdowns and economic activity over a sample of up to 52 advanced, emerging market, and developing economies. Panel 1 of Figure 2.1 shows the correlation between the stringency of lockdowns during the first half of 2020 and the decline in GDP relative to

Figure 2.1. Lockdowns and Economic Activity

More stringent lockdowns are correlated with sharper economic contractions.

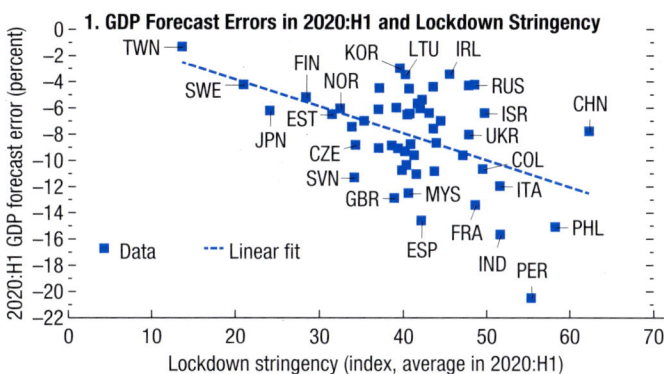

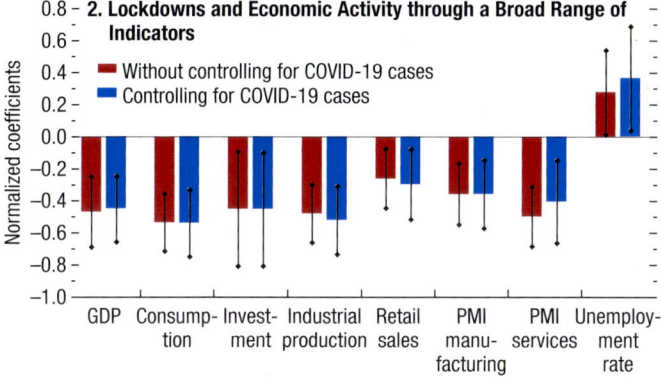

Sources: Haver Analytics; Oxford Coronavirus Government Response Tracker; World Economic Outlook (WEO) database; and IMF staff calculations.
Note: Panel 1: The GDP forecast errors are defined as the deviations from January 2020 WEO projections for the first half of 2020 (2020:H1). Online Annex Table 2.1.2 provides the full list of countries. Panel 2: For GDP, consumption, and investment, the analysis uses data for 2020:H1. For the other indicators that are available at monthly frequency, the analysis considers the first three months after COVID-19 cases reach 100 in a country. The regressions control for the logarithm of the COVID-19 cases normalized by population in 2019. Normalized coefficients reported on the vertical axis show the impact of a one-standard-deviation increase in the lockdown index on each economic variable, normalized by its own standard deviation. Standard deviations are based on the cross-country variation in the sample. The vertical lines refer to 90 percent confidence bands. See Online Annex 2.2 for additional details. PMI = purchasing managers' index. Data labels use International Organization for Standardization (ISO) country codes.

pre-pandemic forecasts.[3] The figure illustrates that countries that implemented more stringent lockdowns experienced sharper GDP contractions.

Panel 2 of Figure 2.1 shows that the negative association between lockdowns and economic activity is robust to using other indicators besides GDP. For example, more stringent lockdowns are associated with lower consumption, investment, industrial production, retail sales, purchasing managers' indices for the manufacturing and service sectors, and higher unemployment rates.[4] These correlations persist with and without controlling for the strength of each country's epidemic based on the total number of confirmed COVID-19 cases scaled by population.

Figure 2.1 thus provides suggestive evidence that lockdowns tend to have a negative short-term economic impact. Nonetheless, these findings should be interpreted with caution given omitted variable concerns that affect cross-country analyses and endogeneity concerns about lockdowns. The decision to deploy lockdowns is indeed not random; rather, it may reflect time-invariant country characteristics that also affect economic outcomes. For example, countries with higher social capital may not require stringent lockdowns—as people take greater precautions against infecting others—and could also better withstand the economic impact of the crisis. This may generate a spurious negative correlation between the stringency of lockdowns and economic activity. To strengthen identification by controlling for such time-invariant country characteristics, the next section reexamines the economic impact of lockdowns using time-series variation in high-frequency data.

[3]The analysis uses a lockdown stringency index that averages several subindicators—school closures, workplace closures, cancellations of public events, restrictions on gatherings, public transportation closures, stay-at-home requirements, restrictions on internal movement, and controls on international travel—provided by the University of Oxford's Coronavirus Government Response Tracker.
[4]Data for GDP, consumption, and investment refer to the first half of 2020. For the other indicators that are available at monthly frequency, the analysis considers the first three months after the first 100 confirmed COVID-19 cases in each country to compare economic outcomes during the same phase of a country's epidemic. See Online Annex 2.2 for additional details. All annexes are available at www.imf.org/en/Publications/WEO.

Assessing the Impact of Lockdowns Using High-Frequency Data

Two types of daily data are used to proxy for economic activity at high frequency. First, the analysis uses mobility data provided by Google, which reports the attendance rate at various locations relative to precrisis levels.[5] These data have the key advantages of covering a large set of countries and being available also at the subnational level. The findings based on mobility data are corroborated using job posting data reported by Indeed, an online job search engine. Indeed data are available for fewer countries but capture labor market conditions more directly.

Lockdowns and Mobility

To assess the impact of lockdowns on mobility, the analysis uses local projections that include country fixed effects and time dummies to control for time-invariant country characteristics and global shocks, respectively. It is important to note that lockdowns are endogenous policy choices that depend on the stage of the epidemic and the degree of mobility. For example, governments are more likely to impose lockdowns when health risks become more acute. At the same time, people tend to reduce mobility because they fear contracting the virus, independent of lockdowns. This may lead to a spurious negative correlation between lockdowns and mobility. To alleviate these endogeneity concerns, the regression framework controls for the number of COVID-19 cases and includes lags of the mobility indicator. In other words, the empirical analysis tries to measure the impact on mobility from a lockdown tightening at a given stage of the country's epidemic. Online Annex 2.3 provides additional details.

The regression is estimated using national-level data for 128 countries. Panel 1 of Figure 2.2 shows that lockdowns tend to have a statistically significant negative effect on mobility. A full lockdown that includes all measures that governments have used during the pandemic—for example, school closures, travel restrictions, business closures, and stay-at-home requirements—tends to generate a reduction in mobility of about

---

[5]Data are based on cell phone locations for people who own smartphones and agree to share location data with Google. Because this category of people may have characteristics that differ from those of the broader population—for example, income level, age, or access to the internet—the mobility indices may not be fully representative of the entire country, especially in poorer countries, where fewer people have smartphones.

Figure 2.2. The Impact of Lockdowns and Voluntary Social Distancing on Mobility
(Percent)

Lockdowns and voluntary social distancing have a substantial negative impact on mobility.

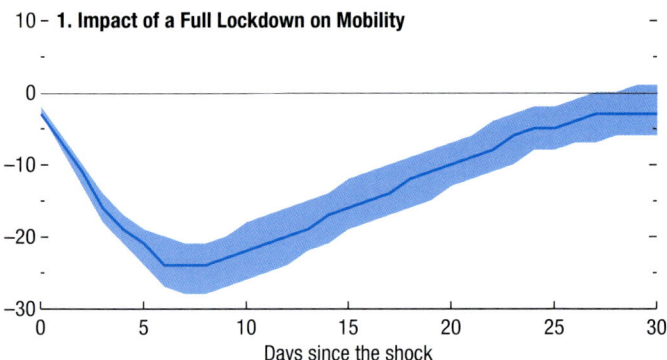

1. Impact of a Full Lockdown on Mobility

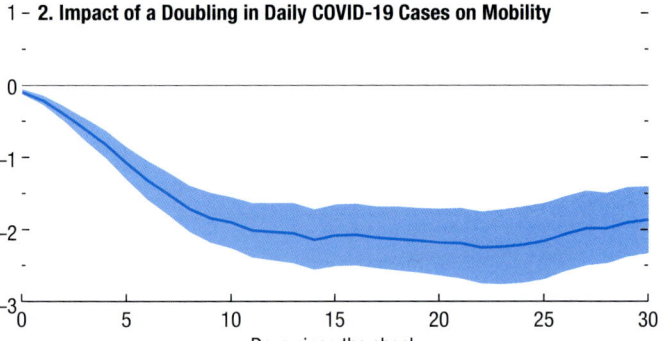

2. Impact of a Doubling in Daily COVID-19 Cases on Mobility

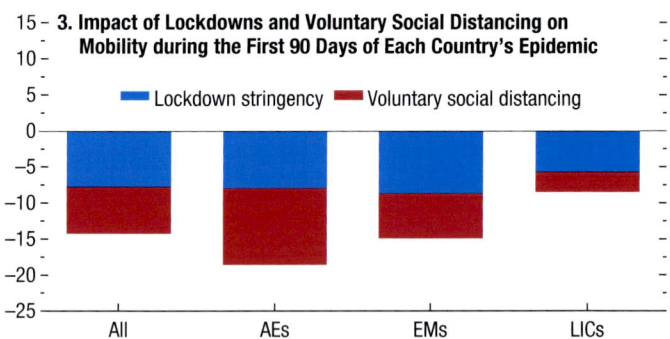

3. Impact of Lockdowns and Voluntary Social Distancing on Mobility during the First 90 Days of Each Country's Epidemic

Source: IMF staff calculations.
Note: The shaded areas in panels 1 and 2 correspond to 90 percent confidence intervals computed with standard errors clustered at the country level. In panel 3, the first 90 days of the epidemic vary across countries as they are counted since the first COVID-19 case in each country. See Online Annex 2.1 for data sources and country coverage. AEs = advanced economies; EMs = emerging markets; LICs = low-income countries.

25 percent within a week. Mobility starts to resume gradually after that as the lockdown tightening shock dissipates, as illustrated in Online Annex 2.3.[6]

To address endogeneity concerns further, the impact of lockdowns is also estimated using subnational data. The analysis considers 15 Group of Twenty countries that imposed national lockdowns in response to severe localized outbreaks and examines the impact on mobility in regions with a relatively low number of COVID-19 cases. This approach strengthens the identification because the adoption of the national lockdown was largely exogenous for regions less affected by the epidemic. As reported in Online Annex 2.3, the results confirm that lockdowns tend to have a strong negative impact on mobility. These findings are robust to controlling for COVID-19 cases at both the regional and national levels.

However, lockdowns are not the only contributing factor to the decline in mobility. During a pandemic, people also voluntarily reduce exposure to one another as infections increase and they fear becoming sick. Several papers document this aspect by showing that mobility has been tightly correlated with the spread of COVID-19, even after controlling for government lockdowns, especially in advanced economies (Aum, Lee, and Shin 2020; Goolsbee and Syverson 2020; Maloney and Taskin 2020). In line with this literature, the regression framework used in the analysis can shed light on the strength of voluntary social distancing by capturing the response of mobility to rising COVID-19 infections for a given lockdown stringency.[7] Panel 2 of Figure 2.2 shows that an increase in COVID-19 cases tends to have a considerable negative effect on mobility. A doubling of daily cases leads to a contraction in mobility by about 2 percent.

To gain further insights into the relative importance of lockdowns and voluntary social distancing tied to rising COVID-19 cases, panel 3 of Figure 2.2 shows their contribution in reducing mobility during the first three months of each country's epidemic. Both lockdowns and voluntary social distancing had a large impact on mobility, playing a roughly similar role in emerging markets. The contribution of voluntary social distancing was smaller in low-income countries and larger in advanced economies. These differences likely reflect that people in more economically developed countries can work from home more easily and can even afford to stop working temporarily by relying on personal savings or social security benefits. Conversely, people in low-income countries are often unable to opt for voluntary social distancing as they do not have the financial means to cope with a temporary income loss. This underscores the importance of international support to ensure that low-income countries have budgetary room for expanding safety nets.

The large contribution of voluntary social distancing in reducing mobility suggests that lifting lockdowns can lead to only a partial rebound in economic activity if health risks persist. In line with this implication, panel 1 in Figure 2.3 shows that the impact of lockdowns on mobility is smaller when infections are relatively high. A likely reason is that people feel uncomfortable with resuming mobility when lockdowns are lifted if they still perceive a considerable risk of contracting or spreading the virus. This insight warns against lifting lockdowns prematurely in hope of jump-starting economic activity. Panel 2 of Figure 2.3 provides additional evidence against expecting a sharp economic recovery just from easing lockdowns. It shows that easing lockdowns tends to have a positive effect on mobility but the magnitude is weaker compared with the impact from a lockdown tightening. As documented in Online Annex 2.3, this difference is statistically significant.

The importance of voluntary social distancing coupled with the modest boost to mobility from easing lockdowns suggest that economies will likely operate below potential as long as health concerns persist.[8] A first implication is that policymakers should be

---

[6]Online Annex 2.3 also shows that the results are robust to controlling for COVID-19 deaths instead of cases; using subindicators of mobility provided by Google; controlling for testing, contact tracing, and public information campaigns; and accounting for possible cross-country heterogeneity in the mobility response depending on population density and indicators of governance and social capital.

[7]Besides reacting to the spread of COVID-19, people may voluntarily opt for social distancing also in response to other factors, such as announcements by public health officials, news about celebrities being infected, or even the adoption of government lockdowns. Therefore, the analysis may underestimate the extent of voluntary social distancing. The results are robust to controlling for COVID-19 deaths instead of cases. Normalizing COVID-19 cases or deaths by population is irrelevant, given that the regressions include country fixed effects and population does not vary during the period of analysis.

[8]Given the severity of the downturn, the crisis may have also reduced the level of potential output, thus leading to permanent losses even after the pandemic is over. This is an important issue for future research.

Figure 2.3. Further Insights into the Impact of Lockdowns on Mobility
(Percent)

The impact of lockdowns on mobility is weaker when COVID-19 cases are higher. Furthermore, a lockdown easing tends to have a smaller impact on mobility relative to a lockdown tightening.

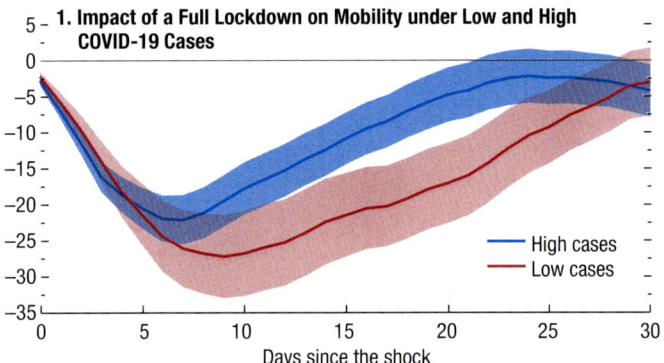

1. Impact of a Full Lockdown on Mobility under Low and High COVID-19 Cases

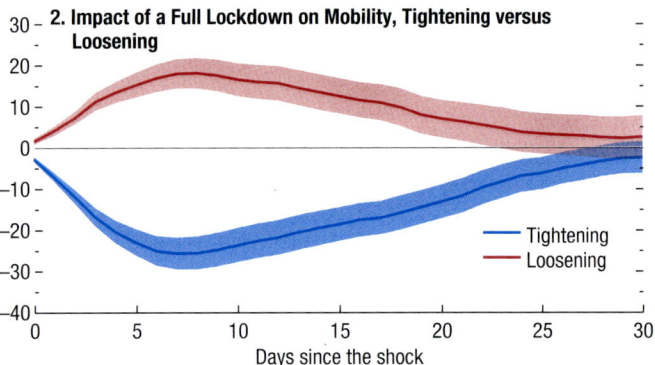

2. Impact of a Full Lockdown on Mobility, Tightening versus Loosening

Source: IMF staff calculations.
Note: See Online Annex 2.1 for data sources and country coverage. High and low cases in panel 1 correspond to the 75th and 25th percentile of the cross-country distribution of log of daily COVID-19 cases, respectively. The shaded areas in panels 1 and 2 correspond to 90 percent confidence intervals computed with standard errors clustered at the country level.

wary of removing policy support too hastily to avoid precipitating a further downturn and should continue to protect the most vulnerable through social safety net spending. Second, it is important to find ways to support economic activity consistent with persistent social distancing. These may include measures to reduce contact intensity and make the workplace safer—for example by promoting contactless payments—and facilitate the reallocation of resources toward less-contact-intensive sectors. Policymakers should also enhance working from home, for example by improving internet access and supporting firm investment in information technology, which, as shown in Box 2.2, can protect employment during the pandemic.

Lockdowns and Job Postings

The importance of lockdowns and voluntary social distancing in the ongoing crisis can also be examined using the daily number of job postings provided by Indeed for 22 countries. The analysis uses a local projection framework that mimics the one used for the analysis of mobility. Panels 1 and 2 of Figure 2.4 show that a lockdown tightening and an increase in COVID-19 cases both lead to a statistically significant negative effect on job postings, corroborating the findings based on mobility. Both lockdowns and voluntary social distancing in response to higher infections appear to have played an important role in driving the reduction in job postings during the first three months of each country's epidemic (panel 3). Consistent with the analysis of mobility, the contribution of voluntary social distancing is relatively higher because the country sample includes mostly advanced economies.

Data from Indeed can also be disaggregated by job categories, providing additional insights consistent with the results presented so far. First, panel 1 of Figure 2.5 suggests that both lockdowns and voluntary social distancing contributed to the reduction in job postings. Contact-intensive jobs—such as those in the hospitality, personal care, and food sectors—declined before stay-at-home orders, likely because of voluntary social distancing as customers grew wary of infection risks. Job postings in the manufacturing sector—that do not involve personal contacts with customers—instead started to decline closer to the adoption of stay-at-home orders, reflecting the impact of lockdown measures. The figure also shows that job postings in contact-intensive sectors declined more than in the manufacturing sector, likely reflecting a larger drop in aggregate demand because of voluntary social distancing. Second, panel 2 provides evidence consistent with the notion that easing lockdowns is unlikely to generate a sharp rebound in economic activity. The removal of stay-at-home orders has coincided with only a marginal increase in job postings, even in the less-contact-intensive manufacturing sector.

The Unequal Effects of Lockdowns across Gender and Age Groups

The pandemic is having disproportional effects on the most economically vulnerable segments of the population. As reviewed in Box 2.1, the literature documents strong negative effects on lower-income

Figure 2.4. The Impact of Lockdowns and Voluntary Social Distancing on Job Postings
(Percent)

Lockdowns and voluntary social distancing have a substantial negative impact on job postings.

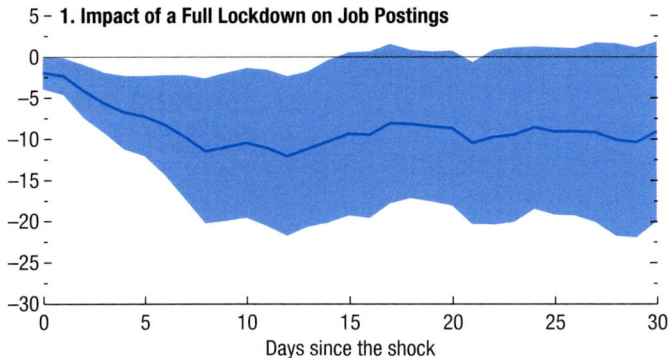

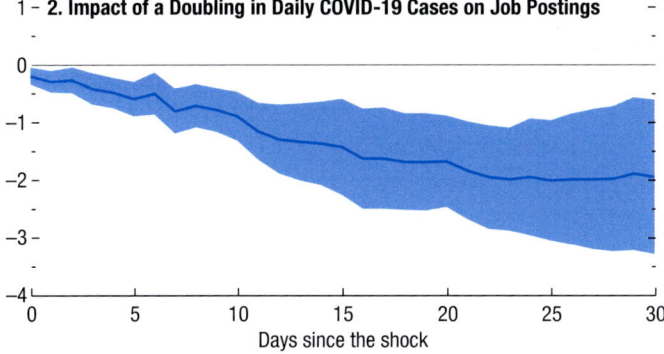

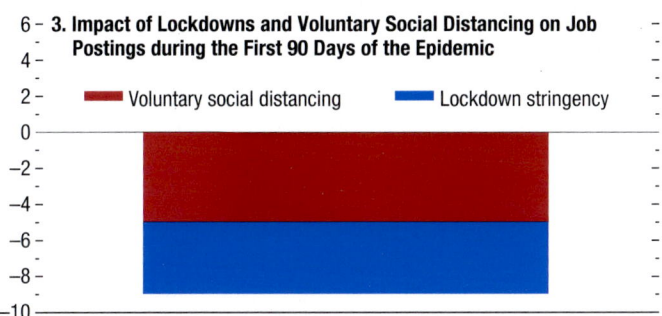

Sources: Indeed; and IMF staff calculations.
Note: See Online Annex 2.1 for data sources and country coverage. The shaded areas in panels 1 and 2 correspond to 90 percent confidence intervals computed with standard errors clustered at the country level.

households, workers with lower educational attainment, minorities, immigrants, and women. For example, unlike during previous recessions, women's employment has generally declined more than men's has. This section provides additional insights on the uneven impact on women using novel mobility data provided by Vodafone

Figure 2.5. Job Postings, by Sector, around Stay-at-Home Orders
(Normalized to 100, 40 days before stay-at-home orders)

Analysis of sectoral job postings confirms the importance of both lockdowns and voluntary social distancing. Jobs in contact-intensive sectors declined before lockdowns, while manufacturing jobs declined around the adoption of stay-at-home orders. Job postings have remained subdued, even after national stay-at-home orders were lifted.

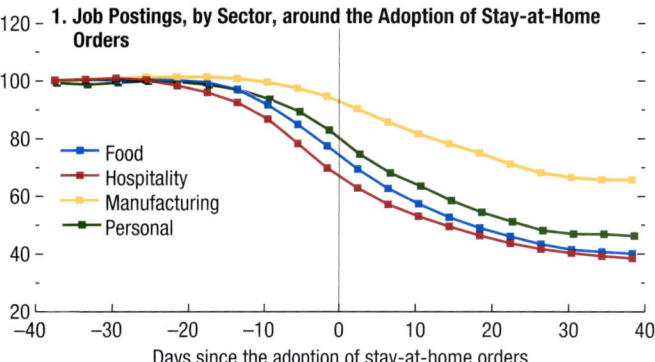

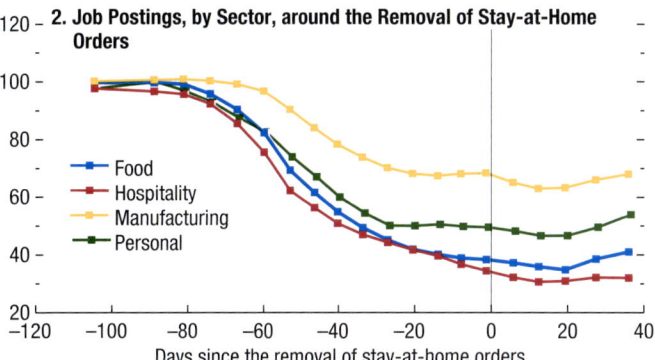

Sources: Indeed; and IMF staff calculations.
Note: This figure reports binned scatter plots showing the evolution over time of the seven-day moving average of job postings in different categories. The x-axis variable is divided into 20 equally sized bins. The sample includes countries that introduced national stay-at-home orders according to the Oxford Coronavirus Government Response Tracker. The countries included are ARE, AUT, BEL, ESP, FRA, GBR, IND, IRL, ITA, MEX, NLD, NZL, POL, and SGP. Country list uses International Organization for Standardization (ISO) country codes.

for Italy, Portugal, and Spain. By analyzing connections across cell towers, Vodafone can create mobility indices by gender based on the information customers provide when subscribing to a phone plan. Data are aggregated at the provincial level to protect customers' privacy. Vodafone data also differentiate mobility indices by age groups, thus providing novel important perspectives on the mobility patterns during the COVID-19 pandemic.

Panel 1 of Figure 2.6 shows mobility levels for men and women 30 days before and after the adoption of

Figure 2.6. Differentiating the Mobility Impact of Lockdowns by Gender and Age Group
(Percent)

Women and younger workers are disproportionately affected by lockdowns.

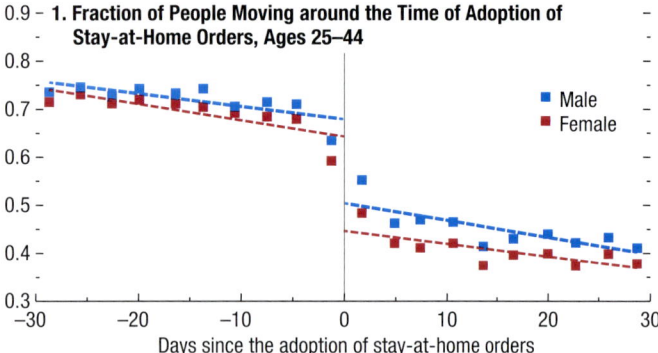

1. Fraction of People Moving around the Time of Adoption of Stay-at-Home Orders, Ages 25–44

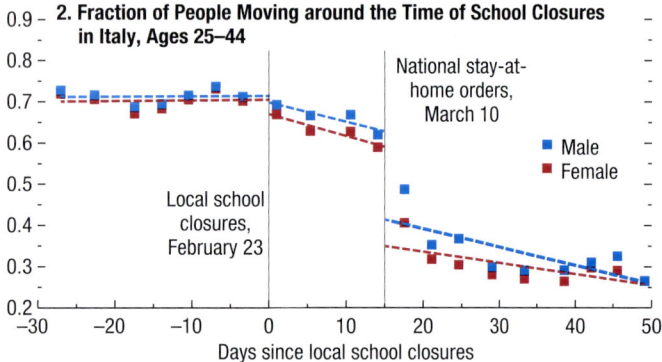

2. Fraction of People Moving around the Time of School Closures in Italy, Ages 25–44

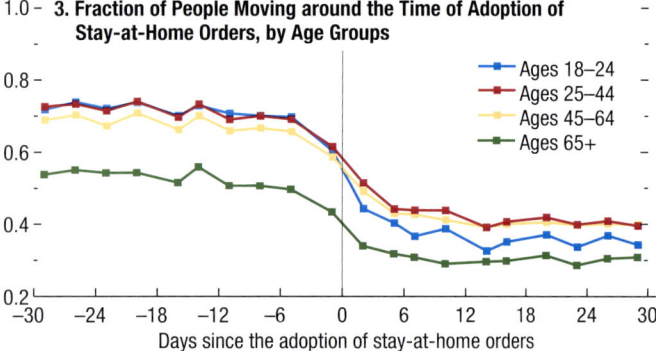

3. Fraction of People Moving around the Time of Adoption of Stay-at-Home Orders, by Age Groups

Sources: Vodafone; and IMF staff calculations.
Note: All panels present binned scatter plots around the time of stay-at-home orders' introduction. In panels 1 and 2, the series are residualized with respect to province and day-of-the-week fixed effects. In panel 2, the sample is restricted to five northern Italian regions where school closures were introduced before stay-at-home orders. The x-axis is divided into 20 equally sized bins.

stay-at-home orders for people aged 25 to 44. These orders coincided with a large drop in mobility for both men and women, leading to a drop of about 20 percent in the number of people who leave their homes on a given day. However, the effect on women was stronger by about 2 percent, a modest but statistically significant difference. Because stay-at-home orders in Italy, Portugal, and Spain coincided with school closures for almost all regions, the higher reduction in women's mobility may reflect that women are more likely to care for children when schools are closed. Consistent with this hypothesis, data show a smaller difference between men and women for people aged 45 to 64, who are less likely to have young children who require supervision at home.

Panel 2 provides additional evidence on women's role in caring for children. Focusing on a few regions in northern Italy that closed schools two weeks before the national lockdown, mobility data show that the gender gap already widened at the time of school closures. The national stay-at-home order increased the gap further, possibly reflecting higher female employment in contact-intensive sectors (such as retail, tourism, and hospitality) that were closed during the national lockdown. The evidence provided in panels 1 and 2 thus points to a disproportionate effect of lockdown measures on women, calling for targeted policy intervention to support women (by offering parental leave, for example) and to avoid long-lasting effects on their employment opportunities.[9]

Vodafone data also reveal uneven effects of lockdowns across age groups. Panel 3 shows that the adoption of stay-at-home orders led to a considerable reduction in mobility across all age categories. Nonetheless, the effects were considerably stronger for younger cohorts. Starting from a higher level of mobility consistent with the need to go to work, working-age people experienced a sharp contraction in mobility around the adoption of stay-at-home orders. The drop was particularly large for people aged 18 to 24 (some of whom, however, are students) and for people aged 25 to 44. The impact was substantially weaker for people aged 65 and above, who generally no longer work and whose level of mobility was already lower before the stay-at-home orders. These findings

[9]The analysis faces several limitations. For example, the sample is restricted to a few European countries, data do not provide information on the employment status before and after lockdowns, and various other factors can amplify or attenuate gender inequality during the pandemic. These are important areas for future research.

highlight that lockdowns tend to have a disproportionate impact on relatively younger workers and could thus widen intergenerational inequality.[10] While older people can rely on retirement income, especially in advanced economies, younger workers depend on labor income and often have temporary job contracts that are more likely to be terminated during a crisis.

Lockdowns and COVID-19 Infections

Lockdowns engender sizable short-term economic costs, but they are also an investment in public health to protect susceptible populations from the highly transmissible virus. The analysis now examines the effectiveness of lockdowns in curbing infections. Growth rates of confirmed COVID-19 cases are regressed using local projections over the stringency of lockdowns while controlling for country and time fixed effects as well as other variables that can affect infections, such as outside temperature and humidity, public information campaigns, testing, and contact tracing. Online Annex 2.5 provides additional details.

Panel 1 of Figure 2.7 shows that lockdowns tend to have a negative impact on infections. A stringent lockdown leads to a reduction in cumulated infections of about 40 percent after 30 days. Note that the effects of lockdowns on confirmed COVID-19 cases tend to materialize after at least two weeks, consistent with the COVID-19 incubation period and the time required for testing. Acknowledging this aspect is important to properly guide people's expectations about the effectiveness of lockdowns. Furthermore, the lagged impact on infections points to the need to adopt lockdowns before infection rates increase too rapidly.

Panels 2 and 3 of Figure 2.7 provide additional evidence of the benefits of adopting lockdowns early in a country's epidemic. Panel 2 shows the evolution of infections since the first COVID-19 case, differentiating countries by the number of days between the first case and the day when lockdown measures reached maximum stringency. Countries that imposed lockdowns faster experienced better epidemiological outcomes. The differences are even more striking if countries are divided with respect to the number of COVID-19 cases at the time of lockdowns (panel 3).

[10]Even though lockdowns had a stronger impact on the mobility of younger people, older people have suffered disproportionately from the health consequences of COVID-19 whose case-fatality rate is much higher in people aged 65 and above.

Figure 2.7. The Impact of Lockdowns on COVID-19 Infections

Lockdowns are an effective tool to reduce infections, especially when they are implemented early in the epidemic.

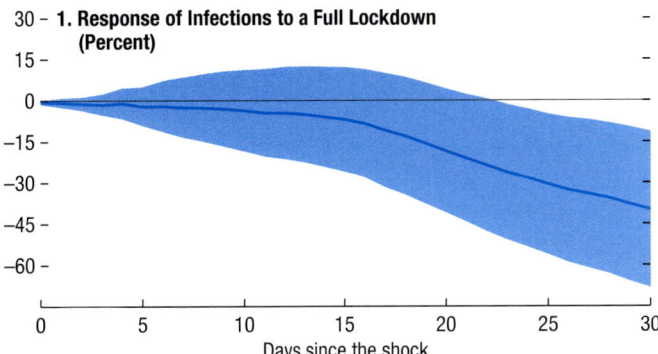

1. Response of Infections to a Full Lockdown (Percent)

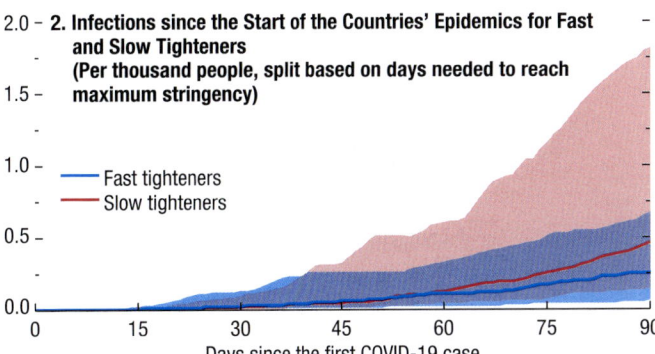

2. Infections since the Start of the Countries' Epidemics for Fast and Slow Tighteners (Per thousand people, split based on days needed to reach maximum stringency)

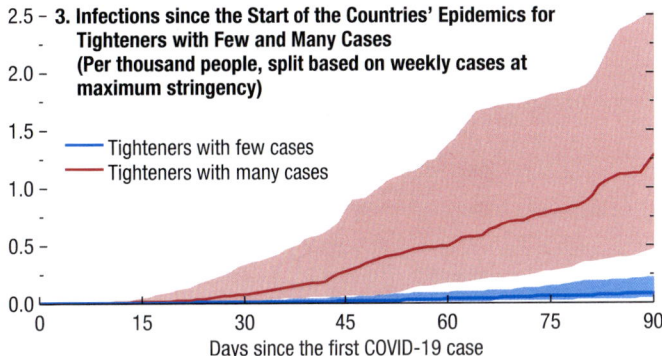

3. Infections since the Start of the Countries' Epidemics for Tighteners with Few and Many Cases (Per thousand people, split based on weekly cases at maximum stringency)

Source: IMF staff calculations.
Note: See Online Annex 2.1 for data sources and country coverage. Panel 1 shows the response of infections to a full lockdown; panels 2 and 3 show the number of infections since the first COVID-19 case. The shaded area in panel 1 corresponds to 90 percent confidence intervals computed with Driscoll-Kraay standard errors; the shaded areas in panels 2 and 3 correspond to the interquartile range.

Countries that adopted lockdowns when COVID-19 cases were still low witnessed considerably fewer infections during the first three months of the epidemic compared with countries that introduced lockdowns when cases were already high.

The observation that lockdowns can reduce infections but involve short-term economic costs is often used to argue that lockdowns involve a trade-off between saving lives and protecting livelihoods. This narrative should be reconsidered in light of the earlier findings showing that rising infections can also have severe detrimental effects on economic activity. By bringing infections under control, lockdowns may thus pave the way to a faster economic recovery as people feel more comfortable about resuming normal activities. In other words, the short-term economic costs of lockdowns could be compensated through higher future economic activity, possibly even leading to positive net effects on the economy. This remains a crucial area for future research as more data become available.

Individual Lockdown Measures and Nonlinear Effects

So far, the analysis has used a lockdown stringency index that combines a broad range of underlying measures. These include, for example, travel restrictions, school and workplace closures, and stay-at-home orders. Disentangling the effects of these measures is an arduous task because they are highly correlated, as countries often introduced them in rapid succession to contain infections. Furthermore, countries have generally followed a similar sequence, from restrictions on international travel to stay-at-home orders, as illustrated in panel 1 of Figure 2.8. Therefore, the empirical analysis tends to capture the marginal impact of a given measure conditional on those that are already in place. As discussed in Online Annex 2.6, this underestimates the importance of measures that are adopted at a later stage. For example, stay-at-home orders are found to have a modest impact on mobility because various other measures are already in place.

An analytically sounder approach is to examine whether further tightening of lockdown measures continues to have similar economic and epidemiological effects. This can inform policymakers on whether it is best to rely on protracted mild lockdowns or to opt for more stringent measures. To shed light on this issue, the analysis uses quadratic terms of the lockdown index in the regression framework. Panel

Figure 2.8. Individual Lockdown Measures and Nonlinear Effects

Countries tend to introduce different lockdown measures following a similar sequence. More stringent lockdowns have a marginally weaker impact on mobility but stronger effects on infections.

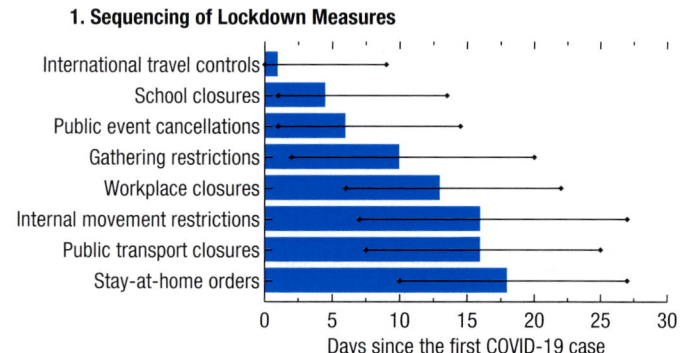

1. Sequencing of Lockdown Measures

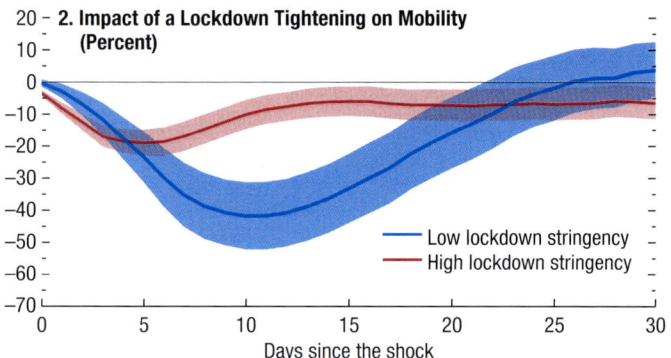

2. Impact of a Lockdown Tightening on Mobility (Percent)

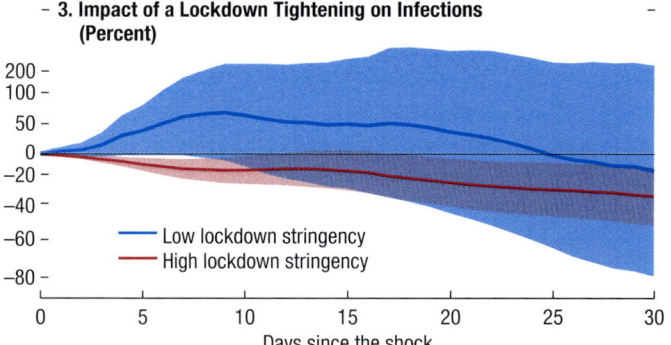

3. Impact of a Lockdown Tightening on Infections (Percent)

Source: IMF staff calculations.
Note: See Online Annex 2.1 for data sources and country coverage. The blue bars in panel 1 represent the median number of days and the horizontal lines the interquartile range. Low and high stringency in panels 2 and 3 refer to the 25th and 75th percentile of lockdown stringency. The shaded areas in panels 2 and 3 correspond to 90 percent confidence intervals computed with standard errors clustered at the country level. A lockdown tightening corresponds to an increase in the index by 100 units.

2 of Figure 2.8 shows that the introduction of additional lockdown measures has a weaker marginal impact on mobility once other measures are already in place—that is, when the lockdown stringency index is already relatively high. This suggests that lockdowns have marginally weaker negative economic effects as they become more and more stringent. For example, stay-at-home orders may have only a modest negative impact on economic activity if governments have already mandated workplace closures.

Conversely, panel 3 shows that lockdowns become progressively more effective in reducing COVID-19 cases when they become sufficiently stringent. Mild lockdowns appear instead ineffective in curbing infections. A possible interpretation is that preventing only a few instances of personal contacts, such as by closing schools alone, is not enough to reduce community spread significantly. Additional measures, such as workplace closures or stay-at-home orders, are needed to effectively bring the virus under control.

These results suggest that to achieve a given reduction in infections, policymakers may want to opt for stringent lockdowns over a shorter period rather than prolonged mild lockdowns. Based on past experience, tighter lockdowns appear indeed to entail only modest additional economic costs while leading to a considerably stronger decline in infections. It will be important to reexamine these results as the pandemic progresses because the relative benefits between mild and tight lockdowns may change. For example, if an expansion of contact tracing and broader use of face masks succeed in limiting infections, mild lockdowns could be sufficient to contain new localized flare-ups of the virus.

Conclusions

This chapter has documented the crucial role that both lockdowns and voluntary social distancing in response to rising infections have played in reducing economic activity during the pandemic. Consistent evidence on the impact of lockdowns is provided by examining cross-country economic indicators and high-frequency proxies for economic activity, such as mobility and job posting data from Google and Indeed. Furthermore, the negative impact of lockdowns on mobility is robust to using subnational data to strengthen identification.

Despite lockdowns having negative short-term economic effects, letting infections grow uncontrolled can also have dire economic consequences. This is because voluntary social distancing in response to rising COVID-19 infections has severe detrimental effects on the economy. The contribution of voluntary social distancing in reducing mobility is particularly high in advanced economies, where people can more easily stay at home thanks to teleworking arrangements, higher personal savings, and more generous social security benefits.

The important contribution of voluntary social distancing to the recession should caution against expecting a quick economic rebound once lockdowns are lifted. This is especially relevant for countries that lift lockdowns prematurely, when infections are still relatively high. In this case, lockdowns tend to have a weaker impact on mobility, likely because people's decisions are driven by fear of contracting the virus. Further tempering the expectations of a sharp economic rebound, the analysis shows that lifting lockdowns tends to have a more modest impact on mobility compared with the impact of a lockdown tightening.

These findings suggest that, as long as significant health risks persist, economic activity is likely to remain subdued. Therefore, policymakers should refrain from withdrawing policy support too quickly and preserve spending on social safety nets. Furthermore, it is important to support economic activity consistent with persistent social distancing, for example by encouraging work from home, facilitating a reallocation of resources toward less-contact-intensive sectors, and promoting the adoption of new technologies to limit the contact intensity within given sectors.

The chapter also provides novel evidence about the unequal effects of lockdowns that severely affect economically vulnerable segments of the population. Mobility data provided by Vodafone for some European countries show that lockdown measures—especially school closures—tend to generate a larger drop in women's mobility. This likely reflects women's disproportionate role in childcare, which could jeopardize their employment opportunities during the crisis. Lockdowns tend to also generate a sharper reduction in the mobility of younger cohorts, a worrisome outcome because younger workers rely on labor income and often have temporary job contracts that are at greater risk of being terminated. Targeted policy intervention, such as strengthening unemployment benefits for vulnerable categories and supporting paid leave for parents, is needed to ensure that the crisis does not contribute to widening gender and intergenerational inequality.

The analysis also finds that lockdowns are powerful instruments to reduce infections, especially when they are introduced early in a country's epidemic and when they are sufficiently stringent. Considering also that lockdowns appear to impose decreasing marginal costs on economic activity as they become more stringent, policymakers may want to lean toward rapidly adopting tight lockdowns when infections increase rather than rely on delayed mild measures. Nonetheless, these recommendations will need to be reassessed as the understanding of the virus and means to counteract it improve. A crucial area of research is to examine the effectiveness of more-targeted instruments compared with blunt lockdowns, for example restrictions on dense indoor gatherings or measures to isolate people who are more vulnerable to the virus.

The effectiveness of lockdowns in reducing infections, coupled with the finding that infections can considerably harm economic activity because of voluntary social distancing, provides an important new perspective on the costs of lockdowns. The prevailing narrative often portrays lockdowns as involving a trade-off between saving lives and supporting the economy. This characterization neglects the point that, despite imposing short-term economic costs, lockdowns may lead to a faster economic recovery by containing the virus and reducing voluntary social distancing.

These medium-term gains may offset the short-term costs of lockdowns, possibly even leading to positive overall effects on the economy. More research is warranted on this important aspect as the crisis evolves and more data become available. Meanwhile, policymakers should also look for alternative ways to contain infections that may have even lower economic costs. In line with the advice of public health experts, these may include expanding testing and contact tracing, promoting the use of face masks, and encouraging working from home.

The analytical results and policy implications presented in this chapter are subject to several caveats. First, the analysis tries to alleviate concerns about the endogeneity of lockdowns by showing that the results hold using cross-sectional and time-series identification and by relying on national and subnational data when available. However, identification concerns cannot be fully dismissed, including regarding the measurement of voluntary social distancing. Second, the analysis relies on short-term indicators, such as mobility and job postings, which provide an imperfect measure of economic activity. The chapter's findings will need to be reexamined as more conventional economic indicators become available. Third, the analysis focuses on the economic consequences of lockdowns, neglecting important side effects, for example, on educational attainment and mental health issues. These are crucial areas for future research.

Box 2.1. An Overview of the Literature on the Economic Impact of Lockdowns

The literature on the economic crisis triggered by the coronavirus pandemic has been expanding at a very rapid pace. This box offers an inexhaustive overview of some of this literature that focuses on the impact of lockdown measures.[1]

Economic Impact of Lockdowns and Inequality Aspects

Several authors point to a substantial role of lockdowns in the United States leading to employment losses, substantial decline in spending, and deterioration in local economic conditions (Baek and others 2020; Baker and others 2020; Béland, Brodeur, and Wright 2020; Chernozhukov, Kasahara, and Schrimpf 2020; Coibion, Gorodnichenko, and Weber 2020; Gupta and others 2020). Similar effects have been documented across different countries (Carvalho and others 2020; Chronopoulos, Lukas, and Wilson 2020; Deb and others 2020a; Demirgüç-Kunt, Lokshin, and Torre 2020).

Other papers argue that voluntary social distancing has had a more important role than lockdowns (Allcott and others 2020; Bartik and others 2020; Kahn, Lange, and Wiczer 2020; Maloney and Taskin 2020). This literature notes that people's mobility and economic activity in the United States contracted before lockdowns (Chetty and others 2020), and that lifting lockdowns led to a limited rebound in mobility (Dave and others 2020b) and economic activity (however, Cajner and others 2020 and Glaeser and others 2020 are exceptions). Goolsbee and Syverson (2020) finds small differences in people's visits to nearby retail establishments that faced different regulatory restrictions because they were located in different jurisdictions. Chen and others (2020b) documents similar results; it expands the analysis to Europe and finds no robust evidence of the impact of lockdowns. Sweden's case also highlights the importance of voluntary social distancing—despite avoiding strict lockdown measures, the country has experienced similar declines in mobility and economic activities compared with comparable countries (Andersen and others 2020a; Born, Dietrich, and Müller 2020; Bricco and others 2020; Chen and others 2020b). Aum, Lee, and Shin (2020) draws relatively similar conclusions analyzing the South Korean experience.

The literature also documents that the early phases of the pandemic have had a harsher effect on more economically vulnerable individuals, both in the United States and other countries (Alstadsæter and others 2020; Béland, Brodeur, and Wright 2020). These individuals include those with lower income and educational attainment (Cajner and others 2020; Chetty and others 2020; Shibata 2020), minorities (Fairlie, Couch, and Xu 2020), immigrants (Borjas and Cassidy 2020), and women (Alon and others 2020a; Del Boca and others 2020; Papanikolaou and Schmidt 2020). One reason is that lower-paid workers are often unable to perform their jobs from home (Barrero, Bloom, and Davis 2020; Dingel and Neiman 2020; Gottlieb and others 2020). This warns of a potential widening of inequality (Mongey, Pilossoph, and Weinberg 2020; Palomino, Rodríguez, and Sebastian 2020).

Some papers use rich structural models of production to predict the damage of lockdowns, mostly finding very large effects on economic activities (Barrot, Grassi, and Sauvagnat 2020; Baqaee and Farhi 2020a; Bonadio and others 2020; Cakmaklı and others 2020; Fadinger and Schymik 2020; Inoue and Todo 2020) and on firms' liquidity and solvency (Carletti and others 2020; Gourinchas and others 2020; Schivardi and Romano 2020). Chen and others (2020a) looks at stock market reactions instead and presents evidence consistent with market beliefs that mitigation policies are good for businesses in the long term. Furthermore, some papers study how supply shocks may cause demand shortage (Guerrieri and others 2020) and interact with nominal rigidities (Baqaee and Farhi 2020b).

Impact of Lockdowns and Social Distancing on Infections

Some empirical analyses also document a significant role of social distancing and lockdowns in slowing the spread of the coronavirus (Chernozhukov, Kasahara, and Schrimpf 2020; Ciminelli and Garcia-Mandico 2020; Dave and others 2020a; Deb and others 2020b; Demirgüç-Kunt, Lokshin, and Torre 2020; di Porto, Naticchioni, and Scrutinio 2020; Fang, Wang, and Yang 2020; Friedson and others 2020; Glaeser, Gorback, and Redding 2020; Imai and others 2020; Jinjarak and others 2020; Yilmazkuday 2020). However, several factors have affected effectiveness and compliance, such as social capital (Barrios and others 2020; Ding and others 2020), availability of high-speed

---

The author of this box is Nicola Pierri.

[1]At the time of writing, most of the cited papers had not yet undergone a peer-review process; thus, their conclusions must be interpreted with caution.

Box 2.1 *(continued)*

internet connections (Chiou and Tucker 2020), electoral concerns (Pulejo and Querubín 2020), labor precariousness (Levy Yeyati and Sartorio 2020), or sick leave policies (Andersen and others 2020b). Some of these papers also argue that less restrictive mitigation policies, such as wearing face masks and mass testing, can play an important role in slowing the spread of infection (Chernozhukov, Kasahara, and Schrimpf 2020; Gapen and others 2020).

Optimal Mitigation Policy and Historical Perspectives

Some studies use theoretical (mostly quantitative) models to characterize optimal mitigation policies while considering the detrimental impact on the economy. For instance, see Acemoglu and others (2020); Akbarpour and others (2020); Alvarez, Argente, and Lippi (2020); Bodenstein, Corsetti, and Guerrieri (2020); Cakmaklı and others (2020); Checo, Grigoli, and Mota (2020); Eichenbaum, Rebelo, and Trabandt (2020); Farboodi, Jarosch, and Shimer (2020); Favero, Ichino, and Rustichini (2020); and Jones, Philippon, and Venkateswaran (2020). The higher risk faced by the elderly, the role of voluntary social distancing, and hospital capacity constraints are among several issues these models study. Many of these papers document an important role for targeted lockdown policies and early interventions. Others focus on how optimal policies may differ in developing economies (Alon and others 2020b; von Carnap and others 2020).

A few papers offer a historical perspective on the economic impact of lockdowns. Correia, Luck, and Verner (2020) finds that lockdowns imposed in US cities to contain the Spanish flu had a positive impact on their subsequent growth, although Lilley, Lilley, and Rinaldi (2020) revisits this evidence and argues that it is inconclusive. Bodenhorn (2020) studies the Spanish flu's impact in the US South and finds no evidence that mandated business closures led to more business failures.

Box 2.2. The Role of Information Technology Adoption during the COVID-19 Pandemic: Evidence from the United States

This box analyzes how firms' adoption of information technology alters the impact of lockdowns and voluntary social distancing on the labor market in the United States. Information technology can dampen the economic effect of the pandemic in several ways: by facilitating teleworking, promoting online sales, or organizing contactless delivery. The analysis finds that employment has been more resilient in US states where firms use information technology more intensively. Panel 1 of Figure 2.2.1 shows the increase in the unemployment rate between February and April for each US state over the stringency of lockdowns during the same period. Similarly, panel 2 illustrates the association between the increase in unemployment and the drop in mobility. In states with low levels of information technology adoption, there is a strong correlation between the intensity of the lockdown, the drop in mobility, and the rise in the unemployment rate. Conversely, lockdowns and mobility are not associated with rising unemployment rates in states with higher levels of information technology adoption. This suggests that information technology may significantly shield local economies during the pandemic.

This pattern is confirmed using individual-level data from the Current Population Survey, a joint survey by the US Census Bureau and US Bureau of Labor Statistics. The probability of being unemployed in April is higher for respondents living in metropolitan statistical areas that experienced larger mobility declines, but companies' information technology adoption mitigates this impact.[1] The increase in the probability of being unemployed associated with a large drop in mobility (one standard deviation, equal to 10 percentage points) is 25 percent larger in metropolitan statistical areas with low levels of information technology adoption than in those with high levels (5 percentage points versus 4 percentage points).

The analysis also explores the impact of information technology adoption across different categories of workers (panel 3 of Figure 2.2.1). Information technology cushions the unemployment impact of mobility for both male and female and for both white and nonwhite workers. However, it does not

The authors of this box are Nicola Pierri and Yannick Timmer. The analysis largely draws from Pierri and Timmer (2020), which includes technical details.

[1] A metropolitan statistical area is defined by the United States Census Bureau as a geographical region with a relatively high population density at its core and close economic ties throughout the area.

Figure 2.2.1. The Dampening Effects of Information Technology Adoption on US Unemployment
(Percent)

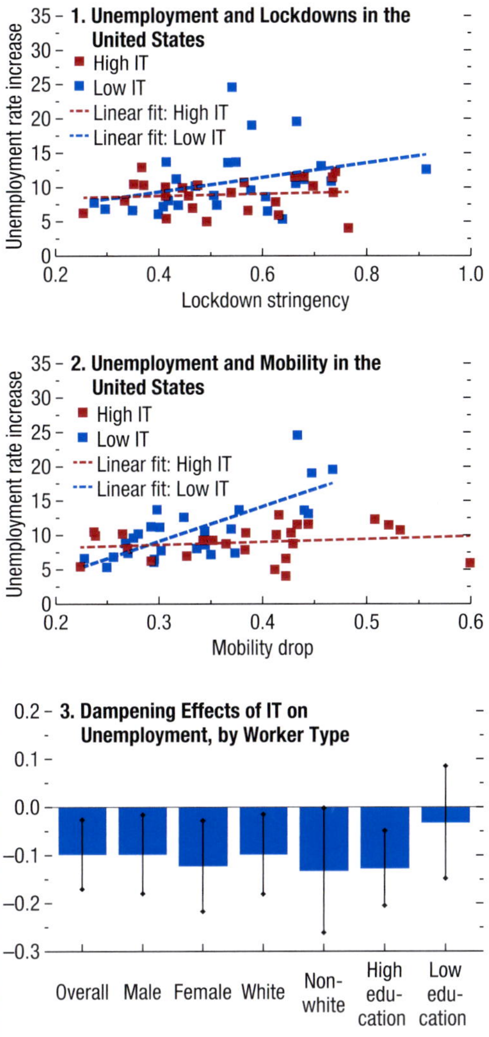

Sources: Google Community Mobility Report; Keystone; and IMF staff calculations.
Note: The *y*-axis in panels 1 and 2 is the increase in the state-level unemployment rate between February and April 2020 in percent. The *x*-axis in panel 1 is the average lockdown stringency between February and April 2020; the *x*-axis in panel 2 is the average drop in mobility. Panel 3 illustrates the results of a regression using data from the Current Population Survey in which the dependent variable is a dummy indicating if the respondent is unemployed in April 2020, and the independent variables are the IT adoption and the drop in mobility in the metropolitan statistical area where the respondent lives, together with their interaction. The *y*-axis of panel 3 reports the magnitude of the coefficient of the interaction term for each subsample. Low education refers to respondents who did not graduate from high school. See Pierri and Timmer (2020) for more details. IT = information technology.

Box 2.2 *(continued)*

mitigate the impact for individuals who have a low level of education. Therefore, even though information technology adoption may, in the aggregate, significantly shield labor markets against the effects of the coronavirus pandemic, it may also contribute to widening inequality between individuals with high and low levels of educational attainment.

References

Acemoglu, Daron, Victor Chernozhukov, Iván Werning, and Michael D. Whinston. 2020. "A Multi-Risk SIR Model with Optimally Targeted Lockdown." NBER Working Paper 27102, National Bureau of Economic Research, Cambridge, MA.

Akbarpour, Mohammad, Cody Cook, Aude Marzuoli, Simon Mongey, Abhishek Nagaraj, Matteo Saccarola, Pietro Tebaldi, Shoshana Vasserman, and Hanbin Yang. 2020. "Socio-economic Network Heterogeneity and Pandemic Policy Response." Becker Friedman Institute for Economics Working Paper 2020–75, University of Chicago, IL.

Allcott, Hunt, Levi Boxell, Jacob Conway, Billy Ferguson, Matthew Gentzkow, and Benjamin Goldman. 2020. "Economic and Health Impacts of Social Distancing Policies during the Coronavirus Pandemic." https://ssrn.com/abstract=3610422.

Alon, Titan M., Matthias Doepke, Jane Olmstead-Rumsey, and Michèle Tertilt. 2020a. "The Impact of COVID-19 on Gender Equality." NBER Working Paper 26947, National Bureau of Economic Research, Cambridge, MA.

Alon, Titan M., Minki Kim, David Lagakos, and Mitchell VanVuren. 2020b. "How Should Policy Responses to the COVID-19 Pandemic Differ in the Developing World?" NBER Working Paper 27273, National Bureau of Economic Research, Cambridge, MA.

Alstadsæter, Annette, Bernt Bratsberg, Gaute Eielsen, Wojciech Kopczuk, Simen Markussen, Oddbjorn Raaum, and Knut Røed. 2020. "The First Weeks of the Coronavirus Crisis: Who Got Hit, When, and Why? Evidence from Norway." NBER Working Paper 27131, National Bureau of Economic Research, Cambridge, MA.

Alvarez, Fernando, David Argente, and Francesco Lippi. 2020. "A Simple Planning Problem for COVID-19 Lockdown." NBER Working Paper 26981, National Bureau of Economic Research, Cambridge, MA.

Andersen, Asger L., Emil T. Hansen, Niels Johannesen, and Adam Sheridan. 2020a. "Pandemic, Shutdown and Consumer Spending: Lessons from Scandinavian Policy Responses to COVID-19." arXiv preprint arXiv:2005.04630.

Andersen, Martin, Johanna Catherine Maclean, Michael F. Pesko, and Kosali I. Simon. 2020b. "Effect of a Federal Paid Sick Leave Mandate on Working and Staying at Home: Evidence from Cellular Device Data." NBER Working Paper 27138, National Bureau of Economic Research, Cambridge, MA.

Anderson, Michael L. 2014. "Subways, Strikes, and Slowdowns: The Impacts of Public Transit on Traffic Congestion." *American Economic Review* 104 (9): 2763–96.

Aum, Sangmin, Sang Yoon (Tim) Lee, and Yongseok Shin. 2020. "COVID-19 Doesn't Need Lockdowns to Destroy Jobs: The Effect of Local Outbreaks in Korea." NBER Working Paper 27264, National Bureau of Economic Research, Cambridge, MA.

Baek, Chaewon, Peter B. McCrory, Todd Messer, and Preston Mui. 2020. "Unemployment Effects of Stay-at-Home Orders: Evidence from High Frequency Claims Data." Institute for Research on Labor and Employment Working Paper 101–20. http://irle.berkeley.edu/files/2020/07/Unemployment-Effects-of-Stay-at-Home-Orders.pdf.

Baker, Scott R., R. A. Farrokhnia, Steffen Meyer, Michaela Pagel, and Constantine Yannelis. 2020. "How Does Household Spending Respond to an Epidemic? Consumption during the 2020 COVID-19 Pandemic." NBER Working Paper 26949, National Bureau of Economic Research, Cambridge, MA.

Baqaee, David, and Emmanuel Farhi. 2020a. "Supply and Demand in Disaggregated Keynesian Economies with an Application to the COVID-19 Crisis." NBER Working Paper 27152, National Bureau of Economic Research, Cambridge, MA.

Baqaee, David, and Emmanuel Farhi. 2020b. "Nonlinear Production Networks with an Application to the COVID-19 Crisis." NBER Working Paper 27281, National Bureau of Economic Research, Cambridge, MA.

Barrero, Jose Maria, Nicholas Bloom, and Steven J. Davis. 2020. "The Future of Working from Home." Unpublished.

Barrios, John M., Efraim Benmelech, Yael V. Hochberg, Paola Sapienza, and Luigi Zingales. 2020. "Civic Capital and Social Distancing during the COVID-19 Pandemic." NBER Working Paper 27320, National Bureau of Economic Research, Cambridge, MA.

Barrot, Jean-Noël, Basile Grassi, and Julien Sauvagnat. 2020. "Sectoral Effects of Social Distancing." CEPR COVID Economics Vetted and Real-Time Papers 3, Centre for Economic Policy Research, London.

Bartik, Alexander W., Marianne Bertrand, Feng Lin, Jesse Rothstein, and Matthew Unrath. 2020. "Measuring the Labor Market at the Onset of the COVID-19 Crisis." NBER Working Paper 27613, National Bureau of Economic Research, Cambridge, MA.

Béland, Louis-Philippe, Abel Brodeur, and Taylor Wright. 2020. "COVID-19, Stay-At-Home Orders, and Employment: Evidence from CPS Data." IZA Discussion Paper 13282, Institute of Labor Economics, Bonn.

Bodenhorn, Howard. 2020. "Business at the Time of the Spanish Influenza." NBER Working Paper 27495, National Bureau of Economic Research, Cambridge, MA.

Bodenstein, Martin, Giancarlo Corsetti, and Luca Guerrieri. 2020. "Social Distancing and Supply Disruptions in a Pandemic." CEPR Discussion Paper 14629, Centre for Economic Policy Research, London.

Bonadio, Barthélémy, Zhen Huo, Andrei A. Levchenko, and Nitya Pandalai-Nayar. 2020. "Global Supply Chains in the Pandemic." NBER Working Paper 27224, National Bureau of Economic Research, Cambridge, MA.

Borjas, George J., and Hugh Cassidy. 2020. "The Adverse Effect of the COVID-19 Labor Market Shock on Immigrant Employment." NBER Working Paper 27243, National Bureau of Economic Research, Cambridge, MA.

Born, Benjamin, Alexander M. Dietrich, and Gernot J. Müller. 2020. "Do Lockdowns Work? A Counterfactual for Sweden." CEPR COVID Economics Vetted and Real-Time Papers 16, Centre for Economic Policy Research, London.

Bricco, Jana, Florian Misch, Khaled Sakr, and Alexandra Solovyeva. 2020. "What are the Economic Effects of Pandemic Containment Policies? Evidence from Sweden." IMF Working Paper 20/191, International Monetary Fund, Washington, DC.

Cajner, Tomaz, Leland D. Crane, Ryan A. Decker, John Grigsby, Adrian Hamins-Puertolas, Erik Hurst, Christopher Kurz, and Ahu Yildirmaz. 2020. "The US Labor Market during the Beginning of the Pandemic Recession." NBER Working Paper 27159, National Bureau of Economic Research, Cambridge, MA.

Cakmaklı, Cam, Selva Demiralp, Sebnem Kalemli-Ozcan, Sevcan Yesiltas, and Muhammed A. Yildirim. 2020. "COVID-19 and Emerging Markets: An Epidemiological Model with International Production Networks and Capital Flows." NBER Working Paper 27191, National Bureau of Economic Research, Cambridge, MA.

Carletti, Elena, Tommaso Oliviero, Marco Pagano, Loriana Pelizzon, and Marti G. Subrahmanyam. 2020. "The COVID-19 Shock and Equity Shortfall: Firm-Level Evidence from Italy." CEPR Discussion Paper 14831, Centre for Economic Policy Research, London.

Carvalho, Vasco M., Stephen Hansen, Álvaro Ortiz, Juan Ramón García, Tomasa Rodrigo, Sevi Rodriguez Mora, and José Ruiz. 2020. "Tracking the COVID-19 Crisis with High-Resolution Transaction Data." CEPR Discussion Paper 14642, Centre for Economic Policy Research, London.

Checo, Ariadne, Francesco Grigoli, Jose M. Mota. 2020. "Assessing Heterogeneous Containment Policies to Fight COVID-19." Unpublished.

Chen, Chen, Sudipto Dasgupta, Thanh D. Huynh, and Ying Xia. 2020a. "Were Stay-at-Home Orders during COVID-19 Harmful for Business?–The Market's View." CEPR COVID Economics Vetted and Real-Time Papers 32, Centre for Economic Policy Research, London.

Chen, Sophia, Deniz Igan, Nicola Pierri, and Andrea Presbitero. 2020b. "Tracking the Economic Impact of COVID-19 and Mitigation Policies in Europe and the United States." IMF Working Paper 20/125, International Monetary Fund, Washington, DC.

Chernozhukov, Victor, Hiroyuki Kasahara, and Paul Schrimpf. 2020. "Causal Impact of Masks, Policies, Behavior on Early COVID-19 Pandemic in the US." CEPR COVID Economics Vetted and Real-Time Papers 35, Centre for Economic Policy Research, London.

Chetty, Raj, John N. Friedman, Nathaniel Hendren, Michael Stepner, and the Opportunity Insights Team. 2020. "How Did COVID-19 and Stabilization Policies Affect Spending and Employment? A New Real-Time Economic Tracker Based on Private Sector Data." NBER Working Paper 27431, National Bureau of Economic Research, Cambridge, MA.

Chiou, Lesley, and Catherine Tucker. 2020. "Social Distancing, Internet Access and Inequality." NBER Working Paper 26982, National Bureau of Economic Research, Cambridge, MA.

Chronopoulos, Dimitris K., Marcel Lukas, and John O. S. Wilson. 2020. "Consumer Spending Responses to the COVID-19 Pandemic: An Assessment of Great Britain." https://ssrn.com/abstract=3586723.

Ciminelli, Gabriele, and Silvia Garcia-Mandico. 2020. "Business Shutdowns and COVID-19 Mortality." Unpublished.

Coibion, Olivier, Yuriy Gorodnichenko, and Michael Weber. 2020. "The Cost of the COVID-19 Crisis: Lockdowns, Macroeconomic Expectations, and Consumer Spending." NBER Working Paper 27141, National Bureau of Economic Research, Cambridge, MA.

Correia, Sergio, Stephan Luck, and Emil Verner. 2020. "Pandemics Depress the Economy, Public Health Interventions Do Not: Evidence from the 1918 Flu." https://ssrn.com/abstract=3561560.

Dave, Dhaval M., Andrew I. Friedson, Kyutaro Matsuzawa, Drew McNichols, and Joseph J. Sabia. 2020a. "Did the Wisconsin Supreme Court Restart a COVID-19 Epidemic? Evidence from a Natural Experiment." NBER Working Paper 27322, National Bureau of Economic Research, Cambridge, MA.

Dave, Dhaval M., Andrew I. Friedson, Kyutaro Matsuzawa, and Joseph J. Sabia. 2020b. "When Do Shelter-in-Place Orders Fight COVID-19 Best? Policy Heterogeneity across States and Adoption Time." NBER Working Paper 27091, National Bureau of Economic Research, Cambridge, MA.

Davis, Lucas W. 2008. "The Effect of Driving Restrictions on Air Quality in Mexico City." *Journal of Political Economy* 116 (1): 38–81.

Deb, Pragyan, Davide Furceri, Jonathan D. Ostry, and Nour Tawk. 2020a. "The Effect of Containment Measures on the COVID-19 Pandemic." CEPR Discussion Paper 15086, Centre for Economic Policy Research, London.

Deb, Pragyan, Davide Furceri, Jonathan D. Ostry, and Nour Tawk. 2020b. "The Economic Effects of COVID-19 Containment Measures." CEPR COVID Economics Vetted and Real-Time Papers 24, Centre for Economic Policy Research, London.

Del Boca, Daniela, Noemi Oggero, Paola Profeta, and Maria Cristina Rossi. 2020. "Women's Work, Housework and Childcare, before and during COVID-19." IZA Discussion Paper 13409, Institute of Labor Economics, Bonn.

Demirgüç-Kunt, Asli, Michael Lokshin, and Iván Torre. 2020. "The Sooner, the Better: The Early Economic Impact of Non-Pharmaceutical Interventions during the COVID-19 Pandemic" World Bank Policy Research Working Paper 9257.

di Porto, Edoardo, Paolo Naticchioni, Vincenzo Scrutinio. 2020. "Partial lockdown and the spread of COVID-19: Lessons from the Italian case" Unpublished.

Ding, Wenzhi, Ross Levine, Chen Lin, and Wensi Xie. 2020. "Social Distancing and Social Capital: Why US Counties Respond Differently to COVID-19." https://ssrn.com/abstract=3624495.

Dingel, Jonathan, and Brent Neiman. 2020. "How Many Jobs Can Be Done at Home?" NBER Working Paper 26948, National Bureau of Economic Research, Cambridge, MA.

Eichenbaum, Martin S., Sergio Rebelo, and Mathias Trabandt. 2020. "The Macroeconomics of Epidemics." NBER Working Paper 26882, National Bureau of Economic Research, Cambridge, MA.

Fadinger, Harald, and Jan Schymik. 2020. "The Costs and Benefits of Home Office during the COVID-19 Pandemic: Evidence from Infections and an Input-Output Model for Germany." CEPR COVID Economics Vetted and Real-Time Papers 9, Centre for Economic Policy Research, London.

Fairlie, Robert W., Kenneth Couch, and Huanan Xu. 2020. "The Impacts of COVID-19 on Minority Unemployment: First Evidence from April 2020 CPS Microdata." NBER Working Paper 27246, National Bureau of Economic Research, Cambridge, MA.

Fang, Hanming, Long Wang, and Yang. 2020. "Human Mobility Restrictions and the Spread of the Novel Coronavirus (2019-nCoV) in China." NBER Working Paper 26906, National Bureau of Economic Research, Cambridge, MA.

Farboodi, Maryam, Gregor Jarosch, and Robert Shimer. 2020. "Internal and External Effects of Social Distancing in a Pandemic." NBER Working Paper 27059, National Bureau of Economic Research, Cambridge, MA.

Favero, Carlo A., Andrea Ichino, and Aldo Rustichini. 2020. "Restarting the Economy while Saving Lives under COVID-19." CEPR Discussion Paper 14664, Centre for Economic Policy Research, London.

Friedson, Andrew I., Drew McNichols, Joseph J. Sabia, and Dhaval Dave. 2020. "Did California's Shelter-in-Place Order Work? Early Coronavirus-Related Public Health Effects." NBER Working Paper 26992, National Bureau of Economic Research, Cambridge, MA.

Gapen, Michael, Jonathan Millar, Blerina Uruçi, and Pooja Sriram. 2020. "Assessing the Effectiveness of Alternative Measures to Slow the Spread of COVID-19 in the United States." CEPR COVID Economics Vetted and Real-Time Papers 40, Centre for Economic Policy Research, London.

Glaeser, Edward L., Caitlin S. Gorback, and Stephen J. Redding. 2020. "How Much Does COVID-19 Increase with Mobility? Evidence From New York and Four Other US Cities." NBER Working Paper 27519, National Bureau of Economic Research, Cambridge, MA.

Glaeser, Edward L., Ginger Zhe Jin, Benjamin T. Leyden, and Michael Luca. 2020. "Learning from Deregulation: The Asymmetric Impact of Lockdown and Reopening on Risky Behavior During COVID-19." NBER Working Paper 27650, National Bureau of Economic Research, Cambridge, MA.

Goolsbee, Austan, and Chad Syverson. 2020. "Fear, Lockdown, and Diversion: Comparing Drivers of Pandemic Economic Decline 2020." NBER Working Paper 27432, National Bureau of Economic Research, Cambridge, MA.

Gottlieb, Charles, Jan Grobovšek, Markus Poschke, and Fernando Saltiel. 2020. "Lockdown Accounting." IZA Discussion Paper 13397, Institute of Labor Economics, Bonn.

Gourinchas, Pierre-Olivier, Sebnem Kalemli-Ozcan, Veronika Penciakova, and Nick Sander. 2020. "COVID-19 and SME Failures." IMF Working Paper 20/207, International Monetary Fund, Washington, DC.

Guerrieri, Veronica, Guido Lorenzoni, Ludwig Straub, and Iván Werning. 2020. "Macroeconomic Implications of COVID-19: Can Negative Supply Shocks Cause Demand Shortages?" NBER Working Paper 26918, National Bureau of Economic Research, Cambridge, MA.

Gupta, Sumedha, Laura Montenovo, Thuy D. Nguyen, Felipe Lozano Rojas, Ian M. Schmutte, Kosali I. Simon, Bruce A. Weinberg, and Coady Wing. 2020. "Effects of Social Distancing Policy on Labor Market Outcomes." NBER Working Paper 27280, National Bureau of Economic Research, Cambridge, MA.

Hausman, Catherine, and David S. Rapson. 2018. "Regression Discontinuity in Time: Considerations for Empirical Applications." *Annual Review of Resource Economics* 10 (1): 533–52.

Imai, Natsuko, Katy A. M. Gaythorpe, Sam Abbott, Sangeeta Bhatia, Sabine van Elsland, Kiesha Prem, Yang Liu, and Neil M. Ferguson. 2020. "Adoption and Impact of Non-Pharmaceutical Interventions for COVID-19." *Wellcome Open Research* 5:59. https://doi.org/10.12688/wellcomeopenres.15808.1.

Inoue, Hiroyasu, and Yasuyuki Todo. 2020. "The Propagation of the Economic Impact through Supply Chains: The Case of a Mega-City Lockdown to Contain the Spread of COVID-19." CEPR COVID Economics Vetted and Real-Time Papers 2, Centre for Economic Policy Research, London.

Jinjarak, Yothin, Rashad Ahmed, Sameer Nair-Desai, Weining Xin, and Joshua Aizenman. 2020. "Accounting for Global COVID-19 Diffusion Patterns, January-April 2020." NBER Working Paper 27185, National Bureau of Economic Research, Cambridge, MA.

Jones, Callum J., Thomas Philippon, and Venky Venkateswaran. 2020. "Optimal Mitigation Policies in a Pandemic: Social Distancing and Working from Home." NBER Working Paper 26984, National Bureau of Economic Research, Cambridge, MA.

Kahn, Lisa, Fabian Lange, and David Wiczer. 2020. "Labor Demand in the Time of COVID-19: Evidence from Vacancy Postings and UI Claims." NBER Working Paper 27061, National Bureau of Economic Research, Cambridge, MA.

Levy Yeyati, Eduardo, and Luca Sartorio. 2020. "Take Me Out: De Facto Limits on Strict Lockdowns in Developing Countries." CEPR COVID Economics Vetted and Real-Time Papers 39, Centre for Economic Policy Research, London.

Lilley, Andrew, Matthew Lilley, and Gianluca Rinaldi. 2020. "Public Health Interventions and Economic Growth: Revisiting the Spanish Flu Evidence." https://ssrn.com/abstract= 3590008Documentos de Trabajo Gobierno Nro 8.

Maloney, William, and Temel Taskin. 2020. "Determinants of Social Distancing and Economic Activity during COVID-19: A Global View." World Bank Policy Research Working Paper 9242, Washington, DC.

Mongey, Simon, Laura Pilossoph, and Alex Weinberg. 2020. "Which Workers Bear the Burden of Social Distancing Policies?" NBER Working Paper 27085, National Bureau of Economic Research, Cambridge, MA.

Palomino, Juan C., Juan G. Rodríguez, and Raquel Sebastian. 2020. "Wage Inequality and Poverty Effects of Lockdown and Social Distancing in Europe." SSRN. https://ssrn.com/ abstract=3615615.

Papanikolaou, Dimitris, and Lawrence D. W. Schmidt. 2020. "Working Remotely and the Supply-Side Impact of COVID-19." NBER Working Paper 27330, National Bureau of Economic Research, Cambridge, MA.

Pierri, Nicola, and Yannick Timmer. 2020. "IT Shields: Technology Adoption and Economic Resilience during the COVID-19 Pandemic." IMF Working Paper 20/208, International Monetary Fund, Washington, DC.

Pulejo, Massimo, and Pablo Querubín. 2020. "Electoral Concerns Reduce Restrictive Measures during the COVID-19 Pandemic." NBER Working Paper 27498, National Bureau of Economic Research, Cambridge, MA.

Schivardi, Fabiano, and Guido Romano. 2020. "A Simple Method to Estimate Firms Liquidity Needs during the COVID-19 Crisis with an Application to Italy." CEPR COVID Economics: Vetted and Real-Time Papers 35, Centre for Economic Policy Research, London.

Shibata, Ippei. 2020. "The Distributional Impact of Recessions: The Global Financial Crisis and the Pandemic Recession." IMF Working Paper 20/96, International Monetary Fund, Washington, DC.

von Carnap, Tillmann, Ingvild Almås, Tessa Bold, Selene Ghisolfi, and Justin Sandefur. 2020. "The Macroeconomics of Pandemics in Developing Countries: An Application to Uganda." CEPR COVID Economics Vetted and Real-Time Papers 27, Centre for Economic Policy Research, London.

Yilmazkuday, Hakan. 2020. "Stay-at-Home Works to Fight against COVID-19: International Evidence from Google Mobility Data." https://ssrn.com/abstract=3571708.

MITIGATING CLIMATE CHANGE—GROWTH- AND DISTRIBUTION-FRIENDLY STRATEGIES

Without further action to reduce greenhouse gas emissions, the planet is on course to reach temperatures not seen in millions of years, with potentially catastrophic implications. The analysis in this chapter suggests that an initial green investment push combined with steadily rising carbon prices would deliver the needed emission reductions at reasonable transitional global output effects, putting the global economy on a stronger and more sustainable footing over the medium term. Carbon pricing is critical to mitigation because higher carbon prices incentivize energy efficiency besides reallocating resources from high- to low-carbon activities. A green investment push up front would strengthen the macroeconomy in the short term and help lower the costs of adjusting to higher carbon prices. The transitional costs of carbon pricing consistent with net zero emissions by mid-century appear manageable and could be reduced further as new technological innovations develop in response to carbon pricing and green research and development subsidies. Governments can protect those most affected by mitigation by providing targeted cash transfers financed by carbon revenues.

Introduction

Global warming continues apace. The increase in the average temperature over the surface of the planet since the industrial revolution is estimated at about 1°C and is believed to be accelerating. Each successive decade since the 1980s has been warmer than the previous one, the past five years (2015–19) were the warmest ever reported, and 2019 was likely the second-warmest year on record. Rising pressure on Earth systems is already evident from more frequent weather-related natural disasters.[1] Global sea levels are rising, and evidence is mounting that the world is closer to abrupt and irreversible changes—so-called tipping points—than previously thought (Lenton and others 2019).

Scientific studies attribute most of global warming to emissions of greenhouse gases associated with human activity, especially from the carbon released by burning fossil fuels (IPCC 2014, 2018a) (see Box 3.1 for a glossary).[2] Scientists have warned that temperature increases relative to preindustrial levels need to be kept well below 2°C—and ideally 1.5°C—to avoid reaching climate tipping points and imposing severe stress on natural and socioeconomic systems (IPCC 2014, 2018a). The objective of limiting temperature increases by 2100 to 1.5°C–2°C was endorsed worldwide by policymakers in the 2015 Paris Agreement. Sizable and rapid reductions in carbon emissions are needed for this goal to be met; specifically, net carbon emissions need to decline to zero by mid-century (IPCC 2014, 2018a). This means that carbon emissions must be eliminated or that any remaining carbon emissions must be removed from the atmosphere by natural (for example, forests and oceans) or artificial (for example, carbon capture and storage) sinks. Even with such drastic reductions, temperatures may temporarily overshoot the target until the stock of accumulated carbon in the atmosphere is sufficiently reduced by absorption by carbon sinks.

The authors of this chapter are Philip Barrett, Christian Bogmans, Benjamin Carton, Johannes Eugster, Florence Jaumotte (lead), Adil Mohommad, Evgenia Pugacheva, Marina M. Tavares, and Simon Voigts, in collaboration with external consultants Warwick McKibbin and Weifeng Liu for modeling simulations, and with contributions from Thomas Brand. Srijoni Banerjee, Eric Bang, and Jaden Kim provided research support, and Daniela Rojas Fernandez provided editorial assistance.

[1]See also Chapter 2 of the April 2020 *Sub-Saharan Africa Regional Economic Outlook*, Chapter 3 of the October 2017 *World Economic Outlook*, and Kahn and others (2019). Adaptation policies are another critical element of the strategy to reduce losses from climate change and, in some cases, can overlap with mitigation policies (such as for the preservation of rain forests). However, these are beyond the scope of this chapter.

[2]Greenhouse gas is any gas that contributes to the greenhouse effect by absorbing infrared radiation (net heat energy) emitted from Earth's surface and radiating it back to Earth's surface. These gases include carbon dioxide, methane, nitrous oxide, and fluorinated gases. The chapter focuses on carbon emissions from the consumption of fossil fuels, which is a main driver of human-made greenhouse gas emissions. IMF (2019) discusses policies to reduce other important sources of greenhouse gas emissions beyond domestic fossil fuel CO_2 emissions (forestry, agriculture, methane leaks, industrial process emissions, F-gases, international aviation/maritime emissions).

Tangible policy responses to reduce greenhouse gas emissions have been grossly insufficient to date.[3] While the COVID-19 crisis has reduced emissions, it is already evident that this decline will be only temporary. Under unchanged policies, emissions will continue to rise relentlessly, and global temperatures could increase by an additional 2–5°C by the end of this century, reaching levels not seen in millions of years, imposing growing physical and economic damage, and increasing the risk of catastrophic outcomes across the planet (Figure 3.1).[4] Damages from climate change include (but are not limited to) lower productivity due to changes in the yield of agricultural crops and fish farming and hotter temperatures for people working outside; more frequent disruption of economic activity and greater physical destruction of productive capital, infrastructure, and buildings as a result of more frequent and severe natural disasters and (for coastal areas) the rise in sea levels; deterioration of health and possible loss of life due to natural disasters and increased prevalence of infectious diseases; and diversion of resources toward adaptation and reconstruction (see, for example, Batten 2018).[5] The response of temperatures to the accumulated stock of carbon emissions in the atmosphere ("climate sensitivity") and the damages that can be expected for given temperature increases are subject to uncertainty; many of the damages—including damages to the natural world and catastrophic risk—are also insufficiently captured by existing estimates, which are based on small historical variations in temperatures. Nevertheless, by all estimates, damages are expected to be substantial, and more recent studies that take account of the possibility

[3]For most countries, the Nationally Determined Contributions pledged under the Paris Agreement are deemed insufficient to meet either the 1.5°C or the 2°C target, and, judging by current policies, unlikely to be met in the first place (see Climate Action Tracker Warming Projections Global Update—December 2019). Views about the shortfalls of stated policies have been echoed by others, such as the International Energy Agency, which points out that significantly more ambitious policies are needed to reach the targets (IEA 2019).

[4]Absent climate change mitigation policies or massive migration, one-third of the global population could experience mean annual temperatures above 29°C by 2070. Such temperatures are currently found in only 0.8 percent of Earth's land surface, mostly in Africa, and are projected to cover 19 percent of land by 2070 (Xu and others 2020).

[5]Climate change will also complicate the management of macro-economic stability, as climatic changes and natural disasters increase output and price volatility and, with the costs of natural disasters—from reconstruction to investment in adaptation—put pressure on fiscal sustainability. Last but not least, it will increase poverty and inequality because lower-income countries and lower-income people in any given country tend to be not only more exposed to but also less able to handle shocks or adapt to climate change.

Figure 3.1. Risks from Unmitigated Climate Change

Under the current trajectory of emissions, the probability of keeping global warming below 1.5°C would drop to 50 percent in about 15 years. Global temperatures under business-as-usual would increase to levels not seen in millions of years, triggering substantial income losses and raising the risk of catastrophic outcomes.

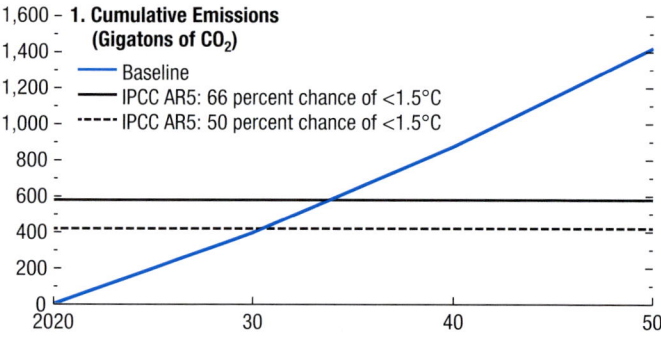

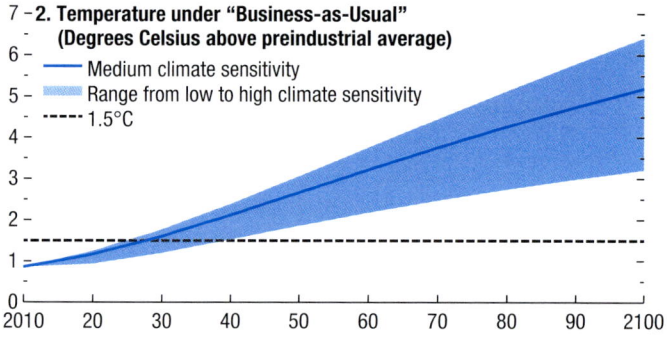

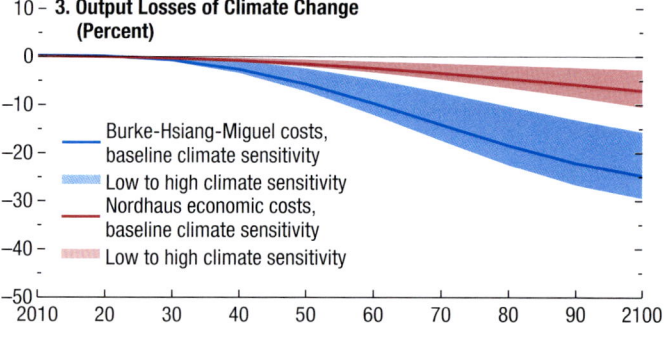

Sources: Burke, Hsiang, and Miguel 2015; IPCC 2014, 2018a; Nordhaus 2010; and IMF staff estimates.
Note: Baseline in panel 1 represents cumulative emissions under the unmitigated climate change scenario based on the G-Cubed model; dashed lines correspond to the emission ceilings needed to limit global warming. AR5 = the Fifth Assessment Report of the Intergovernmental Panel on Climate Change (IPCC). Panel 2 shows global average temperature under business-as-usual. Solid line assumes a climate sensitivity (the long-term increase in temperature caused by a long-term doubling of the atmospheric carbon stock) of 3; the shaded area assumes a range of climate sensitivity from 1.5 to 4.5 (see Heal 2017; Hassler, Krusell, and Olovsson 2018). Panel 3 shows economic losses from climate change relative to holding temperatures fixed at current levels. Solid lines assume a climate sensitivity of 3; the shaded area assumes a range from 1.5 to 4.5 (see Heal 2017; Hassler, Krusell, and Olovsson 2018). Economic costs of given temperature rises are based on either Nordhaus (2010) or Burke, Hsiang, and Miguel (2015).

of nonlinear effects and long-lasting reductions in economic growth (for example, Burke, Hsiang, and Miguel 2015) point to much higher damages than previously projected. Various changes that global warming is setting in motion, such as the melting of the ice caps and rise in sea levels, and the acidification of oceans could themselves reinforce global warming and would be very hard to reverse over human timescales (IPCC 2014, 2018a).

The COVID-19 crisis creates both challenges and opportunities for the climate change mitigation agenda. Though mitigation is likely to boost incomes in the long term by limiting damages and severe physical risks, the economic transformation it requires may lower growth during the transition, especially in countries heavily reliant on fossil fuel exports and in those with rapid economic and population growth. The current global recession makes it more challenging to enact the policies needed for mitigation and raises the urgency of understanding how mitigation can be achieved in an employment- and growth-friendly way and with protection for the poor. However, there are also opportunities in the current context to put the economy on a greener path (see also the October 2020 *Fiscal Monitor*).[6] The crisis has led to a major retrenchment in investment and policies can seek to ensure that the composition of the recovery in capital spending is consistent with decarbonization by providing correct price signals and other financial incentives. In addition, fiscal stimulus—which will likely be needed in the aftermath of the pandemic—can be an opportunity to boost green and resilient public infrastructure.

This chapter takes the goal of reducing net carbon emissions to zero by 2050 as given and looks at possible ways of designing mitigation policies, being mindful of constraints related to political feasibility.[7] Specifically, the chapter asks the following two questions:

- Which combination of policy tools—carbon pricing, a public and private investment push, research and development subsidies—would allow the world to reach net zero carbon emissions by 2050 in a growth-, employment-, and distribution-friendly way?
- Can well-designed and sequenced mitigation policies help with the economic repair from the COVID-19 crisis?

While issues of international coordination are important, the depth of emission reductions targeted in this chapter (reaching net zero emissions) limits the room for differentiation of mitigation efforts across countries, especially across the large ones. Each country/region is thus assumed to reduce emissions to the same extent (with the exception of a group of selected oil-exporting and other economies where emissions are assumed to remain at current levels).

A deep decarbonization of human activity will require both energy efficiency and the share of low-carbon sources in energy supply to increase radically more than in recent decades. Incentivizing these changes will require carbon-intensive energy to become much more expensive relative to both low-carbon energy and other goods and services than it is today. Fossil fuels are now massively underpriced, reflecting undercharging for production and environmental costs—including for air pollution and global warming. Coady and others (2019) estimate global energy subsidies—the gap between existing and efficient prices (that is, prices warranted by supply costs, environmental costs, and revenue considerations)—at a striking $4.7 trillion in 2015, or about 6.3 percent of global GDP. A narrower subsidy measure, reflecting only differences between the amount consumers actually pay for fuel use and the corresponding opportunity cost of supplying the fuel, was estimated by Coady and others (2019) at $305 billion globally in 2015.

Governments can use various measures to raise the relative price of carbon-intensive activities. The first set of policies consists of raising the price of carbon through either carbon taxes or carbon emission trading programs to price the emission externality. Correctly pricing carbon would reduce its use while boosting the supply of low-carbon alternatives. While the chapter focuses on a carbon tax as a way to raise carbon prices, introducing feebates or imposing direct mandates and regulations on emissions are alternative or complementary tools that are less efficient but raise the implicit price of carbon and may face less political resistance (see the October 2019 *Fiscal Monitor* for a discussion

---

[6]For discussions on this, see Batini and others (2020), Bhattacharya and Rydge (2020), Black and Parry (2020), Hepburn and others (2020) and Chapter 5 of the October 2020 Global Financial Stability Report.

[7]Almost all countries are revising their climate strategies under the Paris Agreement (Nationally Determined Contributions) ahead of the 2021 UN Climate Change Conference (COP 26) meeting. About 70 countries have committed to net zero emissions by 2050. Under net zero emissions, positive emissions would need to be offset by negative emissions (such as co-firing biofuels in power generation with carbon capture and storage, expanding forest carbon storage, and direct air capture technologies).

of efficiency/feasibility trade-offs).[8] The second set of policies directly aims at making low-carbon energy sources more abundant and cheaper and tackles broader market failures (such as knowledge spillovers, network externalities, and scale economies) in their provision. The toolkit for this approach includes subsidies and price guarantees to increase demand, investment, and supply in the low-carbon energy sector; direct public investment in low-carbon technologies and infrastructure; and research and development subsidies to spur innovation.[9]

Other policy options include the further development and adoption of negative emission technologies, such as carbon capture and storage, which are assumed to play a role in the modeling of emission reduction strategies in the chapter, and solar radiation modification measures, which can be effective in theory but in practice involve large uncertainties, risks, and knowledge gaps.[10]

The optimal mix and sequencing of mitigation policy tools, along with their macroeconomic implications, are still matters of much debate. Some commentators argue that reining in climate change through carbon pricing, while boosting output and welfare in the long term, could weaken growth in the short to medium term, as higher energy prices raise living costs (especially for the poor), displace workers, and reduce profits in carbon-intensive activities. However, some of these effects can be reduced if carbon pricing revenues are used to boost growth (for example, through funding productive investment or reducing distortionary taxes). Others stress the possibility of "green growth,"

arguing that government support for sustainable investment and technologies—together with higher expected carbon prices—can stimulate activity in the short to medium term through higher net investment, especially when the economy is operating below potential.[11] Another argument is that decarbonization policies focused on innovation policy (such as research subsidies) could trigger waves of technological change that would boost productivity and growth in the medium to long term.

This chapter approaches these questions in three ways. The first takes stock of the mitigation policies implemented in a large sample of countries over the past 25 years or so, and examines their roles in the shift from high- to low-carbon activities and what impact that had on overall activity. The analysis focuses on the power sector, which was the target of many of these policies. The second uses three macroeconomic models to examine mitigation policies needed to get to net zero emissions by 2050 and how to design them to be as growth friendly as possible. The third part of the approach examines the distributional effects of mitigation policies by modeling their impact on both consumption and labor income of households. It also looks at different ways of using carbon revenues to mitigate the adverse effects on those whose livelihoods would be the most affected.

The chapter finds that climate change mitigation policies have made important contributions to reallocating innovation, electricity generation, and employment toward low-carbon activities, broadly without harming overall activity. Supported by these empirical results, the chapter's model simulations suggest that getting to net zero emissions by 2050 is still within reach, though the window to keep temperature increases to safe levels is closing rapidly. This would put the global economy on a sustainable growth path in the second half of the century and

---

[8]Feebates are sectoral measures (for example, on transport, industry, or power) that impose a sliding scale of fees on firms/goods with emission rates (for example, CO_2 per kilowatt-hour) above a "pivot point" level and corresponding subsidies for firms/goods with emission rates below the pivot point. They are a hybrid between carbon pricing and green supply policies and may be more politically acceptable as they avoid an increase in the price of energy. Feebates can be used on their own or play a reinforcing role by complementing other instruments (see the October 2019 *Fiscal Monitor*).

[9]A broad package of measures is likely ideal, as the two types of policies can be expected to work in synergy. For instance, higher carbon prices would be more acceptable to the public—and so more sustainable—if low-carbon energy sources were available at a reasonable cost. Conversely, subsidies may not encourage strong private investment in low-carbon technologies if they are not coupled with expectations of a sufficiently high carbon price in the future.

[10]Solar radiation modification attempts to offset the warming from emissions accumulated in the atmosphere, while carbon capture and storage directly limits atmospheric greenhouse gas accumulation.

[11]While the terms "low" and "high" carbon refer to a specific metric (CO_2), the term "green" originates in the environment literature and generally refers to activities that have a (very) small impact on the environment. While "green" is commonly used to refer to low-carbon activities, these may not be strictly green, but just greener. For instance, wind and solar are low-carbon energy sources, but they are land and resource/material intensive. The same holds for other low-carbon sources of energy, such as hydro or nuclear power, which points to the issue of problem-shifting in a world characterized by multiple environmental problems. "Renewable energy" refers to wind and solar energy and to the fact that these technologies do not require fossil fuels, which are nonrenewable on human timescales.

beyond and immediately yield substantial domestic co-benefits from mitigation policies—mainly thanks to reduced mortality and morbidity from less environmental pollution.[12] An initial green investment push combined with initially moderate and gradually rising carbon prices would deliver the needed emission reductions at reasonable output effects. A green fiscal stimulus would support global GDP and employment during the recovery from the COVID-19 crisis and lay the ground for higher carbon prices by boosting productivity in low-carbon sectors. As the recovery takes hold, preannounced and gradually rising carbon prices become a powerful tool to deliver the quick and substantial reductions in carbon emissions required to reach net zero emissions by 2050.

Along the transition, higher carbon prices would entail global output losses, but these losses would be moderate relative to the expected income gains from avoided climate damage in the second half of the century and beyond. Growth in the medium and long term will be harmed considerably unless climate change is addressed, making the benefits from mitigation much higher than the temporary benefits from inaction.[13] The transitional economic costs would be reduced further if new low-carbon technologies were developed, and a strong case can be made to complement early on the innovation incentives sparked by carbon pricing with green research and development subsidies that help remove obstacles to developing new technologies.

The economic costs of the low-carbon transition differ across the world. Countries with fast economic and population growth (such as India and, to a lesser extent, China), those with heavy reliance on high-carbon energy (such as China), and most oil producers are likely to bear larger transition costs. However, for fast-growing countries, these costs remain small given their projected growth over the next 30 years (even under mitigation) and need to be weighed against substantial avoided damage from climate change and co-benefits from climate change mitigation, such as reduced local pollution and mortality rates. If advanced economies were to enact mitigation policies on their own, they would not be able to keep global emissions and temperature increases to safe levels; joint action

by the largest economies is critical to avoid the worst outcomes of climate change. For fossil fuel producers, the required diversification of their economies will be difficult, but many of them also stand to benefit from global climate change mitigation.

Finally, whereas carbon pricing would disproportionately affect poorer households, recycling one-sixth to one-quarter of carbon revenues as targeted transfers could fully compensate the poorest 20 percent of households. Fully compensating the poorest 40 percent of households would require recycling between 40 and 55 percent of the carbon revenues. In addition, some limited government spending on low-carbon sectors would support job transitions from high-carbon to low-carbon sectors. Conscious and determined action by governments to build inclusion will be key to enhance the social and political acceptability of the transition.

The Mitigation Toolkit: How Have Policies Worked So Far?

Global innovation and investment in clean energy technologies have increased dramatically over the past two decades or so amid tightening environmental policies (Figure 3.2, panel 1).[14] Environmental policies cover a range of instruments used to varying degrees. Emission limits, notably for power (electricity) plants, and research and development subsidies ("nonmarket instruments") have been widely used since the 1990s and have become more stringent over time. The use of "market instruments," such as trading programs and feed-in tariffs, has picked up since the early 2000s, whereas carbon taxes have yet to become binding constraints in most countries (Figure 3.2, panel 2).[15]

---

[12]See Parry, Veung, and Heine (2015) and the October 2019 *Fiscal Monitor* for details on the unilateral costs and domestic net benefits of a $50/ton carbon tax in the Group of Twenty countries.

[13]See also Stern (2007) and Hassler, Krusell, and Olovsson (2018).

[14]This chapter uses the Organisation for Economic Co-operation and Development's Environmental Policy Stringency Index, as published in OECD (2018). For more details, see Botta and Koźluk (2014).

[15]Under feed-in tariffs, producers of renewable electricity are offered long-term contracts that guarantee a fixed price for every unit of electricity delivered to the grid. Trading programs include green and white certificates and those covering emissions of various pollutants. Green and white certificates are titles, respectively, for reaching renewable energy targets (portfolio standards) or energy-saving targets. In an emission trading program, a fixed number of emission permits is allocated or sold by a central institution, and the price adjusts to supply and demand. In contrast, a tax on carbon (or other pollutants) defines a price, or more precisely a markup, and lets the quantity of emissions adjust.

Figure 3.2. Environmental Policies and Share of Clean Innovation and Electricity Generation

Clean innovation and electricity generation increased largely in line with tightening environmental policies. The use of carbon taxes has been very limited historically.

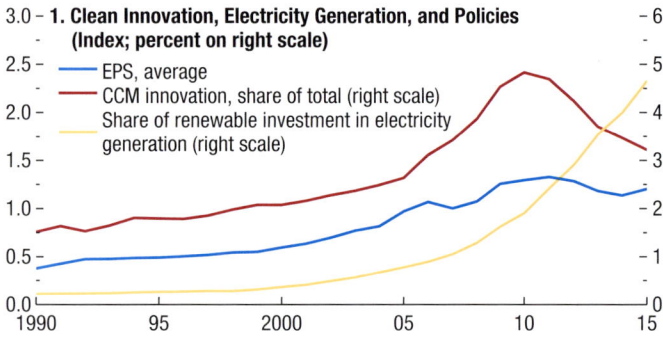

1. Clean Innovation, Electricity Generation, and Policies
(Index; percent on right scale)
- EPS, average
- CCM innovation, share of total (right scale)
- Share of renewable investment in electricity generation (right scale)

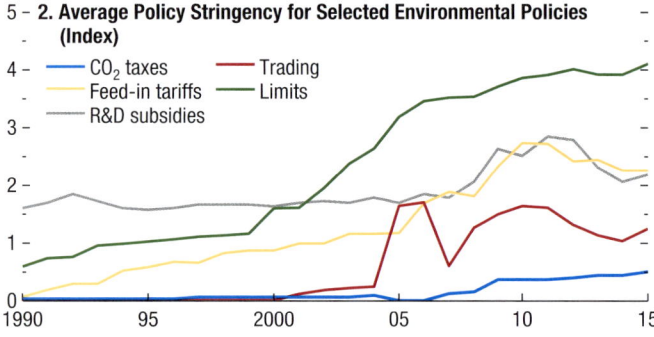

2. Average Policy Stringency for Selected Environmental Policies
(Index)
- CO$_2$ taxes
- Trading
- Feed-in tariffs
- Limits
- R&D subsidies

Sources: International Energy Agency; Organisation for Economic Co-operation and Development; Worldwide Patent Statistical Database; and IMF staff calculations.
Note: CCM innovation = patents in climate change mitigating technologies; EPS = environmental policy stringency index.

Over the same period, clean energy innovation (measured by patent applications)[16] doubled in share of total energy innovation; and clean electricity innovation now accounts for half of total electricity innovation in the top five innovating countries (up from 15 percent in 1990). The global share of solar and wind power in electricity generation has also increased substantially, from virtually zero in 2000 to 6 ½ percent in 2020, with much higher shares in some European Union countries. Furthermore, the transition in electricity generation

[16]The analysis focuses on clean innovation in the energy sector, given the sector's important contribution to total emissions and innovation in clean technologies and its direct exposure to most of the environmental policies analyzed. Clean energy innovation is defined here as the number of patent applications in climate change mitigation technologies related to energy generation, transmission, or distribution, as classified by Haščič and Migotto (2015).

is accelerating: whereas the global renewable share was increasing at a pace of ½ percentage point a year by 2010, that number reached 1 percentage point by 2016.

Econometric analysis suggests that the tightening of environmental policies in many countries has played an important role in the changing composition of energy sector innovation and investment toward low-carbon activities (Figure 3.3; Online Annexes 3.1 and 3.2).[17] Specifically, more stringent environmental policies are estimated to have contributed to the following:

- Thirty percent of the increase in global clean energy innovation, equivalent to the effect of a permanent rise in oil prices of $66 a barrel. Higher oil prices explain the rest of the increase up to 2010, though this reversed after 2010. In the electricity sector, environmental policies increased the share of innovation in clean and "gray" electricity technologies (gray innovations reduce the pollution of dirty technologies) at the expense of dirty technologies.[18] Environmental policies contributed to more electricity innovation overall (Figure 3.3, panel 1).

- Fifty-five percent of the increase in the share of renewables in electricity generation. Tighter environmental policies were associated with declines in the share of coal and an ambiguous effect on the share of natural gas—often a complement to renewable energy (Figure 3.3, panel 2). The intermittent nature of renewables requires backup power in the form of batteries or generators that can dispatch electricity to the grid quickly, such as from hydroelectric or natural gas power plants. By and large, environmental policies do not appear to be associated with a discernible negative impact on total electricity generation.

Various policy instruments are found to be effective in spurring both innovation and investment in renewables.

- Both market and nonmarket policies—in particular research and development subsidies, trading programs, emission limits, and feed-in tariffs—were effective in spurring clean innovation. Oil prices

[17]The analyses cover about 30 advanced economies and emerging market economies during 1990–2015. While the specifications differ somewhat, they generally control for constant country-specific factors and global dynamics (through country and year fixed effects), changes in energy prices, oil and gas reserves, and regulatory changes. All annexes are available at www.imf.org/en/Publications/WEO.

[18]Examples of gray technologies include those that allow the use of heat from fuel or waste incineration or fuels from nonfossil sources. See Dechezleprêtre, Martin, and Mohnen (2017) for details on the classification.

Figure 3.3. Effect of Policy Tightening on Electricity Innovation, Electricity Generation, and Employment, by Type of Technology

More stringent environmental policies stimulated innovation in climate-change-mitigating energy technologies and raised the share of renewable electricity generation. They also raised employment in the "green" sectors and lowered it in the "brown" sectors.

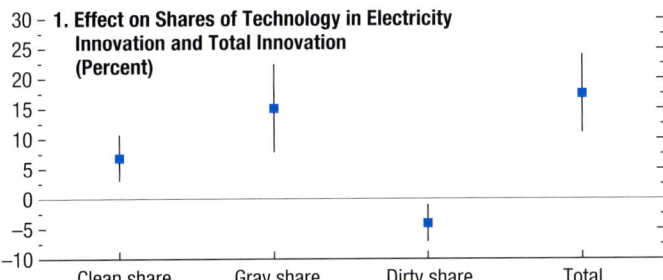

1. Effect on Shares of Technology in Electricity Innovation and Total Innovation
(Percent)

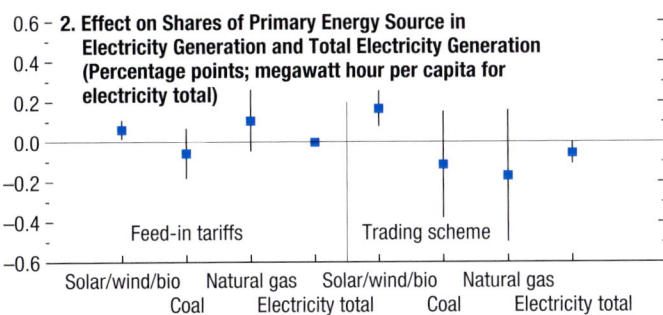

2. Effect on Shares of Primary Energy Source in Electricity Generation and Total Electricity Generation
(Percentage points; megawatt hour per capita for electricity total)

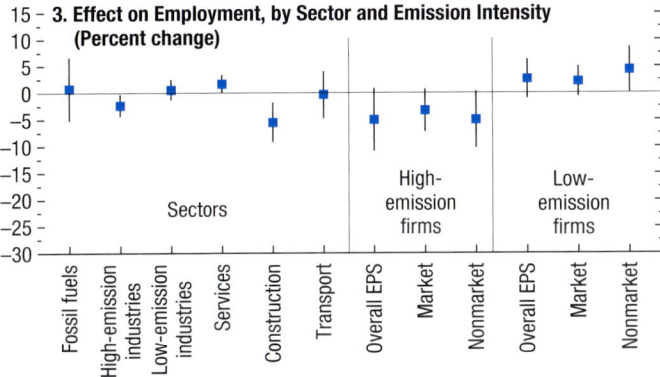

3. Effect on Employment, by Sector and Emission Intensity
(Percent change)

Sources: Dechezleprêtre, Martin, and Mohnen 2017; International Energy Agency; Organisation for Economic Co-operation and Development; Penn World Tables; Worldscope database; Worldwide Patent Statistical Database; and IMF staff calculations.
Note: All panels show point estimate and 90 percent confidence bands. Panel 1 shows the effect of a one-unit tightening in the environmental policy index on innovation in the respective types and total electricity innovation. Panel 2 shows the effect of a one-unit tightening in the policy indicator on the electricity share of the respective primary energy sources and on total electricity generation per capita. Panel 3 shows the effect of tightening policies by one standard deviation on employment. The six bars on the left show the impact of tightening market-based policies on employment among firms in select sectors. The six bars on the right show the impact of tightening aggregate, market-based, and non-market-based policies, respectively, on employment in firms with high (low) CO_2 emissions intensity (based on a smaller sample of firms that report CO_2 emissions). EPS = environmental policy stringency.

were also found to be important determinants of clean energy innovation.[19] Whereas both the tightening in environmental policies and rising oil prices contributed to boosting clean energy innovation up to 2010, the expansion of clean innovation has stalled since then. This has coincided with the partial reversal of regulatory tightening and the shale oil and gas boom in the United States, which capped oil price increases.[20] Popp and others (2020) also point to the possible role of an earlier clean-tech bubble and falling returns on clean innovation. Though the estimated effect of higher carbon prices was far from statistically significant—likely reflecting limited take-up of this instrument and limited statistical power—the significant impact of oil prices on clean innovation suggests that policies that increase the cost of dirty energy may be a strong incentive for clean innovation.

- Instruments that seem to have a clear positive impact on investment in renewable electricity generation are feed-in tariffs and trading programs (which include green certificates to achieve renewable portfolio standards and carbon emission trading programs).[21] Green certificate programs are being phased out in several countries, and carbon tax and carbon trading programs are expected to become more important. As the share of renewables in electricity generation increases, addressing their intermittency will become increasingly relevant, likely requiring significant public investment in grids and innovation (such as storage technologies).

Finally, the analysis examined the impact of tighter environmental policies on employment in high- and low-carbon sectors (see Online Annex 3.3). A concern with decarbonization policies is that they will lead to job losses in carbon-intensive activities, such as coal mining, shale oil and gas production, carbon-intensive

---

[19]The estimation of the effect of oil prices relies on a separate regression, with identical controls but without year fixed effects.
[20]Acemoglu and others (2019) discusses how the shale gas revolution has set back clean innovation.
[21]Under feed-in tariffs, producers of renewable electricity are offered long-term contracts that guarantee a fixed price for every unit of electricity delivered to the grid. Green certificates are a means to implement government-mandated renewable portfolio standards, measured as the percentage of electricity that utilities need to source from renewables.

manufacturing, or transportation.[22] But the net effect of decarbonization policies on jobs also depends on how many new jobs are created in low-carbon activities, in the energy sector (such as solar and wind power generation), and in the economy more broadly. Production in renewable energy is more job intensive than electricity generation based on fossil fuels (see below).[23] But the substitution may not be full (given that mitigation policies curb emissions in part through reduced energy demand and intensity), and the net effect can be insignificant or negative. Evidence from firms suggests that job losses in some high-emission sectors (for example, high-emission manufacturing, transportation) in response to tighter environmental policies can be offset by job creation in some low-emission sectors (for example, low-emission manufacturing and services).[24] The net effect on aggregate jobs is typically small and indeterminate, depending on the extent of substitution between high- and low-emission activities (Figure 3.3, panel 3).[25] In general, the job effects seem larger and net negative in response to changes in nonmarket policies, whereas market policies, such as feed-in tariffs and trading programs, have a more muted and net positive effect. The impact on fossil fuel industry employment is not significant and reflects the opposing effects of tax-based policies (negative) and trading-based policies (positive). All in all, the evidence indicates that environmental policies have succeeded in reallocating jobs from high- to low-carbon sectors. However, job transitions can involve costs for the workers affected, and it will be important to examine distributional consequences arising from the labor market effects of climate policies (see the "How to Build Inclusion" section).

---

[22]The literature suggests that tighter climate change mitigation policies, such as carbon taxation, have led to job losses among the low-skilled and workers in high-emission industries, though effects on overall employment are less clear. See Kahn (1997) and Yamazaki (2017) for employment effects across different sectors, Yip (2018) and Marin and Vona (2019) for effects across skill types, and Metcalf and Stock (2020) for aggregate employment effects. Notably, Yamazaki (2017) shows that a revenue-neutral carbon tax can have a small positive and significant employment effect.

[23]Renewables production and installation tends to be more labor intensive than fossil fuel technologies, as capacity investments in renewable electricity generation tend to be more modular and come in relatively small increments.

[24]High-emission manufacturing sectors include chemicals, metals and minerals, paper and packaging, and food.

[25]Policy tightening would increase costs for high-emission firms and, depending on elasticity of demand, reduce output (and employment). Conversely, labor demand could increase in sectors/firms where energy is substitutable with labor, for example among services (see Yamazaki 2017).

How to Reach Net Zero Emissions by 2050

This part of the chapter examines the combinations of climate change mitigation policies needed to bring net carbon emissions to zero by 2050 and how they may impact the macroeconomy. General equilibrium model analysis is required to simulate the effects of ambitious mitigation policies, given that these affect the economy through various channels and come with both negative and positive effects on output as some sectors contract and others expand. Their net effects cannot be predicted with certainty and depend on the relative strength of various channels.

Mechanisms

At a broad level, mitigation policies affect carbon emissions and the macroeconomy through the difference between the prices of fossil fuel and clean energy and the overall energy price.

Relative Price of Fossil Fuel and Low-Carbon Energy

Both carbon pricing and green supply policies increase the price of fossil fuel energy relative to low-carbon energy by raising the price of carbon and/or lowering the price of renewables and other low-carbon energy. The increase in the price of fossil fuel energy relative to clean energy raises demand for renewable energy and, more generally, activities with low carbon intensity and hence leads to a reallocation of investment, innovation, and employment in that direction. The net effect on economic activity will depend on the relative speed at which high-carbon sectors contract and low-carbon sectors can be scaled up (costs of adjusting capital can hinder a rapid scaling up). The net effect on investment and employment also depends on the relative capital- and labor intensity of the sectors. High-carbon sectors (such as fossil fuel energy and heavy manufacturing) are typically more capital intensive, whereas low-carbon sectors (such as renewable energy and many services) are more labor intensive. All else equal, the net effect of the reallocation of activity from high- to low-carbon sectors could therefore be more positive (less negative) for employment than investment. Finally, widening differences between the price of fossil fuel energy and clean energy can lead to wealth effects and stranded assets. Carbon-intensive activities have large footprints on financial portfolios in advanced economies and the net worth of fuel exporters. In an aggressive decarbonization scenario, early obsolescence of carbon-intensive capital would lead to wealth losses and drag down aggregate demand in some economies. At the same time, countries with comparative advantage in renewable energy and low-carbon technologies could experience positive wealth effects.

Overall Energy Price

Carbon pricing and green supply policies affect the overall energy price differently. While a carbon tax increases the overall energy price and can hurt economic activity, it also encourages energy efficiency and discourages energy usage. That said, revenues from carbon pricing could be used to offset these costs, for instance by directly incentivizing the supply of clean energy or financing green public infrastructure that helps reduce the energy intensity of economic activity or raises the efficiency of renewable power.[26] Revenues can also be used to provide transfers to households to avoid hurting the poor and increase political acceptability (October 2019 *Fiscal Monitor*). In contrast, green supply policies lower the overall price of energy and could potentially boost GDP, depending on how the policy support is financed (taxes versus borrowing). But green supply policies do not incentivize energy efficiency and can be accompanied by greater energy consumption, including of carbon-intensive sources (given the intermittency of renewable power). These differences explain both the greater efficacy of carbon taxes at reducing emissions and their greater output cost.[27] When combined, green supply policies and carbon pricing can, in principle, prompt declines in emissions consistent with substantial climate change mitigation, without major shrinkage of output and consumption during the transition.

In addition to providing price signals through carbon pricing and green supply policies, governments can directly stimulate green technologies by providing incentives for research. Innovation is driven by market size; as such, higher carbon prices (which expand markets for low-carbon activities and shrink those for carbon-intensive ones) would incentivize a shift toward greener research and development, lowering the prices of green technologies over time and

amplifying decarbonization. Importantly, the presence of this amplifying mechanism would mean that a given decline in emissions could be delivered with lower carbon prices. The use of green research and development subsidies alongside carbon taxes is justified on economic grounds to resolve multiple market failures (for example, Acemoglu and others 2012, 2016; Stiglitz and others 2014). These may include knowledge spillovers from innovation that are not taken into account by private firms; path dependency of research, which gives the established technologies an advantage and creates entry barriers (through economies of scale, sunk costs, and network effects); and difficulty accessing financing due to high uncertainty/risk, a long lag until innovation pays off, and lack of knowledge and information among investors. As with other green supply policies, green research and development subsidies would lower the energy price overall, boosting output but also partly offsetting the reduction in emissions through higher energy consumption. Historically, government research programs have had key roles in the development of large technological breakthroughs (for example, landing on the moon, or the prototype of the internet). More active government involvement—including through international cooperation—may be needed to assist in the development of technologies that can support the low-carbon transition.

A Comprehensive Mitigation Package

The goal of bringing net carbon emissions to zero by 2050 in each country can be achieved through a comprehensive policy package that is growth friendly (especially in the short term) and involves compensatory transfers to households to ensure inclusion. The 2050 objective is operationalized as a reduction in gross emissions by 80 percent, assuming that the expansion of natural emission sinks (such as forests) and some deployment of negative emission technologies (for example, carbon capture and storage technologies) will help absorb the remaining carbon emissions (IPCC 2018a, b). To implement such deep reductions in emissions at the global level, each country/region needs to reduce its own emissions by 80 percent, and there is little room for differentiation of mitigation efforts across countries. However, one exception is made for the group of selected oil-exporting and other economies, which are assumed to keep emissions at current levels because economic activity shrinks substantially due to

---

[26]Another option for recycling revenue from carbon taxes is to cut distortionary taxes on labor and capital (for example, Goulder 1995 and Goulder and Parry 2008).

[27]Carbon taxes are a very effective way of reducing emissions also because they automatically impose the highest penalties on the most-polluting fuels.

the fall in global oil demand. The policy package is designed with macroeconomic policy goals and political feasibility in mind and includes (1) a green fiscal stimulus that boosts demand and supply in the economy, supporting the recovery from the COVID-19 crisis, and helps reduce the level of carbon prices required to reach the emission target; (2) gradually phased-in carbon price increases; and (3) compensatory transfers to households. Specifically, it includes the following:

- *Green supply policies*: These consist of an 80 percent subsidy rate on renewables production and a 10-year green public investment program (starting at 1 percent of GDP and linearly declining to zero over 10 years; after that, additional public investment maintains the green capital stock created). Public investment is assumed to take place in the renewable and other low-carbon energy sectors, transport infrastructure, and services—the latter to capture the higher energy efficiency of buildings (see Online Annex 3.4 for more details).[28]

- *Carbon pricing*: Carbon prices are calibrated to achieve the 80 percent reduction in emissions by 2050, after accounting for emission reductions from the green fiscal stimulus. A high annual growth rate of carbon prices (7 percent) is assumed to ensure low initial levels of the carbon price and a gradual phase-in of carbon prices.[29] The needed carbon prices start at between $6 and $20 a ton of CO_2 (depending on the country), reach between $10 and $40 a ton of CO_2 in 2030, and are between $40 and $150 a ton of CO_2 in 2050.[30,31]

- *Compensatory transfers*: Households receive compensation equal to one-fourth of carbon tax revenues, which should protect the purchasing power of poor households through targeted cash transfers (see the "How to Build Inclusion" section).

- *Supportive macroeconomic policies*: The policy package outlined above implies a fiscal easing that requires debt financing for the first decade and occurs amid low-for-long interest rates, given the current context of low inflation.

Model Simulations

Policy simulations are run using the G-Cubed global macroeconomic model (McKibbin and Wilcoxen 1999, 2013; Liu and others 2020; see Online Annex 3.4). The model features 10 countries/regions, detailed energy sectors, forward-looking agents, real and nominal rigidities, and fiscal and monetary policies. It is suited to examining the effect of mitigation policies on carbon emissions related to the burning of fossil fuels and on the macroeconomic dynamics in the short, medium, and long term. The long-term dynamics of temperatures and estimates of the avoided damages from climate change are simulated using the integrated assessment model of Hassler and others (2020) and different climate change damage functions. The goal of the simulations presented in the chapter is to illustrate the main mechanisms at work and provide some order of quantification. The exact magnitudes in these long-term projections are unavoidably subject to substantial uncertainty.

In the absence of new climate change mitigation policies, global carbon emissions are projected to continue to rise at an average annual pace of 1.7 percent and reach 57.5 gigatons by 2050 (Figure 3.4).[32] Improvements in energy efficiency and some penetration of renewables—reflecting a continuation of current policies and some autonomous increases (for example, reflecting consumer preferences)—cannot offset the forces of population and economic growth that are driving emissions. Whereas advanced economies have historically contributed the lion's share of emissions, China and India, as large and fast-growing emerging market economies, are significant emitters and are expected to continue to account for growing shares of carbon emissions. Their per capita emissions, however,

---

[28]IEA (2020a) discusses green investment opportunities in the energy and transportation sectors and in energy efficiency (for example, retrofitting of buildings). See also McCollum and others (2018) for an estimate of energy investment needs for fulfilling the Paris Agreement and achieving the United Nations Sustainable Development Goals.

[29]Gollier (2018a, b) finds that, contrary to the Hotelling rule (according to which greatest efficiency is achieved when the carbon tax grows at a rate equal to the interest rate), most scenarios from the Intergovernmental Panel on Climate Change involve a rate of growth in the carbon tax higher than the interest rate, to reflect political constraints on the initial level of carbon taxes.

[30]The range of estimates of carbon prices needed to reach a certain level of emission reduction is large (see, for instance, IPCC 2014, Figure 6.21.a, or Stiglitz and others 2014). The relatively low levels of carbon prices in this chapter's simulations reflect (1) the combination of carbon prices with other instruments (green infrastructure investment and green subsidies), which achieve part of the emission reduction; (2) the high assumed growth rate of carbon prices, which back-loads their increases; and (3) the fact that the G-Cubed model embeds more substitutability between high- and low-carbon energy (based on econometric evidence) than engineering-based models.

[31]The real price of carbon continues to grow until 2080.

[32]Black and Parry (2020) finds that the required emission reductions for meeting temperature stabilization goals are essentially unchanged by the current economic crisis. But the COVID-19 crisis could lead to long-term behavioral changes that would raise or lower emissions—such as reduced use of public transportation and greater reliance on individual vehicles or greater use of digital communication, leading to reduced commuting and less travel. The baseline assumes (somewhat above) trend increases in energy efficiency.

Figure 3.4. G-Cubed Model Simulations, Baseline

Under unchanged policies, global carbon emissions would keep rising due to economic and population growth. Continued declines in energy intensity would not be sufficient to offset these forces.

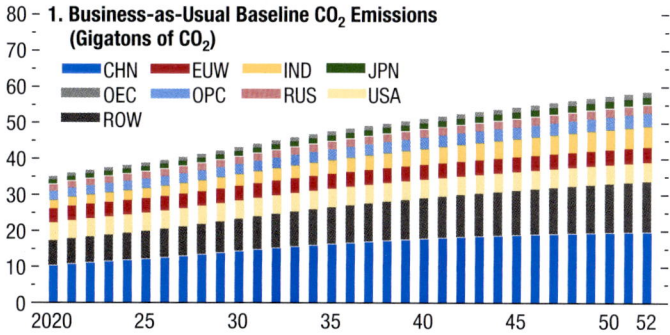

1. Business-as-Usual Baseline CO_2 Emissions (Gigatons of CO_2)

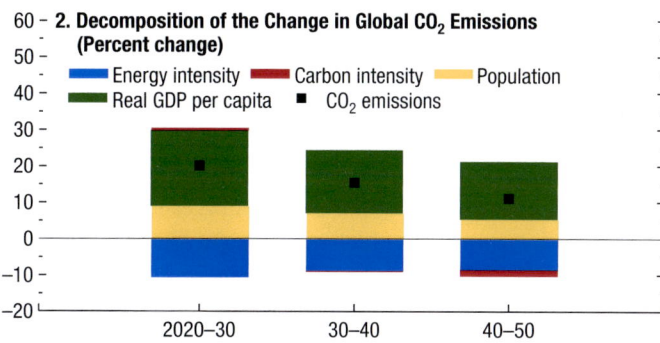

2. Decomposition of the Change in Global CO_2 Emissions (Percent change)

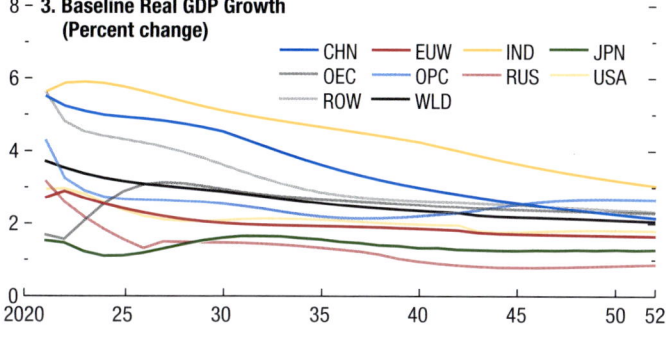

3. Baseline Real GDP Growth (Percent change)

Source: IMF staff estimates.
Note: The baseline simulations are run using the G-Cubed global macroeconomic model of McKibbin and Wilcoxen (1999, 2013) and Liu and others (2020). See Online Annex 3.4 for a description of the baseline assumptions. EUW = EU, Norway, Switzerland, United Kingdom; OEC = Australia, Canada, Iceland, Liechtenstein, and New Zealand; OPC = selected oil-exporting countries and other economies; ROW = rest of the world; WLD = world. Data labels use International Organization for Standardization (ISO) country codes.

Figure 3.5. Global Temperature and CO_2 Emissions

The policy package, combined with some deployment of carbon capture and storage, brings carbon emissions to net zero by mid-century and helps keep temperature increases to 2°C in the long term.

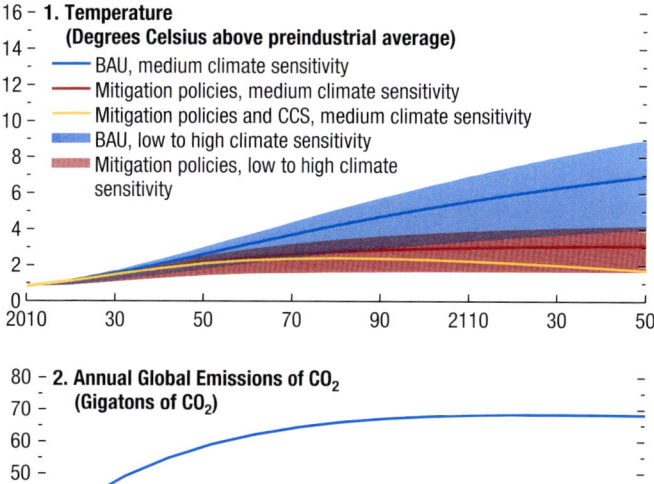

1. Temperature (Degrees Celsius above preindustrial average)

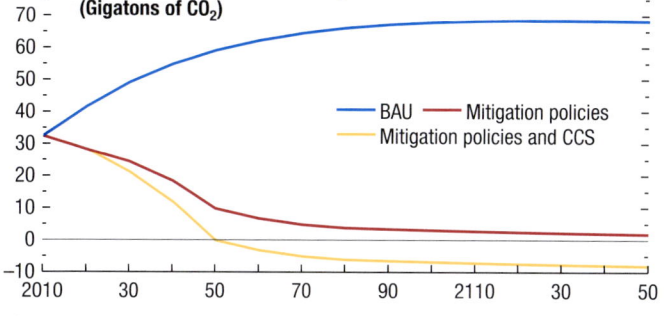

2. Annual Global Emissions of CO_2 (Gigatons of CO_2)

Source: IMF staff estimates.
Note: The calculations use an integrated assessment model with exogenous technical change. Panel 1 shows global average temperature under three policy scenarios: business-as-usual, a mitigation policy package, and a mitigation policy package plus carbon capture and storage (CCS). Solid lines assume a climate sensitivity (the long-term increase in temperature caused by a long-term doubling of the atmospheric carbon stock) of 3; the shaded areas are a range from 1.5 to 4.5 (see Heal 2017; Hassler, Krusell, and Olovsson 2018). BAU = business-as-usual.

still remain relatively small when compared with those of advanced economies. Global growth is assumed to progressively decline from 3.7 percent in 2021 to 2.1 percent in 2050, reflecting a tapering off of growth in emerging market economies as they catch up toward the income levels of advanced economies. Projections

of economic growth over the next 30 years determine the expected growth of future emissions and therefore the scale of effort needed to keep temperature increases to 1.5–2°C. However, most existing scenarios (IPCC 2014, 2018a) indicate that, under unchanged policies, carbon emissions will continue growing strongly, leading to temperature increases well above the safe levels agreed to in the Paris Agreement and raising the risk of catastrophic damage for the planet.

As the simulations show, however, an initial green investment push combined with steadily rising carbon prices would deliver the needed emission reductions at reasonable output effects.

Under the policy package, global carbon emissions are reduced by about 75 percent from current levels, reaching about 9 gigatons by mid-century (Figure 3.5). This brings net emissions to zero around mid-century and to negative levels thereafter with the deployment of carbon capture and storage. Over the long term, temperature increases are kept down to 2°C after some modest initial overshooting. Thus, the policy package allows avoiding much of the severe damage from climate change and especially the risk of catastrophic outcomes, putting the global economy on a higher and sustainable income path from the second half of the century (see below).

A closer look over the next 30 years shows that the costs of the transition are moderate and that both a green fiscal stimulus and carbon pricing play key roles (Figure 3.6). The policy package delivers a net positive effect on global growth in the initial years, suggesting that it can support the recovery from the COVID-19 crisis. After 15 years, GDP is lower by up to about 1 percent relative to its baseline level under unchanged policies. The estimated transitional GDP costs in this chapter's simulation are within the range of other studies (1–6 percent of GDP by 2050), albeit on the lower side of estimates—reflecting the support to activity from green infrastructure investment and higher substitutability between high- and low-carbon energy in G-Cubed than in engineering-based models (see Chapter 6 of IPCC 2014). These are moderate output losses in the context of the expected 120 percent cumulative global GDP growth over the next 30 years (Figure 3.6, panels 2 and 3). From mid-century on, the benefits of climate mitigation in the form of avoided damage grow larger, and the policy package boosts GDP and growth substantially above their baseline levels (Figure 3.7).

Closer examination of the effects of different tools employed in the policy package shows their complementary roles:

- *Emission reductions:* While the green fiscal stimulus helps reduce emissions meaningfully, its effect is much smaller than that of carbon pricing. The latter is a powerful tool to generate rapid and substantial emission reductions because it is effective at increasing energy efficiency, while green supply policies lower the overall energy price and boost energy consumption (Figure 3.6, panel 1).

- *Economic costs:* Whereas carbon pricing lowers real GDP by increasing the cost of energy, the green fiscal stimulus boosts it, both directly and indirectly (Figure 3.6, panel 2). First, the green fiscal stimulus directly adds to GDP through higher investment spending. Second, it indirectly reduces the output costs of the transition to a low-carbon economy by lowering future carbon emissions and the level of carbon taxes needed to meet the emission reduction targets. The green stimulus first boosts economic

activity by increasing aggregate demand; thereafter the green infrastructure investment boosts the productivity of the low-carbon sectors, incentivizing more private investment in these sectors and increasing the potential output of the economy. Its effects are large enough to comfortably offset the economic cost of the carbon tax in the initial years. As a result, the policy package raises output in the first 15 years by about 0.7 percent of global GDP each year (on average over that period). After 15 years the drag from the carbon tax is larger, resulting in small net output losses. The net drag of the policy package on global output—of about 0.7 percent, on average, between 2036–50, and slightly more than 1 percent by 2050—appears manageable in the context of an expected cumulative increase in real GDP of 120 percent over the next 30 years. Average annual growth, after being higher in the 2020s thanks to the green fiscal stimulus, is lower by only one-tenth of a percentage point in the 2030s and by less than one-tenth of a percentage point in the 2040s (Figure 3.6, panel 3). Over time, the economy benefits from avoiding damages from climate change—such as lower productivity due to higher temperatures and more frequent natural disasters—meaning that output would be higher relative to what it would have been under unchanged policies. Estimates of damages from climate change vary with the assumed response of temperatures to the accumulated carbon stock and with methodologies used to relate economic damages to temperatures. The more recent studies (for example, Burke, Hsiang, and Miguel 2015) point to much larger damages than previously estimated and are more in line with the substantial risks scientists have warned about.[33] Based on these estimates, the projected net output gains from mitigating climate change increase rapidly after 2050, reaching up to 13 percent of global GDP by 2100 (Figure 3.7). However, even these estimates are likely to understate benefits from mitigating climate change as they imperfectly take account of—or do not incorporate—some of the damages related to temperature increases, such as

---

[33]The large difference between the various measures comes from uncertainty over two aspects of the costs of climate change: first, whether temperature increases affect the level of output (as in Nordhaus 2010) or its growth rate (as in Dell, Jones, and Olken 2012; and Burke, Hsiang, and Miguel 2015); second, whether the relationships observed in historical data between temperature and output can be relied upon in the future (especially when these are nonlinear). Over long forecast horizons, different stances on these two aspects can lead to very big differences in the costs of climate change and the gains from climate mitigation.

Figure 3.6. G-Cubed Model Simulations of Comprehensive Policy Package, Global Results
(Deviation from baseline, unless noted otherwise)

An initial green investment push, combined with steadily rising carbon prices, would deliver the needed emissions reductions at reasonable output effects. The package would initially boost global GDP, supporting the recovery from the COVID-19 crisis, but then weigh on global activity for a period, as the impact of the investment push wanes and carbon prices continue to rise. In the second half of the century, the reduction in emissions would place the global economy on a stronger and more sustainable path.

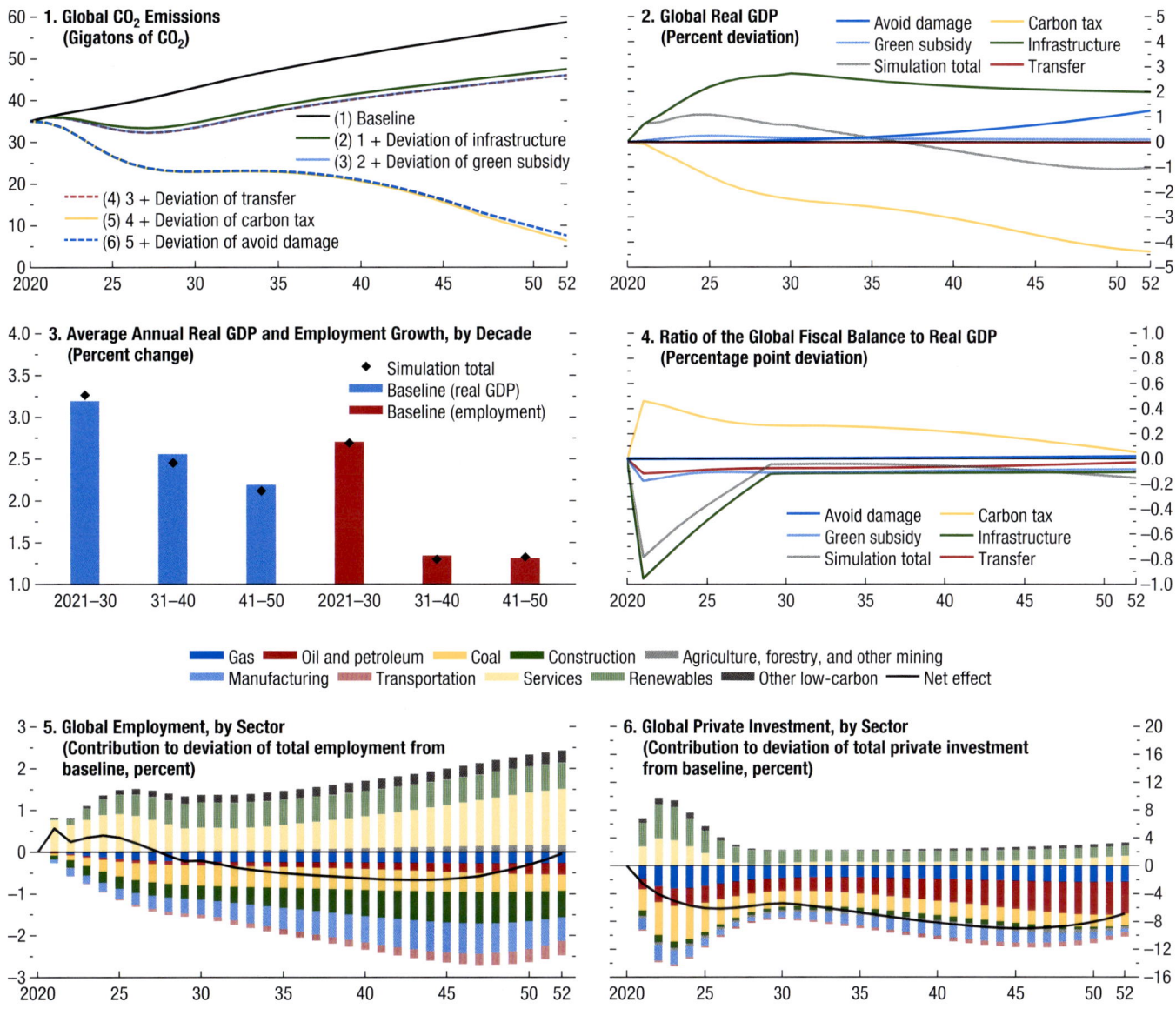

Source: IMF staff estimates.
Note: The simulations are run using the G-Cubed global macroeconomic model of McKibbin and Wilcoxen (1999, 2013) and Liu and others (2020). The climate change mitigation policy package is calibrated to reduce gross emissions by 80 percent in every country/region by 2050 and comprises (1) gradually rising carbon taxes, (2) a green fiscal stimulus consisting of green infrastructure investment and a subsidy for renewables production, and (3) compensatory transfers to households. The figure also shows the effects of avoided damages from climate change resulting from the implementation of the package. See Online Annex 3.4 for more details on the implementation of the simulation.

Figure 3.7. Medium- to Long-Term Output Gains from Climate Change Mitigation
(Percent of baseline GDP)

Climate change mitigation results in substantial output gains in the second half of the century.

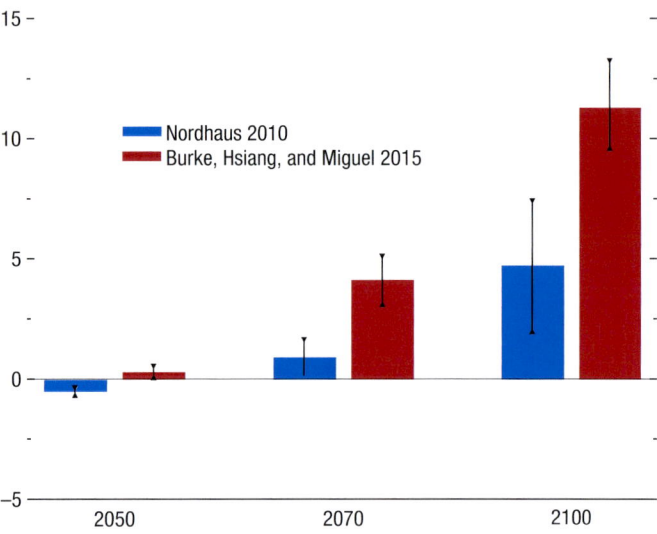

Source: IMF staff estimates.
Note: The figure shows the variation over output gains from climate change mitigation due to uncertainty from two sources: local costs of higher temperatures, from either Nordhaus (2010) or Burke, Hsiang, and Miguel (2015); and climate sensitivity, measured as the increase in long-term temperature with respect to a doubling in CO_2 concentration, with a range of 1.5–4.5 and a midpoint of 3 (see text for discussion).

Figure 3.8. Job Multipliers
(Job-years per gigawatt hour; levelized over lifetime of utility)

Renewable-based electricity generation and energy-efficiency-enhancing investment are more job-intensive than the generation of electricity from fossil fuels.

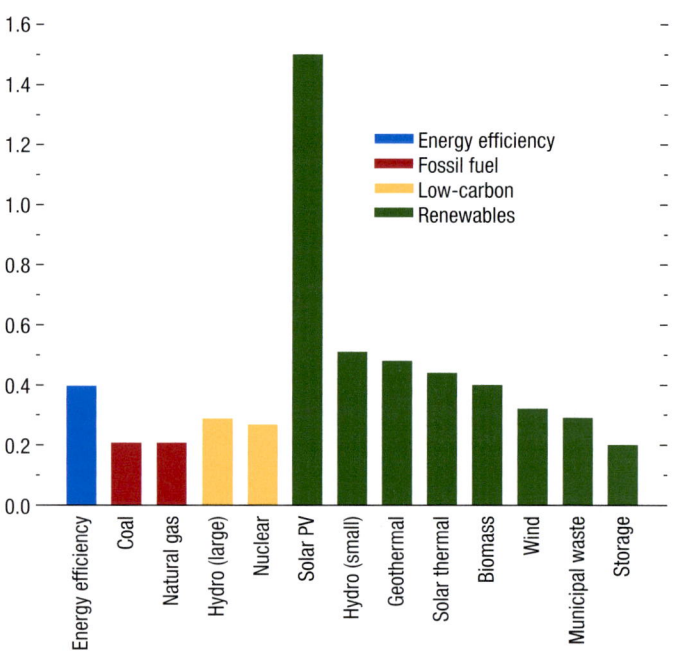

Sources: Wei, Patadia, and Kammen 2010; and IMF staff calculations.
Note: Each bar shows the total number of job-years generated per gigawatt hour of capacity. This includes both direct and indirect jobs, and barring energy efficiency, excludes induced job effects (for example, induced by changing relative prices). The jobs created, both in the initial phase of asset creation and in the subsequent operation and maintenance of new capacities, are averaged (levelized) over a typical lifespan of a utility. PV = photovoltaic.

a higher frequency and severity of natural disasters, a rise in sea levels, and the risk of more catastrophic climate change.

- *Fiscal costs:* On the fiscal front, the policy package initially deteriorates the fiscal balance and requires debt financing, given that the carbon revenues are smaller than the initial spending on infrastructure, subsidies, and compensatory transfers to households. Carbon tax revenues are thereafter broadly sufficient to finance the additional green infrastructure and transfers to poor households (Figure 3.6, panel 4).

The effects of the climate change mitigation policy package on global employment follow largely those on output (Figure 3.6, panel 5). Employment is boosted initially. Global employment would be higher by a total of 12 million people, on average, each year between 2021 and 2027, followed by a small decline relative to the baseline employment path during the transition until the economy reaches a higher output and growth path. Despite the decline relative to baseline, employment

continues to grow strongly throughout the period (Figure 3.6, panel 3). Expanding low-carbon sectors, such as renewable energy, retrofitting of buildings, electric car production, and the services sector, are typically more labor intensive than the shrinking high-carbon sectors (such as fossil fuel energy, transportation, heavy manufacturing)—both in the short and long term—and can create many jobs (Figure 3.8). However, the policy package scenario entails a substantial reallocation of about 2 percent of jobs from high- to low-carbon sectors, which could cause difficult transitions for some workers and require reskilling and government support (see below).

Turning to private investment, the policy package leads to a sharp global contraction because the carbon tax acts as a negative wealth shock and reduces the long-term desired capital stock (Figure 3.6, panel 6). The expanding low-carbon sectors (renewables, services) are also less capital intensive than the contracting sectors (fossil fuel energy, manufacturing), further reducing demand for capital investment. Finally, the renewable energy sector is smaller than the fossil fuel sector and takes time to expand due to capital adjustment costs, although green infrastructure investment and subsidies help incentivize private investment in renewables and other low-carbon energy sectors.[34] Some variation is seen across countries and regions: reductions in private investment are especially large in countries with larger fossil fuel sectors, whereas the policy package elicits more positive responses from private investment where low-carbon energy sectors are already large and the cost of ramping up physical capital relatively low (for example, Europe and Japan; see below). In the current context of depressed private investment and very low interest rates, green support policies could also have a more positive effect on private investment in the near term than modeled here.

To sum up, a mix of carbon pricing and an initial green stimulus would help with economic recovery from the COVID-19 crisis in the near term while putting the global economy on a sustainable growth path at moderate transitional growth costs. The green fiscal easing would help boost growth and employment in the first few years, when the economy is depressed, despite the introduction of the carbon tax. From a macroeconomic and public finance perspective, the next decade is the best time for governments to invest and borrow, given that interest rates for many large emitters are likely to stay low for long, suggesting that an aggressive investment policy would be affordable and desirable. As the recovery takes hold, further increases in carbon taxes would be essential to generate the needed substantial declines in emissions and would imply only moderate growth costs. Over the longer term, the economy would be on a higher growth and output path because substantial damages from climate change would be avoided.

Cross-Country Differences

While the transitional output costs associated with the policy package are relatively moderate in global terms, they are very different across countries (Figure 3.9, panel 1).

Some of the advanced economies may experience smaller economic costs throughout the transition—or

even gain, as does Europe. The more renewables there are already in the economy, the higher the initial capital stocks, so the more they can be ramped up without incurring large adjustment costs.[35] Europe starts with a large renewable sector, implying that the adjustment costs per unit of additional investment are much lower than for other countries.[36] In contrast, the United States and China have a large amount of fossil fuel capital relative to non-fossil-fuel capital, and the investment reductions from these industries offset the investment in renewables, which face larger adjustment costs to ramp up.

Countries with fast economic or population growth (India, especially; China, to a lesser extent) and most oil producers are bound to experience larger economic costs by forgoing cheap forms of energy, such as coal or oil. These output costs nevertheless remain modest relative to baseline growth for most. For example, with the policy package, India's GDP would be 277 percent higher in 2050 than today, only moderately below what it would have been with unchanged policies (287 percent). But more important, these economic costs also need to be weighed against avoided damage from climate change and co-benefits from climate change mitigation.

The countries for which economic costs are larger are also the ones that would enjoy immediate substantial co-benefits from acting to curb carbon emissions (Figure 3.9, panel 2). These are reductions in mortality risks and improved health from less air pollution (thanks to lower use of coal and natural gas) and reduced road congestion, traffic accident risk, and road damage (associated with taxation of gasoline and road diesel). While the value of saving lives goes well beyond economic gains and quantifying the economic value of human life and health is difficult, existing valuations (see, for example, the October 2019 *Fiscal Monitor;* and Parry, Veung, and Heine 2015) indicate that many countries would experience substantial economic gains from co-benefits—on the order of 0.7 percent of GDP immediately and 3.5 percent of GDP by 2050 for China, and 0.3 percent immediately and 1.4 percent by 2050 for India.[37] Combining real GDP

---

[34]In the G-Cubed model, investors are forward looking, and substitutability is high relative to other models (McKibbin and Wilcoxen 1999, 2013; Liu and others 2020).

[35]This is because adjustment costs are quadratic in the rate of investment.

[36]IMF (2020a) examines climate mitigation scenarios for the European Union using the Envisage CGE model. It concludes that a higher carbon price is needed for Europe's climate mitigation objectives and that a subsidy for renewables production would allow the needed carbon price to be reduced. The new European Union recovery fund explicitly aims to address climate change.

[37]Parry, Veung, and Heine (2015) estimates a price on CO_2 that would internalize domestic non-climate-related external costs

Figure 3.9. G-Cubed Model Simulations of Comprehensive Policy Package, Cross-Country Differences

There are large cross-country differences in output effects, with most oil producers and countries with fast economic and population growth bearing larger costs in the medium term. However, these countries also stand to benefit more from avoided damages from climate change and co-benefits.

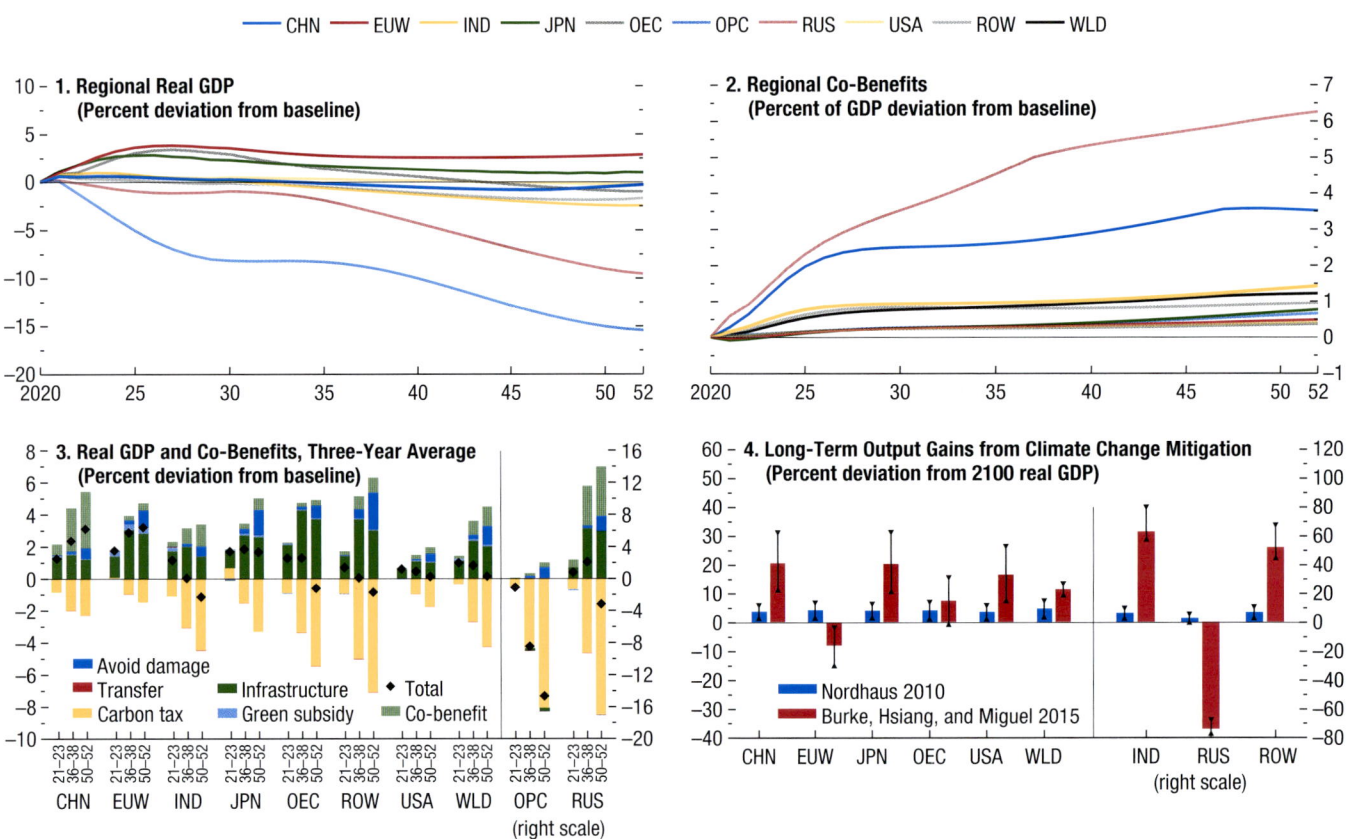

Source: IMF staff estimates.
Note: Panels 1, 2, and 3 are based on simulations run using the G-Cubed global macroeconomic model of McKibbin and Wilcoxen (1999, 2013) and Liu and others (2020). The climate change mitigation policy package is calibrated to reduce gross emissions by 80 percent in every country/region by 2050 and comprises (1) gradually rising carbon taxes, (2) a green fiscal stimulus consisting of green infrastructure investment and a subsidy for renewables production, and (3) compensatory transfers to households. The figure also shows the effects of avoided damages from climate change resulting from the implementation of the package. See Online Annex 3.4 for more details on the simulation. Panel 4 shows the variation over output gains from climate change mitigation by 2100 due to uncertainty from two sources: local costs of higher temperatures, from either Nordhaus (2010) or Burke, Hsiang, and Miguel (2015); and climate sensitivity, measured as the increase in long-term temperature with respect to a doubling in CO_2 concentration, with a range of 1.5–4.5 and a midpoint of 3 (see text for discussion). EUW = European Union, Norway, Switzerland, United Kingdom; OEC = Australia, Canada, Iceland, Liechtenstein, New Zealand; OPC = selected oil-exporting countries and other economies; ROW = rest of the world; WLD = world. Data labels use International Organization for Standardization (ISO) country codes.

associated with fossil fuels around the world. The nationally efficient CO_2 price level is, on average, $57.5 a ton (in 2010)—and ranges between $11 and $85 for the countries/regions in the G-Cubed model. These reflect primarily health co-benefits from reduced air pollution at coal plants and, in some cases, reductions in automobile externalities. The co-benefits differ across countries per unit of abatement and are largest for Russia and China. See Karlsson, Alfredsson, and Westling (2020) for a review of available monetary estimates of air quality co-benefits. Based on quasi-experimental evidence from China, Ebenstein and others (2017) finds that an increase of 10 micrograms a cubic meter in PM10 (particulate matter under 10 micrometers in size) reduces life expectancy by

0.64 year and, consequently, bringing all of China into compliance with its Class I standard for PM10 would save 3.7 billion life-years. In addition to the benefit of reduced mortality, studies also show significant benefits from reduced morbidity (that is, lower health care spending) in response to environmental policies. For example, reducing PM2.5 (particulate matter under 2.5 micrometers in size) concentration in China from the prevailing average to the World Health Organization–recommended level (which is about one-sixth the current average level) would reduce health care spending by $42 billion relative to 2015 spending levels, or about 7 percent of national annual health care spending (see, for example, Barwick and others 2018).

effects and co-benefits yields net benefits throughout the transition for China and smaller transitional costs for India, Russia, and others (Figure 3.9, panel 3).[38]

Without global policy action, damages from climate change increase sharply after 2050. Therefore, all countries would experience substantial benefits from avoided climate damages in the second half of the century under the policy package. The benefits from mitigating climate change are expected to be particularly large for some of the countries with higher transitional costs. India is among those likely to suffer the greatest damage from global warming, reflecting its initially high temperatures. For India, the net gains from climate change mitigation—relative to inaction—would be up to 60–80 percent of GDP by 2100 (Figure 3.9, panel 4). While estimates of losses from climate change are somewhat smaller for colder regions (for example, Europe, North America, and east Asia), these are likely underestimations as they do not include a number of damages (for example, rise in sea levels, natural disasters, damage to infrastructure from thawing of permafrost in Russia) and negative global spillovers from large economic disruptions in other parts of the world.

It is sometimes argued that countries that have contributed the bulk of the stock of global carbon emissions—advanced economies—should shoulder a greater part of the mitigation burden. Advanced economies cannot keep global temperatures to safe levels on their own, as their share in global emissions is set to drop to 23 percent in 2050 from 32 percent of global emissions under unchanged policies. And in a scenario in which only advanced economies enact mitigation policies, the decline in their emissions would be partially offset by an increase in other countries' emissions relative to the baseline. This reflects two types of "leakages": first, lower demand from advanced economies for fossil fuels depresses global fossil fuel prices and so increases their consumption by other countries; and second, some carbon-intensive activities previously carried out in advanced economies are likely to relocate to countries where carbon is not taxed.

In a scenario in which advanced economies are the only ones that reduce their gross carbon emissions by 80 percent by 2050, global emissions still increase to 48 gigatons

[38]Bento, Jacobsen, and Liu (2018) also points out that the costs of implementing a carbon tax are substantially lower with a large informal sector as the carbon tax lowers the relative distortion between the formal and informal sectors—given that even the informal sector must buy energy from the formal sector, these mechanisms can lead to welfare-enhancing expansion of the formal sector.

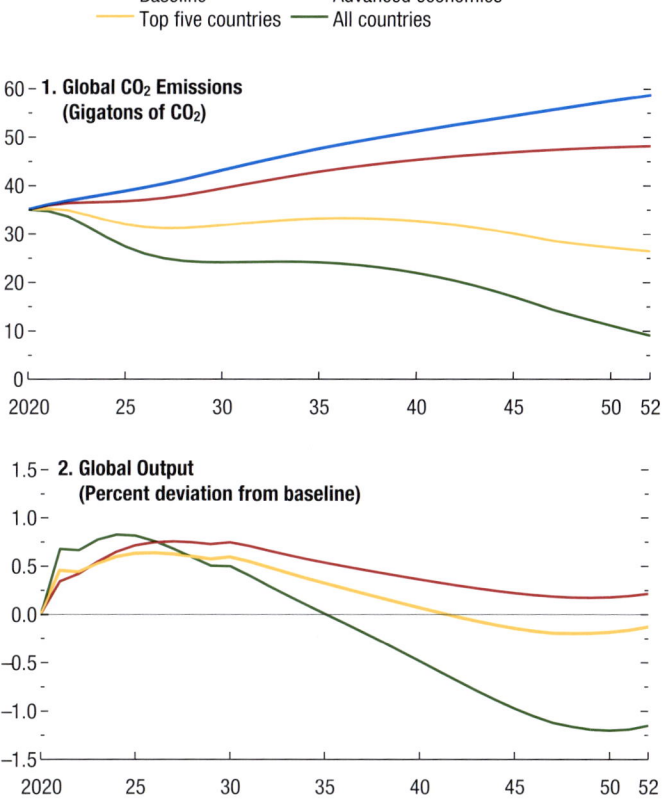

Figure 3.10. G-Cubed Simulations, Partial Participation in Mitigation

Advanced economies mitigating alone cannot keep temperature increases to safe levels. But joint action by the five largest countries (economic region) would make a significant dent in global emissions.

Source: IMF staff estimates.
Note: This figure is based on simulations run using the G-Cubed global macroeconomic model of McKibbin and Wilcoxen (1999, 2013), and Liu and others (2020). The climate change mitigating policy package is calibrated to reduce gross emissions by 80 percent in every country/region except OPEC (the "All countries" scenario) by 2050 and comprises (1) gradually rising carbon taxes, (2) a green fiscal stimulus consisting of green infrastructure investment and a subsidy for renewables production, and (3) compensatory transfers to households. The figure also shows the effects of avoided damages from climate change resulting from the implementation of the package. See Online Annex 3.4 for more details on the simulation. Scenarios "Advanced economies" and "Top five countries" assume that only advanced economies and five countries/regions with the largest GDP (China, European Union, India, Japan, United States) act to mitigate.

by 2050, well above current levels (Figure 3.10). If the United States, Europe, China, Japan, and India—as the five largest countries (economic region)—act together, they can make a significant dent in global emissions over the next three decades. Global emissions would be reduced by about 55 percent from baseline levels and 25 percent from current levels by mid-century, with a very similar effect on each participating country's GDP, as in the scenario of global action. The October 2019

Fiscal Monitor discusses how a carbon price floor among the largest emitters—possibly with a lower price floor or transfers for lower-income countries—would be an effective arrangement to scale up Paris Agreement commitments. It would provide a transparent target based on a common measure and help reassure against potential losses in international competitiveness from higher energy costs.

Fossil fuel exporters are bound to experience the largest economic losses from the transition of the global economy to a low-carbon path (see Mirzoev and others 2020 for a discussion of carbon transition risks in Gulf Cooperation Council countries). Even without a domestic carbon tax, the fall in global demand for fossil fuels would significantly lower these economies' fiscal revenues and economic activity. Moreover, the industrial structure in many fuel exporters is reliant on cheap energy, making the required restructuring and diversification of these economies more difficult and painful. Imposing an export tax (royalty) on oil sales—if this could be agreed upon among oil producers—could maximize the revenue extracted from oil reserves (while demand lasts) and at the same time contribute to the decarbonization of other economies (see the October 2019 *Fiscal Monitor*). Many oil exporters, however, also stand to gain from global climate change mitigation measures. For example, rising temperatures will make oil-exporting countries in the Middle East, where water scarcity is already a growing concern, even hotter. Many oil-exporting countries have recognized the challenges that are being created by the energy transition and are actively seeking to diversify their economies away from the reliance on oil. Policies that seek to strengthen the non-oil sector through better business regulation, greater credit availability, and reforms to the labor market, and increase sources of non-oil revenue for the government, are being implemented.

The Returns to Supporting Technological Innovation

The response of technology ("endogenous technical change") to carbon taxes or research and development subsidies is important in amplifying the effects of carbon pricing and facilitating the low-carbon transition. Given that this mechanism is difficult to integrate into the G-Cubed model, this chapter uses the more stylized representation of Hassler and others (2020) to illustrate the impact of supporting technological innovation (Figure 3.11; see Online Annex 3.5). Assuming a plausible response of technological change to the price of carbon—and combining it with a subsidy (of 70 percent) for green research and development—would allow a similar

Figure 3.11. Role of Green Technological Progress

Policies that contract markets for dirty fuels and expand markets for clean fuels induce a green technological response so that similar emission reductions can be achieved with a lower carbon tax and at a lower cost to output.

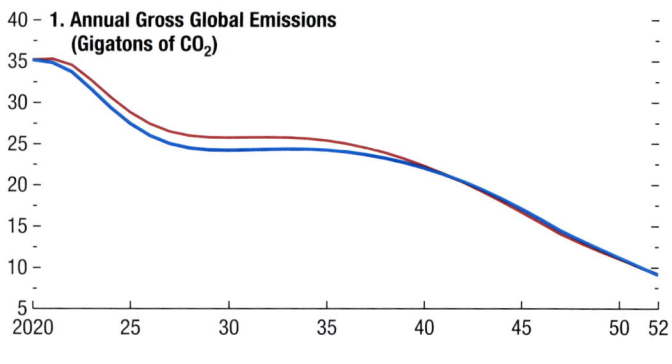

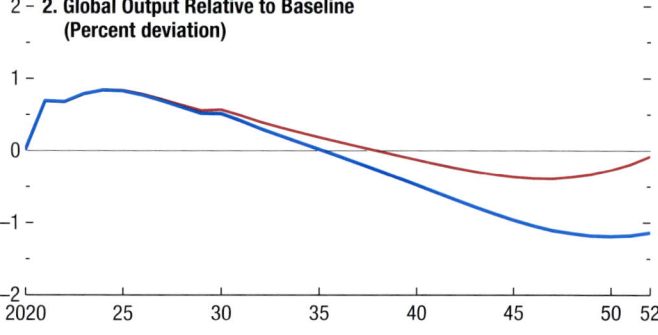

Source: IMF staff estimates.
Note: The panels compare the G-Cubed simulation of the comprehensive policy package with a simulation run using an extension of the Hassler and others (2020) integrated assessment model with endogenous technological change. The second simulation features a lower carbon tax and a green research and development subsidy and includes the endogenous response of technology to policies. See Online Annex 3.5 for more details.

emission target to be achieved with a carbon price path at about half the prices required in the G-Cubed scenario. In the presence of endogenous technical change and research and development subsidies, the transitional costs of mitigation policies are therefore significantly lower, and global GDP rises toward baseline earlier (around the mid-2040s) than in the absence of innovation.

The beneficial impact of this policy is felt mostly in the medium to longer term (after 2030), as the innovation response and the diffusion of new knowledge through the global economy take time to materialize.[39]

[39]The immediate effects of this policy are limited by the modest initial size of the green energy sector.

Figure 3.12. Potential for Emission Reductions in the Electricity Sector

The electricity sector offers substantial scope for emission reductions and better emission-output trade-offs due to the availability of substitute low-carbon technologies.

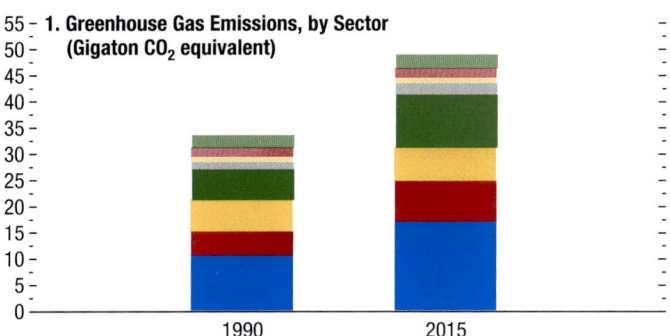

1. Greenhouse Gas Emissions, by Sector (Gigaton CO$_2$ equivalent)

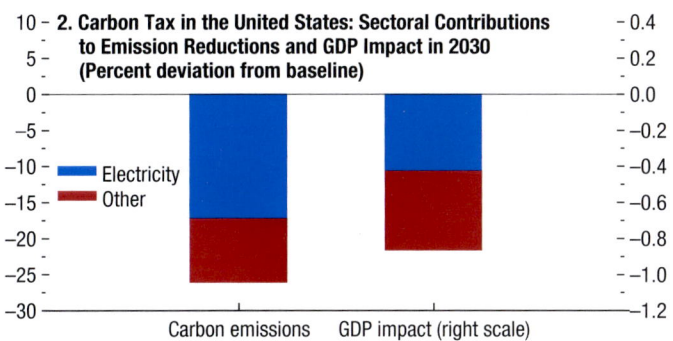

2. Carbon Tax in the United States: Sectoral Contributions to Emission Reductions and GDP Impact in 2030 (Percent deviation from baseline)

Sources: International Energy Agency; and IMF staff estimates.
Note: Panel 2 is based on the carbon tax effect in the G-Cubed simulations of the comprehensive policy package.

Overall, the analysis suggests that a lower carbon price, if combined with early use of green research and development subsidies, may be able to achieve the same lower-emission benefits as a higher tax, at a lower overall transitional cost to output. Research and development subsidies on their own, however, could not generate the quick and substantial reductions in emissions needed to keep temperature increases to safe levels.[40]

A good example of the role of technology in reducing emissions is the electricity sector, which, together with heating, generates roughly 40 percent of total

global carbon emissions (Figure 3.12). Three-quarters of these emissions are from coal-based electricity generation. Raising the share of renewables in the electricity sector is considered the first step toward decarbonization because substitute low-carbon technologies are already available and are economically competitive as a result of a dramatic decline in prices in the past decade—for example, the cost of electricity from wind has declined by 70 percent (Lazard 2019). This makes near-term emission-output trade-offs particularly favorable in this sector, which is also reflected in the G-Cubed simulation, in which about two-thirds of emission reductions in the first 10 years are achieved in electricity generation. Moreover, low-carbon electricity production would generate additional benefits for decarbonization as other end-uses of energy (automobiles, heating, and so on) are electrified. Box 3.2 investigates in more detail how emissions in the electricity sector can be reduced with existing technologies (see also Online Annex 3.6).

How to Build Inclusion

Underlying the moderate macroeconomic effects of mitigation policies discussed in the previous section are differentiated impacts on low- and high-income households and on workers in shrinking versus expanding sectors (such as fossil fuel extraction and manufacturing versus clean-energy and services sectors). For instance, in the absence of compensatory measures, low-income households are more likely than high-income households to be hurt by carbon pricing; in many countries the poor spend a relatively larger share of their income on energy-intensive goods, such as electricity and heating (Figure 3.13, panel 1). Low-income households are also more likely to experience losses in labor income, given that they tend to be employed in low-skill occupations in carbon-intensive sectors (manufacturing, transportation, energy; Figure 3.13, panel 2). Opinion surveys suggest that low-skilled workers are less likely than high-skilled workers to favor protecting the environment over boosting economic growth. Support for protection of the environment is lowest among lower-skilled workers employed in carbon-intensive sectors (Figure 3.14).[41]

The distributional impacts of carbon pricing are likely to vary by country. Carbon pricing is not always regressive, especially in emerging market and

---

[40]See also, for example, Bosetti and others (2011), Newell (2015), and Dechezleprêtre and Popp (2017).

[41]See also IMF (forthcoming).

Figure 3.13. Distribution of Consumption, Employment, and Impact of Carbon Taxes

Households at the bottom quintile of the income distribution spend slightly more on energy than their richer counterparts and they are more likely to be employed in high-energy-intensive sectors. Carbon taxes, when accompanied by transfers to households, can reduce poverty and inequality; when accompanied by government spending on low-energy sectors, they can support job transitions to low-energy-intensive sectors.

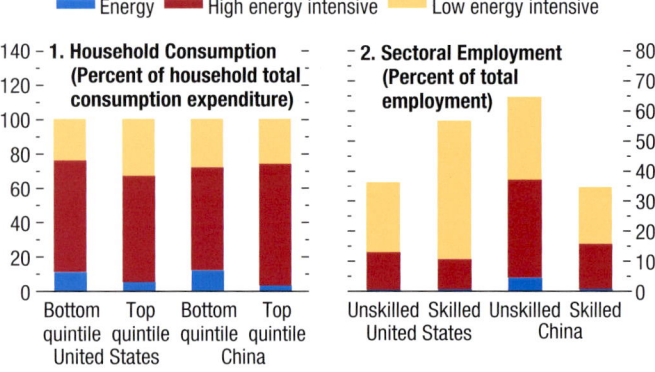

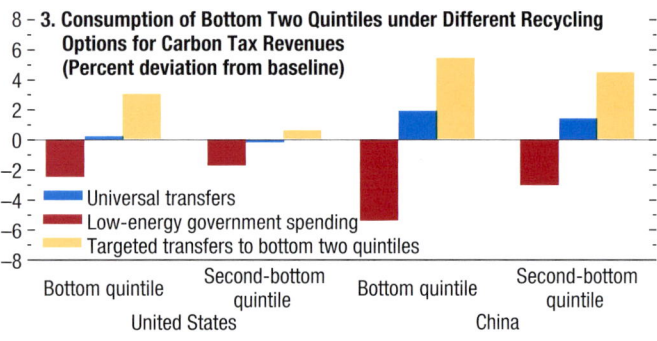

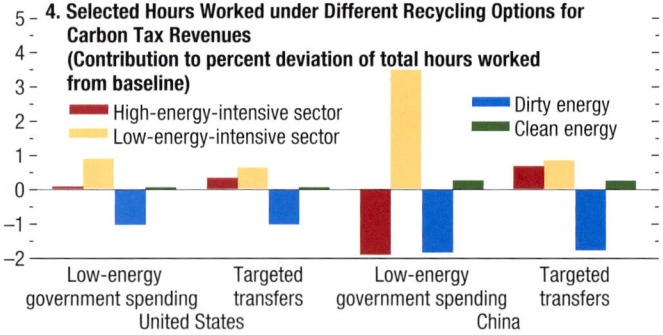

Sources: American Community Survey; China Family Panel Survey; Consumption Expenditure Survey; National Bureau of Statistics of China; and IMF staff calculations.

Note: Panels 1 and 2 are based on survey data. In panel 1, energy goods are electricity, heating, gas, and oil. High-energy-intensive goods are mostly industrial goods and transportation, while low-energy-intensive goods are basically services less transportation. In panel 2, unskilled workers are workers with a high-school education or less, while skilled workers have more than a high-school education. Panels 3 and 4 use a multisector heterogeneous agent model calibrated to generate sectoral output shares to simulate $50 tax per ton of CO_2, where the revenue is used to finance government spending on (1) low-energy-intensive goods, (2) universal cash transfers, and (3) targeted cash transfers to the bottom two quintiles of the income distribution. In panel 3, each bar shows the quintile percentage change in consumption with respect to the baseline. In panel 4, each bar shows the percentage change in workers' hours weighted by sector employment in the baseline with respect to the baseline.

Figure 3.14. Public Opinion in Support of Environmental Protection
(Percent)

Support for the environment tends to be higher among high-skilled individuals, particularly those working in clean industries. Low-skilled individuals working in high-carbon industries, who represent the group most adversely affected by the changes needed for a transition to a green economy, show the lowest levels of support for environmental policies.

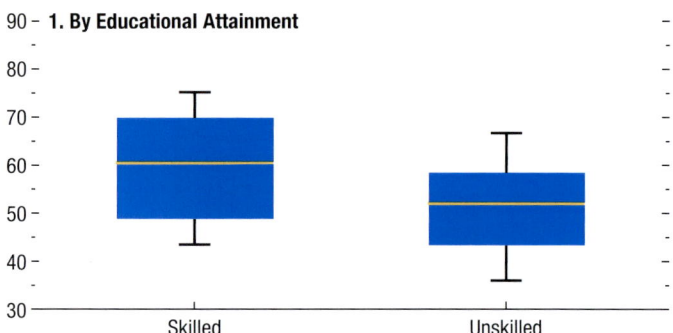

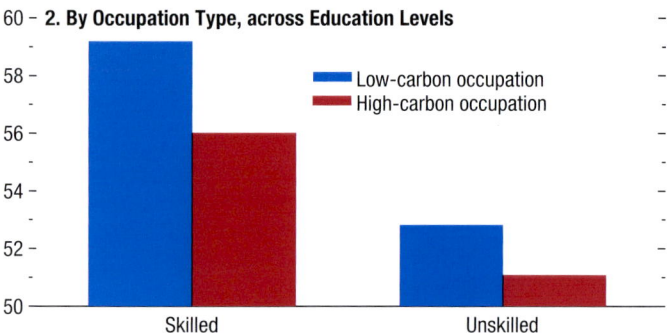

Sources: European Values Study (2017); World Values Survey, wave 7 (2017–20); and IMF staff calculations.

Note: The figure shows the percent of respondents who believe that protecting the environment should be given priority, even if it causes slower economic growth and some loss of jobs. Panel 1 shows the range of values across 77 countries, where the box represents the 25th and 75th percentiles, the whiskers represent the 10th and 90th percentiles, and the horizontal line stands for the median. Educational attainment is used as a proxy for skill level: skilled is post-secondary; unskilled is upper-secondary and below. Panel 2 shows the average across individuals from 47 countries. High-carbon occupations correspond to skilled industry, unskilled, semi-skilled, and farm occupations.

developing economies, where lower access to electricity and ownership of durable goods results in lower direct consumption of energy by poorer households (see the October 2019 *Fiscal Monitor* for additional discussion). Similarly, the distributional impact through the labor income channel can vary across countries. But where carbon pricing is likely to adversely affect vulnerable households and workers, building fairness and inclusion will be crucial to the political acceptability and sustainability of mitigation strategies.

Various policies can limit the adverse effects of higher carbon prices on households. These include fully or partially rebating the carbon pricing revenues through universal or targeted cash transfers—or using some of the revenue to finance higher public spending in low-carbon sectors, which will create jobs and offset employment losses in carbon-intensive sectors. Among the different options for cash transfers, targeted compensation for low-income households is a cost-effective option. Figure 3.13, panel 3, shows the consumption impact of a tax of $50/ton of CO_2 under various revenue recycling options, based on a general equilibrium model with heterogenous agents calibrated to the United States and China that incorporates the carbon tax's impact on consumption and employment (see Online Annex 3.7 and Tavares, forthcoming). Simulations suggest that fully recycling carbon tax revenues in cash transfers targeted to low-income groups (bottom two quintiles) can raise their consumption (see Figure 3.13, panel 3, and Online Annex 3.7 for the impact on the entire consumption distribution). The consumption of households in the lowest quintile could be protected (consumption kept broadly constant) by redistributing about one-quarter and one-sixth of the carbon revenues, respectively, to this group of households in the United States and China. By contrast, it would take, respectively, 55 percent and 40 percent of revenues to protect consumption levels of households in the lowest two quintiles in the United States and China. Fully rebating the carbon revenues through universal transfers would also broadly avert a decline in the consumption of households in the bottom two quintiles, but at a much higher fiscal cost.[42]

While they both protect private consumption, neither universal nor targeted cash transfers help

materially ease job transitions. By contrast, increasing government spending on low-carbon goods and services—similar in spirit to the green supply policies studied in the previous section—would fail to protect the consumption of poorer households but would prevent a decline in aggregate employment and spur further reallocation of workers toward low-carbon sectors (Figure 3.13, panel 4).

In practice, governments seeking to introduce carbon pricing will likely face calls to protect low-income households from higher prices and compensate for job losses in carbon-intensive industries. The simulations here show that carbon pricing can produce enough revenue to spend on both goals if income support is well targeted.

Feebates are an essential complement to other mitigation policies. They are systems of fees and rebates on products or activities with above- or below-average emission intensity, or regulations (such as emission rates or energy efficiency standards) that can be used when carbon pricing is not feasible or cannot be imposed on the necessary scale (October 2019 *Fiscal Monitor*). Feebates can be tailored to specific markets, and their impact on emissions depends on the size and energy intensity of the target market. Feebates are modeled broadly here as consisting of a tax of $50/ton of CO_2 imposed on the dirty energy consumption of firms and households, with the revenue used to finance a subsidy to promote the consumption of clean energy. The only way in which this experiment differs from the previous one is that the revenue is spent on subsidies to promote the consumption of clean energy. The revenue-raising component (carbon tax) is similar.

Simulations show that the effects of the feebates on the consumption of the bottom quintile and inequality are smaller than when carbon taxes are imposed, if no action is taken to mitigate the impact on the distribution (Figure 3.15). The effects are smaller because the impact on energy prices is minimal (taxes and subsidies are levied on different varieties of the same good) and because feebates stimulate employment for low-skilled workers, on net (given that the renewable sector is more labor intensive than the dirty energy sector).

Finally, mitigation policies are likely to affect some communities more than others, adding a geographic dimension to inequality. A just transition is needed also for the most hard-hit communities and regions and may require—beyond reskilling of workers—effective government support for those communities.

---

[42]Iran's 2010 fuel subsidy reform and the introduction of carbon pricing in British Columbia are examples of successful reforms that included compensatory transfers to households (among other measures). See Guillaume, Zytek, and Farzin (2011) and Carl and Fedor (2016).

Figure 3.15. Distributional Impact of Feebates
(Consumption, percent deviation from baseline, and Gini index change)

Feebates can reduce carbon emissions, but they also need to be accompanied by transfers.

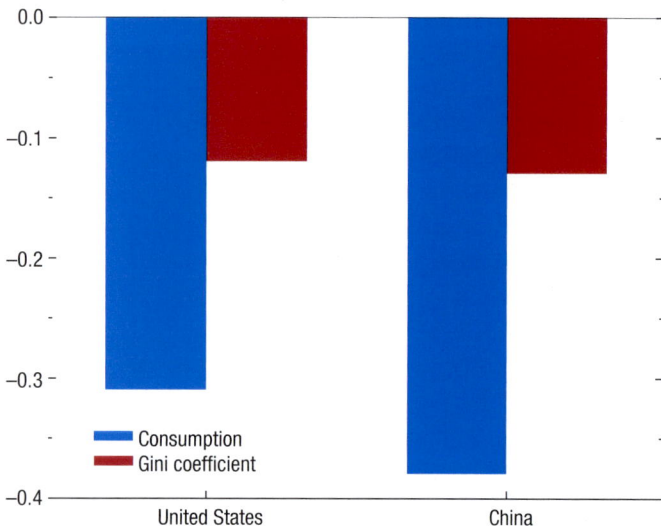

Source: IMF staff calculations.
Note: The figure shows the results of the multisector heterogeneous agent model simulation of a $50 tax per ton of CO_2 levied on dirty energy consumption by households and firms. The revenue is used to finance a subsidy to clean energy. The first bar shows the bottom quintile percentage change in consumption with respect to the baseline, and the second bar shows the change in the Gini coefficient with respect to the baseline. The Gini coefficient is measured on a scale from 0 (perfect equality) to 100 (perfect inequality).

Conclusion

The window for attaining net zero emissions by 2050 and holding temperature increases to safe levels is rapidly closing. The analysis in this chapter suggests that an initial green investment push combined with steadily rising carbon prices would deliver the needed emission reductions at reasonable transitional global output effects. A green fiscal stimulus would strengthen the macroeconomy in the short term and help lower the costs of adjusting to higher carbon prices. Carbon pricing is critical to mitigation because higher carbon prices incentivize energy efficiency in addition to real-locating resources from high- to low-carbon activities. The transitional costs of carbon pricing consistent with net zero emissions by mid-century would be manageable in the context of the projected growth of the global economy over the next three decades and could be reduced further as technological innovations develop in response to carbon pricing and green research and development subsidies. In the medium term, such a strategy would place the global economy on a stronger and more sustainable growth path by avoiding serious damages from climate change and the risk of catastrophic outcomes.

Keeping global temperatures to safe levels requires a global effort. Advanced economies cannot successfully mitigate climate change by themselves, as they account for a declining share of global emissions. But the five largest countries/economic union—the United States, China, the European Union, Japan, and India—acting jointly can make a significant dent in global emissions. While the economic costs of mitigation vary across countries, all stand to gain greatly from avoided damages from climate change and co-benefits from mitigation, such as reduced pollution and mortality. Building sustainably now, rather than having to rebuild infrastructure later, would lower the transitional costs of mitigation. For fossil fuel exporters, smoothing the transition will require accelerating the diversification of their economies. This chapter set out to examine the macroeconomic impacts of climate change mitigation policies. Another important issue is international coordination, which could offer scope for different burden sharing of mitigation costs. International policy coordination on climate change deserves further study—given how elusive it has been for countries to come together and take meaningful action to reduce emissions (see, for example, Barrett 2005, 2013, 2016; Lessmann and others 2015; Nordhaus 2015). Analysis on how to achieve such cooperation is, however, outside the scope of this chapter.

Last but not least, decarbonization involves a structural transformation of economies, with unequal impacts across population subgroups. To build inclusion and ensure the broadest possible support for mitigation policies, governments can use part of their carbon tax revenues to support job transitions and provide targeted cash transfers to protect poorer households against losses in purchasing power. Place-based policies to compensate areas or regions likely to experience more labor shedding due to a retrenchment in high-carbon sectors may also be needed.

Box 3.1. Glossary

Avoided damages. The value of avoided climate-change-induced events, such as crop loss, rises in sea level, and extreme weather.

Carbon dioxide (CO_2). The main greenhouse gas, produced from burning fossil fuels, manufacturing cement, and forestry practices. CO_2 emissions remain in the atmosphere for an average of 100 years.

Carbon tax. A tax imposed on CO_2 emissions released largely through the combustion of carbon-based fossil fuels. Administratively, implementation is easiest by taxing the supply of fossil fuels—coal, oil, and natural gas—in proportion to their carbon content.

Clean energy innovation. The number of patent applications in climate change mitigation technologies related to energy generation, transmission, and distribution.

Co-benefits. Reductions in mortality risks and improved health from less air pollution (as a result of lower use of coal and natural gas) and reduced road congestion, traffic accident risk, and road damage.

Distribution-friendly policy. A policy that attempts to mitigate the policy's negative effects on low-income groups' consumption (or some other measure of household well-being).

Economies of scale. Cost advantages for businesses as a result of their scale of operation, with unit costs of output decreasing with increasing scale.

Emission trading system. A market-based policy to reduce emissions (sometimes referred to as "cap and trade"). Covered sources are required to hold allowances for each ton of their emissions or (in an upstream program) the embodied emission content in fuels. The total quantity of allowances is fixed, and market trading of allowances establishes a market price for emissions. Auctioning the allowances is a valuable source of government revenue.

Externality. A cost imposed by the actions of individuals or firms on other individuals or firms (possibly in the future, as in the case of climate change) that the former does not take into account.

Feebate. A sliding scale of fees on firms with emission rates (for example, CO_2 per kilowatt-hour) above a "pivot point" level and corresponding subsidies for firms with emission rates below the pivot point. Alternatively, a feebate can be applied to energy consumption rates (for example, gasoline per mile driven) rather than emission rates. Feebates can exploit many (but not all) of the mitigation opportunities promoted by carbon taxes but without a large increase in energy prices.

Feed-in tariffs. Long-term contracts that guarantee producers of renewable electricity a fixed price for every unit of electricity delivered to the grid.

Gray technologies. Technologies that tend to improve the pollution effect of "dirty" technologies. Examples include technologies that use the heat from fuel or waste incineration or fuels from nonfossil sources.

Green supply policies. Policies aimed at boosting the supply of renewable energy and energy efficiency, including subsidies and investment programs.

Green/white certificates. Titles, respectively, for reaching renewable energy/energy saving targets.

Greenhouse gas. A gas in the atmosphere that allows incoming solar radiation to pass through but traps and absorbs heat radiated from Earth. CO_2 is easily the most predominant greenhouse gas.

High-carbon activities. Activities that either involve generation of carbon-based energy or emit relatively high amounts of CO_2.

Nationally Determined Contribution (NDC). Climate strategies, including mitigation commitments, submitted by 190 parties to the Paris Agreement. Countries are required to report progress on implementing NDCs every two years and (from 2020 onward) to submit revised NDCs (which are expected to contain progressively more stringent mitigation pledges) every five years.

Paris Agreement. An international accord (ratified in 2016) on climate mitigation, adaptation, and financing. The agreement's central objective is to contain global average temperature increases to 1.5–2°C above preindustrial levels.

Renewable energy. Typically includes energy generated from solar photovoltaic, solar thermal, wind, geothermal, biomass, and hydroelectric sources. Hydroelectric is often subdivided into "large" and "small" because of the major environmental impact of the former.

Research and development. Innovative activities by corporations and governments with the goal of developing new products and technologies.

Revenue recycling. Use of (carbon) tax revenues for purposes such as lowering other taxes on households and firms or funding public investment.

Box 3.2. Zooming In on the Electricity Sector: The First Step toward Decarbonization

This box investigates in more detail how emissions in the electricity sector—which, together with heating, accounts for roughly 40 percent of global emissions—can be reduced with existing technologies. To this end, the analysis modifies the Global Integrated Monetary and Fiscal model (Laxton and others 2010) to include an electricity sector where power is generated from coal, natural gas, renewables or by nuclear or hydro-electric processes. The constraints that intermittency of renewables (the undesired output variation from the varying availability of sun and wind) pose for their market penetration are captured by pairing renewable electricity generation with a flexible backup capacity that covers output shortfalls (see Online Annex 3.6; all annexes are available at www.imf.org/en/Publications/WEO). Studying the same illustrative $50 carbon price in the United States, Europe, and China allows for highlighting how a country's current electricity mix and economic structure affect the impact of introducing a carbon price.

Simulations for the United States show that even a moderate policy of gradually introducing a $50 carbon price over 10 years in the electricity sector, flanked by a front-loaded subsidy for investment in renewables, would unlock substantial decarbonization of the electricity sector at very small output costs (Figure 3.2.1, panels 1–3). The policy mix is budget neutral when the carbon price is fully in place after 10 years, and its revenues (roughly 0.2 percent of GDP) are enough to finance the subsidy. However, before revenues fully emerge, the subsidy is financed through debt, leading to a total increase in the debt-to-output ratio of roughly 1 percent of GDP. The carbon price discriminates according to the carbon intensity of the different technologies, thereby disadvantaging electricity production using coal (and to a lesser extent gas). Accentuated by a decline in renewable prices due to the subsidy, the change in relative prices leads to a rebalancing of the electricity mix away from coal toward renewables technologies, and electricity sector emissions decline by 35 percent relative to baseline by 2030 as a result. The decline of gas is dampened by its role as a backup capacity for renewable electricity.

While investment and employment decline in the coal sector, the subsidy triggers a surge in investment in renewables, offsetting a large portion of

The authors of this box are Benjamin Carton and Simon Voigts.

Figure 3.2.1. Decarbonization of the Electricity Sector

Legend: United States, China, European Union, $50 carbon tax only, $50 carbon tax with policy package

1. Share in Electricity Generation (Percent)

2. Carbon Emissions from the Electricity Sector (Percent deviation from baseline)

3. Real GDP (Percent deviation from baseline)

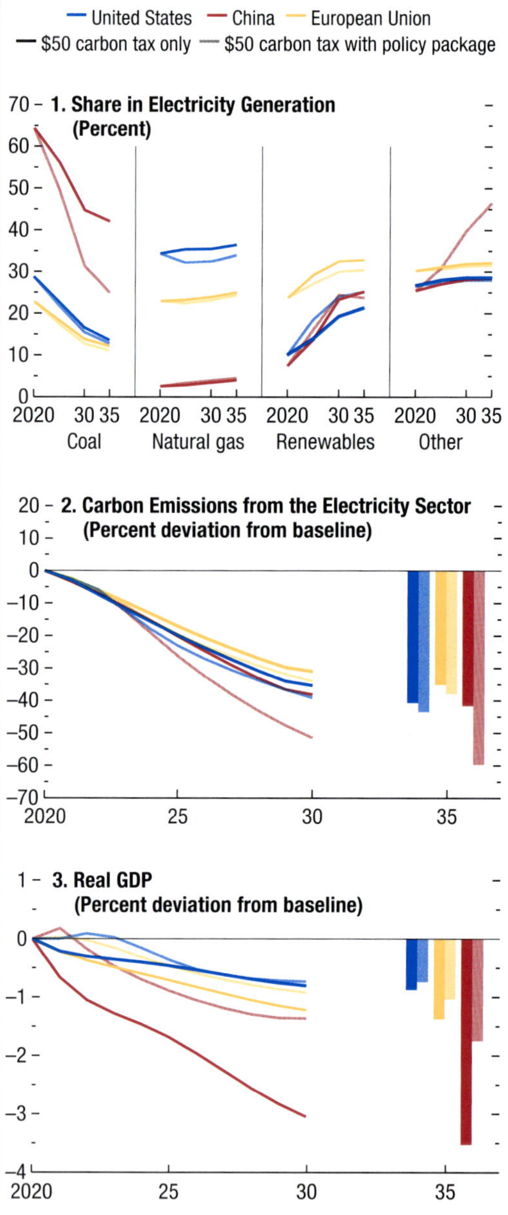

Source: IMF staff estimates.
Note: The figure is based on the CarMMa (Carbon Mitigation Macro Model). Simulation of a $50 tax per ton of carbon dioxide, phased in over 10 years, alone and together with a policy package. The policy package includes, in each of the three regions, frontloaded renewables investment subsidies and, in the short term, an accommodative monetary policy. For China, the policy package also includes a doubling of nuclear and hydro capacities over 20 years.

Box 3.2 *(continued)*

the losses in coal sector investment. Therefore, the policy mix greatly reduces emissions, while economic damage is mitigated (output declines below baseline by ½ percent over 10 years) as the economy adjusts by reallocating labor and investment from coal toward renewables.

The European Union is comparably advanced in its electricity transition (coal and renewables both have a share of about 20 percent). At the same time, the share of natural gas is considerably smaller than in the United States, which constrains further expansion of renewables by making the grid comparably less flexible to accommodate a rise in intermittent electricity generation. With less room to cut coal output and more limited means for renewables to expand, the carbon price achieves a somewhat milder reduction in emissions.

The high share of coal-generated electricity in China—almost 70 percent—amplifies the increase in electricity costs caused by the carbon price, in turn leading to a more pronounced decline in output. The carbon price increases the share of renewables by about 20 percentage points, which alone is not enough to reduce the share of coal to a sustainable level. With limited availability of natural gas, renewables must be backed up by coal itself (assuming the

possibility of flexibility retrofits, as discussed in IEA 2019), reducing the scope for reductions. In addition to renewables subsidies, the macroeconomic package assumes an expansion in nuclear power (accounting for the time it takes to build plants), which crowds out coal-based generation. While the percentage decline in emissions is of the same order as in other regions, in absolute terms, it is about three times greater than in the United States owing to China's greater initial emissions.

Overall, the policy is highly effective at curbing electricity-related emissions at modest macroeconomic costs, especially if labor reallocation can be facilitated. Storage technology for renewable electricity, which could become feasible in the near term, would amplify the penetration of renewables resulting from the carbon price. Given that the macroeconomic costs of a low-carbon electricity transition are modest, it is striking that current policy action and plans for the phasing out of coal generally fall short of what is needed to avoid irreversible climate damage. According to the International Energy Agency, under current and proposed investment plans and policies, power generation from coal alone would use up most of the remaining carbon budget (IEA 2019).

References

Acemoglu, Daron, Philippe Aghion, Leonardo Bursztyn, and David Hémous. 2012. "The Environment and Directed Technical Change." *American Economic Review* 102 (1): 131–66.

Acemoglu, Daron, Ufuk Akcigit, Douglas Hanley, and William Kerr. 2016. "Transition to Clean Technology." *Journal of Political Economy* 124 (1): 52–104.

Acemoglu, Daron, and David Autor. 2011. "Skills, Tasks, and Technologies: Implications for Employment and Earnings." In *Handbook of Labor Economics* 4: 1043–171. North Holland: Elsevier.

Acemoglu, Daron, David Hemous, Lint Barrage, and Philippe Aghion. 2019. "Climate Change, Directed Innovation, and Energy Transition: The Long-Run Consequences of the Shale Gas Revolution." In *2019 Meeting Papers* 1302. New York: Society for Economic Dynamics.

Barrett, Scott. 2005. "The Theory of International Environmental Agreements." In *Handbook of Environmental Economics* 3: 1457–516. Amsterdam: Elsevier.

Barrett, Scott. 2013. "Climate Treaties and Approaching Catastrophes." *Journal of Environmental Economics and Management* 66 (2): 235–50.

Barrett, Scott. 2016. "Coordination vs. Voluntarism and Enforcement in Sustaining International Environmental Cooperation." *Proceedings of the National Academy of Sciences* 113 (5): 14515–22.

Barwick, Panle Jia, Shanjun Li, Deyu Rao, and Nahim Bin Zahur. 2018. "The Morbidity Cost of Air Pollution: Evidence from Consumer Spending in China." NBER Working Paper 24688, National Bureau of Economic Research, Cambridge, MA.

Batini, Nicoletta, Mehdi Benatiya Andaloussi, Pierpaolo Grippa, Andy Jobst, and William Oman. 2020. "Earth Day—The Impact of COVID-19 on Climate Change Policies." SPARK Seminar Presentation, International Monetary Fund, Washington, DC, April 22. http://www-intranet.imf.org/departments/ILU/Documents/SPARK_Earth%20Day.pptx.

Batten, Sandra. 2018. "Climate Change and the Macro-Economy: A Critical Review." Bank of England Working Paper 706, London.

Ben-David, Itzhak, Stefanie Kleimeier, and Michael Viehs. 2018. "Exporting Pollution: Where Do Multinational Firms Emit CO_2?" NBER Working Paper 25063, National Bureau of Economic Research, Cambridge, MA.

Bento, Antonio M., Mark R. Jacobsen, and Antung A. Liu. 2018. "Environmental Policy in the Presence of an Informal Sector." *Journal of Environmental Economics and Management* 90: 61–77.

Bhattacharya, Amar, and James Rydge, under the guidance of Nicholas Stern. 2020. "Better Recovery, Better World: Resetting Climate Action in the Aftermath of the COVID Pandemic." Informal Note for Members of the Coalition of Finance Ministers for Climate Action.

Black, Simon, and Ian Parry. 2020. "Implications of the Global Economic Crisis for Carbon Pricing: A Quantitative Assessment for Coalition Member Countries." Informal Note for Members of the Coalition of Finance Ministers for Climate Action. https://www.cape4financeministry.org/sites/cape/files/inline-files/IMF-WB%20Coalition%20Note%20-%20Implications%20of%20the%20Global%20Economic%20Crisis%20for%20Carbon%20Pricing.pdf.

Bolt, Jutta, Robert Inklaar, Herman J. de Jong, and Jan Luiten van Zanden. 2018. "Rebasing 'Maddison': New Income Comparisons and the Shape of Long-Run Economic Development." GGDC Research Memorandum 174, Groningen Growth and Development Centre, University of Groningen, Netherlands.

Bosetti, Valentina, Carlo Carraro, Romain Duval, and Massimo Tavoni. 2011. "What Should We Expect from Innovation? A Model-Based Assessment of the Environmental and Mitigation Cost Implications of Climate-Related R&D." *Energy Economics* 33 (6): 1313–20.

Botta, Enrico, and Tomasz Koźluk. 2014. "Measuring Environmental Policy Stringency in OECD Countries." OECD Economics Department Working Papers 1177, Organisation for Economic Co-operation and Development, Paris.

Bourcet, Clémence. 2020. "Empirical Determinants of Renewable Energy Deployment: A Systematic Literature Review." *Energy Economics* 85 (104563).

British Petroleum (BP). 2019. *BP Statistical Review of World Energy.* http://www.bp.com/statisticalreview.

Burke, Marshall, Solomon M. Hsiang, and Edward Miguel. 2015. "Global Non-Linear Effect of Temperature on Economic Production." *Nature* 527 (7577): 235–39.

Burke, Paul J. 2010. "Income, Resources, and Electricity Mix." *Energy Economics* 32 (3): 616–26.

Calderón, César, Enrique Moral-Benito, and Luis Servén. 2015. "Is Infrastructure Capital Productive? A Dynamic Heterogeneous Approach." *Journal of Applied Econometrics* 30 (2): 177–98.

Carl, Jeremy, and David Fedor. 2016. "Tracking Global Carbon Revenues: A Survey of Carbon Taxes versus Cap-and-Trade in the Real World." *Energy Policy* 96: 50–77.

Chateau, Jean, Ruben Bibas, and Elisa Lanzi. 2018. "Impacts of Green Growth Policies on Labour Markets and Wage Income Distribution: A General Equilibrium Application to Climate and Energy Policies." OECD Environment Working Papers 137, Organisation for Economic Co-operation and Development, Paris.

Coady, David, Ian Parry, Nghia-Piotr Le, and Baoping Shang. 2019. "Global Fossil Fuel Subsidies Remain Large: An Update Based on Country-Level Estimates." IMF Working Paper 19/89, International Monetary Fund, Washington, DC.

Dechezleprêtre, Antoine, Ralf Martin, and Myra Mohnen. 2017. "Knowledge Spillovers from Clean and Dirty Technologies: A Patent Citation Analysis." Grantham Research Institute on Climate Change and the Environment Working Paper 135, London School of Economics.

Dechezleprêtre, Antoine, and David Popp. 2017. "Fiscal and Regulatory Instruments for Clean Technology Development in the European Union." In *Energy Tax and Regulatory Policy in Europe: Reform Priorities,* edited by Ian Parry, Karen Pittel, and Herman Vollebergh. Cambridge, MA: MIT Press.

Dell, Melissa, Benjamin F. Jones, and Benjamin A. Olken. 2012. "Temperature Shocks and Economic Growth: Evidence from the Last Half Century." *American Economic Journal: Macroeconomics* 4 (3): 66–95.

Deschenes, Olivier. 2018. "Environmental Regulations and Labor Markets." *IZA World of Labor,* Institute of Labor Economics, Bonn.

Ebenstein, Avraham, Maoyong Fan, Michael Greenstone, Guojun He, and Maigeng Zhou. 2017. "New Evidence on the Impact of Sustained Exposure to Air Pollution on Life Expectancy from China's Huai River Policy. *Proceedings of the National Academy of Sciences* 114 (39): 10384–89.

Eggertsson, Gauti B. 2012. "Was the New Deal Contractionary?" *American Economic Review* 102 (1): 524–55.

European Values Survey. 2020. European Values Study 2017: Integrated Dataset (EVS 2017). GESIS Data Archive, Cologne. ZA7500 Data file Version 3.0.0, doi:10.4232/1.13511.

Fremstad, Anders, and Mark Paul. 2019. "The Impact of a Carbon Tax on Inequality." *Ecological Economics* 163: 88–97.

Fried, Stephie, Kevin Novan, and William Peterman. 2018. "The Distributional Effects of a Carbon Tax on Current and Future Generations." *Review of Economic Dynamics* 30: 30–46.

Fuss, Sabine, William F. Lamb, Max W. Callaghan, Jérôme Hilaire, Felix Creutzig, Thorben Amann, Tim Beringer, and others. 2018. "Negative Emissions—Part 2: Costs, Potentials, and Side Effects." *Environmental Research Letters* 13 (6).

Garín, Julio, Robert Lester, and Eric Sims. 2019. "Are Supply Shocks Contractionary at the ZLB? Evidence from Utilization-Adjusted TFP Data." *Review of Economics and Statistics* 101 (1): 160–75.

Gillingham, Kenneth, and James H. Stock. 2018. "The Cost of Reducing Greenhouse Gas Emissions." *Journal of Economic Perspectives* 32 (4): 53–72.

Gollier, Christian. 2018a. "On the Efficient Growth Rate of Carbon Price under a Carbon Budget." Toulouse School of Economics, University of Toulouse-Capitole.

Gollier, Christian. 2018b. "The Cost-Efficiency Carbon Pricing Puzzle." Toulouse School of Economics, University of Toulouse-Capitole.

Goulder, Lawrence H. 1995. "Environmental Taxation and the Double Dividend: A Reader's Guide." *International Tax and Public Finance* 2: 157–83.

Goulder, Lawrence H., and Ian W. H. Parry. 2008. "Instrument Choice in Environmental Policy." *Review of Environmental Economics and Policy* 2: 152–74.

Grainger, Corbett A., and Charles D. Kolstad. 2010. "Who Pays a Price on Carbon?" *Environmental and Resource Economics* 46 (3): 359–76.

Greenstone, Michael. 2002. "The Impacts of Environmental Regulations on Industrial Activity: Evidence from the 1970 and 1977 Clean Air Act Amendments and the Census of Manufactures." *Journal of Political Economy* 110 (6): 1175–219.

Guillaume, Dominique, Roman Zytek, and Mohammad Reza Farzin. 2011. "Iran: The Chronicles of the Subsidy Reform." IMF Working Paper 11/167, International Monetary Fund, Washington, DC.

Haerpfer, C., R. Inglehart, A. Moreno, C. Welzel, K. Kizilova, J. Diez-Medrano, M. Lagos, and others, eds. 2020. *World Values Survey: Round Seven–Country-Pooled Datafile.* Madrid and Vienna: JD Systems Institute and WVSA Secretariat. http://www.worldvaluessurvey.org/WVSDocumentationWV7.jsp.

Haščič, Ivan, and Mauro Migotto. 2015. "Measuring Environmental Innovation Using Patent Data." OECD Environment Working Paper 89, Organisation for Economic Co-operation and Development, Paris.

Hassler, John, Per Krusell, and Conny Olovsson. 2018. "The Consequences of Uncertainty: Climate Sensitivity and Economic Sensitivity to the Climate." *Annual Review of Economics* 10: 189–205.

Hassler, John, Per Krusell, Conny Olovsson, and Michael Reiter. 2020. "On the Effectiveness of Climate Policies." https://www.bde.es/f/webpi/SES/seminars/2020/Fich/sie20200226.pdf.

Heal, Geoffrey. 2017. "The Economics of the Climate." *Journal of Economic Literature* 55 (3): 1046–63.

Hepburn, Cameron, Brian O'Callaghan, Nicholas Stern, Joseph Stiglitz, and Dimitri Zenghelis. 2020. "Will COVID-19 Fiscal Recovery Packages Accelerate or Retard Progress on Climate Change?" *Oxford Review of Economic Policy.* https://doi.org/10.1093/oxrep/graa015.

High-Level Commission on Carbon Prices. 2017. *Report of the High-Level Commission on Carbon Prices.* Washington, DC: World Bank. License: Creative Commons Attribution CC BY 3.0 IGO.

Intergovernmental Panel on Climate Change (IPCC). 2014. "Summary for Policymakers." In *Climate Change 2014: Mitigation of Climate Change. Contribution of Working Group III to the Fifth Assessment Report of the Intergovernmental Panel on Climate Change,* edited by O. Edenhofer, R. Pichs-Madruga, Y. Sokona, E. Farahani, S. Kadner, K. Seyboth, A. Adler, and others. New York.

Intergovernmental Panel on Climate Change (IPCC). 2018a. "Summary for Policymakers. In *Global Warming of 1.5°C. An IPCC Special Report on the Impacts of Global Warming of 1.5°C above Pre-industrial Levels and Related Global Greenhouse Gas Emission Pathways, in the Context of Strengthening the Global Response to the Threat of Climate Change, Sustainable Development, and Efforts to Eradicate Poverty,* edited by V. Masson-Delmotte, P. Zhai, H.-O. Pörtner, D. Roberts, J. Skea, P. R. Shukla, A. Pirani, and others. In press.

Intergovernmental Panel on Climate Change (IPCC). 2018b. Special Report on Global Warming of 1.5 °C (SR15). Chapter 4 in *Strengthening and Implementing the Global Response.* Geneva: Intergovernmental Panel on Climate Change.

International Energy Agency (IEA). 2019. *World Energy Outlook*. Paris. https://www.iea.org/reports/world-energy-outlook-2019.

International Energy Agency (IEA). 2020a. *Sustainable Recovery*. Paris. https://www.iea.org/reports/sustainable-recovery.

International Energy Agency (IEA). 2020b. *World Energy Investment 2020*. Paris. https://www.iea.org/reports/world-energy-investment-2020.

International Energy Agency (IEA). 2020c. *Green Stimulus after the 2008 Crisis*. Paris. https://www.iea.org/articles/green-stimulus-after-the-2008-crisis.

International Hydropower Association (IHA). 2020. *Hydropower Status Report*. London.

International Monetary Fund (IMF). 2019. "Fiscal Policies for Paris Climate Strategies—From Principle to Practice." IMF Policy Paper 19/010, Washington, DC.

International Monetary Fund (IMF). 2020a. "EU Climate Mitigation Policy." IMF Policy Paper, Washington, DC.

International Monetary Fund (IMF). 2020b. Primary Commodity Price Tables, Washington, DC. www.imf.org/external/np/res/commod/index.asp.

International Monetary Fund (IMF). 2020c. "Sectoral Policies for Climate Change Mitigation in the EU." IMF Policy Paper, Washington, DC.

International Monetary Fund (IMF). Forthcoming. "Fiscal Policies to Address Climate Change in Asia and the Pacific: Opportunities and Challenges." IMF Policy Paper, Washington, DC.

International Renewable Energy Agency (IRENA). 2020. *Renewable Capacity and Energy Statistics*. Abu Dhabi.

Johnstone, Nick, Ivan Haščič, and David Popp. 2010. "Renewable Energy Policies and Technological Innovation: Evidence Based on Patent Counts." *Environmental and Resource Economics* 45 (1): 133–55.

Kahn, Matthew E. 1997. "Particulate Pollution Trends in the United States." *Regional Science and Urban Economics* 27: 87–107.

Kahn, Matthew E., Kamiar Mohaddes, N. Ryan, C. Ng, M. Hashem Pesaran, Mehdi Raissi, and Jui-Chung Yang. 2019. "Long-Term Macroeconomic Effects of Climate Change: A Cross-Country Analysis." NBER Working Paper 26167, National Bureau of Economic Research, Cambridge, MA.

Karlsson, Mikael, Eva Alfredsson, and Nils Westling. 2020. "Climate Policy Co-Benefits: A Review." *Climate Policy* 20 (3): 292–316.

Koske, Isabell, Isabelle Wanner, Rosamaria Bitetti, and Omar Barbiero. 2015. "The 2013 Update of the OECD's Database on Product Market Regulation." OECD Economics Department Working Papers 1200, Organisation for Economic Co-operation and Development, Paris.

Laxton, Douglas, Susanna Mursula, Michael Kumhof, and Dirk Muir. 2010. *The Global Integrated Monetary and Fiscal Model (GIMF): Theoretical Structure*. Washington, DC: International Monetary Fund.

Lazard. 2019. "Levelized Cost of Energy Analysis." https://www.lazard.com/perspective/lcoe2019.

Lenton, Timothy M., Johan Rockström, Owen Gaffney, Stefan Rahmstorf, Katherine Richardson, Will Steffen, and Hans Joachim Schellnhuber. 2019. "Climate Tipping Points—Too Risky to Bet Against." https://www.nature.com/articles/d41586-019-03595-0.

Lessmann, Kai, Ulrike Kornek, Valentina Bosetti, Rob Dellink, Johannes Emmerling, Johan Eyckmans, Miyuki Nagashima, and others. 2015. "The Stability and Effectiveness of Climate Coalitions." *Environmental and Resource Economics* 62 (4): 811–36.

Liu, Mengdi, Ronald Shadbegian, and Bing Zhang. 2017. "Does Environmental Regulation Affect Labor Demand in China? Evidence from the Textile Printing and Dyeing Industry." *Journal of Environmental Economics and Management* 86: 277–94.

Liu, Weifeng, Warwick J. McKibbin, Adele Morris, and Peter J. Wilcoxen. 2020. "Global Economic and Environmental Outcomes of the Paris Agreement." *Energy Economics* 90: 1–17.

Marin, Giovanni, and Francesco Vona. 2019. "Climate Policies and Skill-Biased Employment Dynamics: Evidence from EU Countries." *Journal of Environmental Economics and Management* 98 (102253).

McCollum, David L., Wenji Zhou, Christoph Bertram, Harmen-Sytze De Boer, Valentina Bosetti, Sebastian Busch, Jacques Després, and others. 2018. "Energy Investment Needs for Fulfilling the Paris Agreement and Achieving the Sustainable Development Goals." *Nature Energy* 3 (7): 589–99.

McKibbin, Warwick J., and Peter J. Wilcoxen. 1999. "The Theoretical and Empirical Structure of the G-Cubed Model." *Economic Modelling* 16 (1): 123–48.

McKibbin, Warwick J., and Peter J. Wilcoxen. 2013. "A Global Approach to Energy and the Environment: The G-Cubed Model." Chapter 17 in *Handbook of Computable General Equilibrium Modelling*, 995–1068. North Holland: Elsevier.

Metcalf, Gilbert E. 2019. "The Distributional Impacts of US Energy Policy." *Energy Policy* 129: 926–29.

Metcalf, Gilbert E., and James H. Stock. 2020, "Measuring the Macroeconomic Impact of Carbon Taxes." *AEA Papers and Proceedings* 110, American Economic Association, Nashville, TN.

Mirzoev, Tokhir N., Ling Zhu, Yang Takhar, Tian Zhang, Erik Roos, Andrea Pescatori, and Akito Matsumoto. 2020. "The Future of Oil and Fiscal Sustainability in the GCC Region." IMF Departmental Paper 20/01, International Monetary Fund, Washington, DC.

Morris, Jennifer S., John M. Reilly, and Sergey Paltsev. 2010. "Combining a Renewable Portfolio Standard with a Cap-and-Trade Policy: A General Equilibrium Analysis." MIT Joint Program on the Science and Policy of Global Change. http://globalchange.mit.edu/publication/13783.

Newell, Richard G. 2015. "The Role of Energy Technology Policy alongside Carbon Pricing." In *Implementing a US Carbon Tax: Challenges and Debates,* edited by Ian Parry, Adele Morris, and Roberton C. Williams III. New York: Routledge.

Nordhaus, William D. 2010. Excel file for RICE model as of April 26, 2010. Ann Arbor, MI: Interuniversity Consortium for Political and Social Research [distributor], 2010-11-17. https://doi.org/10.3886/ICPSR28461.v1.

Nordhaus, William D. 2015. "Climate Clubs: Overcoming Free-Riding in International Climate Policy." *American Economic Review* 105 (4): 1339–70.

Organisation for Economic Co-operation and Development (OECD). 2018. "Environmental Policy Stringency index (Edition 2017)," OECD Environment Statistics (database).

Papageorgiou, Chris, Marianne Saam, and Patrick Schulte. 2017. "Substitution between Clean and Dirty Energy Inputs: A Macroeconomic Perspective." *Review of Economics and Statistics* 99 (2): 281–90.

Parry, Ian, Chandara Veung, and Dirk Heine. 2015. "How Much Carbon Pricing Is in Countries' Own Interests? The Critical Role of Co-Benefits." *Climate Change Economics* 6 (0) 4: 1550019.

Popp, David, Ivan Haščič, and Neelakshi Medhi. 2011. "Technology and the Diffusion of Renewable Energy." *Energy Economics* 33 (4): 648–62.

Popp, David, Jacquelyn Pless, Ivan Haščič, and Nick Johnstone. 2020. "Innovation and Entrepreneurship in the Energy Sector." NBER Working Paper 27145, National Bureau of Economic Research, Cambridge, MA.

Rodríguez, Miguel Cárdenas, Ivan Haščič, Nick Johnstone, Jérôme Silva, and Antoine Ferey. 2015. "Renewable Energy Policies and Private Sector Investment: Evidence from Financial Microdata." *Environmental and Resource Economics* 62 (1): 163–88.

Smith, Michael G., and Johannes Urpelainen. 2014. "The Effect of Feed-in Tariffs on Renewable Electricity Generation: An Instrumental Variables Approach." *Environmental and Resource Economics* 57 (3): 367–92.

Stavropoulos, Spyridon, and Martijn J. Burger. 2020. "Modelling Strategy and Net Employment Effects of Renewable Energy and Energy Efficiency: A Meta-Regression." *Energy Policy* 136 (111047).

Stern, Nicholas. 2007. *The Economics of Climate Change: The Stern Review.* Cambridge, UK: Cambridge University Press.

Stiglitz, Joseph E., and Bruce C. Greenwald, with commentary and contributions from Philippe Aghion, Kenneth J. Arrow, Robert M. Solow, and Michael Wood Ford. 2014. *Creating a Learning Society: A New Approach to Growth, Development, and Social Progress.* New York: Columbia University Press.

Tavares, Marina M. Forthcoming. "Carbon Pricing Winners and Losers: Workers, Consumers, and Policy Options."

United Nations (UN). 2019. *World Population Prospects 2019: Highlights.* New York: United National Department for Economic Social Affairs.

United States Department of Energy. 2017. *US Energy and Employment Report.* Washington, DC.

Van der Werf, Edwin. 2008. "Production Functions for Climate Policy Modeling: An Empirical Analysis." *Energy Economics* 30 (6): 2964–79.

Van Reenen, John. 1997. "Employment and Technological Innovation: Evidence from UK Manufacturing Firms." *Journal of Labor Economics* 15 (2): 255–84.

Verdolini, Elena, Francesco Vona, and David Popp. 2018. "Bridging the Gap: Do Fast-Reacting Fossil Technologies Facilitate Renewable Energy Diffusion?" *Energy Policy* 116: 242–56.

Wei, Max, Shana Patadia, and Daniel M. Kammen. 2010. "Putting Renewables and Energy Efficiency to Work: How Many Jobs Can the Clean Energy Industry Generate in the US?" *Energy Policy* 38 (2): 919–31.

Wieland, Johannes F. 2019. "Are Negative Supply Shocks Expansionary at the Zero Lower Bound?" *Journal of Political Economy* 127 (3): 973–1007.

Xu, Chi, Timothy A. Kohler, Timothy M. Lenton, Jens-Christian Svenning, and Marten Scheffer. 2020. "Future of the Human Climate Niche." *Proceedings of the National Academy of Sciences* 117 (21): 11350–55.

Yamazaki, Akio. 2017. "Jobs and Climate Policy: Evidence from British Columbia's Revenue-Neutral Carbon Tax." *Journal of Environmental Economics and Management* 83: 197–216.

Yip, Chi Man. 2018. "On the Labor Market Consequences of Environmental Taxes." *Journal of Environmental Economics and Management* 89: 136–52.

STATISTICAL APPENDIX

The Statistical Appendix presents historical data as well as projections. It comprises seven sections: Assumptions, What's New, Data and Conventions, Country Notes, General Features and Composition of Groups in the *World Economic Outlook* Classification, Key Data Documentation, and Statistical Tables.

The first section summarizes the assumptions underlying the estimates and projections for 2020–21. The second section briefly describes the changes to the database and statistical tables since the April 2020 *World Economic Outlook* (WEO). The third section offers a general description of the data and the conventions used for calculating country group composites. The fourth section presents selected key information for each country. The fifth section summarizes the classification of countries in the various groups presented in the WEO. The sixth section provides information on methods and reporting standards for the member countries' national account and government finance indicators included in the report.

The last, and main, section comprises the statistical tables. (Statistical Appendix A is included here; Statistical Appendix B is available online at www.imf.org/en/Publications/WEO.)

Data in these tables have been compiled on the basis of information available through September 28, 2020. The figures for 2020–21 are shown with the same degree of precision as the historical figures solely for convenience; because they are projections, the same degree of accuracy is not to be inferred.

Assumptions

Real effective *exchange rates* for the advanced economies are assumed to remain constant at their average levels measured during July 24–August 21, 2020. For 2020 and 2021 these assumptions imply average US dollar–special drawing right (SDR) conversion rates of 1.391 and 1.430, US dollar–euro conversion rates of 1.143 and 1.230, and yen–US dollar conversion rates of 107.2 and 105.9, respectively.

It is assumed that the *price of oil* will average $41.69 a barrel in 2020 and $46.70 a barrel in 2021.

National authorities' established *policies* are assumed to be maintained. Box A1 describes the more specific policy assumptions underlying the projections for selected economies.

With regard to *interest rates*, it is assumed that the London interbank offered rate (LIBOR) on six-month US dollar deposits will average 0.7 percent in 2020 and 0.4 percent in 2021, the LIBOR on three-month euro deposits will average –0.4 percent in 2020 and –0.5 percent in 2021, and the LIBOR on six-month yen deposits will average 0.0 percent in 2020 and 2021.

As a reminder, in regard to the *introduction of the euro*, on December 31, 1998, the Council of the European Union decided that, effective January 1, 1999, the irrevocably fixed conversion rates between the euro and currencies of the member countries adopting the euro are as described in Box 5.4 of the October 1998 WEO. See Box 5.4 of the October 1998 WEO as well for details on how the conversion rates were established.

1 euro	=	13.7603	Austrian schillings
	=	40.3399	Belgian francs
	=	0.585274	Cyprus pound[1]
	=	1.95583	Deutsche marks
	=	15.6466	Estonian krooni[2]
	=	5.94573	Finnish markkaa
	=	6.55957	French francs
	=	340.750	Greek drachmas[3]
	=	0.787564	Irish pound
	=	1,936.27	Italian lire
	=	0.702804	Latvian lat[4]
	=	3.45280	Lithuanian litas[5]
	=	40.3399	Luxembourg francs
	=	0.42930	Maltese lira[1]
	=	2.20371	Netherlands guilders
	=	200.482	Portuguese escudos
	=	30.1260	Slovak koruna[6]
	=	239.640	Slovenian tolars[7]
	=	166.386	Spanish pesetas

[1]Established on January 1, 2008.
[2]Established on January 1, 2011.
[3]Established on January 1, 2001.
[4]Established on January 1, 2014.
[5]Established on January 1, 2015.
[6]Established on January 1, 2009.
[7]Established on January 1, 2007.

What's New

- Following the recent release of the 2017 International Comparison Program (ICP) survey for new purchasing-power-parity benchmarks, the WEO's estimates of purchasing-power-parity weights and GDP valued at purchasing power parity have been updated. For more details, see Box 1.1 of the October 2020 WEO.
- Starting with the October 2020 WEO, data and forecasts for Bangladesh and Tonga are presented on a fiscal year basis.
- Data for West Bank and Gaza are now included in the WEO. West Bank and Gaza is added to the Middle East and Central Asia regional group.

Data and Conventions

Data and projections for 195 economies form the statistical basis of the WEO database. The data are maintained jointly by the IMF's Research Department and regional departments, with the latter regularly updating country projections based on consistent global assumptions.

Although national statistical agencies are the ultimate providers of historical data and definitions, international organizations are also involved in statistical issues, with the objective of harmonizing methodologies for the compilation of national statistics, including analytical frameworks, concepts, definitions, classifications, and valuation procedures used in the production of economic statistics. The WEO database reflects information from both national source agencies and international organizations.

Most countries' macroeconomic data as presented in the WEO conform broadly to the 2008 version of the *System of National Accounts* (SNA 2008). The IMF's sector statistical standards—the sixth edition of the *Balance of Payments and International Investment Position Manual* (BPM6), the *Monetary and Financial Statistics Manual and Compilation Guide* (MFSMCG), and the *Government Finance Statistics Manual 2014* (GFSM 2014)—have been aligned with the SNA 2008. These standards reflect the IMF's special interest in countries' external positions, financial sector stability, and public sector fiscal positions. The process of adapting country data to the new standards begins in earnest when the manuals are released. However, full concordance with the manuals is ultimately dependent on the provision by national statistical compilers of revised country data; hence, the WEO estimates are only partly adapted to these manuals. Nonetheless, for many countries, conversion to the updated standards will have only a small impact on major balances and aggregates. Many other countries have partly adopted the latest standards and will continue implementation over a number of years.[1]

The fiscal gross and net debt data reported in the WEO are drawn from official data sources and IMF staff estimates. While attempts are made to align gross and net debt data with the definitions in the GFSM, as a result of data limitations or specific country circumstances, these data can sometimes deviate from the formal definitions. Although every effort is made to ensure the WEO data are relevant and internationally comparable, differences in both sectoral and instrument coverage mean that the data are not universally comparable. As more information becomes available, changes in either data sources or instrument coverage can give rise to data revisions that can sometimes be substantial. For clarification on the deviations in sectoral or instrument coverage, please refer to the metadata for the online WEO database.

Composite data for country groups in the WEO are either sums or weighted averages of data for individual countries. Unless noted otherwise, multiyear averages of growth rates are expressed as compound annual rates of change.[2] Arithmetically weighted averages are used for all data for the emerging market and developing economies group—except data on inflation and money growth, for which geometric averages are used. The following conventions apply:

Country group composites for exchange rates, interest rates, and growth rates of monetary aggregates are weighted by GDP converted to US dollars at market exchange rates (averaged over the preceding three years) as a share of group GDP.

Composites for other data relating to the domestic economy, whether growth rates or ratios, are weighted by GDP valued at purchasing power parity as a share

---

[1] Many countries are implementing the SNA 2008 or European System of National and Regional Accounts 2010, and a few countries use versions of the SNA older than that from 1993. A similar adoption pattern is expected for the BPM6 and GFSM 2014. Please refer to Table G, which lists the statistical standards each country adheres to.

[2] Averages for real GDP, inflation, GDP per capita, and commodity prices are calculated based on the compound annual rate of change, except in the case of the unemployment rate, which is based on the simple arithmetic average.

of total world or group GDP.[3] Annual inflation rates are simple percentage changes from the previous years, except in the case of emerging market and developing economies, for which the rates are based on logarithmic differences.

Composites for real GDP per capita in *purchasing power parity* terms are sums of individual country data after conversion to the international dollar in the years indicated.

Unless noted otherwise, composites for all sectors for the euro area are corrected for reporting discrepancies in intra-area transactions. Unadjusted annual GDP data are used for the euro area and for the majority of individual countries, except for Cyprus, Ireland, Portugal, and Spain, which report calendar-adjusted data. For data prior to 1999, data aggregations apply 1995 European currency unit exchange rates.

Composites for fiscal data are sums of individual country data after conversion to US dollars at the average market exchange rates in the years indicated.

Composite unemployment rates and employment growth are weighted by labor force as a share of group labor force.

Composites relating to external sector statistics are sums of individual country data after conversion to US dollars at the average market exchange rates in the years indicated for balance of payments data.

Composites of changes in foreign trade volumes and prices, however, are arithmetic averages of percent changes for individual countries weighted by the US dollar value of exports or imports as a share of total world or group exports or imports (in the preceding year).

Unless noted otherwise, group composites are computed if 90 percent or more of the share of group weights is represented.

Data refer to calendar years, except in the case of a few countries that use fiscal years; Table F lists the economies with exceptional reporting periods for national accounts and government finance data for each country.

For some countries, the figures for 2019 and earlier are based on estimates rather than actual outturns; Table G lists the latest actual outturns for the

indicators in the national accounts, prices, government finance, and balance of payments indicators for each country.

Country Notes

For *Albania*, projections were prepared prior to the first Post-Program Monitoring mission that ended on September 28 and therefore do not reflect updates made during the mission.

For *Argentina*, fiscal and inflation variables are excluded from publication for 2021–25 and 2020–25, respectively, as these are to a large extent linked to still-pending program negotiations. The official national consumer price index (CPI) for Argentina starts in December 2016. For earlier periods, CPI data for Argentina reflect the Greater Buenos Aires Area CPI (prior to December 2013), the national CPI (IPCNu, December 2013 to October 2015), the City of Buenos Aires CPI (November 2015 to April 2016), and the Greater Buenos Aires Area CPI (May 2016 to December 2016). Given limited comparability of these series on account of differences in geographical coverage, weights, sampling, and methodology, the average CPI inflation for 2014–16 and end-of-period inflation for 2015–16 are not reported in the October 2020 WEO. Also, Argentina discontinued the publication of labor market data in December 2015 and new series became available starting in the second quarter of 2016.

For *Australia*, projections do not reflect the October 6 Commonwealth budget, which was released after the cutoff date (September 28) for the October 2020 WEO.

Data and forecasts for *Bangladesh* are presented on a fiscal year basis starting with the October 2020 WEO. However, the real GDP and purchasing-power-parity GDP aggregates that include Bangladesh are based on calendar year data.

For *Belarus*, projections were prepared before the presidential elections of August 9, 2020.

The fiscal series for the *Dominican Republic* have the following coverage: public debt, debt service, and the cyclically adjusted/structural balances are for the consolidated public sector (which includes central government, the rest of the nonfinancial public sector, and the central bank); and the remaining fiscal series are for the central government.

The fiscal data for *Ecuador* reflect net lending/ borrowing for the nonfinancial public sector.

---

[3] See Box 1.1 of the October 2020 WEO for a summary of the revised purchasing-power-parity-based weights as well as "Revised Purchasing Power Parity Weights" in the July 2014 WEO *Update*, Box A2 of the April 2004 WEO, Box A1 of the May 2000 WEO, and Annex IV of the May 1993 WEO. See also Anne-Marie Gulde and Marianne Schulze-Ghattas, "Purchasing Power Parity Based Weights for the *World Economic Outlook*," in *Staff Studies for the World Economic Outlook* (Washington, DC: International Monetary Fund, December 1993), 106–23.

Ecuadorian authorities, with technical support from the IMF, are undertaking revisions of the historical fiscal data for the net lending/borrowing of the nonfinancial public sector over 2012–17, with the view of correcting recently identified statistical errors in data compilation at the subnational level and the consistency between above-the-line and financing data by subsectors.

India's real GDP growth rates are calculated as per national accounts: for 1998 to 2011, with base year 2004/05 and, thereafter, with base year 2011/12.

For *Lebanon*, projections for 2021–25 are omitted due to an unusually high degree of uncertainty.

Against the backdrop of a civil war and weak capacity, the reliability of *Libya's* data, especially regarding national accounts and medium-term projections, is low.

Data for *Syria* are excluded from 2011 onward because of the uncertain political situation.

Ukraine's revised national accounts data are available beginning in 2000 and exclude Crimea and Sevastopol from 2010.

Starting from October 2018 *Uruguay's* public pension system has been receiving transfers in the context of a new law that compensates persons affected by the creation of the mixed pension system. These funds are recorded as revenues, consistent with the IMF's methodology. Therefore, data and projections for 2018–21 are affected by these transfers, which amounted to 1.3 percent of GDP in 2018 and 1.2 percent of GDP in 2019, and are projected to be 0.8 percent of GDP in 2020, 0.2 percent of GDP in 2021, and zero percent thereafter. See IMF Country Report 19/64 for further details.[4] The disclaimer about the public pension system applies only to the revenues and net lending/borrowing series.

The coverage of the fiscal data for *Uruguay* was changed from consolidated public sector to nonfinancial public sector with the October 2019 WEO. In Uruguay, nonfinancial public sector coverage includes central government, local government, social security funds, nonfinancial public corporations, and Banco de Seguros del Estado. Historical data were also revised accordingly. Under this narrower fiscal perimeter—which excludes the central bank—assets and liabilities held by the nonfinancial public sector where the counterpart is the central bank are not netted out in debt

figures. In this context, capitalization bonds issued in the past by the government to the central bank are now part of the nonfinancial public sector debt. Gross and net debt estimates for 2008–11 are preliminary.

Projecting the economic outlook in *Venezuela*, including assessing past and current economic developments as the basis for the projections, is complicated by the lack of discussions with the authorities (the last Article IV consultation took place in 2004), incomplete understanding of the reported data, and difficulties in interpreting certain reported economic indicators given economic developments. The fiscal accounts include the budgetary central government; social security; FOGADE (insurance deposit institution); and a sample of public enterprises, including Petróleos de Venezuela, S.A. (PDVSA); and data for 2018–19 are IMF staff estimates. The effects of hyperinflation and the paucity of reported data mean that the IMF staff's projected macroeconomic indicators need to be interpreted with caution. For example, nominal GDP is estimated assuming the GDP deflator rises in line with the IMF staff's projection of average inflation. Public external debt in relation to GDP is projected using the IMF staff's estimate of the average exchange rate for the year. Wide uncertainty surrounds these projections. Venezuela's consumer prices are excluded from all WEO group composites.

In 2019 *Zimbabwe* authorities introduced the Real Time Gross Settlement dollar, later renamed the Zimbabwe dollar, and are in the process of redenominating their national accounts statistics. Current data are subject to revision. The Zimbabwe dollar previously ceased circulating in 2009 and, between 2009 and 2019, Zimbabwe operated under a multi-currency regime with the US dollar as the unit of account.

Classification of Countries

Summary of the Country Classification

The country classification in the WEO divides the world into two major groups: advanced economies and emerging market and developing economies.[5] This classification is not based on strict criteria, economic or otherwise, and it has evolved over time. The objective is to facilitate analysis by providing a reasonably

---

[4] *Uruguay: Staff Report for the 2018 Article IV Consultation*, Country Report 19/64 (Washington, DC: International Monetary Fund, February 2019).

[5] As used here, the terms "country" and "economy" do not always refer to a territorial entity that is a state as understood by international law and practice. Some territorial entities included here are not states, although their statistical data are maintained on a separate and independent basis.

meaningful method of organizing data. Table A provides an overview of the country classification, showing the number of countries in each group by region and summarizing some key indicators of their relative size (GDP valued at purchasing power parity, total exports of goods and services, and population).

Some countries remain outside the country classification and therefore are not included in the analysis. Cuba and the Democratic People's Republic of Korea are examples of countries that are not IMF members, and the IMF therefore does not monitor their economies.

General Features and Composition of Groups in the *World Economic Outlook* Classification

Advanced Economies

Table B lists the 39 advanced economies. The seven largest in terms of GDP based on market exchange rates—the United States, Japan, Germany, France, Italy, the United Kingdom, and Canada—constitute the subgroup of major advanced economies, often referred to as the Group of Seven. The members of the euro area are also distinguished as a subgroup. Composite data shown in the tables for the euro area cover the current members for all years, even though the membership has increased over time.

Table C lists the member countries of the European Union, not all of which are classified as advanced economies in the WEO.

Emerging Market and Developing Economies

The group of emerging market and developing economies (156) includes all those that are not classified as advanced economies.

The regional breakdowns of emerging market and developing economies are emerging and developing Asia; emerging and developing Europe (sometimes also referred to as "central and eastern Europe"); Latin America and the Caribbean; Middle East and Central Asia (which comprises the regional subgroups Caucasus and Central Asia; and Middle East, North Africa, Afghanistan, and Pakistan); and sub-Saharan Africa.

Emerging market and developing economies are also classified according to *analytical criteria* that reflect the composition of export earnings and a distinction between net creditor and net debtor economies. Tables D and E show the detailed composition of emerging market and developing economies in the regional and analytical groups.

The analytical criterion *source of export earnings* distinguishes between the categories *fuel* (Standard International Trade Classification [SITC] 3) and *nonfuel* and then focuses on *nonfuel primary products* (SITCs 0, 1, 2, 4, and 68). Economies are categorized into one of these groups if their main source of export earnings exceeded 50 percent of total exports on average between 2015 and 2019.

The financial criteria focus on *net creditor economies, net debtor economies, heavily indebted poor countries* (HIPCs), and *low-income developing countries* (LIDCs). Economies are categorized as net debtors when their latest net international investment position, where available, was less than zero or their current account balance accumulations from 1972 (or earliest available data) to 2019 were negative. Net debtor economies are further differentiated on the basis of *experience with debt servicing.*[6]

The HIPC group comprises the countries that are or have been considered by the IMF and the World Bank for participation in their debt initiative known as the HIPC Initiative, which aims to reduce the external debt burdens of all the eligible HIPCs to a "sustainable" level in a reasonably short period of time.[7] Many of these countries have already benefited from debt relief and have graduated from the initiative.

The LIDCs are countries that have per capita income levels below a certain threshold (set at $2,700 in 2016 as measured by the World Bank's Atlas method), structural features consistent with limited development and structural transformation, and external financial linkages insufficiently close for them to be widely seen as emerging market economies.

---

[6] During 2015–19, 27 economies incurred external payments arrears or entered into official or commercial bank debt-rescheduling agreements. This group is referred to as *economies with arrears and/or rescheduling during 2015–19.*

[7] See David Andrews, Anthony R. Boote, Syed S. Rizavi, and Sukwinder Singh, "Debt Relief for Low-Income Countries: The Enhanced HIPC Initiative," IMF Pamphlet Series 51 (Washington, DC: International Monetary Fund, November 1999).

Table A. Classification, by *World Economic Outlook* Groups and Their Shares in Aggregate GDP, Exports of Goods and Services, and Population, 2019[1]
(Percent of total for group or world)

	Number of Economies	GDP Advanced Economies	GDP World	Exports of Goods and Services Advanced Economies	Exports of Goods and Services World	Population Advanced Economies	Population World
Advanced Economies	**39**	**100.0**	**43.1**	**100.0**	**63.0**	**100.0**	**14.1**
United States		37.0	15.9	16.3	10.3	30.7	4.3
Euro Area	19	29.0	12.5	41.7	26.3	31.7	4.5
Germany		8.1	3.5	11.7	7.4	7.8	1.1
France		5.6	2.4	5.8	3.6	6.1	0.9
Italy		4.6	2.0	4.1	2.6	5.6	0.8
Spain		3.5	1.5	3.1	2.0	4.3	0.6
Japan		9.4	4.1	5.8	3.7	11.8	1.7
United Kingdom		5.6	2.4	5.8	3.6	6.2	0.9
Canada		3.3	1.4	3.5	2.2	3.5	0.5
Other Advanced Economies	16	15.7	6.8	26.9	16.9	16.1	2.3
Memorandum							
Major Advanced Economies	7	73.5	31.7	53.0	33.4	71.6	10.1

	Number of Economies	GDP Emerging Market and Developing Economies	GDP World	Exports of Goods and Services Emerging Market and Developing Economies	Exports of Goods and Services World	Population Emerging Market and Developing Economies	Population World
Emerging Market and Developing Economies	**156**	**100.0**	**56.9**	**100.0**	**37.0**	**100.0**	**85.9**
Regional Groups							
Emerging and Developing Asia	30	55.4	31.5	49.1	18.2	56.1	48.2
China		30.5	17.4	29.1	10.8	21.5	18.5
India		12.5	7.1	5.9	2.2	21.0	18.1
ASEAN-5	5	10.0	5.7	12.5	4.6	8.8	7.6
Emerging and Developing Europe	16	13.4	7.6	16.8	6.2	5.8	5.0
Russia		5.4	3.1	5.3	2.0	2.3	1.9
Latin America and the Caribbean	33	13.3	7.6	13.7	5.1	9.7	8.3
Brazil		4.2	2.4	2.9	1.1	3.2	2.8
Mexico		3.4	2.0	5.4	2.0	2.0	1.7
Middle East and Central Asia	32	12.6	7.2	15.9	5.9	12.5	10.7
Saudi Arabia		2.2	1.2	3.1	1.2	0.5	0.4
Sub-Saharan Africa	45	5.4	3.1	4.5	1.7	15.9	13.6
Nigeria		1.4	0.8	0.8	0.3	3.1	2.7
South Africa		1.0	0.6	1.2	0.4	0.9	0.8
Analytical Groups[2]							
By Source of Export Earnings							
Fuel	27	15.7	8.9	20.7	7.7	11.7	10.0
Nonfuel	128	84.3	48.0	79.3	29.3	88.3	75.8
Of Which, Primary Products	36	5.6	3.2	5.2	1.9	9.2	7.9
By External Financing Source							
Net Debtor Economies	123	53.7	30.6	50.5	18.7	68.5	58.8
Net Debtor Economies by Debt-Servicing Experience							
Economies with Arrears and/or Rescheduling during 2015–19	27	3.8	2.2	2.9	1.1	7.6	6.6
Other Groups							
Heavily Indebted Poor Countries	39	2.8	1.6	2.0	0.7	11.9	10.2
Low-Income Developing Countries	59	8.2	4.6	7.4	2.8	23.2	19.9

[1]The GDP shares are based on the purchasing-power-parity valuation of economies' GDP. The number of economies comprising each group reflects those for which data are included in the group aggregates.

[2]Syria is omitted from the source of export earnings, and South Sudan and Syria are omitted from the net external position group composites because of insufficient data.

Table B. Advanced Economies, by Subgroup

Major Currency Areas

United States
Euro Area
Japan

Euro Area

Austria	Greece	Netherlands
Belgium	Ireland	Portugal
Cyprus	Italy	Slovak Republic
Estonia	Latvia	Slovenia
Finland	Lithuania	Spain
France	Luxembourg	
Germany	Malta	

Major Advanced Economies

Canada	Italy	United States
France	Japan	
Germany	United Kingdom	

Other Advanced Economies

Australia	Korea	Singapore
Czech Republic	Macao SAR[2]	Sweden
Denmark	New Zealand	Switzerland
Hong Kong SAR[1]	Norway	Taiwan Province of China
Iceland	Puerto Rico	
Israel	San Marino	

[1]On July 1, 1997, Hong Kong was returned to the People's Republic of China and became a Special Administrative Region of China.

[2]On December 20, 1999, Macao was returned to the People's Republic of China and became a Special Administrative Region of China.

Table C. European Union

Austria	France	Malta
Belgium	Germany	Netherlands
Bulgaria	Greece	Poland
Croatia	Hungary	Portugal
Cyprus	Ireland	Romania
Czech Republic	Italy	Slovak Republic
Denmark	Latvia	Slovenia
Estonia	Lithuania	Spain
Finland	Luxembourg	Sweden

Table D. Emerging Market and Developing Economies, by Region and Main Source of Export Earnings

	Fuel	Nonfuel Primary Products
Emerging and Developing Asia		
	Brunei Darussalam	Kiribati
	Timor-Leste	Lao P.D.R.
		Marshall Islands
		Papua New Guinea
		Solomon Islands
		Tuvalu
Emerging and Developing Europe		
	Russia	
Latin America and the Caribbean		
	Ecuador	Argentina
	Trinidad and Tobago	Bolivia
	Venezuela	Chile
		Guyana
		Paraguay
		Peru
		Suriname
		Uruguay
Middle East and Central Asia		
	Algeria	Afghanistan
	Azerbaijan	Mauritania
	Bahrain	Somalia
	Iran	Sudan
	Iraq	Tajikistan
	Kazakhstan	Uzbekistan
	Kuwait	
	Libya	
	Oman	
	Qatar	
	Saudi Arabia	
	Turkmenistan	
	United Arab Emirates	
	Yemen	
Sub-Saharan Africa		
	Angola	Benin
	Chad	Burkina Faso
	Republic of Congo	Burundi
	Equatorial Guinea	Central African Republic
	Gabon	Democratic Republic of the Congo
	Nigeria	Côte d'Ivoire
	South Sudan	Eritrea
		Guinea
		Guinea-Bissau
		Liberia
		Malawi
		Mali
		Sierra Leone
		South Africa
		Zambia
		Zimbabwe

Table E. Emerging Market and Developing Economies, by Region, Net External Position, and Status as Heavily Indebted Poor Countries and Low-Income Developing Countries

	Net External Position[1]	Heavily Indebted Poor Countries[2]	Low-Income Developing Countries		Net External Position[1]	Heavily Indebted Poor Countries[2]	Low-Income Developing Countries
Emerging and Developing Asia				North Macedonia	*		
Bangladesh	*		*	Poland	*		
Bhutan	*		*	Romania	*		
Brunei Darussalam	•			Russia	•		
Cambodia	*		*	Serbia	*		
China	•			Turkey	*		
Fiji	*			Ukraine	*		
India	*			**Latin America and the Caribbean**			
Indonesia	*			Antigua and Barbuda	*		
Kiribati	•		*	Argentina	•		
Lao P.D.R.	*		*	Aruba	*		
Malaysia	*			The Bahamas	*		
Maldives	*			Barbados	*		
Marshall Islands	*			Belize	*		
Micronesia	•			Bolivia	*	•	
Mongolia	*			Brazil	*		
Myanmar	*		*	Chile	*		
Nauru	*			Colombia	*		
Nepal	•		*	Costa Rica	*		
Palau	*			Dominica	•		
Papua New Guinea	*		*	Dominican Republic	*		
Philippines	*			Ecuador	*		
Samoa	*			El Salvador	*		
Solomon Islands	*		*	Grenada	*		
Sri Lanka	*			Guatemala	*		
Thailand	*			Guyana	*	•	
Timor-Leste	•		*	Haiti	*	•	*
Tonga	*			Honduras	*	•	*
Tuvalu	*			Jamaica	*		
Vanuatu	*			Mexico	*		
Vietnam	*		*	Nicaragua	*	•	*
Emerging and Developing Europe				Panama	*		
Albania	*			Paraguay	*		
Belarus	*			Peru	*		
Bosnia and Herzegovina	*			St. Kitts and Nevis	*		
Bulgaria	*			St. Lucia	*		
Croatia	*			St. Vincent and the Grenadines	*		
Hungary	*			Suriname	*		
Kosovo	*			Trinidad and Tobago	•		
Moldova	*		*	Uruguay	*		
Montenegro	*			Venezuela	•		

Table E. Emerging Market and Developing Economies, by Region, Net External Position, and Status as Heavily Indebted Poor Countries and Low-Income Developing Countries *(continued)*

	Net External Position[1]	Heavily Indebted Poor Countries[2]	Low-Income Developing Countries		Net External Position[1]	Heavily Indebted Poor Countries[2]	Low-Income Developing Countries
Middle East and Central Asia				Cameroon	*	●	*
Afghanistan	●	●	*	Central African Republic	*	●	*
Algeria	●			Chad	*	●	*
Armenia	*			Comoros	*	●	*
Azerbaijan	●			Democratic Republic of the Congo	*	●	*
Bahrain	●			Republic of Congo	*	●	*
Djibouti	*		*	Côte d'Ivoire	*	●	*
Egypt	*			Equatorial Guinea	●		
Georgia	*			Eritrea	●	*	*
Iran	●			Eswatini	●		
Iraq	●			Ethiopia	*	●	*
Jordan	*			Gabon	●		
Kazakhstan	*			The Gambia	*	●	*
Kuwait	●			Ghana	*	●	*
Kyrgyz Republic	*		*	Guinea	*	●	*
Lebanon	*			Guinea-Bissau	*	●	*
Libya	●			Kenya	*		*
Mauritania	*	●	*	Lesotho	*		*
Morocco	*			Liberia	*	●	*
Oman	*			Madagascar	*	●	*
Pakistan	*			Malawi	*	●	*
Qatar	●			Mali	*	●	*
Saudi Arabia	●			Mauritius	●		
Somalia	*	*	*	Mozambique	*	●	*
Sudan	*	*	*	Namibia	*		
Syria[3]	...			Niger	*	●	*
Tajikistan	*		*	Nigeria	*		*
Tunisia	*			Rwanda	*	●	*
Turkmenistan	●			São Tomé and Príncipe	*	●	*
United Arab Emirates	●			Senegal	*	●	*
Uzbekistan	●		*	Seychelles	*		
West Bank and Gaza	*			Sierra Leone	*	●	*
Yemen	*		*	South Africa	●		
Sub-Saharan Africa				South Sudan[3]	...		*
Angola	*			Tanzania	*	●	*
Benin	*	●	*	Togo	*	●	*
Botswana	●			Uganda	*	●	*
Burkina Faso	*	●	*	Zambia	*	●	*
Burundi	*	●	*	Zimbabwe	*		*
Cabo Verde	*						

[1]Dot (star) indicates that the country is a net creditor (net debtor).
[2]Dot instead of star indicates that the country has reached the completion point, which allows it to receive the full debt relief committed to at the decision point.
[3]South Sudan and Syria are omitted from the net external position group composite for lack of a fully developed database.

Table F. Economies with Exceptional Reporting Periods[1]

	National Accounts	Government Finance
The Bahamas		Jul/Jun
Bangladesh	Jul/Jun	Jul/Jun
Barbados		Apr/Mar
Bhutan	Jul/Jun	Jul/Jun
Botswana		Apr/Mar
Dominica		Jul/Jun
Egypt	Jul/Jun	Jul/Jun
Eswatini		Apr/Mar
Ethiopia	Jul/Jun	Jul/Jun
Haiti	Oct/Sep	Oct/Sep
Hong Kong SAR		Apr/Mar
India	Apr/Mar	Apr/Mar
Iran	Apr/Mar	Apr/Mar
Jamaica		Apr/Mar
Lesotho	Apr/Mar	Apr/Mar
Malawi		Jul/Jun
Marshall Islands	Oct/Sep	Oct/Sep
Mauritius		Jul/Jun
Micronesia	Oct/Sep	Oct/Sep
Myanmar	Oct/Sep	Oct/Sep
Namibia		Apr/Mar
Nauru	Jul/Jun	Jul/Jun
Nepal	Aug/Jul	Aug/Jul
Pakistan	Jul/Jun	Jul/Jun
Palau	Oct/Sep	Oct/Sep
Puerto Rico	Jul/Jun	Jul/Jun
Rwanda		Jul/Jun
St. Lucia		Apr/Mar
Samoa	Jul/Jun	Jul/Jun
Singapore		Apr/Mar
Thailand		Oct/Sep
Tonga	Jul/Jun	Jul/Jun
Trinidad and Tobago		Oct/Sep

[1]Unless noted otherwise, all data refer to calendar years.

Table G. Key Data Documentation

Country	Currency	National Accounts					Prices (CPI)	
		Historical Data Source[1]	Latest Actual Annual Data	Base Year[2]	System of National Accounts	Use of Chain-Weighted Methodology[3]	Historical Data Source[1]	Latest Actual Annual Data
Afghanistan	Afghan afghani	NSO	2019	2002/03	SNA 1993		NSO	2019
Albania	Albanian lek	IMF staff	2018	1996	ESA 2010	From 1996	NSO	2019
Algeria	Algerian dinar	NSO	2019	2001	SNA 1993	From 2005	NSO	2019
Angola	Angolan kwanza	NSO and MEP	2018	2002	ESA 1995		NSO	2019
Antigua and Barbuda	Eastern Caribbean dollar	CB	2019	2006[6]	SNA 1993		CB	2019
Argentina	Argentine peso	NSO	2019	2004	SNA 2008		NSO	2019
Armenia	Armenian dram	NSO	2019	2005	SNA 2008		NSO	2019
Aruba	Aruban Florin	NSO	2017	2000	SNA 1993	From 2000	NSO	2019
Australia	Australian dollar	NSO	2019	2017/18	SNA 2008	From 1980	NSO	2019
Austria	Euro	NSO	2019	2015	ESA 2010	From 1995	NSO	2019
Azerbaijan	Azerbaijan manat	NSO	2018	2005	SNA 1993	From 1994	NSO	2018
The Bahamas	Bahamian dollar	NSO	2018	2012	SNA 1993		NSO	2018
Bahrain	Bahrain dinar	NSO	2019	2010	SNA 2008		NSO	2019
Bangladesh	Bangladesh taka	NSO	2018/19	2005/06	SNA 1993		NSO	2018/19
Barbados	Barbados dollar	NSO and CB	2019	2010	SNA 1993		NSO	2019
Belarus	Belarusian ruble	NSO	2019	2014	SNA 2008	From 2005	NSO	2019
Belgium	Euro	CB	2019	2015	ESA 2010	From 1995	CB	2019
Belize	Belize dollar	NSO	2019	2000	SNA 1993		NSO	2019
Benin	CFA franc	NSO	2018	2015	SNA 1993		NSO	2019
Bhutan	Bhutanese ngultrum	NSO	2018/19	2000/01[6]	SNA 1993		CB	2018/19
Bolivia	Bolivian boliviano	NSO	2019	1990	SNA 2008		NSO	2019
Bosnia and Herzegovina	Bosnian convertible marka	NSO	2018	2015	ESA 2010	From 2000	NSO	2019
Botswana	Botswana pula	NSO	2019	2006	SNA 1993		NSO	2019
Brazil	Brazilian real	NSO	2019	1995	SNA 2008		NSO	2019
Brunei Darussalam	Brunei dollar	NSO and GAD	2019	2010	SNA 1993		NSO and GAD	2018
Bulgaria	Bulgarian lev	NSO	2019	2015	ESA 2010	From 1996	NSO	2019
Burkina Faso	CFA franc	NSO and MEP	2018	2015	SNA 1993		NSO	2019
Burundi	Burundi franc	NSO	2015	2005	SNA 1993		NSO	2018
Cabo Verde	Cabo Verdean escudo	NSO	2018	2007	SNA 2008	From 2011	NSO	2019
Cambodia	Cambodian riel	NSO	2018	2000	SNA 1993		NSO	2018
Cameroon	CFA franc	NSO	2019	2005	SNA 2008		NSO	2019
Canada	Canadian dollar	NSO	2019	2012	SNA 2008	From 1980	NSO	2019
Central African Republic	CFA franc	NSO	2017	2005	SNA 1993		NSO	2018
Chad	CFA franc	CB	2017	2005	SNA 1993		NSO	2019
Chile	Chilean peso	CB	2019	2013[6]	SNA 2008	From 2003	NSO	2019
China	Chinese yuan	NSO	2019	2015	SNA 2008		NSO	2018
Colombia	Colombian peso	NSO	2019	2015	SNA 2008	From 2005	NSO	2019
Comoros	Comorian franc	MoF	2018	2007	. . .	From 2007	NSO	2019
Democratic Republic of the Congo	Congolese franc	NSO	2019	2005	SNA 1993		CB	2019
Republic of Congo	CFA franc	NSO	2018	2005	SNA 1993		NSO	2019
Costa Rica	Costa Rican colón	CB	2019	2012	SNA 2008		CB	2019

Table G. Key Data Documentation *(continued)*

Country	Government Finance					Balance of Payments		
	Historical Data Source[1]	Latest Actual Annual Data	Statistics Manual in Use at Source	Subsectors Coverage[4]	Accounting Practice[5]	Historical Data Source[1]	Latest Actual Annual Data	Statistics Manual in Use at Source
Afghanistan	MoF	2019	2001	CG	C	NSO, MoF, and CB	2018	BPM 6
Albania	IMF staff	2018	1986	CG,LG,SS,MPC, NFPC	...	CB	2018	BPM 6
Algeria	MoF	2019	1986	CG	C	CB	2019	BPM 6
Angola	MoF	2018	2001	CG,LG	...	CB	2018	BPM 6
Antigua and Barbuda	MoF	2019	2001	CG	C	CB	2018	BPM 6
Argentina	MEP	2019	1986	CG,SG,SS	C	NSO	2019	BPM 6
Armenia	MoF	2019	2001	CG	C	CB	2019	BPM 6
Aruba	MoF	2019	2001	CG	Mixed	CB	2019	BPM 6
Australia	MoF	2018/19	2014	CG,SG,LG,TG	A	NSO	2019	BPM 6
Austria	NSO	2019	2014	CG,SG,LG,SS	A	CB	2019	BPM 6
Azerbaijan	MoF	2018	...	CG	C	CB	2018	BPM 6
The Bahamas	MoF	2018/19	2014	CG	C	CB	2019	BPM 5
Bahrain	MoF	2019	2001	CG	C	CB	2019	BPM 6
Bangladesh	MoF	2018/19	...	CG	C	CB	2018/19	BPM 6
Barbados	MoF	2019/20	1986	BCG	C	CB	2019	BPM 5
Belarus	MoF	2019	2001	CG,LG,SS	C	CB	2019	BPM 6
Belgium	CB	2019	ESA 2010	CG,SG,LG,SS	A	CB	2019	BPM 6
Belize	MoF	2019	1986	CG,MPC	Mixed	CB	2019	BPM 6
Benin	MoF	2019	1986	CG	C	CB	2018	BPM 6
Bhutan	MoF	2018/19	1986	CG	C	CB	2018/19	BPM 6
Bolivia	MoF	2019	2001	CG,LG,SS,NMPC, NFPC	C	CB	2019	BPM 6
Bosnia and Herzegovina	MoF	2019	2014	CG,SG,LG,SS	Mixed	CB	2019	BPM 6
Botswana	MoF	2018/19	1986	CG	C	CB	2019	BPM 6
Brazil	MoF	2019	2001	CG,SG,LG,SS,NFPC	C	CB	2019	BPM 6
Brunei Darussalam	MoF	2019	...	CG,BCG	C	NSO, MEP, and GAD	2018	BPM 6
Bulgaria	MoF	2019	2001	CG,LG,SS	C	CB	2019	BPM 6
Burkina Faso	MoF	2019	2001	CG	CB	CB	2018	BPM 6
Burundi	MoF	2015	2001	CG	A	CB	2016	BPM 6
Cabo Verde	MoF	2018	2001	CG	A	NSO	2018	BPM 6
Cambodia	MoF	2018	2001	CG,LG	Mixed	CB	2018	BPM 5
Cameroon	MoF	2019	2001	CG,NFPC,NMPC	Mixed	MoF	2018	BPM 6
Canada	MoF	2019	2001	CG,SG,LG,SS,other	A	NSO	2019	BPM 6
Central African Republic	MoF	2018	2001	CG	C	CB	2017	BPM 5
Chad	MoF	2019	1986	CG,NFPC	C	CB	2013	BPM 5
Chile	MoF	2019	2001	CG,LG	A	CB	2019	BPM 6
China	MoF	2019	...	CG,LG	C	GAD	2019	BPM 6
Colombia	MoF	2019	2001	CG,SG,LG,SS	...	CB and NSO	2019	BPM 6
Comoros	MoF	2018	1986	CG	Mixed	CB and IMF staff	2018	BPM 5
Democratic Republic of the Congo	MoF	2019	2001	CG,LG	A	CB	2019	BPM 6
Republic of Congo	MoF	2018	2001	CG	A	CB	2017	BPM 6
Costa Rica	MoF and CB	2019	1986	CG	C	CB	2019	BPM 6

Table G. Key Data Documentation *(continued)*

Country	Currency	National Accounts Historical Data Source[1]	Latest Actual Annual Data	Base Year[2]	System of National Accounts	Use of Chain-Weighted Methodology[3]	Prices (CPI) Historical Data Source[1]	Latest Actual Annual Data
Côte d'Ivoire	CFA franc	NSO	2017	2015	SNA 2008		NSO	2019
Croatia	Croatian kuna	NSO	2019	2015	ESA 2010		NSO	2019
Cyprus	Euro	NSO	2019	2010	ESA 2010	From 1995	NSO	2019
Czech Republic	Czech koruna	NSO	2019	2015	ESA 2010	From 1995	NSO	2019
Denmark	Danish krone	NSO	2019	2010	ESA 2010	From 1980	NSO	2019
Djibouti	Djibouti franc	NSO	2018	2013	SNA 1993		NSO	2019
Dominica	Eastern Caribbean dollar	NSO	2018	2006	SNA 1993		NSO	2019
Dominican Republic	Dominican peso	CB	2018	2007	SNA 2008	From 2007	CB	2019
Ecuador	US dollar	CB	2019	2007	SNA 1993		NSO and CB	2019
Egypt	Egyptian pound	MEP	2018/19	2016/17	SNA 2008		NSO	2019/20
El Salvador	US dollar	CB	2019	2014	SNA 2008		NSO	2019
Equatorial Guinea	CFA franc	MEP and CB	2017	2006	SNA 1993		MEP	2019
Eritrea	Eritrean nakfa	IMF staff	2018	2011	SNA 1993		NSO	2018
Estonia	Euro	NSO	2019	2015	ESA 2010	From 2010	NSO	2019
Eswatini	Swazi lilangeni	NSO	2018	2011	SNA 1993		NSO	2019
Ethiopia	Ethiopian birr	NSO	2018/19	2015/16	SNA 1993		NSO	2019
Fiji	Fijian dollar	NSO	2018	2014	SNA 1993		NSO	2018
Finland	Euro	NSO	2019	2010	ESA 2010	From 1980	NSO	2019
France	Euro	NSO	2019	2014	ESA 2010	From 1980	NSO	2019
Gabon	CFA franc	MoF	2019	2001	SNA 1993		NSO	2019
The Gambia	Gambian dalasi	NSO	2018	2013	SNA 1993		NSO	2018
Georgia	Georgian lari	NSO	2019	2015	SNA 1993	From 1996	NSO	2019
Germany	Euro	NSO	2019	2015	ESA 2010	From 1991	NSO	2019
Ghana	Ghanaian cedi	NSO	2018	2013	SNA 1993		NSO	2018
Greece	Euro	NSO	2019	2010	ESA 2010	From 1995	NSO	2019
Grenada	Eastern Caribbean dollar	NSO	2019	2006	SNA 1993		NSO	2019
Guatemala	Guatemalan quetzal	CB	2019	2013	SNA 1993	From 2001	NSO	2019
Guinea	Guinean franc	NSO	2018	2010	SNA 1993		NSO	2019
Guinea-Bissau	CFA franc	NSO	2018	2015	SNA 1993		NSO	2018
Guyana	Guyanese dollar	NSO	2019	2012[6]	SNA 2008		NSO	2019
Haiti	Haitian gourde	NSO	2017/18	1986/87	SNA 1993		NSO	2018/19
Honduras	Honduran lempira	CB	2019	2000	SNA 1993		CB	2019
Hong Kong SAR	Hong Kong dollar	NSO	2019	2018	SNA 2008	From 1980	NSO	2019
Hungary	Hungarian forint	NSO	2019	2015	ESA 2010	From 1995	IEO	2019
Iceland	Icelandic króna	NSO	2018	2005	ESA 2010	From 1990	NSO	2018
India	Indian rupee	NSO	2019/20	2011/12	SNA 2008		NSO	2019/20
Indonesia	Indonesian rupiah	NSO	2019	2010	SNA 2008		NSO	2019
Iran	Iranian rial	CB	2019/20	2011/12	SNA 1993		CB	2018/19
Iraq	Iraqi dinar	NSO	2019	2007	SNA 1968/93		NSO	2019
Ireland	Euro	NSO	2019	2017	ESA 2010	From 1995	NSO	2019
Israel	New Israeli shekel	NSO	2019	2015	SNA 2008	From 1995	NSO	2019
Italy	Euro	NSO	2019	2015	ESA 2010	From 1980	NSO	2019
Jamaica	Jamaican dollar	NSO	2019	2007	SNA 1993		NSO	2019

Table G. Key Data Documentation *(continued)*

Country	Historical Data Source[1]	Latest Actual Annual Data	Statistics Manual in Use at Source	Subsectors Coverage[4]	Accounting Practice[5]	Historical Data Source[1]	Latest Actual Annual Data	Statistics Manual in Use at Source
	Government Finance					Balance of Payments		
Côte d'Ivoire	MoF	2019	1986	CG	A	CB	2018	BPM 6
Croatia	MoF	2019	2014	CG,LG	A	CB	2019	BPM 6
Cyprus	NSO	2019	ESA 2010	CG,LG,SS	A	CB	2019	BPM 6
Czech Republic	MoF	2019	2014	CG,LG,SS	A	NSO	2019	BPM 6
Denmark	NSO	2019	2014	CG,LG,SS	A	NSO	2019	BPM 6
Djibouti	MoF	2019	2001	CG	A	CB	2018	BPM 5
Dominica	MoF	2019/20	1986	CG	C	CB	2018	BPM 6
Dominican Republic	MoF	2019	2014	CG,LG,SS,NMPC	A	CB	2018	BPM 6
Ecuador	CB and MoF	2019	1986	CG,SG,LG,SS,NFPC	Mixed	CB	2019	BPM 6
Egypt	MoF	2018/19	2001	CG,LG,SS,MPC	C	CB	2018/19	BPM 5
El Salvador	MoF and CB	2019	1986	CG,LG,SS,NFPC	C	CB	2019	BPM 6
Equatorial Guinea	MoF and MEP	2017	1986	CG	C	CB	2017	BPM 5
Eritrea	MoF	2018	2001	CG	C	CB	2018	BPM 5
Estonia	MoF	2019	1986/2001	CG,LG,SS	C	CB	2019	BPM 6
Eswatini	MoF	2018/19	2001	CG	A	CB	2019	BPM 6
Ethiopia	MoF	2018/19	1986	CG,SG,LG,NFPC	C	CB	2019/20	BPM 5
Fiji	MoF	2018	1986	CG	C	CB	2018	BPM 6
Finland	MoF	2019	2014	CG,LG,SS	A	NSO	2019	BPM 6
France	NSO	2019	2014	CG,LG,SS	A	CB	2019	BPM 6
Gabon	IMF staff	2019	2001	CG	A	CB	2019	BPM 5
The Gambia	MoF	2018	1986	CG	C	CB and IMF staff	2018	BPM 5
Georgia	MoF	2019	2001	CG,LG	C	NSO and CB	2019	BPM 6
Germany	NSO	2019	ESA 2010	CG,SG,LG,SS	A	CB	2019	BPM 6
Ghana	MoF	2018	2001	CG	C	CB	2018	BPM 5
Greece	NSO	2019	2014	CG,LG,SS	A	CB	2019	BPM 6
Grenada	MoF	2019	2014	CG	CB	CB	2018	BPM 6
Guatemala	MoF	2019	2001	CG	C	CB	2019	BPM 6
Guinea	MoF	2019	2001	CG	C	CB and MEP	2019	BPM 6
Guinea-Bissau	MoF	2018	2001	CG	A	CB	2018	BPM 6
Guyana	MoF	2019	1986	CG,SS,NFPC	C	CB	2019	BPM 6
Haiti	MoF	2018/19	1986	CG	C	CB	2018/19	BPM 5
Honduras	MoF	2019	2014	CG,LG,SS,other	Mixed	CB	2019	BPM 5
Hong Kong SAR	NSO	2018/19	2001	CG	C	NSO	2019	BPM 6
Hungary	MEP and NSO	2019	ESA 2010	CG,LG,SS,NMPC	A	CB	2019	BPM 6
Iceland	NSO	2018	2001	CG,LG,SS	A	CB	2018	BPM 6
India	MoF and IMF staff	2018/19	1986	CG,SG	C	CB	2018/19	BPM 6
Indonesia	MoF	2019	2001	CG,LG	C	CB	2019	BPM 6
Iran	MoF	2018/19	2001	CG	C	CB	2018/19	BPM 5
Iraq	MoF	2018	2001	CG	C	CB	2018	BPM 6
Ireland	MoF and NSO	2019	2001	CG,LG,SS	A	NSO	2019	BPM 6
Israel	MoF and NSO	2019	2014	CG,LG,SS	...	NSO	2019	BPM 6
Italy	NSO	2019	2001	CG,LG,SS	A	NSO	2019	BPM 6
Jamaica	MoF	2019/20	1986	CG	C	CB	2019/20	BPM 6

Table G. Key Data Documentation *(continued)*

Country	Currency	National Accounts					Prices (CPI)	
		Historical Data Source[1]	Latest Actual Annual Data	Base Year[2]	System of National Accounts	Use of Chain-Weighted Methodology[3]	Historical Data Source[1]	Latest Actual Annual Data
Japan	Japanese yen	GAD	2019	2011	SNA 2008	From 1980	GAD	2019
Jordan	Jordanian dinar	NSO	2019	2016	SNA 2008		NSO	2019
Kazakhstan	Kazakhstani tenge	NSO	2019	2007	SNA 1993	From 1994	CB	2019
Kenya	Kenyan shilling	NSO	2019	2009	SNA 2008		NSO	2019
Kiribati	Australian dollar	NSO	2017	2006	SNA 2008		IMF staff	2017
Korea	South Korean won	CB	2019	2015	SNA 2008	From 1980	NSO	2019
Kosovo	Euro	NSO	2019	2016	ESA 2010		NSO	2019
Kuwait	Kuwaiti dinar	MEP and NSO	2019	2010	SNA 1993		NSO and MEP	2019
Kyrgyz Republic	Kyrgyz som	NSO	2019	2005	SNA 1993		NSO	2019
Lao P.D.R.	Lao kip	NSO	2018	2012	SNA 1993		NSO	2019
Latvia	Euro	NSO	2019	2015	ESA 2010	From 1995	NSO	2019
Lebanon	Lebanese pound	NSO	2018	2010	SNA 2008	From 2010	NSO	2019/20
Lesotho	Lesotho loti	NSO	2017/18	2012/13	SNA 2008		NSO	2018
Liberia	US dollar	CB	2018	2018	SNA 1993		CB	2019
Libya	Libyan dinar	MEP	2017	2007	SNA 1993		NSO	2019
Lithuania	Euro	NSO	2019	2015	ESA 2010	From 2005	NSO	2019
Luxembourg	Euro	NSO	2019	2010	ESA 2010	From 1995	NSO	2019
Macao SAR	Macanese pataca	NSO	2019	2018	SNA 2008	From 2001	NSO	2019
Madagascar	Malagasy ariary	NSO	2018	2007	SNA 1993		NSO	2019
Malawi	Malawian kwacha	NSO	2011	2010	SNA 2008		NSO	2019
Malaysia	Malaysian ringgit	NSO	2019	2015	SNA 2008		NSO	2019
Maldives	Maldivian rufiyaa	MoF and NSO	2019	2014	SNA 1993		CB	2019
Mali	CFA franc	NSO	2018	1999	SNA 1993		NSO	2018
Malta	Euro	NSO	2019	2015	ESA 2010	From 2000	NSO	2019
Marshall Islands	US dollar	NSO	2017/18	2003/04	SNA 1993		NSO	2017/18
Mauritania	New Mauritanian ouguiya	NSO	2018	2014	SNA 2008	From 2014	NSO	2019
Mauritius	Mauritian rupee	NSO	2018	2006	SNA 1993	From 1999	NSO	2018
Mexico	Mexican peso	NSO	2019	2013	SNA 2008		NSO	2019
Micronesia	US dollar	NSO	2017/18	2003/04	SNA 1993		NSO	2017/18
Moldova	Moldovan leu	NSO	2019	1995	SNA 2008		NSO	2019
Mongolia	Mongolian tögrög	NSO	2019	2010	SNA 1993		NSO	2019
Montenegro	Euro	NSO	2019	2006	ESA 2010		NSO	2019
Morocco	Moroccan dirham	NSO	2019	2007	SNA 1993	From 2007	NSO	2019
Mozambique	Mozambican metical	NSO	2019	2014	SNA 1993/ 2008		NSO	2018
Myanmar	Myanmar kyat	MEP	2018/19	2015/16	. . .		NSO	2018/19
Namibia	Namibian dollar	NSO	2019	2000	SNA 1993		NSO	2019
Nauru	Australian dollar	. . .	2018/19	2006/07	SNA 1993		NSO	2019/20
Nepal	Nepalese rupee	NSO	2018/19	2000/01	SNA 1993		CB	2018/19
Netherlands	Euro	NSO	2019	2015	ESA 2010	From 1980	NSO	2019
New Zealand	New Zealand dollar	NSO	2019	2009/10	SNA 2008	From 1987	NSO	2019
Nicaragua	Nicaraguan córdoba	CB	2019	2006	SNA 1993	From 1994	CB	2019
Niger	CFA franc	NSO	2019	2015	SNA 1993		NSO	2019
Nigeria	Nigerian naira	NSO	2019	2010	SNA 2008		NSO	2019
North Macedonia	Macedonian denar	NSO	2019	2005	ESA 2010		NSO	2019
Norway	Norwegian krone	NSO	2018	2017	ESA 2010	From 1980	NSO	2019

Table G. Key Data Documentation *(continued)*

Country	Government Finance					Balance of Payments		
	Historical Data Source[1]	Latest Actual Annual Data	Statistics Manual in Use at Source	Subsectors Coverage[4]	Accounting Practice[5]	Historical Data Source[1]	Latest Actual Annual Data	Statistics Manual in Use at Source
Japan	GAD	2018	2014	CG,LG,SS	A	MoF	2019	BPM 6
Jordan	MoF	2019	2001	CG,NFPC	C	CB	2019	BPM 6
Kazakhstan	NSO	2019	2001	CG,LG	A	CB	2019	BPM 6
Kenya	MoF	2019	2001	CG	C	CB	2019	BPM 6
Kiribati	MoF	2017	1986	CG	C	NSO	2018	BPM 6
Korea	MoF	2019	2001	CG,SS	C	CB	2019	BPM 6
Kosovo	MoF	2019	. . .	CG,LG	C	CB	2019	BPM 6
Kuwait	MoF	2019	2014	CG,SS	Mixed	CB	2018	BPM 6
Kyrgyz Republic	MoF	2019	. . .	CG,LG,SS	C	CB	2019	BPM 6
Lao P.D.R.	MoF	2018	2001	CG	C	CB	2019	BPM 6
Latvia	MoF	2019	ESA 2010	CG,LG,SS	C	CB	2019	BPM 6
Lebanon	MoF	2019	2001	CG	Mixed	CB and IMF staff	2019	BPM 5
Lesotho	MoF	2019/20	2001	CG,LG	C	CB	2018/19	BPM 6
Liberia	MoF	2018	2001	CG	A	CB	2018	BPM 5
Libya	MoF	2019	1986	CG,SG,LG	C	CB	2017	BPM 6
Lithuania	MoF	2019	2014	CG,LG,SS	A	CB	2019	BPM 6
Luxembourg	MoF	2019	2001	CG,LG,SS	A	NSO	2019	BPM 6
Macao SAR	MoF	2018	2014	CG,SS	C	NSO	2018	BPM 6
Madagascar	MoF	2019	1986	CG,LG	C	CB	2019	BPM 6
Malawi	MoF	2018/19	1986	CG	C	NSO and GAD	2018	BPM 6
Malaysia	MoF	2019	2001	CG,SG,LG	C	NSO	2019	BPM 6
Maldives	MoF	2019	1986	CG	C	CB	2019	BPM 6
Mali	MoF	2018	2001	CG	Mixed	CB	2018	BPM 6
Malta	NSO	2019	2001	CG,SS	A	NSO	2019	BPM 6
Marshall Islands	MoF	2017/18	2001	CG,LG,SS	A	NSO	2017/18	BPM 6
Mauritania	MoF	2019	1986	CG	C	CB	2018	BPM 6
Mauritius	MoF	2019/20	2001	CG,LG,NFPC	C	CB	2018	BPM 6
Mexico	MoF	2019	2014	CG,SS,NMPC,NFPC	C	CB	2019	BPM 6
Micronesia	MoF	2017/18	2001	CG,SG	. . .	NSO	2017/18	BPM 6
Moldova	MoF	2019	1986	CG,LG	C	CB	2019	BPM 6
Mongolia	MoF	2019	2001	CG,SG,LG,SS	C	CB	2019	BPM 6
Montenegro	MoF	2019	1986/2001	CG,LG,SS	C	CB	2019	BPM 6
Morocco	MEP	2019	2001	CG	A	GAD	2019	BPM 6
Mozambique	MoF	2018	2001	CG,SG	Mixed	CB	2018	BPM 6
Myanmar	MoF	2018/19	2014	CG,NFPC	C	IMF staff	2018/19	BPM 6
Namibia	MoF	2018/19	2001	CG	C	CB	2019	BPM 6
Nauru	MoF	2019/20	2001	CG	Mixed	IMF staff	2018/19	BPM 6
Nepal	MoF	2018/19	2001	CG	C	CB	2018/19	BPM 5
Netherlands	MoF	2019	2001	CG,LG,SS	A	CB	2019	BPM 6
New Zealand	MoF	2018/19	2014	CG, LG	A	NSO	2019	BPM 6
Nicaragua	MoF	2018	1986	CG,LG,SS	C	IMF staff	2018	BPM 6
Niger	MoF	2019	1986	CG	A	CB	2018	BPM 6
Nigeria	MoF	2019	2001	CG,SG,LG	C	CB	2019	BPM 6
North Macedonia	MoF	2019	1986	CG,SG,SS	C	CB	2019	BPM 6
Norway	NSO and MoF	2019	2014	CG,LG,SS	A	NSO	2018	BPM 6

Table G. Key Data Documentation *(continued)*

Country	Currency	National Accounts					Prices (CPI)	
		Historical Data Source[1]	Latest Actual Annual Data	Base Year[2]	System of National Accounts	Use of Chain-Weighted Methodology[3]	Historical Data Source[1]	Latest Actual Annual Data
Oman	Omani rial	NSO	2019	2010	SNA 1993		NSO	2019
Pakistan	Pakistan rupee	NSO	2019/20	2005/06[6]	. . .		NSO	2019/20
Palau	US dollar	MoF	2018/19	2014/15	SNA 1993		MoF	2018/19
Panama	US dollar	NSO	2019	2007	SNA 1993	From 2007	NSO	2019
Papua New Guinea	Papua New Guinea kina	NSO and MoF	2015	2013	SNA 1993		NSO	2015
Paraguay	Paraguayan guaraní	CB	2018	2014	SNA 2008		CB	2018
Peru	Peruvian sol	CB	2019	2007	SNA 1993		CB	2019
Philippines	Philippine peso	NSO	2019	2018	SNA 2008		NSO	2019
Poland	Polish zloty	NSO	2019	2010	ESA 2010	From 2010	NSO	2019
Portugal	Euro	NSO	2019	2016	ESA 2010	From 1980	NSO	2019
Puerto Rico	US dollar	NSO	2017/18	1954	SNA 1968		NSO	2018/19
Qatar	Qatari riyal	NSO and MEP	2019	2018	SNA 1993		NSO and MEP	2019
Romania	Romanian leu	NSO	2019	2015	ESA 2010	From 2000	NSO	2019
Russia	Russian ruble	NSO	2019	2016	SNA 2008	From 1995	NSO	2019
Rwanda	Rwandan franc	NSO	2018	2017	SNA 2008		NSO	2019
Samoa	Samoan tala	NSO	2018/19	2012/13	SNA 2008		NSO	2018/19
San Marino	Euro	NSO	2018	2007	. . .		NSO	2018
São Tomé and Príncipe	São Tomé and Príncipe dobra	NSO	2019	2008	SNA 1993		NSO	2019
Saudi Arabia	Saudi riyal	NSO	2019	2010	SNA 1993		NSO	2019
Senegal	CFA franc	NSO	2019	2014	SNA 1993		NSO	2019
Serbia	Serbian dinar	NSO	2019	2010	ESA 2010	From 2010	NSO	2019
Seychelles	Seychelles rupee	NSO	2017	2006	SNA 1993		NSO	2019
Sierra Leone	Sierra Leonean leone	NSO	2018	2006	SNA 1993	From 2010	NSO	2019
Singapore	Singapore dollar	NSO	2019	2015	SNA 2008	From 2015	NSO	2019
Slovak Republic	Euro	NSO	2019	2015	ESA 2010	From 1997	NSO	2019
Slovenia	Euro	NSO	2019	2010	ESA 2010	From 2000	NSO	2019
Solomon Islands	Solomon Islands dollar	CB	2019	2012	SNA 1993		NSO	2019
Somalia	US dollar	CB	2019	2013	SNA 1993		CB	2019
South Africa	South African rand	NSO	2019	2010	SNA 2008		NSO	2019
South Sudan	South Sudanese pound	NSO and IMF staff	2018	2010	SNA 1993		NSO	2019
Spain	Euro	NSO	2019	2015	ESA 2010	From 1995	NSO	2019
Sri Lanka	Sri Lankan rupee	NSO	2019	2010	SNA 1993		NSO	2019
St. Kitts and Nevis	Eastern Caribbean dollar	NSO	2019	2006	SNA 1993		NSO	2019
St. Lucia	Eastern Caribbean dollar	NSO	2018	2018	SNA 1993		NSO	2018
St. Vincent and the Grenadines	Eastern Caribbean dollar	NSO	2019	2006	SNA 1993		NSO	2019
Sudan	Sudanese pound	NSO	2019	1982	SNA 1968		NSO	2019
Suriname	Surinamese dollar	NSO	2018	2007	SNA 1993		NSO	2019

Table G. Key Data Documentation *(continued)*

Country	Government Finance					Balance of Payments		
	Historical Data Source[1]	Latest Actual Annual Data	Statistics Manual in Use at Source	Subsectors Coverage[4]	Accounting Practice[5]	Historical Data Source[1]	Latest Actual Annual Data	Statistics Manual in Use at Source
Oman	MoF	2018	2001	CG	C	CB	2018	BPM 5
Pakistan	MoF	2019/20	1986	CG,SG,LG	C	CB	2019/20	BPM 6
Palau	MoF	2018/19	2001	CG	. . .	MoF	2018/19	BPM 6
Panama	MoF	2019	2014	CG,SG,LG,SS,NFPC	C	NSO	2019	BPM 6
Papua New Guinea	MoF	2015	1986	CG	C	CB	2015	BPM 5
Paraguay	MoF	2019	2001	CG,SG,LG,SS,MPC, NFPC	C	CB	2018	BPM 6
Peru	CB and MoF	2019	2001	CG,SG,LG,SS	Mixed	CB	2019	BPM 5
Philippines	MoF	2019	2001	CG,LG,SS	C	CB	2019	BPM 6
Poland	MoF and NSO	2019	ESA 2010	CG,LG,SS	A	CB	2019	BPM 6
Portugal	NSO	2019	2001	CG,LG,SS	A	CB	2019	BPM 6
Puerto Rico	MEP	2015/16	2001	. . .	A	. . .	. . .	. . .
Qatar	MoF	2019	1986	CG	C	CB and IMF staff	2019	BPM 5
Romania	MoF	2019	2001	CG,LG,SS	C	CB	2019	BPM 6
Russia	MoF	2019	2014	CG,SG,SS	Mixed	CB	2019	BPM 6
Rwanda	MoF	2018	1986	CG,LG	Mixed	CB	2018	BPM 6
Samoa	MoF	2018/19	2001	CG	A	CB	2018/19	BPM 6
San Marino	MoF	2018	. . .	CG	. . .	Other	2018	. . .
São Tomé and Príncipe	MoF and Customs	2019	2001	CG	C	CB	2019	BPM 6
Saudi Arabia	MoF	2019	2014	CG	C	CB	2019	BPM 6
Senegal	MoF	2019	2001	CG	C	CB and IMF staff	2019	BPM 6
Serbia	MoF	2019	1986/2001	CG,SG,LG,SS,other	C	CB	2018	BPM 6
Seychelles	MoF	2019	1986	CG,SS	C	CB	2017	BPM 6
Sierra Leone	MoF	2019	1986	CG	C	CB	2018	BPM 5
Singapore	MoF and NSO	2019/20	2014	CG	C	NSO	2019	BPM 6
Slovak Republic	NSO	2019	2001	CG,LG,SS	A	CB	2019	BPM 6
Slovenia	MoF	2019	2001	CG,LG,SS	A	CB	2019	BPM 6
Solomon Islands	MoF	2019	1986	CG	C	CB	2019	BPM 6
Somalia	MoF	2019	2001	CG	C	CB	2019	BPM 5
South Africa	MoF	2019	2001	CG,SG,SS,other	C	CB	2019	BPM 6
South Sudan	MoF and MEP	2019	. . .	CG	C	MoF, NSO, and MEP	2018	BPM 6
Spain	MoF and NSO	2019	ESA 2010	CG,SG,LG,SS	A	CB	2019	BPM 6
Sri Lanka	MoF	2019	2001	CG	C	CB	2019	BPM 6
St. Kitts and Nevis	MoF	2019	1986	CG, SG	C	CB	2018	BPM 6
St. Lucia	MoF	2017/18	1986	CG	C	CB	2018	BPM 6
St. Vincent and the Grenadines	MoF	2019	1986	CG	C	CB	2018	BPM 6
Sudan	MoF	2019	2001	CG	Mixed	CB	2019	BPM 6
Suriname	MoF	2018	1986	CG	Mixed	CB	2019	BPM 5

Table G. Key Data Documentation *(continued)*

Country	Currency	National Accounts					Prices (CPI)	
		Historical Data Source[1]	Latest Actual Annual Data	Base Year[2]	System of National Accounts	Use of Chain-Weighted Methodology[3]	Historical Data Source[1]	Latest Actual Annual Data
Sweden	Swedish krona	NSO	2019	2019	ESA 2010	From 1993	NSO	2019
Switzerland	Swiss franc	NSO	2019	2010	ESA 2010	From 1980	NSO	2019
Syria	Syrian pound	NSO	2010	2000	SNA 1993		NSO	2011
Taiwan Province of China	New Taiwan dollar	NSO	2019	2016	SNA 2008		NSO	2019
Tajikistan	Tajik somoni	NSO	2018	1995	SNA 1993		NSO	2018
Tanzania	Tanzanian shilling	NSO	2018	2015	SNA 2008		NSO	2018
Thailand	Thai baht	MEP	2018	2002	SNA 1993	From 1993	MEP	2019
Timor-Leste	US dollar	NSO	2018	2015[6]	SNA 2008		NSO	2019
Togo	CFA franc	NSO	2016	2007	SNA 1993		NSO	2019
Tonga	Tongan pa'anga	CB	2018/19	2016/17	SNA 1993		CB	2018/19
Trinidad and Tobago	Trinidad and Tobago dollar	NSO	2018	2012	SNA 1993		NSO	2019
Tunisia	Tunisian dinar	NSO	2019	2010	SNA 1993	From 2009	NSO	2019
Turkey	Turkish lira	NSO	2019	2009	ESA 2010	From 2009	NSO	2019
Turkmenistan	New Turkmen manat	NSO	2018	2008	SNA 1993	From 2000	NSO	2018
Tuvalu	Australian dollar	PFTAC advisors	2018	2005	SNA 1993		NSO	2018
Uganda	Ugandan shilling	NSO	2019	2016	SNA 1993		CB	2018/19
Ukraine	Ukrainian hryvnia	NSO	2019	2016	SNA 2008	From 2005	NSO	2019
United Arab Emirates	U.A.E. dirham	NSO	2019	2010	SNA 2008		NSO	2019
United Kingdom	British pound	NSO	2019	2016	ESA 2010	From 1980	NSO	2019
United States	US dollar	NSO	2019	2012	SNA 2008	From 1980	NSO	2019
Uruguay	Uruguayan peso	CB	2019	2005	SNA 1993		NSO	2019
Uzbekistan	Uzbek som	NSO	2019	2015	SNA 1993		NSO and IMF staff	2019
Vanuatu	Vanuatu vatu	NSO	2018	2006	SNA 1993		NSO	2019
Venezuela	Venezuelan bolívar soberano	CB	2018	1997	SNA 2008		CB	2019
Vietnam	Vietnamese dong	NSO	2019	2010	SNA 1993		NSO	2019
West Bank and Gaza	New Israeli shekel	NSO	2019	2015	SNA 2008		NSO	2019
Yemen	Yemeni rial	IMF staff	2019	1990	SNA 1993		NSO,CB, and IMF staff	2019
Zambia	Zambian kwacha	NSO	2018	2010	SNA 2008		NSO	2019
Zimbabwe	Zimbabwe dollar	NSO	2019	2012	. . .		NSO	2019

Table G. Key Data Documentation *(continued)*

Country	Government Finance					Balance of Payments		
	Historical Data Source[1]	Latest Actual Annual Data	Statistics Manual in Use at Source	Subsectors Coverage[4]	Accounting Practice[5]	Historical Data Source[1]	Latest Actual Annual Data	Statistics Manual in Use at Source
Sweden	MoF	2018	2001	CG,LG,SS	A	NSO	2018	BPM 6
Switzerland	MoF	2018	2001	CG,SG,LG,SS	A	CB	2019	BPM 6
Syria	MoF	2009	1986	CG	C	CB	2009	BPM 5
Taiwan Province of China	MoF	2019	2001	CG,LG,SS	C	CB	2019	BPM 6
Tajikistan	MoF	2018	1986	CG,LG,SS	C	CB	2018	BPM 6
Tanzania	MoF	2018	1986	CG,LG	C	CB	2018	BPM 6
Thailand	MoF	2018/19	2001	CG,BCG,LG,SS	A	CB	2018	BPM 6
Timor-Leste	MoF	2018	2001	CG	C	CB	2019	BPM 6
Togo	MoF	2019	2001	CG	C	CB	2018	BPM 6
Tonga	MoF	2018/19	2014	CG	C	CB and NSO	2018/19	BPM 6
Trinidad and Tobago	MoF	2018/19	1986	CG	C	CB	2019	BPM 6
Tunisia	MoF	2019	1986	CG	C	CB	2019	BPM 5
Turkey	MoF	2019	2001	CG,LG,SS,other	A	CB	2019	BPM 6
Turkmenistan	MoF	2018	1986	CG,LG	C	NSO and IMF staff	2015	BPM 6
Tuvalu	MoF	2019	...	CG	Mixed	IMF staff	2012	BPM 6
Uganda	MoF	2019	2001	CG	C	CB	2019	BPM 6
Ukraine	MoF	2019	2001	CG,LG,SS	C	CB	2019	BPM 6
United Arab Emirates	MoF	2018	2001	CG,BCG,SG,SS	Mixed	CB	2018	BPM 5
United Kingdom	NSO	2019	2001	CG,LG	A	NSO	2019	BPM 6
United States	MEP	2019	2014	CG,SG,LG	A	NSO	2019	BPM 6
Uruguay	MoF	2019	1986	CG,LG,SS,NFPC,NMPC	C	CB	2019	BPM 6
Uzbekistan	MoF	2019	2014	CG,SG,LG,SS	C	CB and MEP	2019	BPM 6
Vanuatu	MoF	2019	2001	CG	C	CB	2019	BPM 6
Venezuela	MoF	2017	2001	BCG,NFPC,SS,other	C	CB	2018	BPM 6
Vietnam	MoF	2018	2001	CG,SG,LG	C	CB	2018	BPM 5
West Bank and Gaza	MoF	2019	2001	CG	Mixed	NSO	2019	BPM 6
Yemen	MoF	2019	2001	CG,LG	C	IMF staff	2019	BPM 5
Zambia	MoF	2019	1986	CG	C	CB	2018	BPM 6
Zimbabwe	MoF	2018	1986	CG	C	CB and MoF	2018	BPM 6

Note: BPM = *Balance of Payments Manual*; CPI = consumer price index; ESA = European System of National Accounts; SNA = System of National Accounts.
[1]CB = central bank; Customs = Customs Authority; GAD = General Administration Department; IEO = international economic organization; MEP = Ministry of Economy, Planning, Commerce, and/or Development; MoF = Ministry of Finance and/or Treasury; NSO = National Statistics Office; PFTAC = Pacific Financial Technical Assistance Centre.
[2]National accounts base year is the period with which other periods are compared and the period for which prices appear in the denominators of the price relationships used to calculate the index.
[3]Use of chain-weighted methodology allows countries to measure GDP growth more accurately by reducing or eliminating the downward biases in volume series built on index numbers that average volume components using weights from a year in the moderately distant past.
[4]BCG = budgetary central government; CG = central government; LG = local government; MPC = monetary public corporation, including central bank; NFPC = nonfinancial public corporation; NMPC = nonmonetary financial public corporation; SG = state government; SS = social security fund; TG = territorial governments.
[5]Accounting standard: A = accrual accounting; C = cash accounting; CB = commitments basis accounting; Mixed = combination of accrual and cash accounting.
[6]Base year is not equal to 100 because the nominal GDP is not measured in the same way as real GDP or the data are seasonally adjusted.

Box A1. Economic Policy Assumptions Underlying the Projections for Selected Economies

Fiscal Policy Assumptions

The short-term fiscal policy assumptions used in the *World Economic Outlook* (WEO) are normally based on officially announced budgets, adjusted for differences between the national authorities and the IMF staff regarding macroeconomic assumptions and projected fiscal outturns. When no official budget has been announced, projections incorporate policy measures that are judged likely to be implemented. The medium-term fiscal projections are similarly based on a judgment about the most likely path of policies. For cases in which the IMF staff has insufficient information to assess the authorities' budget intentions and prospects for policy implementation, an unchanged structural primary balance is assumed unless indicated otherwise. Specific assumptions used in regard to some of the advanced economies follow. See also Tables B5 to B9 in the online section of the Statistical Appendix for data on fiscal net lending/borrowing and structural balances.[1]

Argentina: Fiscal projections are based on the available information regarding budget outturn and budget plans for the federal and provincial governments, fiscal measures announced by the authorities, and the IMF staff's macroeconomic projections.

Australia: Fiscal projections are based on data from the Australian Bureau of Statistics, the fiscal year 2019/20 mid-year reviews of the Commonwealth and States, the Economic and Fiscal Outlook in July 2020, and the IMF staff's estimates and projections.

Austria: Fiscal projections are based on data from Statistics Austria, the authorities' projections, and the IMF staff's estimates and projections.

Belgium: Projections are based on the 2020–21 Stability Programme (covering only two years due

to the COVID-19 shock), the Draft Budgetary Plan 2020, and other available information on the authorities' fiscal plans, with adjustments for the IMF staff's assumptions.

Brazil: Fiscal projections for 2020 reflect policy announcements as of July 31. Those for the medium term assume compliance with the constitutional spending ceiling.

Canada: Projections use the baseline forecasts in the 2019 federal budget, the Economic and Fiscal Snapshot 2020, and the latest provincial budget as available. The IMF staff makes some adjustments to these forecasts, including for differences in macroeconomic projections. The IMF staff's forecast also incorporates the most recent data releases from Statistics Canada's Canadian System of National Economic Accounts, including federal, provincial, and territorial budgetary outturns through the first quarter of 2020.

Chile: Projections are based on the authorities' quarterly fiscal reports, adjusted to reflect the IMF staff's projections for GDP and copper prices.

China: A large fiscal expansion is estimated for 2020 based on budgeted and announced tax and expenditure measures in response to offset the health and economic repercussions of the COVID-19 pandemic. For 2021 a mild expansion is projected given that the output gap is expected to remain relatively large.

Denmark: Estimates for 2020 are aligned with the latest official budget numbers, adjusted where appropriate for the IMF staff's macroeconomic assumptions. For 2021 the projections incorporate key features of the medium-term fiscal plan as embodied in the authorities' latest budget.

France: Estimates for 2019 and projections for 2020 onward are based on the measures of the 2018 budget law, the 2019 budget law, and the 2020 budget law, adjusted for differences in assumptions on macroeconomic and financial variables, and revenue projections. Historical fiscal data reflect the May 2019 revisions and update of the historical fiscal accounts, debt data, and national accounts.

Germany: The IMF staff's projections for 2020 and beyond are based on the 2020 Stability Program, supplementary budgets, and data updates from the national statistical agency and ministry of finance, adjusted for the differences in the IMF staff's macroeconomic framework and assumptions concerning revenue elasticities. The estimate of gross debt includes

[1] The output gap is actual minus potential output, as a percentage of potential output. Structural balances are expressed as a percentage of potential output. The structural balance is the actual net lending/borrowing minus the effects of cyclical output from potential output, corrected for one-time and other factors, such as asset and commodity prices and output composition effects. Changes in the structural balance consequently include effects of temporary fiscal measures, the impact of fluctuations in interest rates and debt-service costs, and other noncyclical fluctuations in net lending/borrowing. The computations of structural balances are based on the IMF staff's estimates of potential GDP and revenue and expenditure elasticities. (See Annex I of the October 1993 WEO.) Net debt is calculated as gross debt minus financial assets corresponding to debt instruments. Estimates of the output gap and of the structural balance are subject to significant margins of uncertainty.

Box A1 *(continued)*

portfolios of impaired assets and noncore business transferred to institutions that are winding up, as well as other financial sector and EU support operations.

Greece: Historical data since 2010 reflect adjustments in line with the primary balance definition under the enhanced surveillance framework for Greece.

Hong Kong Special Administrative Region: Projections are based on the authorities' medium-term fiscal projections on expenditures.

Hungary: Fiscal projections include the IMF staff's projections of the macroeconomic framework and fiscal policy plans announced in the 2020 budget.

India: Historical data are based on budgetary execution data. Projections are based on available information on the authorities' fiscal plans, with adjustments for the IMF staff's assumptions. Subnational data are incorporated with a lag of up to one year; general government data are thus finalized well after central government data. IMF and Indian presentations differ, particularly regarding disinvestment and license-auction proceeds, net versus gross recording of revenues in certain minor categories, and some public sector lending.

Indonesia: IMF projections are consistent with gradual unwinding of the large fiscal stimulus in 2020, including returning the fiscal deficit to below 3 percent of GDP by 2023.

Ireland: Fiscal projections are based on the country's Budget 2020 and Stability Programme Update 2020.

Israel: Historical data are based on government finance statistics data prepared by the Central Bureau of Statistics. Projections assume the partial implementation of the two fiscal packages provided by parliament in response to the coronavirus shock.

Italy: The IMF staff's estimates and projections are informed by the fiscal plans included in the government's 2020 budget and approved supplementary budgets. The stock of maturing postal saving bonds is included in the debt projections.

Japan: Projections reflect the fiscal measures already announced by the government, as of September 11, with adjustments for IMF staff assumptions.

Korea: The medium-term forecast incorporates the medium-term path for the overall fiscal balance in the 2021 budget and the medium-term fiscal plan announced in the 2021 budget, and IMF staff's adjustment.

Mexico: Fiscal projections for 2020 are informed by the approved budget but take into account the likely effects of the COVID-19 pandemic on fiscal

outturns; projections for 2021 onward assume compliance with rules established in the Fiscal Responsibility Law. The projections reflect data available until August 31, 2020. Hence, they do not take into account the draft 2021 budget.

Netherlands: Fiscal projections for 2020–25 are based on IMF staff forecasts and informed by the authorities' draft budget plan and Bureau for Economic Policy Analysis projections. Historical data were revised following the June 2014 Central Bureau of Statistics release of revised macro data because of the adoption of the European System of National and Regional Accounts (ESA 2010) and the revisions of data sources.

New Zealand: Fiscal projections are based on the fiscal year 2020/21 budget and IMF staff estimates.

Portugal: The projections for the current year are based on the authorities' approved budget, adjusted to reflect the IMF staff's macroeconomic forecast. Projections thereafter are based on the assumption of unchanged policies.

Puerto Rico: Fiscal projections are based on the Puerto Rico Fiscal and Economic Growth Plans (FEGPs), which were prepared in October 2018, and are certified by the Oversight Board. In line with this plan's assumptions, IMF projections assume federal aid for rebuilding after Hurricane Maria, which devastated the island in September 2017. The projections also assume revenue losses from the following: elimination of federal funding for the Affordable Care Act starting in 2020 for Puerto Rico; elimination of federal tax incentives starting in 2018 that had neutralized the effects of Puerto Rico's Act 154 on foreign firms; and the effects of the Tax Cuts and Jobs Act, which reduce the tax advantage of US firms producing in Puerto Rico. Given sizable policy uncertainty, some FEGP and IMF assumptions may differ, in particular those relating to the effects of the corporate tax reform, tax compliance, and tax adjustments (fees and rates); reduction of subsidies and expenses, freezing of payroll operational costs, and improvement of mobility; reduction of expenses; and increased health care efficiency. On the expenditure side, measures include extension of Act 66, which freezes much government spending, through 2020; reduction of operating costs; decreases in government subsidies; and spending cuts in education. Although IMF policy assumptions are similar to those in the FEGP scenario with full measures, the IMF's projections of fiscal revenues, expenditures, and balance are different from the FEGPs'. This stems from

Box A1 *(continued)*

two main differences in methodologies: first, while IMF projections are on an accrual basis, the FEGPs' are on a cash basis. Second, the IMF and FEGPs make very different macroeconomic assumptions.

Russia: Fiscal policy will be countercyclical in 2020. It will show a degree of consolidation in 2021 and will return to the fiscal rule in 2022.

Saudi Arabia: The IMF staff baseline fiscal projections are based on IMF staff's understanding of government policies as outlined in the 2020 Budget and government measures announced to counter the adverse impact of COVID-19 and the decline in oil prices. Exported oil revenues are based on WEO baseline oil prices and staff's understanding of Saudi Arabia's current oil export policy.

Singapore: For fiscal year 2020 projections are based on the budget (February 18, 2020) and subsequent supplementary budgets (March 26, April 6, April 21, May 26). IMF staff assumes that support packages in fiscal year 2020 are only for one year; for the rest of the projection period, IMF staff assumes unchanged policies.

South Africa: Fiscal assumptions are mostly based on the 2020 Budget Review. Nontax revenue excludes transactions in financial assets and liabilities as they involve primarily revenues associated with realized exchange rate valuation gains from the holding of foreign currency deposits, sale of assets, and conceptually similar items.

Spain: The 2020 fiscal projections include the discretionary measures adopted in response to the COVID-19 crisis, the legislated pension and public wage increases, and the minimal vital income support. Fiscal projections from 2021 onward assume an expiration of the temporary COVID-19 measures and no further policy change. Disbursements under the EU Recovery and Resilience Facility are reflected in the projections for 2021–24.

Sweden: Fiscal estimates for 2019 are based on the data from the Swedish Ministry of Finance. Projections for 2020 are based on preliminary information on the fall 2020 budget bill. The fiscal impact of cyclical developments is calculated using the 2014 Organisation for Economic Co-operation and Development's elasticity[2] to take into account output and employment gaps.

[2] See Robert Price, Thai-Thanh Dang, and Yvan Guillemette, "New Tax and Expenditure Elasticity Estimates for EU Budget Surveillance," OECD Economics Department Working Papers 1174 (Paris: Organisation for Economic Co-operation and Development, December 2019).

Switzerland: The fiscal projections for 2020 reflect the authorities' discretionary stimulus, which is permitted within the context of the debt brake rule in the event of "exceptional circumstances."

Turkey: The basis for the projections in the WEO and *Fiscal Monitor* is the IMF-defined fiscal balance, which excludes some revenue and expenditure items that are included in the authorities' headline balance.

United Kingdom: Fiscal projections are based on the UK's Budget Statement 2020 and revised estimated by the Office for Budget Responsibility. Expenditure projections reflect the measures to respond to the outbreak of the coronavirus. Revenue projections are in addition adjusted for differences between the IMF staff's forecasts of macroeconomic variables (such as GDP growth and inflation) and the forecasts of these variables assumed in the authorities' fiscal projections. Projections assume that the measures taken in response to the coronavirus outbreak expire as announced, but also that there is some additional fiscal loosening relative to the policies announced to date over the next two years to support the economic recovery, and gradual consolidation begins thereafter with the goal of stabilizing public debt within five years. The IMF staff's data exclude public sector banks and the effect of transferring assets from the Royal Mail Pension Plan to the public sector in April 2012. Real government consumption and investment are part of the real GDP path, which, according to the IMF staff, may or may not be the same as projected by the UK Office for Budget Responsibility. Fiscal year GDP is different from current year GDP. The fiscal accounts are presented in terms of fiscal year. Projections do not take into account revisions to the accounting (including on student loans) implemented on September 24, 2019.

United States: Fiscal projections are based on the January 2020 Congressional Budget Office baseline, adjusted for the IMF staff's policy and macroeconomic assumptions. Projections incorporate the effects of the Coronavirus Preparedness and Response Supplemental Appropriations Act, the Families First Coronavirus Response Act, and the Paycheck Protection Program and Health Care Enhancement Act. Finally, fiscal projections are adjusted to reflect the IMF staff's forecasts for key macroeconomic and financial variables and different accounting treatment of financial sector support and of defined-benefit pension plans and are converted to a general government basis. Data are compiled using System of National Accounts 2008, and when translated

Box A1 *(continued)*

into government finance statistics, this is in accordance with the *Government Finance Statistics Manual 2014.* Due to data limitations, most series begin in 2001.

Monetary Policy Assumptions

Monetary policy assumptions are based on the established policy framework in each country. In most cases, this implies a nonaccommodative stance over the business cycle: official interest rates will increase when economic indicators suggest that inflation will rise above its acceptable rate or range; they will decrease when indicators suggest inflation will not exceed the acceptable rate or range, that output growth is below its potential rate, and that the margin of slack in the economy is significant. On this basis, the London interbank offered rate on six-month US dollar deposits is assumed to average 0.7 percent in 2020 and 0.4 percent in 2021 (see Table 1.1). The rate on three-month euro deposits is assumed to average –0.4 percent in 2020 and –0.5 percent in 2021. The interest rate on six-month Japanese yen deposits is assumed to average 0.0 percent in 2020 and in 2021.

Argentina: Monetary policy assumptions are consistent with a modest real appreciation this year and the need for monetary financing of the fiscal deficit and reabsorbing this liquidity.

Australia: Monetary policy assumptions are in line with market expectations.

Brazil: Monetary policy assumptions are consistent with gradual convergence of inflation toward the middle of the target range.

Canada: Monetary policy assumptions are based on the IMF staff's analysis.

Chile: Monetary policy assumptions are based on GDP growth rate.

China: Monetary policy is expected to be accommodative in 2020 and remain supportive in 2021 (but to a lower degree than in 2020).

Denmark: Monetary policy is to maintain the peg to the euro.

Euro area: Monetary policy assumptions for euro area member countries are in line with market expectations.

Greece: Interest rates are based on the WEO LIBOR with an assumption of a spread for Greece. Broad money projections are based on the monetary financial institution balance sheets and deposit flow assumptions.

Hong Kong Special Administrative Region: The IMF staff assumes that the currency board system will remain intact.

India: Monetary policy projections are consistent with achieving the Reserve Bank of India's inflation target over the medium term.

Indonesia: Monetary policy assumptions are in line with the maintenance of inflation within the central bank's targeted band.

Israel: Assumptions include a moderately loose monetary stance in the short term and normalization of nonmonetary policy toward the medium term.

Japan: Monetary policy assumptions are in line with market expectations.

Korea: The projections assume that the policy rate evolves in line with market expectations.

Mexico: Monetary policy assumptions are consistent with attaining the inflation target.

Netherlands: Monetary projections are based on IMF staff six-month euro LIBOR projections.

New Zealand: Monetary projections are based on the growth of nominal GDP estimates.

Portugal: Monetary projections are based on projections for the real and fiscal sectors.

Russia: Monetary projections assume that the Central Bank of Russia is adopting a moderately accommodative monetary policy stance.

Saudi Arabia: Monetary policy projections are based on the continuation of the exchange rate peg to the US dollar.

Singapore: Broad money is projected to grow in line with the projected growth in nominal GDP.

South Africa: Monetary policy assumptions are consistent with maintaining inflation within the 3–6 percent target band.

Sweden: Monetary projections are in line with Riksbank projections.

Switzerland: The projections assume no change in the policy rate in 2020–21.

Turkey: The outlook for monetary and financial conditions assumes no further monetary policy easing in 2020.

United Kingdom: The short-term interest rate path is based on market interest rate expectations.

United States: The IMF staff expects the Federal Open Market Committee to continue to adjust the federal funds target rate in line with the broader macroeconomic outlook.

List of Tables[1]

Output

A1.   Summary of World Output
A2.   Advanced Economies: Real GDP and Total Domestic Demand
A3.   Advanced Economies: Components of Real GDP
A4.   Emerging Market and Developing Economies: Real GDP

Inflation

A5. Summary of Inflation
A6. Advanced Economies: Consumer Prices
A7. Emerging Market and Developing Economies: Consumer Prices

Financial Policies

A8. Major Advanced Economies: General Government Fiscal Balances and Debt

Foreign Trade

A9. Summary of World Trade Volumes and Prices

Current Account Transactions

A10. Summary of Current Account Balances
A11. Advanced Economies: Current Account Balance
A12. Emerging Market and Developing Economies: Current Account Balance

Balance of Payments and External Financing

A13. Summary of Financial Account Balances

Flow of Funds

A14. Summary of Net Lending and Borrowing

Medium-Term Baseline Scenario

A15. Summary of World Medium-Term Baseline Scenario

[1] In the tables, when countries are not listed alphabetically, they are ordered on the basis of economic size.

Table A1. Summary of World Output[1]
(Annual percent change)

	Average 2002–11	2012	2013	2014	2015	2016	2017	2018	2019	Projections 2020	Projections 2021	Projections 2025
World	**4.1**	**3.5**	**3.5**	**3.5**	**3.4**	**3.3**	**3.8**	**3.5**	**2.8**	**−4.4**	**5.2**	**3.5**
Advanced Economies	**1.7**	**1.2**	**1.4**	**2.1**	**2.4**	**1.8**	**2.5**	**2.2**	**1.7**	**−5.8**	**3.9**	**1.7**
United States	1.8	2.2	1.8	2.5	3.1	1.7	2.3	3.0	2.2	−4.3	3.1	1.8
Euro Area	1.1	−0.9	−0.2	1.4	2.0	1.9	2.6	1.8	1.3	−8.3	5.2	1.4
Japan	0.6	1.5	2.0	0.4	1.2	0.5	2.2	0.3	0.7	−5.3	2.3	0.6
Other Advanced Economies[2]	2.9	2.0	2.4	2.9	2.1	2.2	2.8	2.3	1.7	−5.5	4.3	2.1
Emerging Market and Developing Economies	**6.5**	**5.4**	**5.1**	**4.7**	**4.3**	**4.5**	**4.8**	**4.5**	**3.7**	**−3.3**	**6.0**	**4.7**
Regional Groups												
Emerging and Developing Asia	8.6	7.0	6.9	6.8	6.8	6.8	6.7	6.3	5.5	−1.7	8.0	5.9
Emerging and Developing Europe	4.8	3.1	3.1	1.8	1.0	1.9	4.1	3.3	2.1	−4.6	3.9	2.6
Latin America and the Caribbean	3.6	2.9	2.9	1.3	0.4	−0.6	1.4	1.1	0.0	−8.1	3.6	2.5
Middle East and Central Asia	5.6	5.1	3.1	3.1	2.7	4.5	2.6	2.1	1.4	−4.1	3.0	3.3
Sub-Saharan Africa	5.9	4.8	5.1	5.2	3.2	1.5	3.1	3.3	3.2	−3.0	3.1	4.3
Analytical Groups												
By Source of Export Earnings												
Fuel	5.6	5.3	2.6	2.2	0.3	1.5	1.0	0.9	0.2	−5.4	2.8	2.1
Nonfuel	6.7	5.4	5.7	5.3	5.1	5.1	5.6	5.2	4.3	−2.9	6.6	5.1
Of Which, Primary Products	4.5	2.5	4.1	2.2	2.9	1.7	2.8	1.7	1.0	−7.1	4.5	3.3
By External Financing Source												
Net Debtor Economies	5.3	4.4	4.7	4.4	4.1	4.1	4.8	4.4	3.4	−5.6	5.5	4.9
Net Debtor Economies by Debt-Servicing Experience												
Economies with Arrears and/or Rescheduling during 2015–19	4.5	1.8	2.9	1.6	0.3	2.7	3.0	3.6	3.2	−2.4	2.6	4.9
Other Groups												
European Union	1.5	−0.7	0.0	1.7	2.5	2.1	3.0	2.3	1.7	−7.6	5.0	1.6
Low-Income Developing Countries	6.3	4.8	5.9	6.2	4.7	3.9	4.9	5.1	5.3	−1.2	4.9	5.7
Middle East and North Africa	5.3	5.1	2.6	2.8	2.5	4.9	2.0	1.2	0.8	−5.0	3.2	2.9
Memorandum												
Median Growth Rate												
Advanced Economies	2.2	1.0	1.3	2.3	2.2	2.2	3.0	2.7	1.9	−6.1	4.6	1.8
Emerging Market and Developing Economies	4.7	4.3	4.0	3.8	3.3	3.4	3.7	3.5	3.0	−4.8	4.0	3.5
Low-Income Developing Countries	5.3	5.1	5.3	5.4	3.9	4.3	4.5	4.0	4.5	−1.8	3.6	5.0
Output per Capita[3]												
Advanced Economies	1.1	0.6	0.9	1.6	1.8	1.2	2.1	1.8	1.3	−6.2	3.6	1.4
Emerging Market and Developing Economies	4.7	3.7	3.5	3.1	2.8	3.0	3.4	3.2	2.3	−4.7	4.8	3.6
Low-Income Developing Countries	3.6	2.0	3.5	3.9	2.2	1.6	2.6	2.8	2.9	−3.3	2.7	3.4
World Growth Rate Based on Market Exchange Rates	**2.7**	**2.5**	**2.6**	**2.8**	**2.9**	**2.6**	**3.3**	**3.1**	**2.4**	**−4.7**	**4.8**	**2.9**
Value of World Output (billions of US dollars)												
At Market Exchange Rates	53,903	74,805	76,990	79,060	74,829	76,022	80,716	85,690	87,552	83,845	91,031	113,482
At Purchasing Power Parities	75,026	100,032	104,954	108,876	111,126	115,336	121,522	128,712	134,557	130,187	139,824	174,434

[1]Real GDP.
[2]Excludes the United States, euro area countries, and Japan.
[3]Output per capita is in international dollars at purchasing power parity.

Table A2. Advanced Economies: Real GDP and Total Domestic Demand
(Annual percent change)

	Average 2002–11	2012	2013	2014	2015	2016	2017	2018	2019	Projections 2020	2021	2025	Q4 over Q4[1] 2019:Q4	Projections 2020:Q4	2021:Q4
Real GDP															
Advanced Economies	**1.7**	**1.2**	**1.4**	**2.1**	**2.4**	**1.8**	**2.5**	**2.2**	**1.7**	**−5.8**	**3.9**	**1.7**	**1.5**	**−4.9**	**3.8**
United States	1.8	2.2	1.8	2.5	3.1	1.7	2.3	3.0	2.2	−4.3	3.1	1.8	2.3	−4.1	3.2
Euro Area	1.1	−0.9	−0.2	1.4	2.0	1.9	2.6	1.8	1.3	−8.3	5.2	1.4	1.0	−6.6	4.8
Germany	1.1	0.4	0.4	2.2	1.5	2.2	2.6	1.3	0.6	−6.0	4.2	1.2	0.4	−5.2	4.6
France	1.3	0.3	0.6	1.0	1.1	1.1	2.3	1.8	1.5	−9.8	6.0	1.7	0.8	−6.7	4.0
Italy	0.2	−3.0	−1.8	0.0	0.8	1.3	1.7	0.8	0.3	−10.6	5.2	0.9	0.1	−8.0	3.4
Spain	1.6	−3.0	−1.4	1.4	3.8	3.0	2.9	2.4	2.0	−12.8	7.2	1.5	1.8	−10.8	6.6
Netherlands	1.3	−1.0	−0.1	1.4	2.0	2.2	2.9	2.4	1.7	−5.4	4.0	1.5	1.7	−5.6	5.6
Belgium	1.8	0.7	0.5	1.6	2.0	1.5	1.9	1.5	1.4	−8.3	5.4	1.3	1.3	−7.5	5.6
Austria	1.7	0.7	0.0	0.7	1.0	2.1	2.5	2.4	1.6	−6.7	4.6	1.6	0.4	−4.2	2.5
Ireland	2.3	0.0	1.6	8.5	25.4	1.7	9.4	9.3	5.9	−3.0	4.9	2.6	7.7	−6.8	9.6
Portugal	0.4	−4.1	−0.9	0.8	1.8	2.0	3.5	2.6	2.2	−10.0	6.5	1.7	2.2	−9.4	7.9
Greece	0.4	−7.3	−3.2	0.7	−0.4	−0.2	1.5	1.9	1.9	−9.5	4.1	1.0	0.8	−9.2	6.8
Finland	1.8	−1.4	−0.9	−0.4	0.5	2.8	3.3	1.5	1.1	−4.0	3.6	1.3	0.9	−3.6	4.5
Slovak Republic	4.9	1.9	0.7	2.8	4.8	2.1	3.0	3.9	2.4	−7.1	6.9	2.5	2.0	−5.4	7.4
Lithuania	4.3	3.8	3.6	3.5	2.0	2.6	4.2	3.6	3.9	−1.8	4.1	2.2	3.9	−2.9	6.6
Slovenia	2.5	−2.6	−1.0	2.8	2.2	3.1	4.8	4.1	2.4	−6.7	5.2	2.3	0.8	−0.4	2.4
Luxembourg	2.7	−0.4	3.7	4.3	4.3	4.6	1.8	3.1	2.3	−5.8	5.9	2.5	3.0	−4.5	5.3
Latvia	3.7	4.1	2.3	1.9	3.3	1.8	3.8	4.3	2.2	−6.0	5.2	3.0	1.0	−5.9	7.9
Estonia	3.6	3.1	1.3	3.0	1.8	3.2	5.5	4.4	5.0	−5.2	4.5	3.0	4.1	−6.7	7.0
Cyprus	3.0	−3.4	−6.6	−1.9	3.4	6.7	4.4	4.1	3.2	−6.4	4.7	2.5	3.2	−2.5	4.3
Malta	2.6	4.1	5.5	7.6	9.6	3.9	8.0	5.2	4.9	−7.9	4.8	4.5	4.3	−7.9	7.1
Japan	0.6	1.5	2.0	0.4	1.2	0.5	2.2	0.3	0.7	−5.3	2.3	0.6	−0.7	−2.3	0.7
United Kingdom	1.5	1.5	2.1	2.6	2.4	1.9	1.9	1.3	1.5	−9.8	5.9	1.6	1.1	−6.4	3.7
Korea	4.6	2.4	3.2	3.2	2.8	2.9	3.2	2.9	2.0	−1.9	2.9	2.4	2.4	−3.5	5.0
Canada	2.0	1.8	2.3	2.9	0.7	1.0	3.2	2.0	1.7	−7.1	5.2	1.7	1.5	−5.9	4.9
Australia	3.1	3.8	2.1	2.6	2.3	2.8	2.4	2.8	1.8	−4.2	3.0	2.5	2.3	−5.6	5.2
Taiwan Province of China	4.7	2.2	2.5	4.7	1.5	2.2	3.3	2.7	2.7	0.0	3.2	2.1	3.6	−1.3	5.0
Singapore	6.6	4.5	4.8	3.9	3.0	3.2	4.3	3.4	0.7	−6.0	5.0	2.5	1.1	−3.9	3.3
Switzerland	1.9	1.0	1.9	2.5	1.3	1.7	1.9	2.7	1.2	−5.3	3.6	1.3	2.2	−5.2	3.6
Sweden	2.4	−0.6	1.2	2.7	4.5	2.1	2.6	2.0	1.3	−4.7	3.5	2.0	0.7	−5.5	6.6
Hong Kong SAR	4.5	1.7	3.1	2.8	2.4	2.2	3.8	2.8	−1.2	−7.5	3.7	2.9	−3.0	−4.8	4.1
Czech Republic	3.1	−0.8	0.0	2.3	5.4	2.5	5.2	3.2	2.3	−6.5	5.1	2.5	2.0	−6.0	6.3
Norway	1.5	2.7	1.0	2.0	2.0	1.1	2.3	1.3	1.2	−2.8	3.6	1.8	1.8	−4.1	5.5
Israel	3.6	2.3	4.3	3.9	2.2	3.8	3.6	3.5	3.4	−5.9	4.9	4.0	3.9	−7.7	7.5
Denmark	0.8	0.2	0.9	1.6	2.3	3.2	2.0	2.4	2.3	−4.5	3.5	1.7	2.1	−3.7	2.9
New Zealand	2.7	2.5	2.2	3.2	4.1	4.2	3.8	3.2	2.2	−6.1	4.4	2.5	1.8	−5.6	5.6
Puerto Rico	−0.3	0.0	−0.3	−1.2	−1.0	−1.3	−2.7	−4.9	2.0	−7.5	1.5	−0.3	. . .	. . .	. . .
Macao SAR	13.2	9.2	11.2	−1.2	−21.6	−0.7	9.9	5.4	−4.7	−52.3	23.9	6.0	. . .	. . .	. . .
Iceland	2.4	1.3	4.1	2.1	4.7	6.6	4.5	3.9	1.9	−7.2	4.1	1.8	2.9	−9.0	3.5
San Marino	−0.4	−7.2	−0.8	−0.7	2.7	2.3	0.4	1.7	1.1	−11.0	5.7	0.5	. . .	. . .	. . .
Memorandum															
Major Advanced Economies	1.4	1.4	1.4	1.9	2.2	1.5	2.3	2.1	1.6	−5.9	3.8	1.5	1.4	−4.6	3.2
Real Total Domestic Demand															
Advanced Economies	**1.6**	**0.8**	**1.1**	**2.1**	**2.7**	**2.0**	**2.5**	**2.2**	**1.8**	**−5.7**	**4.0**	**1.6**	**1.2**	**−4.7**	**4.0**
United States	1.7	2.2	1.6	2.7	3.7	1.9	2.5	3.2	2.3	−4.5	3.2	1.8	1.9	−3.9	3.2
Euro Area	1.0	−2.4	−0.5	1.4	2.3	2.4	2.3	1.8	1.9	−7.6	4.9	1.3	1.4	−6.4	4.3
Germany	0.6	−0.9	1.1	1.7	1.4	3.1	2.7	1.8	1.2	−4.1	3.4	1.2	0.3	−3.4	3.7
France	1.5	−0.4	0.7	1.5	1.5	1.5	2.4	1.4	1.7	−8.2	6.1	1.3	1.6	−5.1	3.8
Italy	0.3	−5.6	−2.7	0.1	1.2	1.8	1.8	1.1	−0.2	−10.8	5.2	0.9	−0.8	−9.7	6.0
Spain	1.5	−4.9	−2.9	1.9	4.1	2.1	3.1	2.7	1.2	−12.0	7.2	1.1	−0.1	−9.2	6.7
Japan	0.2	2.3	2.4	0.4	0.8	−0.1	1.6	0.3	0.8	−4.8	2.3	0.5	−1.1	−3.2	3.0
United Kingdom	1.4	1.9	2.6	3.2	2.6	2.5	1.2	1.3	1.5	−11.5	7.9	1.6	−1.6	−4.3	3.9
Canada	3.2	2.0	2.2	1.7	−0.2	0.4	4.1	1.9	1.3	−8.3	6.0	1.6	1.6	−6.6	5.5
Other Advanced Economies[2]	3.2	2.0	1.6	2.8	2.5	2.9	3.6	2.6	1.2	−3.5	3.3	2.4	1.6	−3.3	4.4
Memorandum															
Major Advanced Economies	1.3	1.1	1.4	2.0	2.5	1.7	2.3	2.2	1.7	−5.8	3.9	1.5	0.9	−4.3	3.6

[1]From the fourth quarter of the preceding year.
[2]Excludes the Group of Seven (Canada, France, Germany, Italy, Japan, United Kingdom, United States) and euro area countries.

Table A3. Advanced Economies: Components of Real GDP
(Annual percent change)

	Averages		2012	2013	2014	2015	2016	2017	2018	2019	Projections	
	2002–11	2012–21									2020	2021
Private Consumer Expenditure												
Advanced Economies	**1.7**	**1.2**	**1.0**	**1.2**	**1.9**	**2.6**	**2.3**	**2.3**	**2.0**	**1.7**	**−7.1**	**4.4**
United States	2.0	1.8	1.5	1.5	3.0	3.8	2.8	2.6	2.7	2.4	−4.9	2.8
Euro Area	0.9	0.3	−1.1	−0.6	0.9	1.9	2.0	1.8	1.5	1.3	−9.2	5.5
Germany	0.4	0.9	1.5	0.4	1.1	1.9	2.4	1.5	1.5	1.6	−6.9	4.1
France	1.6	0.5	−0.4	0.5	0.8	1.5	1.8	1.5	0.9	1.5	−8.4	6.1
Italy	0.4	−0.8	−3.7	−2.4	0.2	1.9	1.2	1.5	0.9	0.4	−11.8	4.9
Spain	1.4	0.0	−3.3	−2.9	1.7	2.9	2.7	3.0	1.8	1.1	−14.8	9.1
Japan	0.7	0.1	2.0	2.4	−0.9	−0.2	−0.3	1.3	0.0	0.1	−7.8	4.3
United Kingdom	1.4	1.1	1.6	2.7	2.3	3.0	3.6	2.2	1.6	1.0	−12.6	6.7
Canada	3.1	1.8	1.9	2.6	2.6	2.3	2.1	3.6	2.1	1.6	−8.6	8.9
Other Advanced Economies[1]	3.0	1.8	2.1	2.3	2.5	2.9	2.6	2.8	2.8	1.8	−5.8	4.3
Memorandum												
Major Advanced Economies	1.5	1.2	1.1	1.3	1.8	2.6	2.2	2.2	1.9	1.7	−6.9	4.1
Public Consumption												
Advanced Economies	**1.8**	**1.3**	**0.0**	**−0.1**	**0.5**	**1.7**	**2.0**	**1.1**	**1.7**	**2.2**	**2.4**	**1.8**
United States	1.4	0.7	−1.5	−1.9	−0.8	1.6	1.8	0.6	1.5	1.8	1.7	1.9
Euro Area	1.7	1.1	−0.3	0.2	0.8	1.3	1.9	1.1	1.1	1.8	2.2	0.9
Germany	1.4	2.1	1.3	1.4	1.7	2.9	4.0	1.6	1.2	2.7	4.8	−0.4
France	1.6	1.1	1.6	1.5	1.3	1.0	1.4	1.4	0.9	1.7	−3.1	3.6
Italy	0.4	−0.2	−1.8	−1.1	−0.6	−0.6	0.7	−0.1	0.1	−0.4	3.1	−1.0
Spain	4.3	0.5	−4.2	−2.1	−0.7	2.0	1.0	1.0	1.9	2.3	3.7	0.2
Japan	1.3	1.1	1.7	1.5	0.5	1.5	1.4	0.2	0.9	1.9	1.4	−0.4
United Kingdom	2.5	1.6	1.1	−0.4	2.0	1.8	1.0	0.3	0.4	3.4	−2.0	9.1
Canada	2.3	1.4	0.7	−0.8	0.6	1.4	1.8	2.3	3.0	2.1	1.5	1.1
Other Advanced Economies[1]	3.0	3.1	2.3	2.7	2.8	2.8	3.2	3.0	3.5	3.5	5.6	2.3
Memorandum												
Major Advanced Economies	1.5	1.0	−0.2	−0.6	0.1	1.5	1.8	0.7	1.3	1.9	1.4	1.8
Gross Fixed Capital Formation												
Advanced Economies	**0.8**	**2.1**	**2.6**	**1.8**	**3.4**	**3.4**	**2.3**	**3.8**	**2.9**	**2.4**	**−6.0**	**4.6**
United States	0.5	3.1	6.9	3.6	5.1	3.7	1.8	3.5	4.8	2.3	−2.7	2.8
Euro Area	0.4	1.1	−3.2	−2.4	1.4	4.7	4.0	3.8	3.1	5.7	−12.0	7.6
Germany	0.7	1.6	−0.2	−1.3	3.2	1.7	3.8	2.5	3.5	2.5	−5.0	5.8
France	1.2	0.8	0.2	−0.8	0.0	1.0	2.7	4.7	3.2	4.3	−14.2	8.9
Italy	−0.5	−1.0	−9.7	−6.4	−2.2	1.8	4.0	3.2	3.1	1.4	−15.1	12.6
Spain	−0.4	0.4	−7.4	−3.8	4.1	4.9	2.4	5.9	5.3	1.8	−16.2	10.3
Japan	−1.8	1.5	3.5	4.9	3.1	1.6	−0.3	3.0	0.6	1.3	−2.5	0.0
United Kingdom	0.3	1.4	2.0	3.5	6.6	3.7	3.6	1.6	−0.2	0.7	−14.7	9.0
Canada	3.8	0.8	4.9	1.4	2.3	−5.2	−4.7	3.6	1.2	−0.4	−3.9	9.7
Other Advanced Economies[1]	3.5	1.9	3.2	2.6	2.6	2.3	3.1	5.6	0.9	0.0	−4.0	2.8
Memorandum												
Major Advanced Economies	0.3	2.1	3.6	2.2	3.8	2.5	1.8	3.3	3.3	2.0	−5.4	4.6

Table A3. Advanced Economies: Components of Real GDP *(continued)*

(Annual percent change)

	Averages		2012	2013	2014	2015	2016	2017	2018	2019	Projections	
	2002–11	2012–21									2020	2021
Final Domestic Demand												
Advanced Economies	**1.5**	**1.4**	**1.1**	**1.1**	**2.0**	**2.6**	**2.3**	**2.4**	**2.1**	**2.0**	**−5.2**	**3.8**
United States	1.6	1.9	2.0	1.3	2.8	3.5	2.4	2.5	3.0	2.3	−3.6	2.7
Euro Area	1.0	0.7	−1.3	−0.8	1.0	2.3	2.4	2.0	1.7	2.4	−7.4	4.9
Germany	0.7	1.3	1.1	0.2	1.7	2.1	3.1	1.8	1.9	2.0	−4.0	3.4
France	1.5	0.7	0.2	0.5	0.8	1.3	1.9	2.2	1.4	2.2	−8.5	6.1
Italy	0.2	−0.7	−4.5	−2.9	−0.4	1.4	1.6	1.5	1.2	0.4	−9.6	5.0
Spain	1.6	0.0	−4.3	−2.9	1.6	3.1	2.3	3.1	2.5	1.1	−12.1	7.3
Japan	0.2	0.6	2.3	2.8	0.2	0.6	0.0	1.5	0.3	0.8	−4.6	2.4
United Kingdom	1.4	1.2	1.5	2.2	2.9	2.9	3.1	1.7	1.1	1.4	−11.0	7.5
Canada	3.1	1.4	2.3	1.6	2.1	0.3	0.5	3.3	2.1	1.3	−6.1	6.6
Other Advanced Economies[1]	3.1	2.0	2.4	2.4	2.6	2.7	2.9	3.3	2.4	1.5	−3.3	3.4
Memorandum												
Major Advanced Economies	1.3	1.3	1.4	1.2	2.0	2.4	2.1	2.2	2.1	1.8	−5.1	3.6
Stock Building[2]												
Advanced Economies	**0.1**	**−0.1**	**−0.3**	**0.0**	**0.1**	**0.0**	**−0.3**	**0.1**	**0.1**	**−0.2**	**−0.5**	**0.1**
United States	0.1	0.0	0.2	0.2	−0.1	0.3	−0.6	0.0	0.2	0.0	−0.9	0.5
Euro Area	0.0	−0.1	−1.1	0.3	0.4	0.0	0.0	0.3	0.0	−0.5	−0.2	0.0
Germany	0.0	−0.2	−1.8	0.8	0.0	−0.7	0.0	0.8	−0.1	−0.7	0.0	0.0
France	0.0	0.0	−0.6	0.2	0.7	0.3	−0.4	0.2	0.0	−0.4	0.3	0.0
Italy	0.1	−0.2	−1.1	0.2	0.5	−0.1	0.2	0.2	−0.1	−0.6	−1.2	0.1
Spain	0.0	−0.2	−0.8	0.1	0.2	−1.5	−0.1	0.0	0.2	0.1	0.0	0.0
Japan	0.0	0.0	0.0	−0.4	0.1	0.3	−0.1	0.1	0.0	0.1	0.0	0.0
United Kingdom	0.0	0.0	0.4	0.1	0.6	−0.3	−0.6	−0.6	0.2	0.2	0.0	−0.1
Canada	0.1	−0.2	−0.3	0.5	−0.4	−0.5	0.0	0.8	−0.2	0.1	−1.6	−0.6
Other Advanced Economies[1]	0.1	−0.1	−0.4	−0.7	0.2	−0.1	0.0	0.2	0.2	−0.3	−0.2	−0.1
Memorandum												
Major Advanced Economies	0.0	−0.1	−0.2	0.2	0.1	0.1	−0.4	0.1	0.1	−0.1	−0.6	0.2
Foreign Balance[2]												
Advanced Economies	**0.1**	**0.0**	**0.4**	**0.2**	**0.0**	**−0.3**	**−0.1**	**0.0**	**0.0**	**−0.1**	**−0.2**	**0.0**
United States	0.0	−0.2	0.0	0.2	−0.3	−0.8	−0.2	−0.2	−0.3	−0.2	0.3	−0.2
Euro Area	0.2	0.1	1.5	0.3	0.1	−0.2	−0.4	0.4	0.2	−0.5	−1.0	0.5
Germany	0.5	−0.1	1.2	−0.5	0.7	0.3	−0.6	0.1	−0.4	−0.6	−2.1	0.9
France	−0.3	−0.2	0.7	−0.1	−0.5	−0.4	−0.4	−0.1	0.4	−0.2	−1.5	−0.2
Italy	−0.1	0.3	2.6	0.8	−0.1	−0.4	−0.5	0.0	−0.3	0.5	−0.1	0.2
Spain	0.1	0.2	2.0	1.4	−0.5	−0.1	1.0	−0.1	−0.3	0.5	−1.7	0.0
Japan	0.3	0.0	−0.8	−0.4	0.0	0.3	0.6	0.5	−0.1	−0.2	−0.5	0.1
United Kingdom	0.1	−0.2	−0.3	−0.6	−0.7	−0.5	−0.5	0.7	−0.2	0.1	1.9	−1.9
Canada	−1.1	0.1	−0.3	0.1	1.2	0.8	0.4	−1.0	0.1	0.2	0.9	−1.2
Other Advanced Economies[1]	0.5	0.2	0.5	0.7	0.5	0.0	0.0	−0.4	0.4	0.7	−0.4	0.4
Memorandum												
Major Advanced Economies	0.0	−0.1	0.2	0.0	−0.1	−0.4	−0.2	0.0	−0.2	−0.2	−0.1	−0.2

[1]Excludes the Group of Seven (Canada, France, Germany, Italy, Japan, United Kingdom, United States) and euro area countries.
[2]Changes expressed as percent of GDP in the preceding period.

Table A4. Emerging Market and Developing Economies: Real GDP

(Annual percent change)

	Average 2002–11	2012	2013	2014	2015	2016	2017	2018	2019	Projections 2020	2021	2025
Emerging and Developing Asia	**8.6**	**7.0**	**6.9**	**6.8**	**6.8**	**6.8**	**6.7**	**6.3**	**5.5**	**−1.7**	**8.0**	**5.9**
Bangladesh	5.9	6.5	6.0	6.1	6.6	7.1	7.3	7.9	8.2	3.8	4.4	7.3
Bhutan	8.8	6.5	3.6	4.0	6.2	7.4	6.3	3.8	3.8	0.6	−0.5	6.0
Brunei Darussalam	1.5	0.9	−2.1	−2.5	−0.4	−2.5	1.3	0.1	3.9	0.1	3.2	1.8
Cambodia	7.9	7.3	7.4	7.1	7.0	6.9	7.0	7.5	7.0	−2.8	6.8	6.9
China	10.7	7.9	7.8	7.3	6.9	6.8	6.9	6.7	6.1	1.9	8.2	5.5
Fiji	1.4	1.4	4.7	5.6	4.7	2.5	5.4	3.5	−1.3	−21.0	11.5	2.2
India[1]	7.7	5.5	6.4	7.4	8.0	8.3	7.0	6.1	4.2	−10.3	8.8	7.2
Indonesia	5.7	6.0	5.6	5.0	4.9	5.0	5.1	5.2	5.0	−1.5	6.1	5.1
Kiribati	1.0	4.7	4.2	−0.7	10.4	5.1	0.9	2.3	2.3	−1.1	3.0	1.8
Lao P.D.R.	7.5	7.8	8.0	7.6	7.3	7.0	6.8	6.3	5.2	0.2	4.8	6.1
Malaysia	5.1	5.5	4.7	6.0	5.0	4.4	5.8	4.8	4.3	−6.0	7.8	5.0
Maldives	7.0	2.5	7.3	7.3	2.9	6.3	6.8	6.9	5.7	−18.6	12.7	5.9
Marshall Islands	1.0	−2.4	3.7	−0.9	1.6	1.3	4.1	3.6	5.3	−4.5	−0.9	1.8
Micronesia	0.3	−1.9	−3.7	−2.3	4.6	0.9	2.7	0.2	1.2	−3.8	1.2	0.6
Mongolia	7.5	12.3	11.6	7.9	2.4	1.2	5.3	7.2	5.1	−2.0	6.0	4.5
Myanmar	10.0	6.5	7.9	8.2	7.5	6.4	5.8	6.4	6.5	2.0	5.7	6.5
Nauru	. . .	10.4	31.0	27.2	3.4	3.0	−5.5	5.7	1.0	0.7	1.3	0.5
Nepal	3.8	4.8	4.1	6.0	3.3	0.6	8.2	6.7	7.1	0.0	2.5	5.0
Palau	0.3	1.6	−1.7	6.0	5.0	−0.4	−2.0	5.8	−1.8	−11.4	−7.4	2.0
Papua New Guinea	4.1	4.7	3.8	13.5	9.5	4.1	3.5	−0.8	4.9	−3.3	1.2	3.2
Philippines	4.9	6.9	6.8	6.3	6.3	7.1	6.9	6.3	6.0	−8.3	7.4	6.5
Samoa	3.3	−4.1	−0.4	0.1	4.3	8.1	1.0	−2.2	3.5	−5.0	−1.5	2.2
Solomon Islands	4.9	1.9	5.3	1.0	1.4	5.9	5.3	3.9	1.2	−5.0	4.5	3.0
Sri Lanka	6.2	9.1	3.4	5.0	5.0	4.5	3.6	3.3	2.3	−4.6	5.3	4.8
Thailand	4.3	7.2	2.7	1.0	3.1	3.4	4.1	4.2	2.4	−7.1	4.0	3.7
Timor-Leste[2]	3.5	6.0	2.1	4.5	3.1	3.6	−3.8	−0.8	3.1	−6.8	4.0	2.6
Tonga	0.4	0.8	0.3	2.0	1.2	6.6	3.3	0.3	0.7	−2.5	−3.5	1.8
Tuvalu	1.4	−3.9	4.9	1.2	9.2	5.9	4.6	3.7	6.0	−0.5	3.0	3.0
Vanuatu	3.4	1.8	2.0	2.3	0.2	3.5	4.4	2.9	3.3	−8.3	4.3	3.0
Vietnam	6.8	5.5	5.6	6.4	7.0	6.7	6.9	7.1	7.0	1.6	6.7	6.6
Emerging and Developing Europe	**4.8**	**3.1**	**3.1**	**1.8**	**1.0**	**1.9**	**4.1**	**3.3**	**2.1**	**−4.6**	**3.9**	**2.6**
Albania[1]	5.0	1.4	1.0	1.8	2.2	3.3	3.8	4.1	2.2	−7.5	6.1	3.4
Belarus[1]	7.5	1.7	1.0	1.7	−3.8	−2.5	2.5	3.1	1.2	−3.0	2.2	1.3
Bosnia and Herzegovina	3.7	−0.7	2.4	1.1	3.1	3.1	3.2	3.7	2.7	−6.5	5.0	3.5
Bulgaria	4.3	0.4	0.3	1.9	4.0	3.8	3.5	3.1	3.4	−4.0	4.1	2.9
Croatia	2.1	−2.2	−0.5	−0.1	2.4	3.5	3.1	2.7	2.9	−9.0	6.0	3.0
Hungary	1.8	−1.5	2.0	4.2	3.8	2.2	4.3	5.1	4.9	−6.1	3.9	2.6
Kosovo	4.0	2.8	3.4	1.2	4.1	4.1	4.2	3.8	4.0	−7.5	6.0	4.0
Moldova	5.1	−0.6	9.0	5.0	−0.3	4.4	4.7	4.0	3.6	−4.5	4.1	4.2
Montenegro	3.5	−2.7	3.5	1.8	3.4	2.9	4.7	5.1	3.6	−12.0	5.5	3.0
North Macedonia	3.5	−0.5	2.9	3.6	3.9	2.8	1.1	2.7	3.6	−5.4	5.5	3.5
Poland	4.2	1.6	1.4	3.3	3.8	3.1	4.9	5.3	4.1	−3.6	4.6	2.4
Romania	3.9	2.1	3.5	3.4	3.9	4.8	7.1	4.4	4.1	−4.8	4.6	3.5
Russia	4.8	4.0	1.8	0.7	−2.0	0.2	1.8	2.5	1.3	−4.1	2.8	1.8
Serbia	4.7	−0.7	2.9	−1.6	1.8	3.3	2.0	4.4	4.2	−2.5	5.5	4.0
Turkey	5.8	4.8	8.5	4.9	6.1	3.3	7.5	3.0	0.9	−5.0	5.0	3.5
Ukraine[1]	4.0	0.2	0.0	−6.6	−9.8	2.4	2.5	3.4	3.2	−7.2	3.0	4.0
Latin America and the Caribbean	**3.6**	**2.9**	**2.9**	**1.3**	**0.4**	**−0.6**	**1.4**	**1.1**	**0.0**	**−8.1**	**3.6**	**2.5**
Antigua and Barbuda	1.7	3.4	−0.6	3.8	3.8	5.5	3.1	7.0	3.4	−17.3	4.7	3.7
Argentina	4.5	−1.0	2.4	−2.5	2.7	−2.1	2.8	−2.6	−2.1	−11.8	4.9	1.7
Aruba	−0.1	−1.4	4.2	0.9	−0.4	0.5	2.3	1.2	0.4	−19.7	9.0	1.1
The Bahamas	0.5	3.1	−2.7	1.1	0.2	1.4	3.1	3.0	1.2	−14.8	4.6	1.5
Barbados	0.8	−0.4	−1.4	−0.1	2.4	2.5	0.5	−0.6	−0.1	−11.6	7.4	1.8
Belize	3.4	2.4	1.3	3.6	2.8	0.1	1.9	2.1	−2.0	−16.0	8.0	2.0
Bolivia	4.2	5.1	6.8	5.5	4.9	4.3	4.2	4.2	2.2	−7.9	5.6	3.7
Brazil	3.9	1.9	3.0	0.5	−3.5	−3.3	1.3	1.3	1.1	−5.8	2.8	2.2
Chile	4.5	5.3	4.0	1.8	2.3	1.7	1.2	4.0	1.1	−6.0	4.5	2.5
Colombia	4.6	3.9	5.1	4.5	3.0	2.1	1.4	2.5	3.3	−8.2	4.0	3.7

Table A4. Emerging Market and Developing Economies: Real GDP *(continued)*

(Annual percent change)

	Average 2002–11	2012	2013	2014	2015	2016	2017	2018	2019	Projections 2020	Projections 2021	Projections 2025
Latin America and the												
Caribbean (continued)	**3.6**	**2.9**	**2.9**	**1.3**	**0.4**	**−0.6**	**1.4**	**1.1**	**0.0**	**−8.1**	**3.6**	**2.5**
Costa Rica	4.4	4.8	2.3	3.5	3.6	4.2	3.9	2.7	2.1	−5.5	2.3	3.2
Dominica	2.4	−1.1	−0.6	4.4	−2.6	2.5	−9.5	0.5	8.4	−8.8	3.3	1.5
Dominican Republic	4.7	2.7	4.9	7.1	6.9	6.7	4.7	7.0	5.1	−6.0	4.0	5.0
Ecuador	4.5	5.6	4.9	3.8	0.1	−1.2	2.4	1.3	0.1	−11.0	4.8	2.3
El Salvador	1.9	2.8	2.2	1.7	2.4	2.5	2.3	2.4	2.4	−9.0	4.0	2.2
Grenada	2.1	−1.2	2.4	7.3	6.4	3.7	4.4	4.1	3.0	−11.8	3.0	2.7
Guatemala	3.6	3.1	3.5	4.4	4.1	2.7	3.0	3.2	3.8	−2.0	4.0	3.3
Guyana	2.7	5.0	3.7	1.7	0.7	3.8	3.7	4.4	5.4	26.2	8.1	1.1
Haiti	0.7	2.9	4.2	2.8	1.2	1.5	1.2	1.5	−1.2	−4.0	1.2	1.4
Honduras	4.2	4.1	2.8	3.1	3.8	3.9	4.8	3.7	2.7	−6.6	4.9	3.7
Jamaica	0.6	−0.5	0.2	0.6	0.9	1.5	0.7	1.9	0.9	−8.6	3.6	2.1
Mexico	1.9	3.6	1.4	2.8	3.3	2.6	2.1	2.2	−0.3	−9.0	3.5	2.1
Nicaragua	3.2	6.5	4.9	4.8	4.8	4.6	4.6	−4.0	−3.9	−5.5	−0.5	2.1
Panama	6.9	9.8	6.9	5.1	5.7	5.0	5.6	3.7	3.0	−9.0	4.0	5.0
Paraguay	4.2	−0.5	8.4	4.9	3.1	4.3	5.0	3.4	0.0	−4.0	5.5	4.0
Peru	6.2	6.0	5.8	2.4	3.3	4.1	2.5	4.0	2.2	−13.9	7.3	3.8
St. Kitts and Nevis	1.7	−2.2	5.4	6.3	1.0	2.8	−2.0	2.9	2.8	−18.7	8.0	2.7
St. Lucia	2.8	−0.3	−2.2	1.3	−0.2	3.8	3.5	2.6	1.7	−16.9	7.2	1.8
St. Vincent and the Grenadines	2.7	1.4	1.8	1.2	1.3	1.9	1.0	2.2	0.4	−7.0	3.7	2.7
Suriname	5.1	2.7	2.9	0.3	−3.4	−5.6	1.8	2.6	0.3	−13.1	1.5	2.1
Trinidad and Tobago	5.3	−0.7	2.2	−0.9	1.8	−6.3	−2.3	−0.2	0.0	−5.6	2.6	1.5
Uruguay	4.1	3.5	4.6	3.2	0.4	1.7	2.6	1.6	0.2	−4.5	4.3	2.4
Venezuela	3.2	5.6	1.3	−3.9	−6.2	−17.0	−15.7	−19.6	−35.0	−25.0	−10.0	. . .
Middle East and Central Asia	**5.6**	**5.1**	**3.1**	**3.1**	**2.7**	**4.5**	**2.6**	**2.1**	**1.4**	**−4.1**	**3.0**	**3.3**
Afghanistan	. . .	14.0	5.7	2.7	1.0	2.2	2.6	1.2	3.9	−5.0	4.0	4.0
Algeria	3.8	3.4	2.8	3.8	3.7	3.2	1.3	1.4	0.8	−5.5	3.2	0.9
Armenia	7.6	7.1	3.4	3.6	3.3	0.2	7.5	5.2	7.6	−4.5	3.5	4.5
Azerbaijan	13.5	2.2	5.8	2.8	1.0	−3.1	0.2	1.5	2.2	−4.0	2.0	1.7
Bahrain	5.3	3.7	5.4	4.4	2.5	3.6	4.3	1.8	1.8	−4.9	2.3	3.3
Djibouti	4.1	4.8	5.0	7.1	7.7	6.7	5.4	8.4	7.5	−1.0	7.0	6.0
Egypt	4.7	2.2	3.3	2.9	4.4	4.3	4.1	5.3	5.6	3.5	2.8	5.6
Georgia	6.5	6.4	3.6	4.4	3.0	2.9	4.8	4.8	5.1	−5.0	5.0	5.2
Iran	4.9	−7.7	−0.3	3.2	−1.6	12.5	3.7	−5.4	−6.5	−5.0	3.2	1.2
Iraq	13.7	13.9	7.6	0.7	2.5	15.2	−2.5	−0.1	4.4	−12.1	2.5	0.9
Jordan	6.1	2.4	2.6	3.4	2.5	2.0	2.1	1.9	2.0	−5.0	3.4	3.3
Kazakhstan	7.7	4.8	6.0	4.2	1.2	1.1	4.1	4.1	4.5	−2.7	3.0	3.1
Kuwait	5.5	6.6	1.2	0.5	0.6	2.9	−4.7	1.2	0.4	−8.1	0.6	2.4
Kyrgyz Republic	4.1	−0.1	10.9	4.0	3.9	4.3	4.7	3.5	4.5	−12.0	9.8	4.1
Lebanon[1]	5.4	2.5	3.8	2.5	0.2	1.5	0.9	−1.9	−6.9	−25.0	. . .	. . .
Libya[1]	−8.6	124.7	−36.8	−53.0	−13.0	−7.4	64.0	17.9	9.9	−66.7	76.0	0.3
Mauritania	4.3	4.5	4.2	4.3	5.4	1.3	3.5	2.1	5.9	−3.2	2.0	4.3
Morocco	4.7	3.0	4.5	2.7	4.5	1.0	4.2	3.0	2.2	−7.0	4.9	3.7
Oman	2.8	9.1	5.1	1.4	4.7	4.9	0.3	0.9	−0.8	−10.0	−0.5	3.1
Pakistan	4.7	3.8	3.7	4.1	4.1	4.6	5.2	5.5	1.9	−0.4	1.0	5.0
Qatar	14.2	4.7	5.6	5.3	4.8	3.1	−1.5	1.2	0.8	−4.5	2.5	2.5
Saudi Arabia	4.5	5.4	2.7	3.7	4.1	1.7	−0.7	2.4	0.3	−5.4	3.1	2.6
Somalia	. . .	1.2	1.9	2.4	3.5	2.9	1.4	2.8	2.9	−1.5	2.9	3.9
Sudan[3]	3.6	−17.0	2.0	4.7	1.9	3.5	0.7	−2.3	−2.5	−8.4	0.8	4.5
Syria[4]	. . .	. . .	. . .	. . .	. . .	. . .	. . .	. . .	. . .	. . .	. . .	. . .
Tajikistan	7.7	7.5	7.4	6.7	6.0	6.9	7.1	7.3	7.5	1.0	6.0	4.0
Tunisia	3.6	4.1	2.8	2.9	1.2	1.2	1.9	2.7	1.0	−7.0	4.0	3.0
Turkmenistan	12.7	11.1	10.2	10.3	6.5	6.2	6.5	6.2	6.3	1.8	4.6	5.0
United Arab Emirates	4.4	4.5	5.1	4.3	5.1	3.1	2.4	1.2	1.7	−6.6	1.3	2.6
Uzbekistan	7.2	7.4	7.6	7.2	7.4	6.1	4.5	5.4	5.6	0.7	5.0	5.5
West Bank and Gaza	6.5	6.1	4.7	−0.2	3.7	8.9	1.4	1.2	0.9	−12.0	8.2	2.0
Yemen	2.5	2.4	4.8	−0.2	−28.0	−9.4	−5.1	0.8	2.1	−5.0	0.5	6.2

Table A4. Emerging Market and Developing Economies: Real GDP *(continued)*
(Annual percent change)

	Average 2002–11	2012	2013	2014	2015	2016	2017	2018	2019	Projections 2020	2021	2025
Sub-Saharan Africa	**5.9**	**4.8**	**5.1**	**5.2**	**3.2**	**1.5**	**3.1**	**3.3**	**3.2**	**−3.0**	**3.1**	**4.3**
Angola	8.7	8.5	5.0	4.8	0.9	−2.6	−0.2	−1.2	−0.9	−4.0	3.2	2.9
Benin	3.6	4.8	7.2	6.4	1.8	3.3	5.7	6.7	6.9	2.0	5.0	7.0
Botswana	4.7	4.5	11.3	4.1	−1.7	4.3	2.9	4.5	3.0	−9.6	8.7	4.1
Burkina Faso	5.9	6.5	5.8	4.3	3.9	6.0	6.2	6.8	5.7	−2.0	3.9	5.6
Burundi	4.0	4.4	5.9	4.3	−3.9	−0.6	0.5	1.6	1.8	−3.2	3.1	2.6
Cabo Verde	5.2	1.1	0.8	0.6	1.0	4.7	3.7	4.5	5.7	−6.8	4.5	6.2
Cameroon	3.9	4.5	5.4	5.9	5.7	4.6	3.5	4.1	3.9	−2.8	3.4	5.4
Central African Republic	2.5	5.1	−36.4	0.1	4.3	4.7	4.5	3.8	3.0	−1.0	3.0	5.0
Chad	8.6	8.8	5.8	6.9	1.8	−5.6	−2.4	2.3	3.0	−0.7	6.1	3.8
Comoros	2.9	3.2	4.5	2.1	1.3	3.5	4.2	3.6	1.9	−1.8	2.9	4.2
Democratic Republic of the Congo	5.6	7.1	8.5	9.5	6.9	2.4	3.7	5.8	4.4	−2.2	3.6	4.3
Republic of Congo	4.0	9.9	−0.7	6.7	−3.6	−10.7	−4.4	−6.4	−0.6	−7.0	−0.8	2.3
Côte d'Ivoire	0.6	10.9	9.3	8.8	8.8	7.2	7.4	6.8	6.5	1.8	6.2	6.5
Equatorial Guinea	10.6	8.3	−4.1	0.4	−9.1	−8.8	−5.7	−5.8	−6.1	−6.0	2.2	−2.2
Eritrea	2.8	1.9	−10.5	30.9	−20.6	7.4	−10.0	13.0	3.8	−0.6	5.7	3.9
Eswatini	3.7	5.4	3.9	0.9	2.3	1.3	2.0	2.4	1.1	−3.5	1.4	2.1
Ethiopia	8.9	8.7	9.9	10.3	10.4	8.0	10.2	7.7	9.0	1.9	0.0	8.0
Gabon	1.9	5.3	5.5	4.4	3.9	2.1	0.5	1.0	3.8	−2.7	2.1	4.5
The Gambia	2.0	5.2	2.9	−1.4	4.1	1.9	4.8	7.2	6.1	−1.8	6.0	5.8
Ghana	6.7	8.5	7.2	2.9	2.2	3.4	8.1	6.3	6.5	0.9	4.2	4.5
Guinea	3.3	5.9	3.9	3.7	3.8	10.8	10.3	6.2	5.6	1.4	6.6	5.0
Guinea-Bissau	3.7	−1.7	3.3	1.0	6.1	5.3	4.8	3.4	4.5	−2.9	3.0	5.0
Kenya	4.4	4.6	5.9	5.4	5.7	5.9	4.8	6.3	5.4	1.0	4.7	5.8
Lesotho	4.4	6.1	3.9	2.8	3.3	3.4	−1.0	0.4	1.0	−4.8	3.9	2.1
Liberia	2.5	8.4	8.8	0.7	0.0	−1.6	2.5	1.2	−2.5	−3.0	3.2	5.4
Madagascar	2.2	3.0	2.3	3.3	3.1	4.0	3.9	4.6	4.8	−3.2	3.2	5.0
Malawi	5.8	1.9	5.2	5.7	2.9	2.3	4.0	3.2	4.5	0.6	2.5	6.2
Mali	4.6	−0.7	2.2	6.8	6.6	5.9	5.0	5.2	5.1	−2.0	4.0	5.0
Mauritius	4.1	3.5	3.4	3.7	3.6	3.8	3.8	3.8	3.0	−14.2	9.9	3.3
Mozambique	7.6	7.3	7.0	7.4	6.7	3.8	3.7	3.4	2.3	−0.5	2.1	11.2
Namibia	4.3	5.1	5.6	5.8	4.5	−0.3	−0.3	0.7	−1.0	−5.9	3.4	2.7
Niger	4.4	10.5	5.3	6.6	4.4	5.7	5.0	7.2	5.9	0.5	6.9	6.0
Nigeria	8.7	4.3	5.4	6.3	2.7	−1.6	0.8	1.9	2.2	−4.3	1.7	2.5
Rwanda	7.3	8.6	5.9	7.8	8.9	6.0	4.0	8.6	9.4	2.0	6.3	6.1
São Tomé and Príncipe	5.4	3.1	4.8	6.5	3.8	4.2	3.9	3.0	1.3	−6.5	3.0	4.5
Senegal	3.7	5.1	2.8	6.6	6.4	6.4	7.4	6.4	5.3	−0.7	5.2	6.0
Seychelles	2.8	3.7	6.0	4.5	4.9	4.6	4.4	3.8	3.9	−13.8	4.2	4.0
Sierra Leone	7.8	15.2	20.7	4.6	−20.5	6.4	3.8	3.5	5.4	−3.1	2.7	4.6
South Africa	3.5	2.2	2.5	1.8	1.2	0.4	1.4	0.8	0.2	−8.0	3.0	2.3
South Sudan	. . .	−52.4	29.3	2.9	−0.2	−13.5	−5.8	−1.9	0.9	4.1	−2.3	5.4
Tanzania	6.8	5.1	6.8	6.7	6.2	6.9	6.8	7.0	7.0	1.9	3.6	6.7
Togo	2.8	6.5	6.1	5.9	5.7	5.6	4.4	4.9	5.3	0.0	3.0	5.5
Uganda	7.8	2.3	3.9	5.7	6.8	0.4	7.3	6.1	6.7	−0.3	4.9	9.3
Zambia	7.5	7.6	5.1	4.7	2.9	3.8	3.5	4.0	1.4	−4.8	0.6	1.2
Zimbabwe[1]	−2.6	16.7	2.0	2.4	1.8	0.7	4.7	3.5	−6.5	−10.4	4.2	2.2

[1]See country-specific notes for Albania, Belarus, India, Lebanon, Libya, Ukraine, and Zimbabwe in the "Country Notes" section of the Statistical Appendix.
[2]Data for Timor-Leste exclude projections for oil exports from the Joint Petroleum Development Area.
[3]Data for 2011 exclude South Sudan after July 9. Data for 2012 and onward pertain to the current Sudan.
[4]Data for Syria are excluded for 2011 onward owing to the uncertain political situation.

Table A5. Summary of Inflation
(Percent)

	Average 2002–11	2012	2013	2014	2015	2016	2017	2018	2019	Projections 2020	2021	2025
GDP Deflators												
Advanced Economies	**1.6**	**1.3**	**1.3**	**1.5**	**1.2**	**1.0**	**1.5**	**1.7**	**1.5**	**1.3**	**1.4**	**1.8**
United States	2.1	1.9	1.8	1.9	1.0	1.0	1.9	2.4	1.8	1.4	2.2	2.0
Euro Area	1.8	1.3	1.2	0.9	1.4	0.9	1.1	1.4	1.7	1.6	1.2	1.8
Japan	−1.2	−0.8	−0.3	1.7	2.1	0.3	−0.2	−0.1	0.6	0.3	0.3	0.4
Other Advanced Economies[1]	2.1	1.3	1.5	1.4	1.2	1.3	1.9	1.7	1.3	1.2	0.9	1.9
Consumer Prices												
Advanced Economies	**2.0**	**2.0**	**1.4**	**1.4**	**0.3**	**0.7**	**1.7**	**2.0**	**1.4**	**0.8**	**1.6**	**1.9**
United States	2.4	2.1	1.5	1.6	0.1	1.3	2.1	2.4	1.8	1.5	2.8	2.2
Euro Area[2]	2.1	2.5	1.3	0.4	0.2	0.2	1.5	1.8	1.2	0.4	0.9	1.7
Japan	−0.2	−0.1	0.3	2.8	0.8	−0.1	0.5	1.0	0.5	−0.1	0.3	1.0
Other Advanced Economies[1]	2.3	2.1	1.7	1.5	0.5	0.9	1.8	1.9	1.4	0.5	1.2	1.9
Emerging Market and Developing Economies[3]	**6.4**	**5.8**	**5.4**	**4.7**	**4.7**	**4.3**	**4.4**	**4.9**	**5.1**	**5.0**	**4.7**	**4.0**
Regional Groups												
Emerging and Developing Asia	4.6	4.6	4.6	3.4	2.6	2.8	2.4	2.7	3.3	3.2	2.9	3.1
Emerging and Developing Europe	9.9	6.3	5.5	6.5	10.6	5.5	5.6	6.4	6.6	5.2	5.2	5.3
Latin America and the Caribbean	5.6	4.6	4.6	4.9	5.4	5.5	6.3	6.6	7.7	6.2	6.7	4.3
Middle East and Central Asia	7.6	8.8	8.3	6.4	5.5	5.7	6.9	9.5	7.8	9.3	9.3	6.5
Sub-Saharan Africa	9.4	9.0	6.5	6.3	6.8	10.4	10.7	8.4	8.5	10.6	7.9	6.1
Analytical Groups												
By Source of Export Earnings												
Fuel	9.1	7.7	7.7	6.3	8.8	7.4	5.4	6.5	6.2	6.4	6.7	5.8
Nonfuel	5.7	5.3	4.8	4.3	3.9	3.7	4.2	4.6	5.0	4.7	4.3	3.7
Of Which, Primary Products[4]	6.4	6.8	6.4	6.9	5.1	6.0	11.5	13.9	17.6	18.7	16.9	7.0
By External Financing Source												
Net Debtor Economies	7.2	6.9	6.1	5.6	5.4	5.1	5.6	5.5	5.3	5.4	4.9	4.4
Net Debtor Economies by Debt-Servicing Experience												
Economies with Arrears and/or Rescheduling during 2015–19	9.1	7.4	6.1	10.0	15.0	9.8	17.2	16.7	13.4	15.5	12.7	6.4
Other Groups												
European Union	2.4	2.6	1.4	0.4	0.1	0.2	1.6	1.9	1.4	0.8	1.2	1.8
Low-Income Developing Countries	9.8	9.9	7.8	7.2	6.5	8.4	9.2	8.8	8.4	11.3	9.2	5.9
Middle East and North Africa	7.3	9.0	8.7	6.3	5.6	5.4	6.9	10.7	8.2	9.4	9.9	6.9
Memorandum												
Median Inflation Rate												
Advanced Economies	2.3	2.6	1.4	0.7	0.1	0.6	1.6	1.8	1.5	0.5	1.2	1.9
Emerging Market and Developing Economies[3]	5.2	4.6	3.7	3.1	2.6	2.7	3.3	3.1	2.6	2.9	2.9	3.0

[1]Excludes the United States, euro area countries, and Japan.
[2]Based on Eurostat's harmonized index of consumer prices.
[3]Excludes Venezuela but includes Argentina from 2017 onward. See country-specific notes for Venezuela and Argentina in the "Country Notes" section of the Statistical Appendix.
[4]Includes Argentina from 2017 onward. See country-specific note for Argentina in the "Country Notes" section of the Statistical Appendix.

Table A6. Advanced Economies: Consumer Prices[1]

(Annual percent change)

	Average 2002–11	2012	2013	2014	2015	2016	2017	2018	2019	Projections 2020	Projections 2021	Projections 2025	End of Period[2] 2019	End of Period[2] Projections 2020	End of Period[2] Projections 2021
Advanced Economies	**2.0**	**2.0**	**1.4**	**1.4**	**0.3**	**0.7**	**1.7**	**2.0**	**1.4**	**0.8**	**1.6**	**1.9**	**1.5**	**0.9**	**1.5**
United States	2.4	2.1	1.5	1.6	0.1	1.3	2.1	2.4	1.8	1.5	2.8	2.2	2.1	2.1	2.2
Euro Area[3]	2.1	2.5	1.3	0.4	0.2	0.2	1.5	1.8	1.2	0.4	0.9	1.7	1.3	0.1	1.1
Germany	1.7	2.1	1.6	0.8	0.7	0.4	1.7	2.0	1.3	0.5	1.1	2.0	1.5	0.3	1.2
France	1.9	2.2	1.0	0.6	0.1	0.3	1.2	2.1	1.3	0.5	0.6	1.6	1.6	−0.5	1.1
Italy	2.3	3.3	1.2	0.2	0.1	−0.1	1.3	1.2	0.6	0.1	0.6	1.4	0.5	0.1	0.6
Spain	2.8	2.4	1.4	−0.2	−0.5	−0.2	2.0	1.7	0.7	−0.2	0.8	1.7	0.8	−0.3	0.8
Netherlands	1.9	2.8	2.6	0.3	0.2	0.1	1.3	1.6	2.7	1.2	1.5	1.7	2.8	1.3	1.5
Belgium	2.2	2.6	1.2	0.5	0.6	1.8	2.2	2.3	1.2	0.6	1.2	1.6	0.9	0.6	1.1
Austria	2.0	2.6	2.1	1.5	0.8	1.0	2.2	2.1	1.5	1.2	1.8	2.0	1.8	1.0	1.9
Ireland	2.0	1.9	0.5	0.3	0.0	−0.2	0.3	0.7	0.9	−0.2	0.6	2.0	1.1	0.7	0.6
Portugal	2.4	2.8	0.4	−0.2	0.5	0.6	1.6	1.2	0.3	0.0	1.1	1.5	0.4	0.0	1.2
Greece	3.4	1.0	−0.9	−1.4	−1.1	0.0	1.1	0.8	0.5	−0.6	0.7	1.8	1.1	−1.1	1.2
Finland	1.8	3.2	2.2	1.2	−0.2	0.4	0.8	1.2	1.1	0.7	1.3	1.9	1.1	1.2	1.3
Slovak Republic	3.8	3.7	1.5	−0.1	−0.3	−0.5	1.4	2.5	2.8	1.5	1.5	2.1	3.2	0.2	1.8
Lithuania	3.3	3.2	1.2	0.2	−0.7	0.7	3.7	2.5	2.2	1.3	1.7	2.1	2.7	1.3	1.7
Slovenia	3.5	2.6	1.8	0.2	−0.5	−0.1	1.4	1.7	1.6	0.5	1.8	1.9	1.8	1.2	1.6
Luxembourg	2.8	2.9	1.7	0.7	0.1	0.0	2.1	2.0	1.7	0.4	1.4	1.9	1.8	0.5	1.3
Latvia	5.5	2.3	0.0	0.7	0.2	0.1	2.9	2.6	2.7	0.6	1.8	2.2	2.1	1.3	2.2
Estonia	4.2	4.2	3.2	0.5	0.1	0.8	3.7	3.4	2.3	0.2	1.4	1.9	1.8	0.2	1.4
Cyprus	2.6	3.1	0.4	−0.3	−1.5	−1.2	0.7	0.8	0.6	−0.6	1.0	1.7	0.8	−0.5	0.6
Malta	2.4	3.2	1.0	0.8	1.2	0.9	1.3	1.7	1.5	0.8	1.1	2.0	1.3	0.5	1.6
Japan	−0.2	−0.1	0.3	2.8	0.8	−0.1	0.5	1.0	0.5	−0.1	0.3	1.0	0.5	−0.6	0.7
United Kingdom	2.4	2.8	2.6	1.5	0.0	0.7	2.7	2.5	1.8	0.8	1.2	2.0	1.4	0.3	1.5
Korea	3.2	2.2	1.3	1.3	0.7	1.0	1.9	1.5	0.4	0.5	0.9	2.0	0.7	0.4	0.8
Canada	2.1	1.5	0.9	1.9	1.1	1.4	1.6	2.3	1.9	0.6	1.3	2.0	2.1	0.3	1.4
Australia	2.9	1.7	2.5	2.5	1.5	1.3	2.0	1.9	1.6	0.7	1.3	2.4	1.8	0.6	1.2
Taiwan Province of China	1.1	1.6	1.0	1.3	−0.6	1.0	1.1	1.5	0.5	−0.1	1.0	1.4	1.1	−0.1	1.0
Singapore	2.0	4.6	2.4	1.0	−0.5	−0.5	0.6	0.4	0.6	−0.4	0.3	1.5	0.8	−0.5	0.7
Switzerland	0.8	−0.7	−0.2	0.0	−1.1	−0.4	0.5	0.9	0.4	−0.8	0.0	1.0	0.2	−0.8	−0.3
Sweden	1.8	0.9	0.4	0.2	0.7	1.1	1.9	2.0	1.6	0.8	1.4	1.8	1.7	0.9	1.5
Hong Kong SAR	1.1	4.1	4.3	4.4	3.0	2.4	1.5	2.4	2.9	0.3	2.4	2.4	2.9	0.3	2.4
Czech Republic	2.3	3.3	1.4	0.4	0.3	0.7	2.5	2.2	2.9	3.3	2.4	2.0	3.2	3.2	2.4
Norway	1.8	0.7	2.1	2.0	2.2	3.6	1.9	2.8	2.2	1.4	3.3	2.0	1.4	2.0	1.8
Israel	2.4	1.7	1.5	0.5	−0.6	−0.5	0.2	0.8	0.8	−0.5	0.2	0.8	0.6	−0.6	0.5
Denmark	2.0	2.4	0.5	0.4	0.2	0.0	1.1	0.7	0.7	0.4	0.9	1.6	0.8	0.4	0.9
New Zealand	2.8	1.1	1.1	1.2	0.3	0.6	1.9	1.6	1.6	1.7	0.6	2.0	1.9	1.7	0.0
Puerto Rico	3.0	1.3	1.1	0.6	−0.8	−0.3	1.8	1.3	0.1	−1.6	0.6	1.2	0.5	−1.6	0.6
Macao SAR	3.0	6.1	5.5	6.0	4.6	2.4	1.2	3.0	2.8	1.7	1.8	2.8	2.6	1.7	1.8
Iceland	6.0	5.2	3.9	2.0	1.6	1.7	1.8	2.7	3.0	2.7	2.8	2.5	2.0	3.1	2.5
San Marino	. . .	2.8	1.6	1.1	0.1	0.6	1.0	1.8	1.0	0.5	0.8	1.2	0.7	0.5	0.8
Memorandum															
Major Advanced Economies	1.9	1.9	1.3	1.5	0.3	0.8	1.8	2.1	1.5	0.9	1.8	1.9	1.6	1.1	1.6

[1]Movements in consumer prices are shown as annual averages.
[2]Monthly year-over-year changes and, for several countries, on a quarterly basis.
[3]Based on Eurostat's harmonized index of consumer prices.

Table A7. Emerging Market and Developing Economies: Consumer Prices[1]

(Annual percent change)

	Average 2002–11	2012	2013	2014	2015	2016	2017	2018	2019	Projections 2020	Projections 2021	Projections 2025	End of Period[2] 2019	End of Period[2] Projections 2020	End of Period[2] Projections 2021
Emerging and Developing Asia	**4.6**	**4.6**	**4.6**	**3.4**	**2.6**	**2.8**	**2.4**	**2.7**	**3.3**	**3.2**	**2.9**	**3.1**	**4.7**	**1.9**	**2.9**
Bangladesh	7.3	8.9	6.8	7.3	6.4	5.9	5.4	5.8	5.5	5.6	5.9	5.5	5.5	6.0	6.0
Bhutan	5.0	10.1	8.1	9.6	6.7	3.3	4.3	3.7	2.6	3.6	4.6	3.2	2.7	4.5	4.7
Brunei Darussalam	0.4	0.1	0.4	−0.2	−0.3	−0.4	−1.3	1.1	−0.4	0.3	0.5	0.3	0.3	0.3	0.5
Cambodia	5.7	2.9	3.0	3.9	1.2	3.0	2.9	2.4	2.0	2.5	2.9	3.0	3.1	2.1	2.8
China	2.6	2.6	2.6	2.0	1.4	2.0	1.6	2.1	2.9	2.9	2.7	2.6	4.5	1.4	2.5
Fiji	4.0	3.4	2.9	0.5	1.4	3.9	3.4	4.1	1.8	−1.3	1.1	2.0	−0.9	−1.8	1.5
India	7.0	10.0	9.4	5.8	4.9	4.5	3.6	3.4	4.8	4.9	3.7	4.0	6.7	3.4	4.0
Indonesia	7.9	4.0	6.4	6.4	6.4	3.5	3.8	3.3	2.8	2.1	1.6	3.0	2.6	1.5	2.1
Kiribati	2.6	−3.0	−1.5	2.1	0.6	1.9	0.4	0.6	−1.9	1.5	2.0	2.4	−1.2	1.2	1.9
Lao P.D.R.	7.6	4.3	6.4	4.1	1.3	1.8	0.7	2.0	3.3	6.5	4.9	3.1	6.3	6.3	3.5
Malaysia	2.4	1.7	2.1	3.1	2.1	2.1	3.8	1.0	0.7	−1.1	2.4	2.0	1.0	−1.1	2.4
Maldives	5.0	10.9	3.8	2.1	1.9	0.8	2.3	1.4	1.3	0.4	2.7	2.0	1.3	1.5	2.1
Marshall Islands	. . .	4.3	1.9	1.1	−2.2	−1.5	0.1	0.8	1.2	0.9	1.1	2.0	1.2	0.9	1.1
Micronesia	3.5	6.3	2.2	0.7	−0.2	−0.6	0.1	1.5	1.9	−0.8	2.5	2.0	1.9	−0.8	2.5
Mongolia	9.3	14.3	10.5	12.3	5.7	0.7	4.3	6.8	7.3	5.0	5.5	7.5	5.2	4.5	6.6
Myanmar	16.6	0.4	5.8	5.1	7.3	9.1	4.6	5.9	8.6	6.1	6.2	6.0	9.5	3.3	7.7
Nauru	. . .	0.3	−1.1	0.3	9.8	8.2	5.1	0.5	4.3	0.9	1.2	2.0	4.5	−0.9	1.2
Nepal	6.8	8.3	9.9	9.0	7.2	9.9	4.5	4.1	4.6	6.4	6.0	5.3	6.0	6.0	6.0
Palau	3.0	5.4	2.8	4.0	2.2	−1.3	1.1	2.0	0.6	0.0	0.0	2.0	−0.4	0.0	0.0
Papua New Guinea	6.0	4.5	5.0	5.2	6.0	6.7	5.4	4.7	3.7	3.4	3.9	3.2	2.7	3.6	4.4
Philippines	5.0	3.0	2.6	3.6	0.7	1.3	2.9	5.2	2.5	2.4	3.0	3.0	2.5	2.6	3.3
Samoa	5.8	6.2	−0.2	−1.2	1.9	0.1	1.3	3.7	2.2	2.8	2.5	2.8	−0.1	2.9	1.9
Solomon Islands	8.5	5.9	5.4	5.2	−0.6	0.5	0.5	3.5	1.8	3.9	3.0	4.2	2.8	3.1	3.5
Sri Lanka	9.0	7.5	6.9	2.8	2.2	4.0	6.6	4.3	4.3	4.7	4.6	5.0	4.8	4.5	4.8
Thailand	2.8	3.0	2.2	1.9	−0.9	0.2	0.7	1.1	0.7	−0.4	1.8	1.8	0.9	0.8	0.7
Timor-Leste	5.5	10.9	9.5	0.8	0.6	−1.5	0.5	2.3	0.9	0.9	2.0	2.0	0.3	1.5	2.4
Tonga	7.7	3.3	0.7	2.3	0.1	−0.6	7.2	6.8	3.3	0.5	0.8	2.4	−0.1	0.1	2.5
Tuvalu	2.8	1.4	2.0	1.1	3.1	3.5	4.1	2.1	2.2	1.5	2.2	2.0	2.2	1.5	2.3
Vanuatu	2.6	1.3	1.5	0.8	2.5	0.8	3.1	2.3	2.7	2.9	2.4	2.3	3.5	2.6	2.2
Vietnam	9.6	9.1	6.6	4.1	0.6	2.7	3.5	3.5	2.8	3.8	4.0	4.0	5.2	3.1	3.7
Emerging and Developing Europe	**9.9**	**6.3**	**5.5**	**6.5**	**10.6**	**5.5**	**5.6**	**6.4**	**6.6**	**5.2**	**5.2**	**5.3**	**5.3**	**5.3**	**5.2**
Albania[3]	3.1	2.0	1.9	1.6	1.9	1.3	2.0	2.0	1.4	1.4	1.7	3.0	1.1	1.2	2.2
Belarus	19.5	59.2	18.3	18.1	13.5	11.8	6.0	4.9	5.6	5.1	5.1	4.1	4.7	5.5	4.9
Bosnia and Herzegovina	2.5	2.1	−0.1	−0.9	−1.0	−1.6	0.8	1.4	0.6	−0.8	0.4	2.0	0.7	−0.8	0.4
Bulgaria[4]	5.6	2.4	0.4	−1.6	−1.1	−1.3	1.2	2.6	2.5	1.2	1.7	2.0	3.1	0.5	2.4
Croatia	2.7	3.4	2.2	−0.2	−0.5	−1.1	1.1	1.5	0.8	0.3	0.8	2.1	1.4	0.2	0.9
Hungary	5.1	5.7	1.7	−0.2	−0.1	0.4	2.4	2.8	3.4	3.6	3.4	3.0	4.0	3.7	3.1
Kosovo	2.3	2.5	1.8	0.4	−0.5	0.3	1.5	1.1	2.7	0.8	1.2	1.9	1.2	1.5	1.2
Moldova	9.3	4.6	4.6	5.1	9.6	6.4	6.6	3.1	4.8	2.8	2.3	5.0	7.5	0.5	6.0
Montenegro	5.4	4.1	2.2	−0.7	1.5	−0.3	2.4	2.6	0.4	−0.1	0.7	1.7	1.1	−0.4	0.9
North Macedonia	2.0	3.3	2.8	−0.3	−0.3	−0.2	1.4	1.5	0.8	0.9	1.3	2.2	0.4	1.0	1.4
Poland	2.6	3.7	0.9	0.0	−0.9	−0.6	2.0	1.6	2.3	3.3	2.3	2.4	3.4	2.2	2.0
Romania	9.4	3.3	4.0	1.1	−0.6	−1.6	1.3	4.6	3.8	2.9	2.5	2.5	4.0	2.7	2.7
Russia	11.2	5.1	6.8	7.8	15.5	7.0	3.7	2.9	4.5	3.2	3.2	4.0	3.0	3.8	3.3
Serbia	9.3	7.3	7.7	2.1	1.4	1.1	3.1	2.0	1.9	1.5	1.9	3.0	1.9	1.6	2.0
Turkey	13.2	8.9	7.5	8.9	7.7	7.8	11.1	16.3	15.2	11.9	11.9	11.0	11.8	12.0	12.0
Ukraine[3]	10.7	0.6	−0.3	12.1	48.7	13.9	14.4	10.9	7.9	3.2	6.0	5.0	4.1	5.2	5.8
Latin America and the Caribbean[5]	**5.6**	**4.6**	**4.6**	**4.9**	**5.4**	**5.5**	**6.3**	**6.6**	**7.7**	**6.2**	**6.7**	**4.3**	**7.7**	**5.6**	**6.8**
Antigua and Barbuda	2.3	3.4	1.1	1.1	1.0	−0.5	2.4	1.2	1.5	1.0	1.0	2.0	1.5	0.7	1.3
Argentina[3]	10.7	10.0	10.6	. . .	. . .	. . .	25.7	34.3	53.5	. . .	. . .	. . .	53.8	. . .	. . .
Aruba	3.5	0.6	−2.4	0.4	0.5	−0.9	−1.0	3.6	4.3	1.2	1.8	2.2	5.2	−1.1	3.3
The Bahamas	2.3	1.9	0.4	1.2	1.9	−0.3	1.5	2.3	1.3	1.8	2.1	2.2	1.8	1.7	2.5
Barbados	4.7	4.5	1.8	1.8	−1.1	1.5	4.4	3.7	4.1	2.9	1.6	2.3	7.2	−0.8	2.4
Belize	2.6	1.2	0.5	1.2	−0.9	0.7	1.1	0.3	0.2	0.8	0.7	2.2	0.2	1.1	1.3
Bolivia	5.4	4.5	5.7	5.8	4.1	3.6	2.8	2.3	1.8	1.7	4.1	3.5	1.5	3.3	3.8
Brazil	6.6	5.4	6.2	6.3	9.0	8.7	3.4	3.7	3.7	2.7	2.9	3.3	4.3	2.0	2.9
Chile	3.2	3.0	1.8	4.7	4.3	3.8	2.2	2.3	2.3	2.9	2.7	3.0	3.0	2.4	2.9
Colombia	5.1	3.2	2.0	2.9	5.0	7.5	4.3	3.2	3.5	2.4	2.1	2.9	3.8	1.4	2.4

Table A7. Emerging Market and Developing Economies: Consumer Prices[1] (continued)
(Annual percent change)

	Average 2002–11	2012	2013	2014	2015	2016	2017	2018	2019	Projections 2020	Projections 2021	Projections 2025	End of Period[2] 2019	End of Period[2] Projections 2020	End of Period[2] Projections 2021
Latin America and the Caribbean (continued)[5]	**5.6**	**4.6**	**4.6**	**4.9**	**5.4**	**5.5**	**6.3**	**6.6**	**7.7**	**6.2**	**6.7**	**4.3**	**7.7**	**5.6**	**6.8**
Costa Rica	9.7	4.5	5.2	4.5	0.8	0.0	1.6	2.2	2.1	0.8	0.9	2.8	1.5	0.5	1.2
Dominica	2.2	1.4	0.0	0.8	−0.9	0.0	0.6	1.4	1.6	1.8	1.9	2.0	1.8	1.8	2.0
Dominican Republic	12.1	3.7	4.8	3.0	0.8	1.6	3.3	3.6	1.8	3.3	4.0	4.0	3.7	4.0	4.0
Ecuador	5.2	5.1	2.7	3.6	4.0	1.7	0.4	−0.2	0.3	0.0	1.0	1.0	−0.1	−0.3	2.0
El Salvador	3.6	1.7	0.8	1.1	−0.7	0.6	1.0	1.1	0.1	0.2	1.1	1.0	0.0	0.7	1.5
Grenada	3.1	2.4	0.0	−1.0	−0.6	1.7	0.9	0.8	0.6	−0.2	1.1	1.9	0.1	−0.8	1.2
Guatemala	6.7	3.8	4.3	3.4	2.4	4.4	4.4	3.8	3.7	2.1	2.1	4.0	3.4	2.3	3.1
Guyana	6.1	2.4	1.9	0.7	−0.9	0.8	1.9	1.3	2.1	1.0	2.7	3.1	2.1	1.3	2.9
Haiti	13.1	6.8	6.8	3.9	7.5	13.4	14.7	12.9	17.3	22.4	23.8	11.3	19.7	25.0	22.0
Honduras	7.3	5.2	5.2	6.1	3.2	2.7	3.9	4.3	4.4	3.3	3.7	4.0	4.1	3.2	4.2
Jamaica	11.5	6.9	9.3	8.3	3.7	2.4	4.4	3.7	3.9	5.1	5.4	5.0	6.2	4.1	5.7
Mexico	4.4	4.1	3.8	4.0	2.7	2.8	6.0	4.9	3.6	3.4	3.3	3.0	2.8	3.7	2.9
Nicaragua	8.4	7.2	7.1	6.0	4.0	3.5	3.9	4.9	5.4	4.4	4.0	3.5	6.1	4.0	3.5
Panama	3.1	5.7	4.0	2.6	0.1	0.7	0.9	0.8	−0.4	−0.8	0.2	2.0	−0.1	−0.5	0.5
Paraguay	7.9	3.7	2.7	5.0	3.1	4.1	3.6	4.0	2.8	2.9	3.2	3.3	2.8	3.0	3.3
Peru	2.5	3.7	2.8	3.2	3.5	3.6	2.8	1.3	2.1	1.8	1.9	2.0	1.9	1.8	2.0
St. Kitts and Nevis	3.7	0.8	1.1	0.2	−2.3	−0.7	0.7	−1.0	−0.2	0.7	1.1	2.0	0.4	1.0	1.3
St. Lucia	2.4	4.2	1.5	3.5	−1.0	−3.1	0.1	2.4	0.5	0.3	2.1	2.0	0.9	1.5	2.1
St. Vincent and the Grenadines	3.1	2.6	0.8	0.2	−1.7	−0.2	2.2	2.3	0.9	0.9	1.6	2.0	0.5	1.5	2.0
Suriname	11.7	5.0	1.9	3.4	6.9	55.5	22.0	6.9	4.4	49.8	51.0	9.0	4.2	104.9	20.9
Trinidad and Tobago	6.9	9.3	5.2	5.7	4.7	3.1	1.9	1.0	1.0	0.0	1.0	1.0	0.4	0.0	1.0
Uruguay	9.1	8.1	8.6	8.9	8.7	9.6	6.2	7.6	7.9	10.0	8.2	4.0	8.8	9.5	7.5
Venezuela[3]	23.4	21.1	40.6	62.2	121.7	254.9	438.1	65,374.1	19,906	6,500	6,500	. . .	9,585.5	6,500	6,500
Middle East and Central Asia	**7.6**	**8.8**	**8.3**	**6.4**	**5.5**	**5.7**	**6.9**	**9.5**	**7.8**	**9.3**	**9.3**	**6.5**	**6.9**	**10.7**	**8.9**
Afghanistan	11.1	6.4	7.4	4.7	−0.7	4.4	5.0	0.6	2.3	5.4	4.8	4.0	2.8	5.0	4.5
Algeria	3.6	8.9	3.3	2.9	4.8	6.4	5.6	4.3	2.0	3.5	3.8	7.0	2.4	5.2	2.5
Armenia	4.8	2.5	5.8	3.0	3.7	−1.4	1.0	2.4	1.4	0.9	2.0	3.8	0.7	1.5	2.5
Azerbaijan	8.0	1.0	2.4	1.4	4.0	12.4	12.8	2.3	2.7	3.0	3.1	3.2	2.7	3.0	3.1
Bahrain	1.9	2.8	3.3	2.6	1.8	2.8	1.4	2.1	1.0	0.0	2.8	2.2	1.7	2.0	2.4
Djibouti	4.0	4.2	1.1	1.3	−0.8	2.7	0.6	0.1	3.3	2.9	2.4	2.0	3.3	2.5	2.2
Egypt	8.8	8.7	6.9	10.1	11.0	10.2	23.5	20.9	13.9	5.7	6.2	7.4	9.4	5.6	8.0
Georgia	7.0	−0.9	−0.5	3.1	4.0	2.1	6.0	2.6	4.9	5.3	2.5	3.0	7.0	3.5	3.0
Iran	15.6	30.6	34.7	15.6	11.9	9.1	9.6	31.2	41.0	30.5	30.0	25.0	26.0	35.0	25.0
Iraq	. . .	6.1	1.9	2.2	1.4	0.5	0.1	0.4	−0.2	0.8	1.0	2.0	0.1	1.0	1.0
Jordan	4.1	4.6	4.9	3.0	−1.1	−0.6	3.6	4.5	0.7	−0.3	1.4	2.5	0.7	−1.7	1.4
Kazakhstan	8.6	5.1	5.8	6.7	6.7	14.6	7.4	6.0	5.2	6.9	6.2	4.0	5.4	7.5	5.9
Kuwait	3.6	3.2	2.7	3.1	3.7	3.5	1.5	0.6	1.1	1.0	2.3	2.5	1.5	1.4	2.5
Kyrgyz Republic	8.3	2.8	6.6	7.5	6.5	0.4	3.2	1.5	1.1	8.0	5.5	5.0	3.1	7.7	7.0
Lebanon[3]	3.1	6.6	4.8	1.8	−3.7	−0.8	4.5	4.6	2.9	85.5	. . .	. . .	7.0	144.5	. . .
Libya[3]	2.9	6.1	2.6	2.4	14.8	24.0	28.0	−1.2	4.6	22.3	15.1	12.2	4.6	22.3	15.1
Mauritania	6.6	4.9	4.1	3.8	0.5	1.5	2.3	3.1	2.3	3.9	4.5	4.0	2.7	5.0	4.0
Morocco	2.0	0.7	1.6	0.4	1.4	1.5	0.7	1.6	0.2	0.2	0.8	2.0	1.0	0.2	0.8
Oman	3.4	2.9	1.2	1.0	0.1	1.1	1.6	0.9	0.1	1.0	3.4	2.5	0.1	1.0	3.4
Pakistan	9.0	11.0	7.4	8.6	4.5	2.9	4.1	3.9	6.7	10.7	8.8	6.5	8.0	8.6	10.2
Qatar	5.1	1.8	3.2	4.2	1.0	2.7	0.5	0.2	−0.6	−2.2	1.8	2.0	. . .	. . .	. . .
Saudi Arabia	3.2	2.9	3.6	2.2	1.2	2.0	−0.8	2.5	−2.1	3.6	3.7	2.0	−0.1	3.6	3.7
Somalia	. . .	. . .	. . .	. . .	. . .	. . .	. . .	. . .	. . .	. . .	. . .	. . .	3.1	3.0	2.5
Sudan[6]	12.4	35.6	36.5	36.9	16.9	17.8	32.4	63.3	51.0	141.6	129.7	16.8	57.0	198.9	103.0
Syria[7]	. . .	. . .	. . .	. . .	. . .	. . .	. . .	. . .	. . .	. . .	. . .	. . .	. . .	. . .	. . .
Tajikistan	11.1	5.8	5.0	6.1	5.8	5.9	7.3	3.8	7.8	8.1	7.0	6.5	8.0	7.5	7.0
Tunisia	3.5	4.6	5.3	4.6	4.4	3.6	5.3	7.3	6.7	5.8	5.3	4.0	6.1	5.4	4.9
Turkmenistan	6.6	5.3	6.8	6.0	7.4	3.6	8.0	13.3	5.1	8.0	6.0	6.0	6.3	8.0	6.0
United Arab Emirates	5.3	0.7	1.1	2.3	4.1	1.6	2.0	3.1	−1.9	−1.5	1.5	2.1	−1.9	−1.5	1.5
Uzbekistan	13.1	11.9	11.7	9.1	8.5	8.8	13.9	17.5	14.5	13.0	10.7	5.1	15.2	12.1	9.3
West Bank and Gaza	4.3	2.8	1.7	1.7	1.4	−0.2	0.2	−0.2	1.6	−1.2	0.3	2.0	1.3	−1.7	0.9
Yemen	11.7	9.9	11.0	8.2	22.0	21.3	30.4	27.6	10.0	26.4	31.0	8.0	6.2	45.4	21.0

Table A7. Emerging Market and Developing Economies: Consumer Prices[1] *(continued)*

(Annual percent change)

	Average 2002–11	2012	2013	2014	2015	2016	2017	2018	2019	Projections 2020	Projections 2021	Projections 2025	End of Period[2] 2019	End of Period[2] Projections 2020	End of Period[2] Projections 2021
Sub-Saharan Africa	**9.4**	**9.0**	**6.5**	**6.3**	**6.8**	**10.4**	**10.7**	**8.4**	**8.5**	**10.6**	**7.9**	**6.1**	**9.7**	**10.5**	**7.3**
Angola	31.5	10.3	8.8	7.3	9.2	30.7	29.8	19.6	17.1	21.0	20.6	6.0	16.9	22.2	19.6
Benin	3.0	6.7	1.0	−1.1	0.2	−0.8	1.8	0.8	−0.9	2.5	2.0	2.0	0.3	2.5	2.0
Botswana	8.7	7.5	5.9	4.4	3.1	2.8	3.3	3.2	2.8	1.6	3.0	4.0	2.2	1.6	3.0
Burkina Faso	2.6	3.8	0.5	−0.3	0.9	−0.2	0.4	2.0	−3.2	2.0	2.0	2.5	−2.6	3.5	2.5
Burundi	9.1	18.2	7.9	4.4	5.6	5.5	16.6	−2.8	−0.7	7.6	5.2	3.2	5.1	7.9	3.0
Cabo Verde	2.5	2.5	1.5	−0.2	0.1	−1.4	0.8	1.3	1.1	1.0	1.2	1.7	1.9	1.0	1.2
Cameroon	2.4	2.4	2.1	1.9	2.7	0.9	0.6	1.1	2.5	2.8	2.2	2.0	2.4	2.4	2.1
Central African Republic	3.0	5.5	7.0	14.9	1.4	4.9	4.2	1.6	2.7	2.9	2.5	2.5	−2.8	4.6	2.5
Chad	2.2	7.5	0.2	1.7	4.8	−1.6	−0.9	4.0	−1.0	2.8	3.0	3.0	−1.7	1.6	4.4
Comoros	3.8	5.9	0.4	0.0	0.9	0.8	0.1	1.7	3.7	3.0	2.1	2.0	6.3	−5.5	4.1
Democratic Republic of the Congo	19.1	0.9	0.9	1.2	0.7	3.2	35.8	29.3	4.7	11.5	12.1	5.0	4.6	17.1	8.0
Republic of Congo	3.0	5.0	4.6	0.9	3.2	3.2	0.4	1.2	2.2	2.5	2.6	3.0	3.8	2.5	2.7
Côte d'Ivoire	3.0	1.3	2.6	0.4	1.2	0.7	0.7	0.4	0.8	1.2	1.4	2.0	1.6	1.2	1.4
Equatorial Guinea	5.2	3.4	3.2	4.3	1.7	1.4	0.7	1.3	1.2	3.0	2.2	2.1	4.1	2.1	2.2
Eritrea	17.1	4.8	5.9	10.0	28.5	−5.6	−13.3	−14.4	−16.4	4.7	2.6	2.0	27.2	4.0	2.0
Eswatini	7.1	8.9	5.6	5.7	5.0	7.8	6.2	4.8	2.6	4.1	4.2	4.9	2.0	4.5	4.1
Ethiopia	15.3	24.1	8.1	7.4	9.6	6.6	10.7	13.8	15.8	20.2	11.5	8.0	19.5	16.1	8.0
Gabon	1.1	2.7	0.5	4.5	−0.1	2.1	2.7	4.8	2.0	3.0	3.0	2.5	1.0	3.0	3.0
The Gambia	7.0	4.6	5.2	6.3	6.8	7.2	8.0	6.5	7.1	6.1	6.0	5.0	7.7	6.5	5.8
Ghana	13.4	7.1	11.7	15.5	17.2	17.5	12.4	9.8	7.2	10.6	8.7	6.0	7.9	11.6	8.7
Guinea	17.6	15.2	11.9	9.7	8.2	8.2	8.9	9.8	9.5	9.1	8.0	7.8	9.1	8.7	8.0
Guinea-Bissau	2.5	2.1	0.8	−1.0	1.5	2.7	−0.2	0.4	0.2	2.0	2.0	2.0	−0.1	2.5	2.0
Kenya	7.8	9.4	5.7	6.9	6.6	6.3	8.0	4.7	5.2	5.3	5.0	5.0	5.8	4.5	5.0
Lesotho	6.9	6.1	4.9	5.4	3.2	6.6	4.4	4.8	5.2	4.3	4.5	5.5	4.0	4.5	5.0
Liberia	9.6	6.8	7.6	9.9	7.7	8.8	12.4	23.5	27.0	11.9	9.5	5.0	20.3	11.0	8.0
Madagascar	10.4	5.7	5.8	6.1	7.4	6.1	8.6	8.6	5.6	4.3	5.5	5.4	4.0	5.2	5.5
Malawi	8.1	21.3	28.3	23.8	21.9	21.7	11.5	9.2	9.4	9.3	9.5	5.0	11.5	9.2	9.5
Mali	2.5	5.3	−2.4	2.7	1.4	−1.8	1.8	1.7	−2.9	0.5	1.5	2.0	−3.3	1.8	1.7
Mauritius	5.8	3.9	3.5	3.2	1.3	1.0	3.7	3.2	0.5	2.5	3.2	3.3	0.9	3.5	3.7
Mozambique	11.2	2.6	4.3	2.6	3.6	19.9	15.1	3.9	2.8	3.6	5.6	5.5	3.5	4.4	5.5
Namibia	6.6	6.7	5.6	5.3	3.4	6.7	6.1	4.3	3.7	2.3	3.4	4.5	2.6	2.9	3.4
Niger	2.4	0.5	2.3	−0.9	1.0	0.2	0.2	2.8	−2.5	4.4	1.7	2.0	−2.3	2.2	2.0
Nigeria	12.2	12.2	8.5	8.0	9.0	15.7	16.5	12.1	11.4	12.9	12.7	10.6	12.0	13.7	11.6
Rwanda	8.1	6.3	4.2	1.8	2.5	5.7	4.8	1.4	2.4	6.9	1.0	5.0	6.7	5.0	5.0
São Tomé and Príncipe	16.7	10.6	8.1	7.0	5.3	5.4	5.7	8.3	8.4	7.9	8.0	3.0	7.7	8.0	8.0
Senegal	2.1	1.4	0.7	−1.1	0.9	1.2	1.1	0.5	1.0	2.0	2.0	1.5	0.6	2.5	0.9
Seychelles	7.3	7.1	4.3	1.4	4.0	−1.0	2.9	3.7	1.8	3.9	2.9	3.0	1.7	6.6	3.0
Sierra Leone	8.7	6.6	5.5	4.6	6.7	10.9	18.2	16.0	14.8	15.7	15.5	8.4	13.9	17.5	13.5
South Africa	5.9	5.6	5.8	6.1	4.6	6.3	5.3	4.6	4.1	3.3	3.9	4.5	3.7	3.3	4.3
South Sudan	. . .	45.1	0.0	1.7	52.8	379.8	187.9	83.5	51.2	27.1	33.1	11.9	30.0	20.0	23.8
Tanzania	7.4	16.0	7.9	6.1	5.6	5.2	5.3	3.5	3.4	3.6	3.7	4.2	3.8	3.6	3.7
Togo	2.4	2.6	1.8	0.2	1.8	0.9	−0.2	0.9	0.7	1.4	1.5	2.0	−0.3	1.1	4.5
Uganda	7.7	12.7	4.9	3.1	5.4	5.5	5.6	2.6	2.9	4.2	4.8	5.0	3.6	5.0	5.2
Zambia	14.2	6.6	7.0	7.8	10.1	17.9	6.6	7.0	9.8	14.5	13.3	7.0	11.7	13.0	11.2
Zimbabwe[3]	−0.8	3.7	1.6	−0.2	−2.4	−1.6	0.9	10.6	255.3	622.8	3.7	3.0	521.1	495.0	3.0

[1]Movements in consumer prices are shown as annual averages.
[2]Monthly year-over-year changes and, for several countries, on a quarterly basis.
[3]See country-specific notes for Albania, Argentina, Lebanon, Libya, Ukraine, Venezuela, and Zimbabwe in the "Country Notes" section of the Statistical Appendix.
[4]Based on Eurostat's harmonized index of consumer prices.
[5]Excludes Venezuela but includes Argentina from 2017 onward. See country-specific notes for Venezuela and Argentina in the "Country Notes" section of the Statistical Appendix.
[6]Data for 2011 exclude South Sudan after July 9. Data for 2012 and onward pertain to the current Sudan.
[7]Data for Syria are excluded for 2011 onward owing to the uncertain political situation.

Table A8. Major Advanced Economies: General Government Fiscal Balances and Debt[1]

(Percent of GDP, unless noted otherwise)

	Average 2002–11	2012	2013	2014	2015	2016	2017	2018	2019	Projections 2020	2021	2025
Major Advanced Economies												
Net Lending/Borrowing	−5.2	−6.5	−4.3	−3.6	−3.0	−3.3	−3.2	−3.7	−4.2	−16.2	−7.6	−4.0
Output Gap[2]	−1.8	−3.8	−3.5	−2.7	−1.8	−1.5	−0.5	0.2	0.4	−3.6	−2.2	−0.1
Structural Balance[2]	−4.3	−4.6	−3.2	−2.6	−2.4	−2.9	−3.0	−3.6	−4.3	−12.5	−6.2	−3.9
United States												
Net Lending/Borrowing[3]	−6.1	−8.0	−4.6	−4.1	−3.6	−4.4	−4.6	−5.8	−6.3	−18.7	−8.7	−5.5
Output Gap[2]	−3.1	−6.0	−5.4	−4.1	−2.3	−1.9	−1.0	0.4	1.0	−3.2	−1.5	−0.1
Structural Balance[2]	−4.4	−4.9	−3.0	−2.6	−2.6	−3.7	−4.3	−5.7	−6.8	−15.0	−7.6	−5.4
Net Debt	52.3	80.8	81.5	81.2	80.8	81.8	81.9	83.2	84.0	106.8	107.3	113.8
Gross Debt	73.0	103.3	104.9	104.5	104.6	106.6	105.7	106.9	108.7	131.2	133.6	136.9
Euro Area												
Net Lending/Borrowing	−3.2	−3.7	−3.0	−2.5	−2.0	−1.5	−1.0	−0.5	−0.6	−10.1	−5.0	−1.8
Output Gap[2]	0.1	−2.2	−3.1	−2.8	−2.2	−1.5	−0.4	0.2	0.1	−5.1	−3.2	0.0
Structural Balance[2]	−3.3	−2.0	−1.1	−0.7	−0.6	−0.6	−0.6	−0.5	−0.6	−5.3	−3.1	−1.8
Net Debt	58.8	73.2	75.7	75.9	74.7	74.3	72.1	70.4	69.2	85.1	84.7	80.9
Gross Debt	73.5	90.7	92.6	92.8	90.9	90.0	87.6	85.7	84.0	101.1	100.0	94.3
Germany												
Net Lending/Borrowing	−2.4	0.0	0.0	0.6	1.0	1.2	1.4	1.8	1.5	−8.2	−3.2	1.0
Output Gap[2]	−0.2	0.3	−0.8	−0.3	−0.3	0.2	1.0	1.2	0.4	−3.5	−1.8	0.0
Structural Balance[2]	−2.1	0.0	0.6	1.2	1.2	1.2	1.2	1.3	1.3	−5.8	−1.8	1.0
Net Debt	55.7	59.6	58.6	55.0	52.2	49.3	45.5	42.7	41.1	54.1	54.2	43.8
Gross Debt	68.7	81.1	78.7	75.7	72.2	69.2	65.0	61.6	59.5	73.3	72.2	59.5
France												
Net Lending/Borrowing	−4.2	−5.0	−4.1	−3.9	−3.6	−3.6	−2.9	−2.3	−3.0	−10.8	−6.5	−4.7
Output Gap[2]	−0.1	−1.3	−1.9	−2.1	−2.2	−2.3	−1.3	−0.5	0.0	−5.6	−4.0	0.0
Structural Balance[2]	−4.2	−4.0	−2.9	−2.6	−2.2	−2.1	−2.1	−1.7	−2.0	−4.5	−4.0	−4.7
Net Debt	61.8	80.0	83.0	85.5	86.3	89.2	89.4	89.3	89.4	110.0	109.8	114.6
Gross Debt	71.2	90.6	93.4	94.9	95.6	98.0	98.3	98.1	98.1	118.7	118.6	123.3
Italy												
Net Lending/Borrowing	−3.4	−2.9	−2.9	−3.0	−2.6	−2.4	−2.4	−2.2	−1.6	−13.0	−6.2	−2.5
Output Gap[2]	−0.1	−2.8	−4.1	−4.1	−3.4	−2.5	−1.2	−0.7	−0.7	−5.4	−5.4	−0.5
Structural Balance[2]	−4.0	−1.6	−0.5	−1.0	−0.6	−1.3	−1.8	−1.9	−1.3	−3.8	−3.4	−2.5
Net Debt	101.0	114.6	120.0	122.3	123.1	122.4	122.0	122.9	123.0	148.8	146.1	141.5
Gross Debt	109.6	126.5	132.5	135.4	135.3	134.8	134.1	134.8	134.8	161.8	158.3	152.6
Japan												
Net Lending/Borrowing	−6.7	−8.6	−7.9	−5.6	−3.8	−3.7	−3.1	−2.5	−3.3	−14.2	−6.4	−2.7
Output Gap[2]	−1.9	−3.1	−1.7	−1.9	−1.5	−1.8	−0.3	−0.8	−0.7	−3.0	−2.1	0.0
Structural Balance[2]	−6.2	−7.6	−7.5	−5.5	−4.3	−4.1	−3.3	−2.5	−3.0	−12.7	−5.6	−2.7
Net Debt	105.8	145.3	144.7	146.6	146.4	152.0	149.8	153.5	154.9	177.1	178.9	179.7
Gross Debt[4]	183.3	228.7	232.2	235.8	231.3	236.4	234.5	236.6	238.0	266.2	264.0	264.0
United Kingdom												
Net Lending/Borrowing	−4.9	−7.6	−5.5	−5.6	−4.6	−3.3	−2.5	−2.3	−2.2	−16.5	−9.2	−4.4
Output Gap[2]	0.4	−2.0	−1.5	−0.7	−0.1	0.0	0.3	0.0	0.0	−3.9	−3.5	0.0
Structural Balance[2]	−5.2	−6.1	−4.3	−4.9	−4.3	−3.3	−2.6	−2.3	−2.2	−14.0	−6.4	−4.3
Net Debt	44.4	74.8	75.9	78.0	78.4	77.8	76.7	75.9	75.4	98.1	101.6	107.1
Gross Debt	49.7	83.2	84.2	86.2	86.9	86.8	86.2	85.7	85.4	108.0	111.5	117.0
Canada												
Net Lending/Borrowing	−0.6	−2.5	−1.5	0.2	−0.1	−0.5	−0.1	−0.4	−0.3	−19.9	−8.7	−0.3
Output Gap[2]	0.0	−0.4	0.0	1.0	−0.1	−0.9	0.4	0.6	0.4	−3.8	−1.4	0.0
Structural Balance[2]	−0.6	−2.3	−1.5	−0.6	0.0	0.0	−0.3	−0.7	−0.6	−16.5	−7.9	−0.3
Net Debt[5]	28.3	28.9	29.7	28.5	28.4	28.7	27.9	26.5	25.9	46.4	48.4	42.9
Gross Debt	74.5	85.4	86.1	85.6	91.2	91.7	90.5	89.7	88.6	114.6	115.0	106.2

Note: The methodology and specific assumptions for each country are discussed in Box A1. The country group composites for fiscal data are calculated as the sum of the US dollar values for the relevant individual countries.

[1]Debt data refer to the end of the year and are not always comparable across countries. Gross and net debt levels reported by national statistical agencies for countries that have adopted the System of National Accounts 2008 (Australia, Canada, Hong Kong SAR, United States) are adjusted to exclude unfunded pension liabilities of government employees' defined-benefit pension plans. Fiscal data for the aggregated major advanced economies and the United States start in 2001, and the average for the aggregate and the United States is therefore for the period 2001–07.

[2]Percent of potential GDP.

[3]Figures reported by the national statistical agency are adjusted to exclude items related to the accrual-basis accounting of government employees' defined-benefit pension plans.

[4]Nonconsolidated basis.

[5]Includes equity shares.

Table A9. Summary of World Trade Volumes and Prices

(Annual percent change)

	Averages		2012	2013	2014	2015	2016	2017	2018	2019	Projections	
	2002–11	2012–21									2020	2021
Trade in Goods and Services												
World Trade[1]												
Volume	5.7	2.3	3.0	3.6	3.9	2.9	2.2	5.6	3.9	1.0	−10.4	8.3
Price Deflator												
In US Dollars	5.4	−1.5	−1.8	−0.7	−1.7	−13.3	−4.1	4.3	5.4	−2.7	−2.8	3.3
In SDRs	3.2	−0.6	1.3	0.1	−1.7	−5.8	−3.4	4.6	3.2	−0.3	−3.5	0.5
Volume of Trade												
Exports												
Advanced Economies	4.5	1.9	2.9	3.1	3.9	3.7	2.0	4.8	3.5	1.3	−11.6	7.0
Emerging Market and Developing Economies	8.7	2.9	3.4	4.7	3.3	1.7	2.7	6.6	4.1	0.9	−7.7	9.5
Imports												
Advanced Economies	4.1	2.0	1.7	2.6	3.9	4.8	2.6	4.8	3.6	1.7	−11.5	7.3
Emerging Market and Developing Economies	9.9	2.8	5.4	5.1	4.3	−0.8	1.7	7.4	5.0	−0.6	−9.4	11.0
Terms of Trade												
Advanced Economies	−0.2	0.4	−0.6	1.0	0.3	1.8	1.2	−0.2	−0.5	0.1	0.6	0.3
Emerging Market and Developing Economies	1.6	−0.7	0.6	−0.5	−0.6	−4.3	−1.4	1.4	1.2	−1.1	−2.6	0.3
Trade in Goods												
World Trade[1]												
Volume	5.8	2.3	2.8	3.3	3.0	2.3	2.1	5.6	3.8	0.2	−8.1	8.4
Price Deflator												
In US Dollars	5.5	−1.9	−1.9	−1.2	−2.4	−14.5	−4.8	4.9	5.7	−3.1	−3.5	2.9
In SDRs	3.3	−1.0	1.1	−0.4	−2.3	−7.2	−4.2	5.1	3.6	−0.7	−4.2	0.1
World Trade Prices in US Dollars[2]												
Manufactures	2.7	−1.1	2.3	−2.8	−0.4	−3.0	−5.1	0.1	1.9	0.4	−3.1	−1.3
Oil	15.6	−7.7	0.9	−0.9	−7.5	−47.2	−15.7	23.3	29.4	−10.2	−32.1	12.0
Nonfuel Primary Commodities	11.6	−2.0	−7.6	−5.8	−5.5	−17.1	−0.4	6.4	1.3	0.8	5.6	5.1
Food	7.7	−1.8	−3.3	−0.3	−1.6	−16.9	1.5	3.8	−1.2	−3.1	0.4	4.3
Beverages	13.2	−3.6	−18.1	−13.7	20.1	−7.2	−3.1	−4.7	−8.2	−3.8	3.6	3.9
Agricultural Raw Materials	9.3	−4.8	−20.5	−4.4	−7.5	−11.5	0.0	5.2	2.0	−5.4	−4.2	1.7
Metal	17.5	−3.9	−17.8	−3.9	−12.2	−27.3	−5.3	22.2	6.6	3.7	0.8	3.0
World Trade Prices in SDRs[2]												
Manufactures	0.5	−0.1	5.5	−2.0	−0.3	5.3	−4.5	0.4	−0.2	2.9	−3.7	−4.0
Oil	13.2	−6.8	4.0	−0.1	−7.5	−42.7	−15.1	23.6	26.7	−8.0	−32.5	9.0
Nonfuel Primary Commodities	9.3	−1.0	−4.7	−5.1	−5.5	−10.0	0.3	6.6	−0.8	3.3	4.9	2.2
Food	5.4	−0.8	−0.3	0.5	−1.5	−9.8	2.2	4.1	−3.3	−0.7	−0.2	1.4
Beverages	10.8	−2.7	−15.6	−13.0	20.1	0.7	−2.5	−4.5	−10.1	−1.4	3.0	1.1
Agricultural Raw Materials	7.0	−3.8	−18.1	−3.7	−7.5	−4.0	0.6	5.5	−0.1	−3.1	−4.8	−1.1
Metal	15.0	−3.0	−15.3	−3.1	−12.1	−21.1	−4.7	22.5	4.4	6.2	0.1	0.2
World Trade Prices in Euros[2]												
Manufactures	−1.8	0.1	10.8	−5.9	−0.4	16.2	−4.8	−1.9	−2.6	6.0	−5.1	−8.3
Oil	10.7	−6.5	9.2	−4.1	−7.6	−36.8	−15.4	20.8	23.7	−5.2	−33.5	4.1
Nonfuel Primary Commodities	6.8	−0.8	0.0	−8.9	−5.6	−0.7	−0.1	4.2	−3.1	6.4	3.4	−2.3
Food	3.0	−0.6	4.7	−3.5	−1.6	−0.5	1.8	1.7	−5.6	2.3	−1.6	−3.1
Beverages	8.4	−2.4	−11.4	−16.4	20.0	11.1	−2.8	−6.6	−12.2	1.5	1.5	−3.4
Agricultural Raw Materials	4.6	−3.6	−14.0	−7.5	−7.6	5.9	0.3	3.1	−2.5	−0.2	−6.1	−5.5
Metal	12.4	−2.7	−11.0	−7.0	−12.2	−12.9	−5.0	19.7	1.9	9.4	−1.3	−4.2

Table A9. Summary of World Trade Volumes and Prices *(continued)*
(Annual percent change)

	Averages 2002–11	Averages 2012–21	2012	2013	2014	2015	2016	2017	2018	2019	Projections 2020	Projections 2021
Trade in Goods												
Volume of Trade												
Exports												
Advanced Economies	4.5	1.8	2.7	2.6	3.1	3.1	1.5	4.6	3.1	0.7	−9.7	7.3
Emerging Market and Developing Economies	8.5	2.8	3.8	4.6	2.7	1.2	2.7	6.6	4.0	−0.5	−5.5	8.8
Fuel Exporters	5.4	0.3	2.6	1.9	−0.5	3.1	1.2	1.5	1.0	−4.3	−7.8	5.3
Nonfuel Exporters	9.8	3.5	4.3	5.8	4.1	0.5	3.1	7.9	4.8	0.6	−4.9	9.6
Imports												
Advanced Economies	4.2	1.9	1.1	2.3	3.3	3.7	2.3	4.9	3.6	0.5	−9.4	7.6
Emerging Market and Developing Economies	10.0	3.0	5.2	4.7	2.6	−0.5	2.1	7.4	5.0	−0.4	−6.4	10.9
Fuel Exporters	10.3	−0.3	8.6	3.0	0.4	−6.4	−5.5	3.2	−2.0	0.7	−8.4	4.9
Nonfuel Exporters	9.9	3.6	4.5	5.1	3.1	0.8	3.7	8.2	6.3	−0.6	−6.0	11.9
Price Deflators in SDRs												
Exports												
Advanced Economies	2.3	−0.7	−0.4	0.4	−1.9	−6.4	−2.2	4.4	2.8	−1.4	−3.1	1.2
Emerging Market and Developing Economies	5.8	−1.3	3.1	−1.1	−3.1	−9.0	−7.0	6.9	4.8	0.3	−6.4	−0.7
Fuel Exporters	10.7	−4.6	4.4	−2.4	−6.7	−29.9	−12.7	17.0	15.3	−2.7	−21.3	3.8
Nonfuel Exporters	3.9	−0.3	2.6	−0.5	−1.6	−1.0	−5.4	4.4	2.1	1.1	−2.4	−1.7
Imports												
Advanced Economies	2.6	−1.1	0.6	−0.6	−2.0	−8.1	−3.6	4.4	3.5	−1.3	−3.6	0.5
Emerging Market and Developing Economies	4.0	−0.8	2.4	−0.6	−2.6	−4.9	−5.5	5.7	3.6	0.4	−4.4	−1.4
Fuel Exporters	4.6	−0.4	3.0	0.9	−2.1	−4.0	−3.1	4.0	1.0	2.0	−3.6	−1.5
Nonfuel Exporters	3.8	−0.9	2.3	−0.9	−2.8	−5.1	−6.0	6.1	4.0	0.1	−4.6	−1.4
Terms of Trade												
Advanced Economies	−0.3	0.4	−1.0	1.0	0.2	1.8	1.4	−0.1	−0.7	−0.1	0.6	0.7
Emerging Market and Developing Economies	1.8	−0.5	0.7	−0.5	−0.5	−4.3	−1.6	1.1	1.2	−0.1	−2.0	0.7
Regional Groups												
Emerging and Developing Asia	−1.4	1.0	1.4	1.1	2.5	8.4	0.2	−3.3	−2.3	1.0	2.4	−0.6
Emerging and Developing Europe	2.8	−1.6	1.4	−3.2	−0.7	−10.7	−5.8	2.7	4.5	0.3	−3.3	−0.1
Middle East and Central Asia	3.2	−0.7	−1.8	−1.1	−2.5	−8.7	1.1	4.2	0.0	0.2	−1.3	3.4
Latin America and the Caribbean	4.8	−3.7	0.4	−0.9	−4.6	−24.3	−6.1	10.1	10.7	−4.3	−15.4	3.3
Sub-Saharan Africa	5.1	−1.1	−0.2	−0.5	−2.7	−13.5	−0.4	7.3	4.0	−2.0	−5.8	4.4
Analytical Groups												
By Source of Export Earnings												
Fuel	5.9	−4.3	1.3	−3.3	−4.7	−27.0	−9.9	12.5	14.1	−4.6	−18.3	5.3
Nonfuel	0.0	0.6	0.3	0.4	1.2	4.3	0.6	−1.6	−1.9	1.0	2.3	−0.3
Memorandum												
World Exports in Billions of US Dollars												
Goods and Services	14,972	22,916	22,631	23,363	23,798	21,127	20,743	22,854	25,006	24,555	21,302	23,778
Goods	11,859	17,692	18,130	18,552	18,640	16,200	15,734	17,429	19,090	18,538	16,373	18,233
Average Oil Price[3]	15.6	−7.7	0.9	−0.9	−7.5	−47.2	−15.7	23.3	29.4	−10.2	−32.1	12.0
In US Dollars a Barrel	62.22	66.99	105.01	104.07	96.25	50.79	42.84	52.81	68.33	61.39	41.69	46.70
Export Unit Value of Manufactures[4]	2.7	−1.1	2.3	−2.8	−0.4	−3.0	−5.1	0.1	1.9	0.4	−3.1	−1.3

[1]Average of annual percent change for world exports and imports.
[2]As represented, respectively, by the export unit value index for manufactures of the advanced economies and accounting for 83 percent of the advanced economies' trade (export of goods) weights; the average of UK Brent, Dubai Fateh, and West Texas Intermediate crude oil prices; and the average of world market prices for nonfuel primary commodities weighted by their 2014–16 shares in world commodity imports.
[3]Percent change of average of UK Brent, Dubai Fateh, and West Texas Intermediate crude oil prices.
[4]Percent change for manufactures exported by the advanced economies.

Table A10. Summary of Current Account Balances
(Billions of US dollars)

	2012	2013	2014	2015	2016	2017	2018	2019	Projections 2020	2021	2025
Advanced Economies	**50.7**	**244.1**	**248.1**	**297.2**	**391.1**	**480.5**	**392.6**	**339.3**	**242.2**	**314.1**	**435.0**
United States	−418.1	−336.9	−367.8	−407.4	−394.9	−365.3	−449.7	−480.2	−441.7	−463.0	−518.5
Euro Area	129.5	278.1	319.6	322.9	390.0	393.4	418.7	354.8	242.0	344.5	432.4
Germany	251.6	244.8	280.3	288.8	295.1	286.7	292.4	273.2	217.6	294.9	336.0
France	−25.9	−14.3	−27.3	−9.0	−12.0	−19.9	−15.6	−18.1	−48.9	−51.7	−28.9
Italy	−4.8	23.7	41.1	26.1	48.7	50.5	52.0	59.2	59.6	63.2	70.4
Spain	1.1	27.6	23.3	24.2	39.1	35.1	27.5	27.5	6.7	13.4	32.2
Japan	59.7	45.9	36.8	136.4	197.9	203.5	176.6	184.3	143.5	165.6	187.0
United Kingdom	−92.8	−132.7	−144.8	−143.7	−140.9	−93.1	−110.7	−113.5	−54.0	−107.6	−111.8
Canada	−64.6	−58.0	−41.9	−54.4	−47.2	−46.4	−42.8	−35.4	−31.8	−42.9	−48.6
Other Advanced Economies[1]	273.9	342.3	358.4	364.7	345.6	323.7	344.2	392.0	314.2	337.5	400.5
Emerging Market and Developing Economies	**334.5**	**165.9**	**173.9**	**−57.9**	**−82.3**	**7.4**	**−46.2**	**62.8**	**−39.5**	**−144.7**	**−208.7**
Regional Groups											
Emerging and Developing Asia	119.0	98.9	228.3	308.6	223.3	173.1	−49.2	133.0	201.2	64.8	−7.5
Emerging and Developing Europe	−28.4	−56.2	−8.0	36.3	−6.6	−16.3	69.3	54.9	−9.2	4.3	−10.4
Latin America and the Caribbean	−148.3	−172.9	−186.0	−171.9	−99.7	−86.2	−130.2	−89.7	−21.6	−37.3	−71.3
Middle East and Central Asia	418.7	333.7	201.9	−138.9	−143.2	−26.9	108.4	26.8	−133.3	−106.7	−57.8
Sub-Saharan Africa	−26.6	−37.6	−62.4	−92.0	−56.1	−36.3	−44.4	−62.2	−76.6	−69.8	−61.7
Analytical Groups											
By Source of Export Earnings											
Fuel	593.8	460.6	311.3	−75.9	−74.9	83.7	311.0	146.3	−95.6	−41.4	16.7
Nonfuel	−259.2	−294.7	−137.4	18.0	−7.4	−76.4	−357.2	−83.6	56.1	−103.3	−225.5
Of Which, Primary Products	−63.4	−87.5	−53.2	−64.2	−43.7	−56.6	−74.6	−45.7	−32.0	−32.3	−33.9
By External Financing Source											
Net Debtor Economies	−413.6	−379.1	−348.6	−312.2	−219.2	−243.0	−333.8	−228.1	−167.5	−233.4	−347.6
Net Debtor Economies by Debt-Servicing Experience											
Economies with Arrears and/or Rescheduling during 2015–19	−56.5	−62.2	−43.0	−51.3	−55.2	−46.3	−46.0	−47.4	−41.7	−49.5	−40.0
Memorandum											
World	**385.2**	**410.0**	**422.0**	**239.2**	**308.9**	**487.9**	**346.4**	**402.0**	**202.6**	**169.4**	**226.3**
European Union	314.1	435.9	456.1	448.3	479.7	505.3	500.6	434.7	350.7	469.3	571.5
Low-Income Developing Countries	−32.8	−38.6	−40.6	−74.1	−41.1	−34.7	−57.0	−61.2	−88.6	−85.7	−76.4
Middle East and North Africa	408.4	326.5	191.5	−122.6	−120.2	−7.9	125.3	43.8	−117.3	−86.7	−33.6

Table A10. Summary of Current Account Balances *(continued)*
(Percent of GDP)

	2012	2013	2014	2015	2016	2017	2018	2019	Projections 2020	Projections 2021	Projections 2025
Advanced Economies	**0.1**	**0.5**	**0.5**	**0.7**	**0.8**	**1.0**	**0.8**	**0.7**	**0.5**	**0.6**	**0.7**
United States	−2.6	−2.0	−2.1	−2.2	−2.1	−1.9	−2.2	−2.2	−2.1	−2.1	−2.0
Euro Area	1.0	2.1	2.4	2.8	3.3	3.1	3.1	2.7	1.9	2.4	2.5
Germany	7.1	6.6	7.2	8.6	8.5	7.8	7.4	7.1	5.8	6.8	6.7
France	−1.0	−0.5	−1.0	−0.4	−0.5	−0.8	−0.6	−0.7	−1.9	−1.8	−0.8
Italy	−0.2	1.1	1.9	1.4	2.6	2.6	2.5	3.0	3.2	3.0	2.9
Spain	0.1	2.0	1.7	2.0	3.2	2.7	1.9	2.0	0.5	0.9	1.8
Japan	1.0	0.9	0.8	3.1	4.0	4.2	3.6	3.6	2.9	3.2	3.1
United Kingdom	−3.4	−4.8	−4.7	−4.9	−5.2	−3.5	−3.9	−4.0	−2.0	−3.8	−3.3
Canada	−3.5	−3.1	−2.3	−3.5	−3.1	−2.8	−2.5	−2.0	−2.0	−2.4	−2.2
Other Advanced Economies[1]	4.1	5.0	5.1	5.7	5.2	4.6	4.6	5.4	4.5	4.4	4.3
Emerging Market and Developing Economies	**1.2**	**0.5**	**0.6**	**−0.2**	**−0.3**	**0.0**	**−0.1**	**0.2**	**−0.1**	**−0.4**	**−0.4**
Regional Groups											
Emerging and Developing Asia	0.9	0.7	1.5	2.0	1.4	1.0	−0.3	0.6	1.0	0.3	0.0
Emerging and Developing Europe	−0.7	−1.2	−0.2	1.1	−0.2	−0.4	1.8	1.4	−0.3	0.1	−0.2
Latin America and the Caribbean	−2.5	−2.9	−3.1	−3.3	−2.0	−1.6	−2.5	−1.7	−0.5	−0.8	−1.3
Middle East and Central Asia	11.2	8.6	5.1	−4.0	−4.2	−0.8	2.8	0.7	−3.7	−2.7	−1.2
Sub-Saharan Africa	−1.7	−2.2	−3.5	−5.8	−3.8	−2.3	−2.7	−3.6	−4.8	−4.1	−2.5
Analytical Groups											
By Source of Export Earnings											
Fuel	9.6	7.3	5.1	−1.5	−1.6	1.7	5.9	2.7	−2.0	−0.8	0.3
Nonfuel	−1.2	−1.2	−0.5	0.1	0.0	−0.3	−1.2	−0.3	0.2	−0.3	−0.5
Of Which, Primary Products	−3.3	−4.4	−2.7	−3.3	−2.4	−2.8	−3.8	−2.4	−1.9	−1.8	−1.5
By External Financing Source											
Net Debtor Economies	−3.0	−2.7	−2.4	−2.3	−1.6	−1.7	−2.2	−1.5	−1.2	−1.5	−1.7
Net Debtor Economies by Debt-Servicing Experience											
Economies with Arrears and/or Rescheduling during 2015–19	−6.6	−6.9	−4.8	−5.9	−6.5	−5.9	−5.6	−5.3	−4.8	−5.4	−3.4
Memorandum											
World	**0.5**	**0.5**	**0.5**	**0.3**	**0.4**	**0.6**	**0.4**	**0.5**	**0.2**	**0.2**	**0.2**
European Union	2.1	2.8	2.9	3.3	3.5	3.4	3.1	2.8	2.3	2.8	2.8
Low-Income Developing Countries	−1.9	−2.1	−2.0	−3.8	−2.2	−1.8	−2.8	−2.8	−3.9	−3.6	−2.2
Middle East and North Africa	13.3	10.3	6.0	−4.3	−4.3	−0.3	4.0	1.3	−3.9	−2.7	−0.9

Table A10. Summary of Current Account Balances *(continued)*
(Percent of exports of goods and services)

	2012	2013	2014	2015	2016	2017	2018	2019	Projections 2020	Projections 2021	Projections 2025
Advanced Economies	**0.4**	**1.7**	**1.7**	**2.2**	**2.9**	**3.3**	**2.5**	**2.2**	**1.8**	**2.1**	**2.3**
United States	−18.6	−14.6	−15.4	−17.9	−17.6	−15.3	−17.7	−19.0	−20.8	−20.2	−18.4
Euro Area	4.0	8.2	9.0	10.0	12.0	11.1	10.8	9.3	. . .	. . .	. . .
Germany	15.4	14.4	15.8	18.3	18.5	16.5	15.6	15.1	13.4	15.7	14.7
France	−3.2	−1.7	−3.1	−1.2	−1.5	−2.4	−1.7	−2.0	−6.7	−6.6	−2.9
Italy	−0.8	3.9	6.5	4.8	8.8	8.4	7.9	9.4	11.4	10.0	8.8
Spain	0.3	6.2	5.1	6.0	9.4	7.6	5.5	5.7	1.8	3.1	5.2
Japan	6.5	5.5	4.3	17.4	24.4	23.2	19.0	20.4	18.6	19.3	18.2
United Kingdom	−11.4	−15.9	−16.6	−17.7	−18.3	−11.5	−12.6	−12.7	−6.9	−12.4	−11.2
Canada	−11.6	−10.4	−7.3	−11.0	−9.8	−9.0	−7.8	−6.4	−7.1	−8.5	−7.1
Other Advanced Economies[1]	6.8	8.2	8.6	9.8	9.5	8.2	8.0	9.4	8.5	8.4	8.1
Emerging Market and Developing Economies	**3.6**	**1.9**	**2.2**	**−0.6**	**−1.1**	**0.1**	**−0.5**	**0.7**	**−0.3**	**−1.6**	**−1.8**
Regional Groups											
Emerging and Developing Asia	3.3	2.6	5.7	8.1	6.1	4.2	−1.1	3.0	4.8	1.4	−0.1
Emerging and Developing Europe	−2.0	−3.8	−0.5	3.0	−0.6	−1.2	4.5	3.6	−0.7	0.3	−0.5
Latin America and the Caribbean	−11.7	−13.7	−15.0	−15.9	−9.5	−7.3	−10.3	−7.2	−2.0	−3.0	−4.8
Middle East and Central Asia	22.2	18.8	12.9	−10.3	−11.8	−2.2	7.0	1.9	−11.3	−8.3	−3.5
Sub-Saharan Africa	−5.6	−7.8	−13.7	−26.7	−17.6	−9.9	−10.6	−15.3	−23.7	−18.5	−12.0
Analytical Groups											
By Source of Export Earnings											
Fuel	22.5	18.3	13.8	−4.1	−4.8	4.7	15.2	7.8	−6.0	−2.2	1.2
Nonfuel	−4.3	−4.6	−2.1	0.3	−0.1	−1.2	−5.0	−1.2	0.9	−1.4	−2.4
Of Which, Primary Products	−12.9	−18.0	−11.3	−15.9	−10.9	−12.6	−15.5	−9.7	−7.7	−6.9	−5.6
By External Financing Source											
Net Debtor Economies	−10.3	−9.2	−8.4	−8.5	−6.0	−5.8	−7.3	−5.0	−4.3	−5.2	−5.8
Net Debtor Economies by Debt-Servicing Experience											
Economies with Arrears and/or Rescheduling during 2015–19	−21.3	−22.9	−17.0	−24.4	−28.5	−21.2	−18.2	−18.2	−19.5	−21.6	−11.3
Memorandum											
World	**1.6**	**1.8**	**1.9**	**1.2**	**1.5**	**2.1**	**1.4**	**1.6**	**1.0**	**0.7**	**0.8**
European Union	4.8	6.3	6.3	7.0	7.4	7.1	6.3	5.6	5.2	6.1	5.9
Low-Income Developing Countries	−6.9	−7.5	−7.6	−15.4	−8.5	−6.2	−8.9	−9.0	−15.0	−12.8	−7.9
Middle East and North Africa	24.6	20.9	13.9	−10.1	−11.0	−0.9	9.1	3.5	−11.2	−7.6	−2.2

[1]Excludes the Group of Seven (Canada, France, Germany, Italy, Japan, United Kingdom, United States) and euro area countries.

Table A11. Advanced Economies: Current Account Balance
(Percent of GDP)

	2012	2013	2014	2015	2016	2017	2018	2019	Projections 2020	2021	2025
Advanced Economies	**0.1**	**0.5**	**0.5**	**0.7**	**0.8**	**1.0**	**0.8**	**0.7**	**0.5**	**0.6**	**0.7**
United States	−2.6	−2.0	−2.1	−2.2	−2.1	−1.9	−2.2	−2.2	−2.1	−2.1	−2.0
Euro Area[1]	1.0	2.1	2.4	2.8	3.3	3.1	3.1	2.7	1.9	2.4	2.5
Germany	7.1	6.6	7.2	8.6	8.5	7.8	7.4	7.1	5.8	6.8	6.7
France	−1.0	−0.5	−1.0	−0.4	−0.5	−0.8	−0.6	−0.7	−1.9	−1.8	−0.8
Italy	−0.2	1.1	1.9	1.4	2.6	2.6	2.5	3.0	3.2	3.0	2.9
Spain	0.1	2.0	1.7	2.0	3.2	2.7	1.9	2.0	0.5	0.9	1.8
Netherlands	10.2	9.8	8.2	6.3	8.1	10.8	10.8	9.9	7.6	9.0	8.7
Belgium	−0.1	1.0	0.8	1.4	0.6	1.2	−1.4	−1.2	0.0	−0.8	−1.6
Austria	1.5	1.9	2.5	1.7	2.7	1.6	2.3	2.6	2.4	2.5	2.2
Ireland	−3.4	1.6	1.1	4.4	−4.2	0.5	6.0	−11.4	5.0	5.5	5.5
Portugal	−1.6	1.6	0.2	0.2	1.2	1.3	0.4	−0.1	−3.1	−3.5	−3.7
Greece	−2.4	−2.6	−2.3	−1.5	−2.3	−2.5	−3.5	−2.1	−7.7	−4.5	−3.6
Finland	−2.1	−1.8	−1.3	−0.9	−2.0	−0.9	−1.7	−0.5	−1.8	−0.7	0.3
Slovak Republic	0.9	1.9	1.1	−2.1	−2.7	−1.9	−2.6	−2.9	−3.1	−4.1	−2.8
Lithuania	−1.4	0.8	3.2	−2.8	−0.8	0.6	0.3	4.3	7.2	4.5	−1.7
Slovenia	1.3	3.3	5.1	3.8	4.8	6.2	5.9	5.7	4.5	3.9	1.1
Luxembourg	5.6	5.4	5.2	5.1	4.9	4.9	4.8	4.5	3.8	4.3	4.6
Latvia	−3.6	−2.7	−2.3	−0.9	1.4	1.0	−0.7	−0.5	2.0	−0.8	−1.2
Estonia	−1.9	0.3	0.7	1.8	1.6	2.7	2.0	2.6	4.0	2.0	−0.1
Cyprus	−3.9	−1.5	−4.1	−0.4	−4.2	−5.1	−4.4	−6.7	−10.6	−9.1	−3.5
Malta	1.7	2.6	8.5	2.7	3.7	10.2	11.0	9.6	7.6	8.3	10.3
Japan	1.0	0.9	0.8	3.1	4.0	4.2	3.6	3.6	2.9	3.2	3.1
United Kingdom	−3.4	−4.8	−4.7	−4.9	−5.2	−3.5	−3.9	−4.0	−2.0	−3.8	−3.3
Korea	3.8	5.6	5.6	7.2	6.5	4.6	4.5	3.6	3.3	3.4	4.3
Canada	−3.5	−3.1	−2.3	−3.5	−3.1	−2.8	−2.5	−2.0	−2.0	−2.4	−2.2
Australia	−4.3	−3.4	−3.1	−4.6	−3.3	−2.6	−2.1	0.6	1.8	−0.1	−2.0
Taiwan Province of China	8.7	9.7	11.3	13.6	13.1	14.1	11.6	10.7	9.6	9.8	9.2
Singapore	17.6	15.7	18.0	18.7	17.6	16.3	17.2	17.0	15.0	14.5	14.0
Switzerland	10.7	11.6	8.6	11.3	9.9	6.4	8.2	11.5	8.5	9.0	9.3
Sweden	5.5	5.1	4.5	4.1	3.5	3.1	2.5	4.2	3.2	4.2	3.0
Hong Kong SAR	1.6	1.5	1.4	3.3	4.0	4.6	3.7	6.2	4.4	4.7	4.0
Czech Republic	−1.5	−0.5	0.2	0.2	1.5	1.6	0.4	−0.4	−0.7	−0.5	1.0
Norway	12.6	10.3	10.8	8.0	4.5	4.6	7.1	4.1	2.8	4.4	4.3
Israel	0.3	3.0	4.0	5.1	3.3	3.1	2.1	3.4	3.5	3.5	2.8
Denmark	6.3	7.8	8.9	8.2	7.8	7.8	7.0	7.8	6.4	6.6	7.2
New Zealand	−3.9	−3.2	−3.1	−2.9	−2.2	−3.0	−4.3	−3.4	−2.0	−2.4	−2.9
Puerto Rico	...	...	...	...	...	...	...	...	...	...	...
Macao SAR	39.3	40.2	34.2	25.3	28.1	32.3	34.6	34.8	−23.5	−6.7	28.0
Iceland	−3.8	5.8	3.9	5.1	7.6	3.8	3.2	6.2	0.0	0.2	0.1
San Marino	...	...	...	...	...	−0.1	−1.6	0.7	−4.5	−1.2	−0.1
Memorandum											
Major Advanced Economies	−0.8	−0.6	−0.6	−0.5	−0.1	0.0	−0.3	−0.3	−0.4	−0.3	−0.2
Euro Area[2]	2.3	2.9	3.0	3.4	3.6	3.6	3.5	2.9	2.5	2.9	3.1

[1]Data corrected for reporting discrepancies in intra-area transactions.
[2]Data calculated as the sum of the balances of individual euro area countries.

Table A12. Emerging Market and Developing Economies: Current Account Balance
(Percent of GDP)

	2012	2013	2014	2015	2016	2017	2018	2019	Projections 2020	2021	2025
Emerging and Developing Asia	**0.9**	**0.7**	**1.5**	**2.0**	**1.4**	**1.0**	**−0.3**	**0.6**	**1.0**	**0.3**	**0.0**
Bangladesh	−0.3	1.6	0.8	1.8	1.9	−0.5	−3.5	−1.7	−1.5	−2.8	−1.9
Bhutan	−21.9	−25.6	−27.1	−27.9	−30.3	−23.9	−19.1	−22.5	−21.4	−13.5	8.9
Brunei Darussalam	29.8	20.9	31.9	16.7	12.9	16.4	6.9	6.6	0.0	2.8	9.6
Cambodia	−8.6	−8.5	−8.6	−8.7	−8.5	−7.9	−12.2	−15.8	−25.4	−16.3	−7.5
China	2.5	1.5	2.2	2.7	1.8	1.6	0.2	1.0	1.3	0.7	0.5
Fiji	−1.4	−8.9	−5.8	−3.5	−3.6	−6.7	−8.5	−12.9	−15.3	−12.1	−7.6
India	−4.8	−1.7	−1.3	−1.0	−0.6	−1.8	−2.1	−0.9	0.3	−0.9	−2.5
Indonesia	−2.7	−3.2	−3.1	−2.0	−1.8	−1.6	−2.9	−2.7	−1.3	−2.4	−1.8
Kiribati	1.9	−5.5	31.1	32.8	10.8	37.6	38.7	32.0	−1.6	2.8	11.5
Lao P.D.R.	−21.3	−26.5	−23.3	−22.4	−11.0	−10.6	−12.0	−6.4	−8.7	−7.7	−6.7
Malaysia	5.1	3.4	4.3	3.0	2.4	2.8	2.2	3.4	0.9	1.8	0.7
Maldives	−6.6	−4.3	−3.7	−7.5	−23.6	−21.7	−26.4	−26.0	−31.8	−17.0	−5.5
Marshall Islands	−0.4	−6.2	3.4	17.2	16.1	7.5	6.5	8.0	1.6	1.2	−2.3
Micronesia	−13.6	−9.9	6.1	4.5	7.2	10.3	21.0	16.0	1.6	3.5	−3.9
Mongolia	−27.4	−25.4	−11.3	−4.0	−6.3	−10.1	−16.8	−15.6	−12.3	−13.5	−4.1
Myanmar	−1.8	−1.2	−4.5	−3.5	−4.2	−6.8	−4.7	−2.6	−3.5	−4.4	−4.0
Nauru	35.7	49.5	25.2	−21.3	2.0	12.7	−4.6	10.5	4.2	3.4	−1.0
Nepal	4.8	3.3	4.5	5.0	6.3	−0.4	−8.1	−7.7	−2.5	−7.0	−4.7
Palau	−15.2	−14.1	−17.8	−8.5	−13.4	−18.7	−15.2	−26.6	−32.7	−35.4	−29.0
Papua New Guinea	−36.7	−30.9	15.1	25.6	29.4	29.9	26.2	22.2	14.7	18.9	16.7
Philippines	2.7	4.0	3.6	2.4	−0.4	−0.7	−2.5	−0.1	1.6	−1.5	−2.2
Samoa	−9.5	−1.5	−9.1	−2.8	−4.5	−2.0	0.8	2.3	−7.1	−7.0	−1.3
Solomon Islands	1.4	−3.0	−3.7	−2.7	−3.5	−4.3	−3.0	−9.6	−11.3	−16.4	−8.0
Sri Lanka	−5.8	−3.4	−2.5	−2.3	−2.1	−2.6	−3.2	−2.2	−3.6	−3.2	−2.4
Thailand	−1.2	−2.1	2.9	6.9	10.5	9.6	5.6	7.1	4.2	4.6	4.0
Timor-Leste	230.7	171.4	75.6	12.8	−32.9	−21.1	−12.2	8.2	−13.7	−27.6	−36.2
Tonga	−14.9	−9.6	−6.3	−10.1	−6.5	−6.4	−5.6	−4.8	−4.6	−17.5	−12.1
Tuvalu	18.4	−6.7	3.0	−53.5	21.5	24.0	7.1	12.4	17.0	−11.0	−8.0
Vanuatu	−6.5	−3.3	6.2	−1.6	0.8	−6.4	9.4	13.1	−0.3	−1.6	−4.0
Vietnam	4.7	3.6	3.7	−0.9	0.2	−0.6	1.9	3.4	1.2	1.7	0.0
Emerging and Developing Europe	**−0.7**	**−1.2**	**−0.2**	**1.1**	**−0.2**	**−0.4**	**1.8**	**1.4**	**−0.3**	**0.1**	**−0.2**
Albania[1]	−10.2	−9.3	−10.8	−8.6	−7.6	−7.5	−6.8	−7.6	−11.7	−8.5	−7.5
Belarus[1]	−2.8	−10.0	−6.6	−3.3	−3.4	−1.7	0.0	−1.8	−3.3	−2.2	−2.2
Bosnia and Herzegovina	−8.7	−5.3	−7.3	−5.1	−4.7	−4.4	−3.7	−3.6	−4.4	−6.1	−3.8
Bulgaria	−0.9	1.3	1.2	0.1	3.2	3.5	1.4	4.0	1.9	2.3	0.5
Croatia	−1.8	−1.1	0.3	3.3	2.1	3.5	1.8	2.8	−3.2	−3.1	1.6
Hungary	1.6	3.5	1.2	2.4	4.5	2.3	0.0	−0.8	−1.6	−0.9	−0.5
Kosovo	−5.8	−3.4	−6.9	−8.6	−7.9	−5.4	−7.6	−5.5	−6.0	−5.5	−4.2
Moldova	−7.4	−5.2	−6.0	−6.0	−3.5	−5.7	−10.7	−8.9	−8.3	−10.6	−7.3
Montenegro	−15.3	−11.4	−12.4	−11.0	−16.2	−16.1	−17.0	−15.2	−14.2	−13.6	−9.1
North Macedonia	−3.2	−1.6	−0.5	−2.0	−2.9	−1.0	−0.1	−2.8	−4.7	−3.8	−2.3
Poland	−3.7	−1.3	−2.1	−0.6	−0.5	0.0	−1.0	0.4	3.0	1.8	0.1
Romania	−4.8	−0.8	−0.2	−0.6	−1.4	−2.8	−4.4	−4.6	−5.3	−4.5	−3.9
Russia	3.3	1.5	2.8	5.0	1.9	2.0	6.9	3.8	1.2	1.8	1.8
Serbia	−10.8	−5.7	−5.6	−3.5	−2.9	−5.2	−4.8	−6.9	−6.4	−6.5	−5.2
Turkey	−5.4	−5.8	−4.1	−3.2	−3.1	−4.7	−2.7	1.2	−3.7	−0.9	−1.4
Ukraine[1]	−8.1	−9.2	−3.9	1.7	−1.5	−2.2	−3.3	−2.7	4.3	−3.0	−3.4
Latin America and the Caribbean	**−2.5**	**−2.9**	**−3.1**	**−3.3**	**−2.0**	**−1.6**	**−2.5**	**−1.7**	**−0.5**	**−0.8**	**−1.3**
Antigua and Barbuda	...	...	0.3	2.2	−2.4	−7.8	−13.7	−6.5	−22.0	−24.7	−8.4
Argentina	−0.4	−2.1	−1.6	−2.7	−2.7	−4.8	−5.2	−0.9	0.7	1.2	0.7
Aruba	3.5	−12.9	−5.0	4.3	5.1	1.1	−0.7	2.1	−20.8	−17.2	−5.6
The Bahamas	−14.3	−14.3	−19.7	−13.8	−6.0	−12.1	−11.4	0.6	−17.5	−15.9	−7.7
Barbados	−8.5	−8.4	−9.2	−6.1	−4.3	−3.8	−4.0	−3.1	−11.1	−6.8	−3.1
Belize	−2.2	−4.6	−8.2	−10.1	−9.2	−8.6	−8.1	−9.6	−15.3	−11.4	−7.8
Bolivia	7.2	3.4	1.7	−5.8	−5.6	−4.8	−4.6	−3.3	−2.6	−3.5	−4.0
Brazil	−3.4	−3.2	−4.1	−3.0	−1.3	−0.7	−2.2	−2.8	0.3	0.0	−0.7
Chile	−4.4	−4.8	−2.0	−2.4	−2.0	−2.3	−3.6	−3.8	−1.6	−2.9	−0.9
Colombia	−3.1	−3.3	−5.2	−6.3	−4.3	−3.3	−3.9	−4.2	−4.0	−3.9	−3.8

Table A12. Emerging Market and Developing Economies: Current Account Balance *(continued)*
(Percent of GDP)

	2012	2013	2014	2015	2016	2017	2018	2019	Projections		
									2020	2021	2025
Latin America and the Caribbean											
(continued)	**−2.5**	**−2.9**	**−3.1**	**−3.3**	**−2.0**	**−1.6**	**−2.5**	**−1.7**	**−0.5**	**−0.8**	**−1.3**
Costa Rica	−5.1	−4.8	−4.8	−3.5	−2.2	−3.3	−3.3	−2.4	−4.5	−4.1	−2.9
Dominica	...	...	−5.4	−4.7	−7.7	−8.8	−44.6	−27.2	−27.8	−26.3	−11.4
Dominican Republic	−6.5	−4.1	−3.2	−1.8	−1.1	−0.2	−1.4	−1.4	−6.0	−4.5	−1.0
Ecuador	−0.2	−1.0	−0.7	−2.2	1.1	−0.1	−1.2	−0.1	−2.0	−0.1	0.6
El Salvador	−5.8	−6.9	−5.4	−3.2	−2.3	−1.9	−4.7	−2.1	−4.9	−4.5	−5.0
Grenada	...	...	−11.6	−12.5	−11.0	−14.4	−15.9	−15.8	−25.3	−24.9	−10.1
Guatemala	−3.7	−4.2	−3.3	−1.2	1.0	1.1	0.8	2.4	3.8	2.3	−0.4
Guyana	−7.9	−9.3	−6.7	−3.4	1.5	−4.9	−29.2	−33.9	−22.0	−16.2	5.3
Haiti	−5.7	−6.6	−8.6	−3.0	−0.9	−1.0	−3.9	−1.4	−2.5	−0.4	−2.6
Honduras	−8.5	−9.5	−6.9	−4.7	−2.6	−0.8	−5.4	−1.4	−2.2	−2.8	−4.4
Jamaica	−9.8	−9.5	−8.0	−3.0	−0.3	−2.7	−1.6	−2.0	−5.2	−7.2	−3.0
Mexico	−1.6	−2.5	−1.9	−2.7	−2.3	−1.8	−2.1	−0.3	1.2	−0.1	−2.0
Nicaragua	−11.7	−12.6	−8.0	−9.9	−8.5	−7.2	−1.9	6.0	0.5	−0.2	−2.2
Panama	−9.2	−9.0	−13.4	−9.0	−7.8	−5.9	−8.2	−5.2	−7.0	−6.2	−3.1
Paraguay	−0.9	1.6	−0.1	−0.4	3.6	3.1	0.0	−1.0	−0.7	0.0	0.0
Peru	−3.2	−5.1	−4.5	−5.0	−2.6	−1.3	−1.7	−1.4	−1.1	−0.3	−1.0
St. Kitts and Nevis	...	...	0.1	−8.7	−12.7	−11.2	−5.7	−2.1	−21.0	−20.0	−12.4
St. Lucia	...	...	−2.5	0.0	−6.5	−1.0	2.2	5.3	−16.8	−9.3	−0.3
St. Vincent and the Grenadines	...	...	−26.1	−15.3	−13.9	−11.6	−12.0	−10.0	−18.7	−16.9	−7.0
Suriname	3.3	−3.8	−7.9	−16.4	−5.1	1.9	−3.4	−11.1	−8.0	−6.2	−8.1
Trinidad and Tobago	13.4	19.3	13.8	7.0	−4.4	5.3	5.8	4.8	−3.3	1.5	3.6
Uruguay	−4.0	−3.6	−3.2	−0.9	0.6	0.7	0.0	0.6	−1.7	−3.3	−2.2
Venezuela	0.7	1.8	2.4	−5.0	−1.4	6.1	8.8	8.4	−4.1	−4.1	...
Middle East and Central Asia	**11.2**	**8.6**	**5.1**	**−4.0**	**−4.2**	**−0.8**	**2.8**	**0.7**	**−3.7**	**−2.7**	**−1.2**
Afghanistan	10.9	1.4	6.6	3.8	9.0	7.6	12.2	11.7	9.5	7.8	7.0
Algeria	5.9	0.4	−4.4	−16.4	−16.5	−13.2	−9.6	−10.1	−10.8	−16.6	−12.2
Armenia	−10.0	−7.3	−7.8	−2.7	−2.1	−3.0	−9.4	−8.2	−8.8	−7.3	−6.0
Azerbaijan	21.4	16.6	13.9	−0.4	−3.6	4.1	12.8	9.1	−3.6	−4.4	−0.4
Bahrain	8.4	7.4	4.6	−2.4	−4.6	−4.1	−6.5	−2.1	−8.0	−5.7	−4.5
Djibouti	−23.4	−30.8	24.0	29.3	−1.0	−4.8	14.2	13.0	−3.2	−2.5	0.0
Egypt	−3.6	−2.2	−0.9	−3.7	−6.0	−6.1	−2.4	−3.6	−3.2	−4.2	−2.7
Georgia	−11.4	−5.6	−10.2	−11.8	−12.5	−8.1	−6.8	−5.1	−10.8	−8.5	−7.0
Iran	5.6	5.8	3.2	0.3	3.8	3.5	6.1	1.1	−0.5	0.3	0.7
Iraq	5.1	1.1	2.6	−6.5	−8.3	1.8	6.7	1.1	−12.6	−12.1	−7.5
Jordan	−14.9	−10.2	−7.1	−9.0	−9.7	−10.6	−6.9	−2.3	−6.8	−5.7	−3.0
Kazakhstan	1.1	0.8	2.8	−3.3	−5.9	−3.1	−0.1	−3.6	−3.3	−2.8	−2.1
Kuwait	45.5	40.3	33.4	3.5	−4.6	8.0	14.5	9.4	−6.8	−2.8	1.4
Kyrgyz Republic	−15.5	−13.9	−17.0	−15.9	−11.6	−6.2	−12.1	−5.6	−13.4	−12.8	−7.8
Lebanon[1]	−25.9	−28.0	−28.8	−19.9	−23.5	−26.3	−28.2	−27.4	−16.3	...	...
Libya[1]	29.9	0.0	−78.4	−54.3	−24.6	8.0	1.8	−0.3	−59.8	−22.4	−8.6
Mauritania	−18.8	−17.2	−22.2	−15.5	−11.0	−10.0	−13.8	−10.6	−15.3	−17.3	−2.5
Morocco	−9.3	−7.6	−5.9	−2.1	−4.1	−3.4	−5.3	−4.1	−7.3	−5.2	−4.1
Oman	10.2	6.6	5.2	−15.9	−19.1	−15.6	−5.4	−4.6	−14.6	−12.9	−3.2
Pakistan	−2.1	−1.1	−1.3	−1.0	−1.8	−4.1	−6.4	−4.9	−1.1	−2.5	−2.7
Qatar	33.2	30.4	24.0	8.5	−5.5	4.0	9.1	2.4	−0.6	2.6	3.4
Saudi Arabia	22.4	18.1	9.8	−8.7	−3.7	1.5	9.2	5.9	−2.5	−1.6	−0.6
Somalia	...	−13.6	−8.3	−8.3	−9.3	−9.7	−7.5	−10.5	−12.8	−12.9	−15.0
Sudan	−12.8	−11.0	−5.8	−8.4	−7.6	−10.0	−13.1	−15.1	−12.7	−10.7	−7.2
Syria[2]	...	...	...	...	...	...	...	...	...	...	...
Tajikistan	−9.0	−10.4	−3.4	−6.1	−4.2	2.2	−5.0	−2.3	−7.1	−4.5	−3.9
Tunisia	−9.1	−9.7	−9.8	−9.7	−9.3	−10.2	−11.2	−8.5	−8.3	−8.7	−5.4
Turkmenistan	−0.9	−7.3	−6.1	−15.6	−20.2	−10.4	5.5	5.1	1.0	1.8	−3.2
United Arab Emirates	19.5	18.8	13.5	4.9	3.7	7.1	9.6	8.4	3.6	7.5	8.5
Uzbekistan	0.9	2.4	3.3	1.3	0.4	2.5	−7.1	−5.6	−6.4	−7.4	−4.0
West Bank and Gaza	−14.9	−14.8	−13.6	−13.9	−13.9	−13.2	−13.1	−10.8	−11.1	−13.7	−12.2
Yemen	−1.7	−3.1	−0.7	−6.2	−2.9	−0.2	−2.0	−3.9	−6.5	−8.3	−0.3

Table A12. Emerging Market and Developing Economies: Current Account Balance *(continued)*
(Percent of GDP)

	2012	2013	2014	2015	2016	2017	2018	2019	Projections 2020	2021	2025
Sub-Saharan Africa	**−1.7**	**−2.2**	**−3.5**	**−5.8**	**−3.8**	**−2.3**	**−2.7**	**−3.6**	**−4.8**	**−4.1**	**−2.5**
Angola	10.8	6.1	−2.6	−8.8	−4.8	−0.5	7.0	5.7	−1.3	0.1	1.1
Benin	−5.2	−5.4	−6.7	−6.0	−3.0	−4.2	−4.6	−4.3	−5.5	−4.8	−4.5
Botswana	0.3	8.9	15.4	7.8	7.7	5.3	0.6	−7.6	−2.5	−3.1	1.4
Burkina Faso	−1.3	−10.0	−7.2	−7.6	−6.1	−5.0	−4.1	−4.8	−3.5	−3.5	−5.3
Burundi	−18.6	−19.7	−19.5	−20.7	−13.5	−15.0	−14.5	−17.9	−20.7	−20.8	−17.7
Cabo Verde	−12.6	−4.9	−9.1	−3.2	−3.8	−7.8	−5.2	0.3	−15.2	−10.0	−2.9
Cameroon	−3.3	−3.5	−4.0	−3.8	−3.2	−2.7	−3.6	−4.4	−5.4	−4.5	−1.2
Central African Republic	−5.6	−2.9	−13.3	−9.1	−5.3	−7.8	−8.0	−4.9	−5.6	−5.3	−5.6
Chad	−7.8	−9.1	−8.9	−13.8	−10.4	−7.1	−1.4	−4.9	−13.3	−9.7	−5.1
Comoros	−3.2	−4.0	−3.8	−0.3	−4.3	−2.1	−2.8	−3.8	−2.1	−1.5	−0.2
Democratic Republic of the Congo	−4.3	−9.5	−4.8	−3.9	−4.1	−3.3	−3.6	−3.8	−4.8	−4.0	−3.8
Republic of Congo	13.6	10.8	1.0	−39.0	−48.7	−3.3	1.5	3.5	−5.7	−1.9	1.5
Côte d'Ivoire	−0.9	−1.0	1.0	−0.4	−0.9	−2.0	−3.6	−2.7	−3.7	−2.9	−2.1
Equatorial Guinea	−1.1	−2.4	−4.3	−16.4	−13.0	−5.8	−5.4	−5.9	−9.6	−5.8	−16.9
Eritrea	12.4	2.3	17.3	20.8	15.3	24.0	15.4	12.1	10.1	10.8	9.1
Eswatini	5.0	10.8	11.6	12.9	7.8	6.2	1.3	4.2	1.0	5.7	5.4
Ethiopia	−7.1	−6.1	−6.6	−11.7	−9.4	−8.5	−6.5	−5.3	−4.5	−4.6	−3.3
Gabon	17.9	7.3	7.6	−5.6	−10.4	−7.0	−3.2	−0.3	−9.1	−6.0	−0.5
The Gambia	−4.5	−6.7	−7.3	−9.9	−9.2	−7.4	−9.5	−5.3	−8.5	−10.8	−7.4
Ghana	−8.7	−9.0	−7.0	−5.8	−5.2	−3.4	−3.1	−2.7	−3.4	−2.9	−2.1
Guinea	−19.9	−12.5	−12.9	−12.9	−31.9	−6.7	−18.7	−13.7	−20.5	−15.7	−10.1
Guinea-Bissau	−7.9	−4.3	0.5	1.8	1.4	0.3	−3.6	−8.5	−12.1	−4.2	−4.0
Kenya	−8.4	−8.8	−10.4	−6.9	−5.8	−7.2	−5.7	−5.8	−4.9	−5.4	−5.8
Lesotho	−8.8	−5.2	−5.1	−3.9	−6.5	−2.5	−1.3	−8.4	−13.3	−11.9	−4.7
Liberia	−12.3	−14.7	−20.5	−22.2	−19.2	−22.6	−22.5	−21.5	−21.4	−21.6	−20.5
Madagascar	−7.6	−5.5	−0.3	−1.6	0.5	−0.4	0.7	−2.3	−4.2	−2.9	−3.4
Malawi	−9.2	−8.4	−8.2	−17.2	−18.5	−25.6	−20.5	−17.1	−19.2	−19.3	−16.2
Mali	−2.2	−2.9	−4.7	−5.3	−7.2	−7.3	−4.9	−4.2	−2.0	−1.2	−5.8
Mauritius	−7.1	−6.2	−5.4	−3.6	−4.0	−4.6	−3.9	−5.4	−13.3	−10.7	−4.9
Mozambique	−41.8	−40.5	−36.5	−37.4	−32.2	−19.7	−29.6	−20.4	−60.0	−68.9	−27.7
Namibia	−5.7	−4.2	−11.1	−12.6	−15.7	−3.9	−2.8	−2.3	−4.4	−2.1	−2.0
Niger	−10.8	−11.3	−12.0	−15.3	−11.4	−11.4	−12.6	−12.6	−16.8	−19.2	−6.9
Nigeria	3.8	3.7	0.2	−3.1	0.7	2.8	1.0	−3.8	−3.6	−2.0	−0.5
Rwanda	−9.5	−7.1	−11.4	−14.8	−15.5	−7.5	−7.9	−9.2	−16.7	−10.5	−8.3
São Tomé and Príncipe	−21.8	−14.5	−20.7	−12.0	−6.1	−13.2	−12.3	−12.5	−17.0	−11.7	−7.1
Senegal	−8.7	−8.2	−7.0	−5.7	−4.2	−7.3	−8.8	−7.7	−9.2	−9.9	−4.1
Seychelles	−21.1	−11.9	−23.1	−18.6	−20.6	−20.1	−17.9	−16.7	−28.3	−25.7	−19.1
Sierra Leone	−31.8	−17.3	−9.3	−15.5	−9.1	−21.0	−18.7	−13.5	−12.1	−13.3	−10.7
South Africa	−5.1	−5.8	−5.1	−4.6	−2.9	−2.5	−3.5	−3.0	−1.6	−1.8	−2.4
South Sudan	−15.9	−3.9	0.0	−0.8	7.1	−3.1	−7.5	0.9	14.6	−9.2	−14.8
Tanzania	−12.0	−10.7	−10.0	−7.8	−4.1	−2.6	−3.0	−2.3	−3.2	−4.4	−2.3
Togo	−7.6	−13.2	−10.0	−11.0	−9.8	−2.0	−3.5	−4.3	−6.3	−4.4	−3.8
Uganda	−5.4	−5.7	−6.5	−6.1	−2.8	−4.8	−6.8	−6.5	−8.0	−5.9	−0.9
Zambia	4.9	−0.8	2.1	−2.7	−3.3	−1.7	−1.3	0.6	−1.0	0.0	0.6
Zimbabwe[1]	−10.7	−13.2	−11.6	−7.6	−3.6	−1.3	−5.9	1.1	−3.6	−2.0	−5.5

[1]See country-specific notes for Albania, Belarus, Lebanon, Libya, Ukraine, and Zimbabwe in the "Country Notes" section of the Statistical Appendix.
[2]Data for Syria are excluded for 2011 onward owing to the uncertain political situation.

Table A13. Summary of Financial Account Balances
(Billions of US dollars)

	2012	2013	2014	2015	2016	2017	2018	2019	Projections 2020	Projections 2021
Advanced Economies										
Financial Account Balance	−129.8	245.6	334.4	347.6	441.3	456.5	329.1	298.2	137.3	326.0
Direct Investment, Net	126.0	178.5	244.6	−2.2	−302.3	316.8	−78.7	−114.7	−183.4	−126.6
Portfolio Investment, Net	−247.0	−560.6	54.8	194.1	528.0	38.7	413.4	233.0	375.7	603.4
Financial Derivatives, Net	−97.3	74.8	1.3	−82.3	32.7	21.4	56.5	21.5	−3.2	16.7
Other Investment, Net	−185.0	399.8	−106.2	11.8	4.6	−164.5	−189.7	84.3	−107.3	−232.9
Change in Reserves	273.5	153.2	140.1	226.6	178.5	244.5	127.5	74.2	55.5	65.4
United States										
Financial Account Balance	−448.0	−400.1	−297.1	−333.1	−363.6	−334.1	−419.7	−395.5	−539.3	−463.7
Direct Investment, Net	126.9	104.7	135.7	−209.4	−174.6	38.4	−412.8	−163.2	−214.8	−221.8
Portfolio Investment, Net	−498.3	−30.7	−114.9	−53.5	−195.0	−221.4	32.2	−133.4	219.6	355.7
Financial Derivatives, Net	7.1	2.2	−54.3	−27.0	7.8	24.0	−20.4	−38.3	−33.2	−20.0
Other Investment, Net	−88.2	−473.2	−259.9	−37.0	−4.0	−173.4	−23.7	−65.3	−510.6	−577.5
Change in Reserves	4.5	−3.1	−3.6	−6.3	2.1	−1.7	5.0	4.7	−0.2	0.0
Euro Area										
Financial Account Balance	171.7	426.8	339.1	310.2	358.4	392.3	450.0	309.4	...	...
Direct Investment, Net	59.4	37.3	90.3	254.8	97.1	−45.8	149.0	17.0	...	...
Portfolio Investment, Net	−201.6	−184.1	40.1	142.1	609.0	421.9	264.7	−67.0	...	...
Financial Derivatives, Net	38.8	41.9	76.2	101.4	23.2	28.7	109.2	41.2	...	...
Other Investment, Net	258.7	523.4	127.9	−199.9	−387.9	−11.0	−102.4	314.5	...	...
Change in Reserves	16.4	8.3	4.6	11.8	17.0	−1.4	29.6	3.6	...	...
Germany										
Financial Account Balance	194.2	300.8	318.1	259.5	288.8	319.9	279.9	230.1	217.6	294.9
Direct Investment, Net	33.6	26.1	88.0	68.4	47.1	42.2	5.2	62.3	36.5	39.0
Portfolio Investment, Net	66.8	209.5	177.7	210.0	220.1	234.4	185.7	106.6	137.9	173.8
Financial Derivatives, Net	30.9	31.8	50.8	33.8	31.6	12.5	27.3	25.1	17.0	28.1
Other Investment, Net	61.1	32.2	4.8	−50.4	−11.9	32.3	61.2	36.7	26.3	53.9
Change in Reserves	1.7	1.2	−3.3	−2.4	1.9	−1.5	0.5	−0.6	0.0	0.0
France										
Financial Account Balance	−48.0	−19.2	−10.3	−0.8	−18.6	−36.1	−27.6	−32.3	−46.7	−49.4
Direct Investment, Net	19.4	−13.9	47.2	7.9	41.8	11.1	67.5	4.7	15.0	23.3
Portfolio Investment, Net	−50.6	−79.3	−23.8	43.2	0.2	30.3	11.1	−104.1	−70.6	−51.8
Financial Derivatives, Net	−18.4	−22.3	−31.8	14.5	−17.6	−1.4	−30.5	4.1	−0.9	−3.8
Other Investment, Net	−3.6	98.2	−2.9	−74.2	−45.4	−72.7	−87.9	59.8	6.1	−21.7
Change in Reserves	5.2	−1.9	1.0	8.0	2.5	−3.4	12.3	3.2	3.7	4.6
Italy										
Financial Account Balance	−4.1	32.4	73.0	43.1	36.2	53.8	35.9	51.6	60.9	64.9
Direct Investment, Net	6.8	0.9	3.1	2.0	−12.3	0.5	−0.2	−1.6	5.3	6.2
Portfolio Investment, Net	−22.4	−5.1	−2.2	105.7	154.8	95.0	141.7	−56.7	−52.8	−63.2
Financial Derivatives, Net	7.5	4.0	−1.9	1.2	−3.6	−8.2	−3.2	2.8	1.7	1.2
Other Investment, Net	2.1	30.5	75.2	−66.5	−101.4	−36.5	−105.5	103.5	106.7	120.8
Change in Reserves	1.9	2.0	−1.3	0.6	−1.3	3.0	3.1	3.6	0.0	0.0

Table A13. Summary of Financial Account Balances *(continued)*
(Billions of US dollars)

	2012	2013	2014	2015	2016	2017	2018	2019	Projections 2020	Projections 2021
Spain										
Financial Account Balance	11.0	41.2	22.8	31.8	39.2	36.9	37.0	34.4	10.8	33.7
Direct Investment, Net	−23.1	−14.1	14.2	33.4	12.4	13.5	−17.9	12.1	−2.0	3.3
Portfolio Investment, Net	53.6	−85.0	−8.8	12.0	64.9	37.1	25.6	−56.0	39.7	46.6
Financial Derivatives, Net	−10.7	1.4	1.3	4.2	2.8	8.4	1.9	−9.6	0.0	0.0
Other Investment, Net	−11.9	138.0	10.9	−23.3	−50.1	−26.3	24.8	87.0	−26.9	−16.2
Change in Reserves	3.1	0.9	5.2	5.5	9.1	4.1	2.6	0.8	0.0	0.0
Japan										
Financial Account Balance	53.9	−4.3	58.9	180.9	266.8	168.3	182.7	223.2	140.1	161.7
Direct Investment, Net	117.5	144.7	118.6	133.3	137.5	154.9	133.4	212.0	156.4	163.9
Portfolio Investment, Net	28.8	−280.6	−42.2	131.5	276.5	−50.6	92.2	87.1	99.1	110.7
Financial Derivatives, Net	6.7	58.1	34.0	17.7	−16.1	30.4	0.9	3.3	3.3	3.3
Other Investment, Net	−61.1	34.8	−60.1	−106.7	−125.4	10.0	−67.9	−104.7	−130.2	−127.7
Change in Reserves	−37.9	38.7	8.5	5.1	−5.7	23.6	24.0	25.5	11.5	11.5
United Kingdom										
Financial Account Balance	−78.4	−132.8	−153.1	−158.2	−161.1	−101.8	−111.1	−142.3	−56.2	−109.8
Direct Investment, Net	−34.8	−11.2	−176.1	−106.0	−297.4	16.3	−23.9	−88.3	−68.6	28.6
Portfolio Investment, Net	281.2	−284.6	15.9	−230.1	−201.5	−121.9	−360.0	57.4	−105.5	−153.6
Financial Derivatives, Net	−65.8	63.4	31.2	−128.6	29.3	13.3	11.2	11.3	10.6	5.0
Other Investment, Net	−271.2	91.8	−35.8	274.3	299.8	−18.4	236.9	−121.6	97.6	−0.4
Change in Reserves	12.1	7.8	11.7	32.2	8.8	8.8	24.8	−1.1	9.8	10.6
Canada										
Financial Account Balance	−63.9	−57.2	−43.1	−51.8	−45.4	−41.6	−35.4	−32.9	−31.7	−42.9
Direct Investment, Net	12.8	−12.0	1.3	23.6	33.5	51.8	6.4	25.9	13.7	12.3
Portfolio Investment, Net	−68.3	−34.8	−32.8	−36.2	−103.6	−76.4	3.1	−3.4	−94.2	−45.4
Financial Derivatives, Net	...	...	...	...	...	...	...	...	...	...
Other Investment, Net	−10.1	−15.2	−16.9	−47.8	19.1	−17.9	−43.4	−54.1	48.7	−9.8
Change in Reserves	1.7	4.7	5.3	8.6	5.6	0.8	−1.5	−1.3	0.0	0.0
Other Advanced Economies[1]										
Financial Account Balance	252.2	377.1	344.2	300.8	338.7	312.8	328.2	330.7	314.6	333.8
Direct Investment, Net	−33.3	31.2	−6.0	−96.1	−64.5	−162.5	12.3	−58.7	7.9	−35.6
Portfolio Investment, Net	150.0	139.6	175.5	334.6	258.4	157.7	345.2	280.5	235.9	241.0
Financial Derivatives, Net	−28.3	−33.5	−22.3	−11.9	3.5	−1.8	32.1	21.4	−6.5	−2.4
Other Investment, Net	−110.9	138.7	85.7	−101.4	−8.6	106.7	−111.0	48.8	51.0	103.1
Change in Reserves	274.7	101.3	111.5	176.0	150.2	213.1	49.5	38.7	26.3	27.7

Table A13. Summary of Financial Account Balances *(continued)*
(Billions of US dollars)

	2012	2013	2014	2015	2016	2017	2018	2019	Projections 2020	2021
Emerging Market and Developing Economies										
Financial Account Balance	87.3	−24.6	12.0	−306.1	−405.8	−242.1	−220.7	−163.1	26.1	−81.9
Direct Investment, Net	−495.2	−483.7	−428.8	−346.4	−260.3	−303.2	−371.8	−356.3	−276.6	−301.2
Portfolio Investment, Net	−243.7	−147.6	−89.7	127.7	−53.5	−208.4	−94.2	−98.3	53.1	−165.4
Financial Derivatives, Net	...	...	...	...	...	...	...	...	...	...
Other Investment, Net	424.2	64.7	406.3	468.8	381.8	97.5	125.5	116.7	55.1	154.7
Change in Reserves	407.9	541.4	111.7	−562.6	−467.1	168.2	116.4	175.1	195.4	228.7
Regional Groups										
Emerging and Developing Asia										
Financial Account Balance	13.0	28.5	153.2	72.4	−24.8	−53.6	−256.5	−84.0	199.7	63.1
Direct Investment, Net	−220.5	−271.2	−201.6	−139.6	−25.5	−104.2	−165.8	−148.2	−128.8	−140.2
Portfolio Investment, Net	−115.5	−64.6	−125.2	81.6	31.1	−70.1	−99.6	−70.9	−37.5	−117.2
Financial Derivatives, Net	1.3	−2.1	0.8	0.6	−4.6	2.2	4.6	−6.1	−11.9	−5.6
Other Investment, Net	217.2	−81.7	282.0	458.8	352.9	−83.5	−20.4	42.3	−1.0	60.0
Change in Reserves	136.8	444.8	195.6	−329.4	−379.6	201.6	25.6	99.1	379.0	266.8
Emerging and Developing Europe										
Financial Account Balance	−24.9	−66.5	−28.9	65.6	3.8	−19.1	99.9	60.7	6.3	26.0
Direct Investment, Net	−37.4	−15.4	0.3	−22.1	−45.8	−28.7	−25.4	−52.5	−5.6	−18.6
Portfolio Investment, Net	−92.6	−37.9	23.4	54.5	−7.4	−34.6	12.9	−3.6	21.6	−14.7
Financial Derivatives, Net	−1.6	−0.9	5.8	5.0	0.3	−2.5	−3.0	1.5	5.3	0.5
Other Investment, Net	55.1	−4.5	64.1	35.6	21.1	30.3	67.9	22.0	20.2	43.1
Change in Reserves	51.6	−7.8	−122.7	−7.4	35.5	16.5	47.4	93.3	−35.2	15.6
Latin America and the Caribbean										
Financial Account Balance	−155.4	−196.8	−194.0	−192.6	−105.4	−101.1	−148.3	−108.6	−11.6	−33.6
Direct Investment, Net	−159.5	−151.1	−136.6	−136.1	−126.9	−119.5	−148.8	−117.8	−109.8	−92.3
Portfolio Investment, Net	−80.3	−99.8	−109.2	−48.1	−48.5	−39.9	−12.2	5.0	29.0	−17.4
Financial Derivatives, Net	2.5	1.8	6.8	1.2	−2.9	3.9	4.1	5.0	8.6	8.8
Other Investment, Net	22.9	39.8	5.2	19.1	51.7	36.9	−5.1	31.3	47.3	57.9
Change in Reserves	59.0	12.4	39.8	−28.7	21.0	17.1	13.6	−32.0	13.4	9.4
Middle East and Central Asia										
Financial Account Balance	278.8	263.8	159.8	−184.1	−218.5	−31.8	110.9	21.0	−107.0	−80.0
Direct Investment, Net	−43.2	−22.7	−42.7	−10.6	−29.1	−13.6	−9.7	−10.4	−11.4	−20.0
Portfolio Investment, Net	72.6	75.3	130.4	61.6	−11.9	−41.4	6.1	−10.7	19.4	−13.1
Financial Derivatives, Net	...	...	...	...	...	...	...	...	...	...
Other Investment, Net	108.5	121.7	65.9	−52.5	−42.7	104.1	88.5	33.5	−1.0	10.8
Change in Reserves	140.8	89.6	6.8	−182.4	−134.3	−80.6	26.4	8.9	−113.9	−57.5
Sub-Saharan Africa										
Financial Account Balance	−24.2	−53.6	−78.1	−67.5	−60.8	−36.5	−26.7	−52.2	−61.3	−57.3
Direct Investment, Net	−34.6	−23.3	−48.3	−38.0	−33.1	−37.3	−22.0	−27.3	−21.0	−30.0
Portfolio Investment, Net	−27.9	−20.7	−9.1	−21.9	−16.8	−22.4	−1.4	−18.1	20.8	−3.0
Financial Derivatives, Net	−1.7	−0.8	−1.5	−0.4	0.9	0.3	−0.5	0.3	0.2	0.3
Other Investment, Net	20.4	−10.6	−10.9	7.8	−1.3	9.7	−5.5	−12.3	−10.5	−17.1
Change in Reserves	19.8	2.4	−7.8	−14.7	−9.7	13.6	3.5	5.9	−48.0	−5.7

Table A13. Summary of Financial Account Balances *(continued)*
(Billions of US dollars)

	2012	2013	2014	2015	2016	2017	2018	2019	Projections 2020	Projections 2021
Analytical Groups										
By Source of Export Earnings										
Fuel										
Financial Account Balance	426.3	332.8	210.4	−110.7	−161.1	65.0	312.0	140.5	−75.5	−27.9
Direct Investment, Net	−28.1	14.8	6.6	5.5	−27.8	21.5	35.6	−5.9	4.1	−2.0
Portfolio Investment, Net	41.2	87.6	177.9	94.0	−12.1	−42.0	17.6	−25.7	20.3	−10.4
Financial Derivatives, Net	. . .	. . .	. . .	. . .	. . .	. . .	. . .	. . .	. . .	. . .
Other Investment, Net	198.9	174.2	145.4	0.6	25.2	140.2	182.6	84.9	47.4	61.2
Change in Reserves	212.7	55.7	−124.5	−218.0	−146.4	−54.8	77.2	84.6	−145.7	−76.6
Nonfuel										
Financial Account Balance	−339.0	−357.4	−198.4	−195.5	−244.6	−307.1	−532.7	−303.6	101.6	−54.0
Direct Investment, Net	−467.1	−498.5	−435.4	−351.9	−232.6	−324.7	−407.4	−350.4	−280.8	−299.1
Portfolio Investment, Net	−284.9	−235.2	−267.6	33.7	−41.4	−166.4	−111.8	−72.7	32.9	−155.1
Financial Derivatives, Net	−1.0	−2.3	6.7	−0.6	−6.2	3.5	5.8	−1.9	3.0	3.6
Other Investment, Net	225.3	−109.5	260.9	468.2	356.5	−42.7	−57.2	31.9	7.6	93.5
Change in Reserves	195.2	485.7	236.2	−344.6	−320.7	223.0	39.2	90.5	341.1	305.3
By External Financing Source										
Net Debtor Economies										
Financial Account Balance	−409.8	−409.4	−352.7	−288.5	−231.0	−266.6	−319.0	−243.5	−119.9	−178.4
Direct Investment, Net	−277.0	−268.0	−274.6	−287.5	−287.3	−263.7	−308.4	−291.5	−240.0	−259.9
Portfolio Investment, Net	−220.5	−175.9	−188.8	−26.0	−53.3	−117.0	−11.1	−31.8	69.4	−98.5
Financial Derivatives, Net	. . .	. . .	. . .	. . .	. . .	. . .	. . .	. . .	. . .	. . .
Other Investment, Net	−16.1	−38.9	−3.3	41.5	29.2	2.0	−9.0	−35.4	−8.8	74.7
Change in Reserves	112.3	72.2	104.8	−13.9	93.6	108.5	10.7	118.4	59.0	104.2
Net Debtor Economies by Debt-Servicing Experience										
Economies with Arrears and/or Rescheduling during 2015–19										
Financial Account Balance	−56.8	−55.7	−34.3	−45.4	−58.9	−41.2	−36.6	−43.7	−29.3	−32.9
Direct Investment, Net	−32.6	−26.0	−23.3	−25.4	−26.6	−25.8	−27.6	−27.8	−15.9	−24.0
Portfolio Investment, Net	−0.1	−11.8	−4.4	0.7	−8.6	−29.5	−12.8	−14.7	2.2	−6.1
Financial Derivatives, Net	. . .	. . .	. . .	. . .	. . .	. . .	. . .	. . .	. . .	. . .
Other Investment, Net	−3.8	−17.4	0.0	−20.8	−28.1	9.9	−1.5	4.9	2.9	−12.2
Change in Reserves	−20.4	−0.2	−6.4	0.4	4.6	4.6	5.7	−5.7	−18.0	9.9
Memorandum										
World										
Financial Account Balance	−42.5	221.0	346.4	41.5	35.6	214.4	108.4	135.1	163.3	244.1

Note: The estimates in this table are based on individual countries' national accounts and balance of payments statistics. Country group composites are calculated as the sum of the US dollar values for the relevant individual countries. Some group aggregates for the financial derivatives are not shown because of incomplete data. Projections for the euro area are not available because of data constraints.

[1]Excludes the Group of Seven (Canada, France, Germany, Italy, Japan, United Kingdom, United States) and euro area countries.

Table A14. Summary of Net Lending and Borrowing
(Percent of GDP)

	Averages								Projections		
	2002–11	2006–13	2014	2015	2016	2017	2018	2019	2020	2021	Average 2022–25
Advanced Economies											
Net Lending and Borrowing	−0.7	−0.4	0.5	0.6	0.8	1.0	0.7	0.6	0.5	0.6	0.7
Current Account Balance	−0.7	−0.4	0.5	0.7	0.8	1.0	0.8	0.7	0.5	0.6	0.6
Savings	21.6	21.5	22.6	22.8	22.4	23.0	22.9	22.7	21.7	22.0	22.5
Investment	22.2	21.8	21.5	21.6	21.4	21.8	22.0	22.1	21.4	21.6	22.1
Capital Account Balance	0.0	0.0	0.0	−0.1	0.0	0.0	−0.1	−0.1	0.0	0.0	0.0
United States											
Net Lending and Borrowing	−4.4	−3.6	−2.1	−2.3	−2.1	−1.8	−2.2	−2.3	−2.1	−2.1	−2.1
Current Account Balance	−4.4	−3.6	−2.1	−2.2	−2.1	−1.9	−2.2	−2.2	−2.1	−2.1	−2.1
Savings	17.0	17.0	20.4	20.1	18.7	19.2	19.1	18.6	17.7	17.8	18.5
Investment	21.2	20.4	20.8	21.2	20.4	20.5	21.0	21.0	20.3	20.6	21.1
Capital Account Balance	0.0	0.0	0.0	0.0	0.0	0.1	0.0	0.0	0.0	0.0	0.0
Euro Area											
Net Lending and Borrowing	0.0	0.1	2.5	2.9	3.3	2.9	2.8	2.5	...	...	...
Current Account Balance	−0.1	0.0	2.4	2.8	3.3	3.1	3.1	2.7	1.9	2.4	2.5
Savings	22.8	22.7	23.0	23.8	24.2	24.9	25.2	25.2	23.7	24.8	25.8
Investment	22.3	21.7	20.0	20.3	20.7	21.3	21.8	22.3	21.3	21.9	22.7
Capital Account Balance	0.1	0.1	0.1	0.2	0.0	−0.2	−0.3	−0.2	...	...	...
Germany											
Net Lending and Borrowing	4.8	6.2	7.3	8.6	8.6	7.7	7.4	7.1	5.8	6.8	6.9
Current Account Balance	4.9	6.2	7.2	8.6	8.5	7.8	7.4	7.1	5.8	6.8	6.9
Savings	25.3	26.7	27.6	28.3	28.5	28.6	29.0	28.5	27.1	28.7	29.6
Investment	20.4	20.4	20.4	19.7	20.0	20.8	21.6	21.4	21.4	21.9	22.7
Capital Account Balance	0.0	0.0	0.1	0.0	0.1	−0.1	0.0	0.0	0.0	0.0	0.0
France											
Net Lending and Borrowing	0.0	−0.5	−1.0	−0.4	−0.4	−0.8	−0.5	−0.6	−1.8	−1.7	−1.1
Current Account Balance	0.0	−0.5	−1.0	−0.4	−0.5	−0.8	−0.6	−0.7	−1.9	−1.8	−1.1
Savings	22.5	22.4	21.8	22.3	22.1	22.7	23.3	23.5	20.8	21.4	22.6
Investment	22.5	22.9	22.7	22.7	22.6	23.4	23.9	24.2	22.7	23.2	23.8
Capital Account Balance	0.0	0.0	−0.1	0.0	0.1	0.0	0.1	0.1	0.1	0.1	0.1
Italy											
Net Lending and Borrowing	−1.6	−1.5	2.1	1.8	2.4	2.6	2.5	2.9	3.3	3.1	3.1
Current Account Balance	−1.6	−1.6	1.9	1.4	2.6	2.6	2.5	3.0	3.2	3.0	3.0
Savings	19.5	18.6	18.9	18.5	20.2	20.6	20.8	20.9	19.5	21.2	22.3
Investment	21.2	20.2	17.0	17.1	17.6	18.1	18.3	18.0	16.3	18.2	19.3
Capital Account Balance	0.1	0.1	0.2	0.4	−0.2	0.1	0.0	−0.1	0.1	0.1	0.1
Spain											
Net Lending and Borrowing	−5.2	−4.0	2.1	2.7	3.4	2.9	2.4	2.3	0.9	2.3	2.8
Current Account Balance	−5.8	−4.4	1.7	2.0	3.2	2.7	1.9	2.0	0.5	0.9	1.8
Savings	20.9	19.5	19.6	21.0	21.9	22.1	22.3	22.8	20.8	21.7	23.0
Investment	26.8	23.9	17.9	19.0	18.8	19.4	20.4	20.8	20.3	20.8	21.2
Capital Account Balance	0.6	0.4	0.4	0.6	0.2	0.2	0.5	0.3	0.3	1.4	1.0
Japan											
Net Lending and Borrowing	3.2	2.7	0.7	3.1	3.9	4.1	3.5	3.6	2.9	3.2	3.0
Current Account Balance	3.3	2.7	0.8	3.1	4.0	4.2	3.6	3.6	2.9	3.2	3.0
Savings	27.0	25.8	24.7	27.1	27.4	28.2	27.9	28.2	27.8	27.6	26.9
Investment	23.7	23.0	23.9	24.0	23.4	24.0	24.3	24.6	24.9	24.3	23.9
Capital Account Balance	−0.1	−0.1	0.0	−0.1	−0.1	−0.1	0.0	−0.1	−0.1	−0.1	−0.1
United Kingdom											
Net Lending and Borrowing	−2.7	−3.3	−4.8	−5.0	−5.3	−3.6	−4.0	−4.0	−2.1	−3.8	−3.5
Current Account Balance	−2.6	−3.3	−4.7	−4.9	−5.2	−3.5	−3.9	−4.0	−2.0	−3.8	−3.5
Savings	14.5	13.2	12.4	12.5	12.2	14.0	13.2	13.3	13.7	12.6	13.4
Investment	17.1	16.5	17.1	17.4	17.4	17.5	17.1	17.3	15.7	16.3	16.9
Capital Account Balance	0.0	0.0	−0.1	−0.1	−0.1	−0.1	−0.1	0.0	−0.1	−0.1	−0.1

Table A14. Summary of Net Lending and Borrowing *(continued)*
(Percent of GDP)

	Averages								Projections		
	2002–11	2006–13	2014	2015	2016	2017	2018	2019	2020	2021	Average 2022–25
Canada											
Net Lending and Borrowing	0.1	−1.7	−2.3	−3.5	−3.1	−2.8	−2.5	−2.0	−2.0	−2.4	−2.4
Current Account Balance	0.0	−1.7	−2.3	−3.5	−3.1	−2.8	−2.5	−2.0	−2.0	−2.4	−2.3
Savings	22.6	22.2	22.6	20.3	19.7	20.7	20.6	20.7	19.4	19.1	19.8
Investment	22.5	23.9	24.9	23.8	22.8	23.5	23.1	22.7	21.4	21.6	22.1
Capital Account Balance	0.0	0.0	0.0	0.0	0.0	0.0	0.0	0.0	0.0	0.0	0.0
Other Advanced Economies[1]											
Net Lending and Borrowing	4.0	4.1	5.0	5.2	5.4	4.6	4.7	5.3	4.4	4.3	4.3
Current Account Balance	4.0	4.1	5.1	5.7	5.2	4.6	4.6	5.4	4.5	4.4	4.3
Savings	30.0	30.4	30.6	30.9	30.4	30.4	30.2	30.4	29.4	29.0	28.9
Investment	25.8	26.1	25.4	25.0	25.0	25.6	25.5	24.9	24.5	24.1	24.2
Capital Account Balance	0.0	0.0	−0.1	−0.4	0.1	0.1	0.1	−0.1	0.0	0.0	0.0
Emerging Market and Developing Economies											
Net Lending and Borrowing	2.6	2.3	0.6	0.0	−0.2	0.1	0.0	0.3	0.0	−0.3	−0.3
Current Account Balance	2.5	2.2	0.6	−0.2	−0.3	0.0	−0.1	0.2	−0.1	−0.4	−0.4
Savings	30.9	32.6	32.6	31.6	31.2	31.7	32.5	32.5	32.9	32.3	31.8
Investment	28.6	30.6	32.2	32.1	31.4	31.8	32.8	32.5	33.1	32.8	32.3
Capital Account Balance	0.2	0.2	0.0	0.1	0.1	0.1	0.1	0.1	0.1	0.1	0.1
Regional Groups											
Emerging and Developing Asia											
Net Lending and Borrowing	3.6	3.3	1.5	2.0	1.4	1.0	−0.2	0.6	1.0	0.3	0.1
Current Account Balance	3.5	3.3	1.5	2.0	1.4	1.0	−0.3	0.6	1.0	0.3	0.1
Savings	40.3	42.9	42.7	41.1	39.9	40.0	39.8	39.6	40.4	39.0	37.4
Investment	37.1	39.7	41.2	39.2	38.6	39.1	40.0	39.0	39.4	38.7	37.3
Capital Account Balance	0.1	0.1	0.0	0.0	0.0	0.0	0.0	0.0	0.0	0.0	0.0
Emerging and Developing Europe											
Net Lending and Borrowing	−0.2	−0.7	−0.6	1.8	0.1	−0.1	2.3	1.9	0.3	0.7	0.4
Current Account Balance	−0.2	−0.9	−0.2	1.1	−0.2	−0.4	1.8	1.4	−0.3	0.1	−0.1
Savings	23.0	23.2	23.4	24.7	23.5	24.1	25.6	24.2	22.3	22.6	23.1
Investment	22.8	24.0	23.5	23.5	23.7	24.5	23.5	22.7	22.6	22.6	23.4
Capital Account Balance	0.0	0.2	−0.4	0.7	0.3	0.3	0.5	0.5	0.6	0.6	0.5
Latin America and the Caribbean											
Net Lending and Borrowing	−0.1	−1.0	−3.1	−3.2	−1.9	−1.5	−2.4	−1.7	−0.4	−0.8	−1.1
Current Account Balance	−0.2	−1.1	−3.1	−3.3	−2.0	−1.6	−2.5	−1.7	−0.5	−0.8	−1.1
Savings	20.8	20.8	17.8	16.4	16.7	16.4	16.9	17.2	17.1	17.7	18.1
Investment	20.9	21.9	21.5	21.1	18.3	18.3	19.4	19.0	17.7	18.6	19.3
Capital Account Balance	0.1	0.1	0.0	0.0	0.0	0.0	0.0	0.1	0.1	0.0	0.0
Middle East and Central Asia											
Net Lending and Borrowing	8.2	9.1	5.8	−3.6	−4.0	−0.7	3.0	0.8	−3.2	−2.5	−1.2
Current Account Balance	8.4	9.4	5.1	−4.0	−4.2	−0.8	2.8	0.7	−3.7	−2.7	−1.4
Savings	35.2	36.8	32.5	24.7	24.1	27.0	29.6	28.2	24.4	24.6	26.0
Investment	27.5	28.1	26.8	28.3	27.6	27.7	26.8	27.8	28.3	27.8	27.7
Capital Account Balance	0.2	0.2	0.1	0.1	0.1	0.0	0.0	0.0	0.1	0.1	0.1
Sub-Saharan Africa											
Net Lending and Borrowing	1.8	1.0	−3.1	−5.4	−3.4	−1.9	−2.3	−3.3	−4.3	−3.6	−2.6
Current Account Balance	0.5	−0.3	−3.5	−5.8	−3.8	−2.3	−2.7	−3.6	−4.8	−4.1	−3.0
Savings	21.3	21.5	19.3	17.5	18.4	19.0	19.6	20.2	18.1	18.8	20.5
Investment	21.1	22.0	22.7	23.0	21.8	21.3	22.3	24.1	23.0	22.9	23.6
Capital Account Balance	1.3	1.3	0.4	0.4	0.4	0.4	0.4	0.4	0.5	0.5	0.4

Table A14. Summary of Net Lending and Borrowing *(continued)*
(Percent of GDP)

	Averages								Projections		
	2002–11	2006–13	2014	2015	2016	2017	2018	2019	2020	2021	Average 2022–25
Analytical Groups											
By Source of Export Earnings											
Fuel											
Net Lending and Borrowing	9.2	9.1	4.7	−1.5	−1.6	1.6	5.9	2.7	−1.7	−0.7	0.3
Current Account Balance	9.6	9.3	5.1	−1.5	−1.6	1.7	5.9	2.7	−2.0	−0.8	0.2
Savings	33.9	34.4	30.5	24.9	24.8	27.2	31.2	29.5	25.3	25.8	26.6
Investment	24.7	25.5	25.5	27.6	25.3	25.6	25.2	26.9	27.4	26.9	26.6
Capital Account Balance	−0.1	0.0	−0.7	−0.1	0.0	0.0	0.0	0.0	0.0	0.0	0.0
Nonfuel											
Net Lending and Borrowing	0.8	0.3	−0.4	0.2	0.1	−0.2	−1.1	−0.2	0.3	−0.2	−0.4
Current Account Balance	0.6	0.1	−0.5	0.1	0.0	−0.3	−1.2	−0.3	0.2	−0.3	−0.5
Savings	30.1	32.1	33.2	33.0	32.4	32.5	32.8	33.0	34.1	33.3	32.5
Investment	29.6	32.0	33.8	33.0	32.4	32.8	34.1	33.4	34.0	33.7	33.1
Capital Account Balance	0.2	0.2	0.2	0.2	0.1	0.1	0.1	0.1	0.1	0.1	0.1
By External Financing Source											
Net Debtor Economies											
Net Lending and Borrowing	−0.8	−1.6	−2.1	−2.0	−1.4	−1.5	−2.0	−1.3	−0.9	−1.3	−1.4
Current Account Balance	−1.1	−2.0	−2.4	−2.3	−1.6	−1.7	−2.2	−1.5	−1.2	−1.5	−1.7
Savings	23.3	23.8	22.7	22.4	22.4	22.6	22.7	22.7	22.1	22.3	23.2
Investment	24.6	25.8	25.1	24.8	24.1	24.4	25.0	24.3	23.4	24.0	25.0
Capital Account Balance	0.3	0.3	0.3	0.3	0.2	0.2	0.2	0.2	0.2	0.2	0.2
Net Debtor Economies by Debt-Servicing Experience											
Economies with Arrears and/or Rescheduling during 2015–19											
Net Lending and Borrowing	−1.3	−3.3	−4.2	−5.4	−6.1	−5.4	−5.1	−5.0	−4.4	−5.1	−3.9
Current Account Balance	−2.3	−4.4	−4.8	−5.9	−6.5	−5.9	−5.6	−5.3	−4.8	−5.4	−4.2
Savings	19.9	18.4	14.7	12.9	12.6	13.7	14.8	13.7	13.2	13.6	16.2
Investment	22.6	22.9	19.4	19.0	19.5	20.0	20.7	19.5	18.5	19.6	20.9
Capital Account Balance	1.0	1.0	0.6	0.5	0.3	0.6	0.4	0.3	0.4	0.4	0.4
Memorandum											
World											
Net Lending and Borrowing	0.2	0.4	0.5	0.4	0.4	0.6	0.4	0.4	0.3	0.3	0.3
Current Account Balance	0.2	0.4	0.5	0.3	0.4	0.6	0.4	0.4	0.2	0.2	0.2
Savings	24.3	25.2	26.5	26.3	25.8	26.4	26.7	26.7	26.3	26.2	26.4
Investment	24.1	24.8	25.7	25.7	25.2	25.7	26.3	26.3	26.1	26.1	26.4
Capital Account Balance	0.0	0.1	0.0	0.0	0.0	0.0	0.0	0.0	0.0	0.1	0.0

Note: The estimates in this table are based on individual countries' national accounts and balance of payments statistics. Country group composites are calculated as the sum of the US dollar values for the relevant individual countries. This differs from the calculations in the April 2005 and earlier issues of the *World Economic Outlook*, in which the composites were weighted by GDP valued at purchasing power parities as a share of total world GDP. The estimates of gross national savings and investment (or gross capital formation) are from individual countries' national accounts statistics. The estimates of the current account balance, the capital account balance, and the financial account balance (or net lending/net borrowing) are from the balance of payments statistics. The link between domestic transactions and transactions with the rest of the world can be expressed as accounting identities. Savings (S) minus investment (I) is equal to the current account balance (CAB) (S - I = CAB). Also, net lending/net borrowing (NLB) is the sum of the current account balance and the capital account balance (KAB) (NLB = CAB + KAB). In practice, these identities do not hold exactly; imbalances result from imperfections in source data and compilation as well as from asymmetries in group composition due to data availability.
[1]Excludes the Group of Seven (Canada, France, Germany, Italy, Japan, United Kingdom, United States) and euro area countries.

Table A15. Summary of World Medium-Term Baseline Scenario

	Averages				Projections		Averages	
	2002–11	2012–21	2018	2019	2020	2021	2018–21	2022–25
	Annual Percent Change							
World Real GDP	**4.1**	**2.8**	**3.5**	**2.8**	**–4.4**	**5.2**	**1.7**	**3.8**
Advanced Economies	1.7	1.3	2.2	1.7	–5.8	3.9	0.4	2.2
Emerging Market and Developing Economies	6.5	3.9	4.5	3.7	–3.3	6.0	2.7	4.9
Memorandum								
Potential Output								
Major Advanced Economies	1.8	1.0	1.3	1.3	–2.0	2.3	0.7	1.5
World Trade, Volume[1]	**5.7**	**2.3**	**3.9**	**1.0**	**–10.4**	**8.3**	**0.4**	**4.3**
Imports								
Advanced Economies	4.1	2.0	3.6	1.7	–11.5	7.3	0.0	3.8
Emerging Market and Developing Economies	9.9	2.8	5.0	–0.6	–9.4	11.0	1.2	5.2
Exports								
Advanced Economies	4.5	1.9	3.5	1.3	–11.6	7.0	–0.2	3.9
Emerging Market and Developing Economies	8.7	2.9	4.1	0.9	–7.7	9.5	1.5	4.9
Terms of Trade								
Advanced Economies	–0.2	0.4	–0.5	0.1	0.6	0.3	0.2	0.0
Emerging Market and Developing Economies	1.6	–0.7	1.2	–1.1	–2.6	0.3	–0.6	0.0
World Prices in US Dollars								
Manufactures	2.7	–1.1	1.9	0.4	–3.1	–1.3	–0.5	1.5
Oil	15.6	–7.7	29.4	–10.2	–32.1	12.0	–3.0	2.3
Nonfuel Primary Commodities	11.6	–2.0	1.3	0.8	5.6	5.1	3.2	0.4
Consumer Prices								
Advanced Economies	2.0	1.3	2.0	1.4	0.8	1.6	1.4	1.7
Emerging Market and Developing Economies	6.4	4.9	4.9	5.1	5.0	4.7	4.9	4.1
Interest Rates				*Percent*				
Real Six-Month LIBOR[2]	0.3	–0.7	0.1	0.6	–0.5	–1.6	–0.4	–1.5
World Real Long-Term Interest Rate[3]	1.7	0.1	–0.1	–0.2	–0.4	–1.2	–0.5	–0.4
Current Account Balances				*Percent of GDP*				
Advanced Economies	–0.7	0.6	0.8	0.7	0.5	0.6	0.6	0.6
Emerging Market and Developing Economies	2.5	0.1	–0.1	0.2	–0.1	–0.4	–0.1	–0.4
Total External Debt								
Emerging Market and Developing Economies	29.3	30.2	31.0	30.0	32.7	30.8	31.1	28.3
Debt Service								
Emerging Market and Developing Economies	8.9	10.9	10.9	10.8	11.6	10.8	11.0	9.8

[1]Data refer to trade in goods and services.
[2]London interbank offered rate on US dollar deposits minus percent change in US GDP deflator.
[3]GDP-weighted average of 10-year (or nearest-maturity) government bond rates for Canada, France, Germany, Italy, Japan, the United Kingdom, and the United States.

WORLD ECONOMIC OUTLOOK
SELECTED TOPICS

World Economic Outlook Archives

I. Methodology—Aggregation, Modeling, and Forecasting

II. Historical Surveys

III. Economic Growth—Sources and Patterns

IV. Inflation and Deflation and Commodity Markets

V. Fiscal Policy

VI. Monetary Policy, Financial Markets, and Flow of Funds

VII. Labor Markets, Poverty, and Inequality

VIII. Exchange Rate Issues

IX. External Payments, Trade, Capital Movements, and Foreign Debt

X. Regional Issues

XI. Country-Specific Analyses

XII. Climate Change Issues

XIII. Special Topics

IMF EXECUTIVE BOARD DISCUSSION OF THE OUTLOOK, OCTOBER 2020

The following remarks were made by the Chair at the conclusion of the Executive Board's discussion of the
Fiscal Monitor, Global Financial Stability Report, *and* World Economic Outlook *on September 30, 2020.*

Executive Directors broadly concurred with the assessment of the global economic outlook, risks, and policy priorities. While noticing the stronger-than-expected economic activity in the second quarter, especially in advanced economies, they agreed that the path to prepandemic activity will be long and precarious with persistent scarring effects on output and employment. They noted that the projections assume that social distancing will continue into 2021 and then fade over time as therapies improve and vaccines become more broadly available. Directors noted with concern that the pandemic is having dramatic effects on vulnerable people, leading to higher inequality, and a sharp increase in the number of people living in extreme poverty.

Directors agreed that the uncertainty surrounding the baseline projections remains exceptionally large as the economic recovery will be shaped primarily by the path of the pandemic, the efficacy of containment measures, and pharmaceutical innovations. More rapid development of new therapeutics and wide distribution of effective vaccines could accelerate the economic recovery, while medical setbacks and new waves of infections could require new lockdowns. Other important sources of uncertainty include the extent of global spillovers, the damage to the supply potential, the efficacy and duration of policy support, and potential shifts in financial market sentiment. Directors also noted prepandemic risks stemming from trade and technology tensions, geopolitical challenges, and climate change.

Directors agreed that effective and decisive policy support is needed to ensure stronger, more equitable, and resilient growth. Key near-term priorities include supporting the economic recovery, protecting vulnerable people, and strengthening health care systems. They stressed the need to reduce the scarring effects of the crisis on potential output and employment and to reverse the development toward greater inequality and

setbacks to human capital accumulation. Most Directors also saw the crisis as an opportunity to stimulate innovation, develop the digital infrastructure, and to transition to lower carbon emissions using different climate tools, such as green investment and a gradual increase of the carbon price, with due consideration to offsetting negative social impact.

Directors welcomed the unprecedented fiscal actions in response to the pandemic. Directors emphasized that, as economies tentatively reopen, governments should ensure that lifelines are not withdrawn prematurely. Support should gradually shift from protecting jobs to helping displaced workers find new jobs through retraining and reskilling. Directors noted that when the pandemic is under control, governments will need to address the legacies of the crisis, including record deficits and public debt levels, elevated unemployment, and increased poverty. Directors agreed that public investment should play a crucial role in supporting the postpandemic recovery, noted its sizable job creation potential, and underlined that good governance, budget execution, and communication, remain crucial to reap the full benefits of fiscal support and maintain public trust.

Directors emphasized that governments will need to do more with less and prepare credible and equitable measures to reduce fiscal deficits and debts over the medium term. Countries with limited fiscal space should protect public investment and support lower-income households that have been disproportionately hit by the pandemic. Governments could consider increasing progressive taxation as well as reforms to modernize business taxation, including multilateral cooperation on the design of international corporate taxation to respond to the challenges of the digital economy. LICs in particular are faced with significant financing constraints, and many countries will require external support, including in the form of debt relief, grants, and concessional financing.

Directors agreed that bold policy actions taken by central banks to ease monetary policy, provide ample liquidity, and maintain the flow of credit have helped contain the near-term risks to global financial stability. They noted, however, that vulnerabilities are rising, most notably in the nonfinancial corporate sector as liquidity pressures may morph into insolvencies, especially for small and medium-sized enterprises. The credit outlook will ultimately be shaped by the extent of continued policy support and the pace of the recovery, which is expected to be uneven across sectors and countries. Rising defaults could lead to significant losses at banks and nonbank financial institutions. While the global banking system is overall well capitalized, some banks and banking systems may experience aggregate capital shortfalls in the WEO adverse scenario. Directors also highlighted the importance of improving access of emerging markets and frontier economies to capital markets.

Directors emphasized that as economies reopen, accommodative policies and the continued flow of credit to borrowers will be essential to sustaining the recovery. Once the pandemic is under control, policy support can be gradually withdrawn. The postpandemic financial reform agenda should focus on strengthening the regulatory framework to address vulnerabilities in the nonbank financial sector exposed by the crisis and stepping up prudential supervision to contain excessive risk taking in the lower-for-longer interest rate environment.

Directors underscored the importance of international cooperation in the fight against the global health and economic crisis. A key priority is to scale up production capacity and develop distribution channels to ensure that all countries have access to an effective, affordable, and safe vaccine. Directors noted that several emerging market and developing countries require international assistance through debt relief, grants, and concessional financing. They pointed out that the IMF has rapidly scaled up its lending facilities since the onset of the pandemic, providing swift financial assistance to more than 80 countries. Directors discussed opportunities for multilateral cooperation to alleviate trade and technology tensions between countries and to collectively implement climate change mitigation policies.

IMF Special Series on COVID-19

The IMF has responded to the COVID-19 crisis by quickly deploying financial assistance, developing policy advice, and creating special tools to assist member countries. The Special Notes Series (**IMF.org/COVID19notes**) features the latest analysis and research from IMF staff in response to the pandemic. Below are four recent Notes from the dozens published to date.

Options to Support the Income of Informal Workers during COVID-19

Federico Díez, Romain Duval, Chiara Maggi, Yi Ji, Ippei Shibata, and Marina Medes Tavares

This note reviews available options to support informal workers during COVID-19, as well as potential costs and selected financing options. A transfer to cover the basic food and energy needs of all informal workers for two months could cost over 2 and 5 percentage points of annual GDP in the median emerging market and low-income economies, respectively.

The Disconnect Between Financial Markets and the Real Economy

Deniz Igan, Divya Kirti, and Soledad Martinez Peria

This note examines several prominent hypotheses to explain the disconnect between financial markets and the real economy in 2020. The note concludes that monetary policy actions—and the associated decline in discount rates—have lifted asset valuations.

Emerging Market Capital Flows under COVID: What to Expect Given What We Know

Sebnem Kalemli-Ozcan

This note summarizes recent empirical research that focuses on emerging market capital flows before and during the COVID-19 shock, examining the complex interaction between domestic fiscal and external financing needs in those economies.

COVID-19 and Government Debt Dynamics in Low-Income Developing Countries

Gabriela Cugat, Giovanni Melina, and Felipe Zanna

This note assesses the potential medium-term impact of the COVID-19 pandemic on government debt in developing countries. The estimates are based on calibrations of a structural model. Absent more multilateral support, restructurings, and/or fiscal consolidations, government debt may increase significantly in many developing economies.

COVID-19 Policy Tracker

This periodically updated policy tracker summarizes the key economic responses 196 governments are taking to limit the human and economic impact of the pandemic. **IMF.org/COVID19policytracker**

INTERNATIONAL MONETARY FUND